ROME GUIDE

BE A TRAVELER - NOT A TOURIST!

ABOUT THE AUTHOR

Having spent more than eight years living in Italy roaming through the country, Douglas E. Morris is the author of Open Road's *Italy Guide* and *Rome Guide*. Published in a wide variety of media, Mr. Morris gives you accurate, up-to-date, and comprehensive information.

ACKNOWLEDGMENTS

Many people assisted considerably in the development of this book, but I wish to extend my special thanks to Heddi Goodrich for her unique insight into the heart of Naples. My parents, Don and Denise, and my brother Dan were invaluable for their support, information, suggestions, and numerous leads. Special thanks for Alain DeCock's editorial and creative assistance. I am exteremly indebted to Anamaria Porcaro for her intimate knowledge of Rome, as well as Theresa Luis and the MMI class of '76 for their thoughtful insights. And most of all this book is better for the invaluable suggestions and feedback offered by our many readers, including Jack Sawinski, Pamela A. Motta, Hugh L. Curtin, and Senator Paul Simon. Keep your e-mails coming to *Roma79@aol.com*.

ROME GUIDE

BE A TRAVELER - NOT A TOURIST!

Douglas Morris

OPEN ROAD PUBLISHING

3rd Edition

Library of Congress Control No. 00-136194
ISBN 1-892975-45-9

The author has made every effort to be as accurate as possible, but neither the author nor the publisher assume responsibility for the services provided by any business listed in this guide; for any errors or omissions; or any loss, damage, or disruptions in your travels for any reason.

TABLE OF CONTENTS

MAPS

SIDEBARS

1. INTRODUCTION

If you're looking for a wide variety of entertainment, stunning architecture, passionate people, soul-refreshing relaxation, unparalleled artwork, dazzling museums, ruins from ancient civilizations, world-class accommodations, superb restaurants, accessible ski resorts, championship golf courses and continuous recreation, then a vacation to Rome is what you are looking for. Besides all of this, the food in Rome is in my opinion the best in Italy, which means the best in the world. Created with the freshest ingredients and always with a distinctly local flair, not only is the cooking healthy and nutritious, but the variety of flavors and tastes will tantalize and satisfy like no other cuisine. And don't forget great wines like Chianti, Orvieto, and Frascati which all come from vineyards not too far afield. Mix in the Roman passion for living, and in the eternal city you have an ideal vacation destination.

There is so much to see, so much to do, so many great dishes to try and different wines to sample that a trip to Rome is always an adventure. With this guide, your days and nights will be filled with all the exciting possibilities the land of "La Dolce Vita" has to offer. I've given you a multiplicity of options for shopping, eating, traveling and much more so that you can tailor the perfect vacation for your particular needs.

You will not want for things to do and sights to see – Roman ruins, awe-inspiring Renaissance palazzi, winding medieval streets, incredible churches and monuments (including the many wonders of the Vatican City), fun and varied neighborhoods to wander about, and all manner of piazzas, fountains and gardens. All are part of the wonderful tapestry of life that is modern Rome.

And if you have more time, I've also included several chapters worth of terrific excursions, including a number of hill towns and beachs not far from Rome. There are also a few destinations a bit farther away, including the splendor of Florence, the majesty of Orvieto, and the timeless expanses of Pompeii and Herculaneum, preserved through the ages by lava and ash spewed out in the massive volcanic eruption of Mt. Vesuvius nearly two thousands years ago.

So read on, and have a trip of a lifetime in Rome.

2. OVERVIEW

ROME, THE ETERNAL CITY

Rome is a city you can come back to again and again and it will never lose its luster. Take it from one who knows. I spent eight years there and still I return every year, always finding something new to share with you each time. Rome is truly a timeless place, and is aptly called the Eternal City.

Rome has so many adventures to choose from that it's easy to miss something spectacular. You might neglect to see a certain sight, or take the time to go to a specific restaurant, or make the effort to visit a one of Rome's ambiant and charming late night spots. Realizing this, if you do not have the time to sift through the rest of this chapter – which is filled with the most authentic and enjoyable places to stay, eat, and see while in Rome – I have conveniently listed the best options Rome has to offer below.

Even if you are the furthest thing from being religious, make the effort to see **St. Peter's** and the **Vatican Museum**, which will take the better part of a day if you do a proper tour. No church is more magnificent and no museum is more complete. All others in Rome as well as the rest of Italy, the exception being the Uffizzi in Florence, will pale in comparison.

Make sure you get to the **Trastevere** district and sample the atmosphere of **La Canonica**, a converted chapel and now a restaurant that also has many tables spilling out along the street. Reserve a spot inside since this may be your last chance to have a meal in a quaint converted chapel. Try their *spaghetti alla carbonara* (with a light cream sauce, covered with ham, peas, and grated parmesan cheese) for *primo* and for your main course sample the light fish dish, *sogliola alla griglia* (grilled Sole). Then sojourn to one of the cafés in the **Piazza Santa Maria in Trastevere**, grab a drink, and savor the evening.

During another day it is imperative that you visit **Piazza Navona** and grab an ice cream at one of the cafés there, and either lounge on their terraces or take it with you while you sit on the edge of one of the fountains. The best vantage point is on Bernini's magnificent **Fontana Dei Quattro Fiumi** (Fountain of Four Rivers). The four figures supporting the large obelisk (a Bernini trademark) represent the Danube, the Ganges, the Nile, and the Plata rivers. Notice the figure representing the Nile. It is shielding its eyes from the facade of the church it is facing, **Santa Agnese in Agone**, which was designed by Bernini's rival at the time, Borromini. An ancient artistic quarrel comes to life everyday in Piazza Navona.

From there, only a few blocks away is the quaint piazza **Campo dei Fiori** where you'll find one of Rome's best fruit and vegetable markets every day until 1:00pm, except Sundays. Make sure you get here to shop or just to enjoy the atmosphere of a boisterous Roman market.

There is a restaurant in the square where you should enjoy at least one meal, **La Carbonara**. Even though the name would lead you to believe that the best dish to get is the *spaghetti alla carbonara*, it is my impression that their best dish is the *spaghetti alla vongole verace* (a spicy oil, garlic, and clam sauce). If you want to sit outside, you'll have to wait until about 2:00pm, because that is when all the debris from the outdoor market has been swept up from the piazza.

Other dishes you need to sample while in Rome are the *penne all'arrabbiata* (literally means angry pasta and is a tubular pasta made with a spicy garlic, oil, and tomato-based sauce), *tortellini alla panna* (meat or cheese filled pasta in a thick cream sauce), and any *abbacchio* (lamb) or *maiale alla griglia* (grilled pork).

In the evening, don't miss the **Trevi Fountain** all lit up and surrounded by locals and tourists strumming on guitars and drinking wine. It's definitely a party atmosphere. Come here with friends or arrive and meet new ones. For one of your evening meals, there's a place a little past the **Spanish Steps**, where, if you're here in Spring, you should stop for a minute and admire the floral display covering the steps.

At **La Capriciossa** you can sit in a peaceful little piazza just off the Via del Corso, Rome's main shopping street, while you enjoy your meal. They are known for making excellent pizza (only in the evening) as well as preparing perfect Roman pasta dishes and exquisite meat plates. If you haven't already sampled the *penne all'arrabbiata,* do so here, and try the succulent *abbacchio arrosto* (roast lamb), another staple of the Roman diet. And to finish the meal, order a *sambucca con mosce* (this is a sweet liquor with three flies with three coffee beans floating in it). Remember to bite into the beans as you have the sweet liquor in your mouth. The combination of tastes is exquisite.

There is obviously much more to do in Rome than this, such as the **Colosseum** and **Forum,** but if you only have only a little time, make sure you get to the places mentioned above. Then you can say you really have seen Rome.

ROME'S JUBILEE CLEAN-UP

Rome has scrubbed itself clean from years of smog and soot; the monuments haven't gleamed like this since they were first built. The city has introduced new red buses, complete with air conditioning and much more comfortable seating for the year 2000 celebrations. On top of cleaning all their monuments, adding new buses, introducing the fast and efficient EUROSTAR train service, creating covered waiting areas for taxis and buses at the train station, Romans have made everything much more efficient and intuitive for travelers, from signs describing train schedules and layouts, to Metro ticket dispensers with instruction in English. Florence, Siena, Perugia, and other cities have also gone through the same cleansing and organizing to accommodate the massive influx of pilgrims and tourists that visited in the year 2000. Rome and all of Italy have never looked better. This is the time to visit.

EXCURSIONS - FLORENCE, ORVIETO, & MORE

Rome is basically right in the middle of Italy. From here it is an easy train ride to a number of different world-famous destinations including Florence, Siena, Orvieto, Frascati, Pompeii and Herculaneum. You could spend an eternity in Rome and still only scrape the surface of everything that it has to offer, but if you want to sample other parts of this stunning peninsula, I've included some excursions for you to sample.

Most people believe that a visit to Italy is not complete without a trip to **Florence**, one of the most awe-inspiring cities in all of Europe. And at less than three hours away by train it is an easy day trip or overnight excursion from Rome. The Renaissance reached its full heights of artistic expression here, and strolling through the cobblestone streets of Florence is like being in an art history book come to life. The sights, smells, and sounds of this wonderful medieval city must be experienced first-hand to appreciate and understand the magical atmosphere.

Siena is generally described as the feminine counterpart to the masculine Florence, and even its nickname, City of the Virgin, belies this feminine quality. Located 42 miles south of Florence, and thus that much closer to Rome, this picturesque walled city is known for its many beautiful buildings, narrow streets, immense churches, and quaint little

restaurants; but the main reason why I love Siena are that cars are banned from the center of the city, making for a pleasant automobile-free environment. Some people have described the peace and serenity of Siena as being similar to Venice but without the water, and I heartily agree.

An easy hour train ride from Rome's Termini station takes you to the splendid Umbrian hill town of **Orvieto**. A simply enchanting city, resting peacefully on the top of hill bordered by protective cliffs, Orvieto is the perfect antidote for the hectic pace of Rome. Here you can relax in a favorite summer residence of the popes, while enjoying a vast array of medieval streets and stunning architecture, especially the world-famous Duomo. Also home to the ever popular Orvieto wines, a visit to this wonderful town will be memorable.

Another beautiful hill town also known for its wine, **Frascati** is a 40-minute local train ride from Rome. Though not nearly as picturesque and scenic as Orvieto, Frascati will offer you the same peace and tranquility. Come here to wander the twisting medieval streets and savor the popular vintages grown on the hills surrounding the town. Some of you may even wish to stay here and commute back and forth to Rome.

Pompeii & Herculaneum are a bit further afield but they are well worth the visit. Similar to the nearby **Ostia Antica**, which can be reached by Rome's Metro system, but far more extensive, these two towns were buried in time when Mt. Vesuvius erupted in the 2nd century AD. If you are an archaeology buff or simply interested in seeing firsthand how people of that era lived, a trip to Pompeii & Herculaneum is a great experience. I would recommend taking a guided tour bus from Rome so that you do not have to worry about driving or catching the right trains to get there.

Well, in a nutshell, that's what you'll find inside *Rome Guide*. This book has everything you will need so that you can plan the best possible trip to Rome.

MOVIES TO SET THE SCENE FOR YOUR TRIP!

As you're planning your trip, you might want to rent a few movies to get you in the mood for your travels (save the novels for the airplane trips and beach visits!). Some modern classics include:

- ***Amarcord**, Fellini's great film about youth and coming of age*
- ***Christ Stopped at Eboli**, about a sophisticated left-wing doctor sent to a small hill town during the Fascist era*
- ***Cinema Paradiso**, about growing up in southern Italy*
- ***The Garden of the Finzi-Cantinis**, tale of what happens to a wealthy Jewish family before and during World War II*
- ***Caligula**, a bit rough and not for kids, but an interesting take on the debauchery of aristocrats in the Roman Empire*
- ***Il Postino**, a romantic movie about a postman, a poet, and the island of Procida*
- ***Life is Beautiful**, a celebration of living, Italian-style, even in the worst of times*

3. ROMAN ITINERARIES

If you only have a short period of time in **Rome** and you want to fill it up with the best sights, restaurants, hotels, cafés at which to lounge, and pubs from which you can crawl back to your bed, all you have to do is follow the itineraries listed below. The hotels, sights, and restaurants mentioned are all described in more detail later in the book.

The places listed in these itineraries are among my favorites in Rome, but there were plenty of close calls! So follow my advice if you wish, or plow through the rest of the information included here and find the perfect itinerary tailor made for your needs.

THE PERFECT THREE DAYS

Day One

This is going to be a somewhat slow day since you'll have just arrived and will be slightly jet-lagged.

- Arrive at Rome's Leonardo da Vinci airport in the morning.
- Take a cab to the **Hotel Locarno** near **Piazza del Popolo**, shower and unpack.
- Stop at the café next to the excellent restaurant **Dal Bolognese** in the Piazza del Popolo and grab a cappuccino, café, or espresso to get you going.
- Take the **Via del Babuino** to the **Spanish Steps**.
- Get your picture taken while you lean over and grab a drink from the fountain in front of the steps.
- Walk to the top of the steps for the magnificent view over the city
- It should be about lunch time now, so walk back down the steps, cross the street, and take a left into the third street at the edge of the piazza, **Via delle Croce**. Follow this to the end, find an outside seat at the superb local restaurant **Otello alla Concordia**, *Via Della Croce 81. Tel. 06/679-1178*. Try any of their exquisite Roman pasta specialties – *arrabiata, amatriciana,* or *vongole verace*.
- After lunch it should be about nap time. But remember to only take a 2-3 hour nap, wake up right away, take a shower and get out again –

otherwise you'll sleep until 10:00pm and be wide awake because jet-lag will have set in.

- Now it's time to explore the streets around the **Piazza di Spagna**, **Via della Croce**, **Via del Corso**, **Via dei Condotti** and admire all the different shops.
- After shopping/exploring, take a small walk (or short cab ride) to **Piazza Navona**.
- Stop at **Le Tre Scalini** and sample some of the world famous Italian *gelato* (ice cream). If you sit at the tables outside the cost will double or triple.
- If some liquid refreshment is more your style, exit the Piazza Navona on the other side, cross the **Via Vittorio Emanuele**, visit the **Campo dei Fiori** (where they have a superb market in the mornings which we'll get to in a few days) and stop in at the **Drunken Ship** for some Guiness, Harp, or Kilkenny. Enjoy the lovely English speaking female bartenders, and have a few ales for me.
- From here you are within striking distance of **Trastevere**, the place for Roman nightlife, on the other side the river. Cross the pedestrian bridge **Ponte Sisto** and make your way to **Piazza Santa Maria** in Trastevere.
- If it's too early for dinner (7:30pm or 8:00pm is the beginning time) stop at one of the outdoor cafés and replenish your fluids.
- For dinner stop at **La Canonica** just outside of the piazza. Here you should also try one of the typical Roman pasta specialties, *arrabiata, amatriciana*, or *vongole verace*; as well as some *sogliola alla griglia* (grilled sole) for seconds.
- After dinner, if you're not too tired, let's go to the **Trevi Fountain**. It is beautiful lit up at night. To do so walk down the long road leading to the Piazza, **Via della Lungaretta**, to the large main road **Viale Trastevere**. From here catch a cab to Piazza Colonna, near the fountain. The side streets leading up to the fountain are usually packed and the cab wouldn't be able to move through the crowds anyway. Go across the big road, Via del Corso and take Via di Sabini to the fountain.

Day Two

- Today is museum day. Start off at the best in the city, the **Vatican Museum** and the **Sistine Chapel**. This should take you all morning.
- Instead of a long sit-down meal, stop at one of the cafés around the museum and St. Peter's and order a light snack. My suggestion is getting a *Medallione*, a grilled ham and cheese concoction that is tasty and filling. You don't order at the counter, you first pay for your order with the cashier (order your drink at the same time), then bring the

receipt up to the counter and tell the bartender what you'll have. A good tip to leave is about L500.

- After your meal, let's explore **St. Peter's**. Guys will need slacks and cannot wear tank tops for this adventure, and women cannot wear short skirts, shorts or tank top-like shirts either. While here, make a point of walking to the top, or taking the elevator, to get a great view over St. Peter's square.
- Once done here, which should be late afternoon, let's stop at **Castel St. Angelo** and explore the ancient armaments museum and fortifications of the fortress that protected the Vatican in the past.
- Now it's time to go home for a 2-3 hour nap, if you need it.
- Dinner tonight is at the nearby **La Buca di Ripetta**, on Via di Ripetta, where you should try either the *Lasagna al Forno, Saltimbocca alla Romana,* or the *Ossobuco di Vitello*.
- After dinner, if you missed the **Trevi Fountain** last night, go there tonight. It's about a 20 minute walk (if you're staying at the Locarno), or a short cab ride away.
- If not, you must return to the **Piazza Navona** to soak up the ambiance there at night with its fountains lit up. Either bring your own bottle of wine and sit at one of the benches or grab a table at one of the cafés and enjoy a beautiful Roman evening.

Day Three

- Time to explore some serious ruins. On the way, stop at the market in the **Piazza Venezia**.
- From here make your way down **Via dei Foro Imperiali** to the entrance to the Forum on the right hand side. Up ahead you'll see the **Colosseum**, our next destination.
- See the Colosseum.
- Lunch. Time to hail a cab and go back up the Via dei Foro Imperiali, to Piazza Venezia, then on to **Gino ai Funari** on Via dei Funari. This is a small local place in the Jewish Ghetto that makes the Roman pasta specialties perfectly (*carbonara, amatriciana, vongole verace, and arrabiata*). Or you can try the *conniglio alla cacciatore* (rabbit hunter style made with brandy tomatoes and spices). It is superb.
- After lunch, before we go back up the Via di Teatro Marcello to go to the second best museum in Rome – the Campidoglio – since it's so close by, let's pay a visit to the **Isola Tiberina**.
- After a quick exploration of this island, let's get to the **Campidoglio**. Remember to find *La Buca della Verita*. This should take most of the afternoon.
- When completed, make your way to the **Pantheon** (or back to the hotel if you're tired) and sit at one of the outside cafés and savor the sight

of one of Rome's oldest buildings in a quaint medieval square. If it is super hot, sit by the pillars at the entrance of the Pantheon since it is always wonderfully cool there.

- Back to the hotel to freshen up for your meal this evening at **La Carbonara** in **Campo dei Fiori**. Remember you were here on Day One at the Drunken Ship? They make the best *spaghetti alla vongole verace* I've ever had.
- You can stay in Campo dei Fiori for the whole evening and take in the sights and sounds of one of Rome's most popular nighttime piazzas. Most evenings they have live bands playing. You've already been to Navona, Santa Maria in Trastevere, and Trevi, the other three great piazzas where you can get a true taste of Roman nightlife.

THE PERFECT FOUR DAYS

Follow the above itinerary and add Day Four immediately below.

Day Four

- Time to go to church (you don't have to pray if you that's not your thing). To get to these churches you're going to need to take the metro and buses or rely on Roman taxis. Our first stop is **Saint Paul's Outside the Walls**. Get your picture taken in the middle courtyard with one of the trees in the background. When you next return to Rome, do the same thing and trace how long it has been by how far the tree has grown. My family has been doing that for over 40 years now.
- From here cab it back into town to **Santa Maria Sopra Minerva**.
- Next is **Santa Maria Maggiore** near the train station.
- On to **San Pietro in Vincoli** close to the Colosseum.
- Located between the Colosseum and San Giovanni in Laterano is our next stop, **Church of San Clemente**
- Our next church is the cathedral of Rome, which isn't St. Peter's, it is **San Giovanni in Laterano**.
- Time to get ourselves to Trastevere for a late lunch, and **Sabatini's** is the perfect choice. Here we can sit in their large outdoor terrace on the Piazza and enjoy a fine meal.
- Most people don't come to Trastevere to look at churches. They come for the more bacchanalian aspects of the area. But we religious types have first come to see **Santa Maria in Trastevere** in the same piazza as Sabatini's, then the **Church of Santa Cecilia in Trastevere**.
- Since you've been traveling all over town, let's return to the hotel for brief siesta, since everything is closed anyway, or stop off at **Babbington's Tea Room** near the Spanish Steps for a "cuppa."

- When the stores re-open, let's do some antique shopping on the nearby streets of **Via del Babuino** and the **Via Margutta**, Rome's best for antiques.
- If you want to buy a book, stop into the **Lion Bookshop** at Via del Babuino 181.
- For dinner try the ever popular **Otello Alla Concordia** at nearby Via Della Croce 81, where you can get some of the most succulent *abbacchio alla griglia* anywhere in Rome.
- For an after-dinner vino, sample **Antica Bottigleria Placidi,** a great wine bar on the same street.

THE PERFECT SEVEN DAYS

Follow the above itinerary for the first four days, then add Days Five through Seven immediately below.

Day Five

- If you don't feel as if you are able to truly appreciate some of the activities listed above, by all means return and enjoy them today, but before you run off and do that we're all starting together by waking up early and going back to the **Campo dei Fiori** to see how different it is in the mornings. Here you'll find one of Rome's best food and flower markets. Don't miss it.
- For lunch, return back into the city and find this great place located between Piazza Navona and the Spanish Steps, Orso "80" at Via dell'Orso. Here they make great *spaghetti alla carbonara* as well as the *abbacchio alla griglia*.
- Now the fun begins. We're going to a terrific town – **Frascati**. If we are lucky and it's September, we may stumble into their wine festival (and definitely stumble out).
- To get to Frascati, go to the train station, buy a ticket, go to track 27, board the small local train (takes 35 minutes and costs L6,500), and enjoy the scenery along the way.
- Enjoy the views, exploring the winding medieval streets and the relative peace and quiet compared to Rome. Don't forget to search out some of the little wine stores. My favorite is **Cantina Via Campania**.
- For dinner, let's give the wild and raucous **Pergatolo** at Via del Castello 20 a try. If you're into something more sedate, **Zaraza** at Viale Regina Margherita 21 should be your choice.
- Once dinner is done, make your way back to Rome.
- After arriving at the train station, let's go to a nearby Irish pub, **The Fiddler's Elbow** on Via dell'Olmata, that serves up fine ales, an authentic atmosphere, English conversation, and a fun evening to end an adventurous day.

Day Six

- Let's start off the day at the nearby **Mercato de Stampe**, at Piazza Fontanella, which is open from 9:00am–6:00pm Monday through Saturday. Here you can find maps, stamps, books, almost anything on the intellectual side.
- When done here, take a cab or stroll the short distance to the **Piazza Barberini** at the base of the **Via Veneto**.
- First we'll stop in the **Palazzo Barberini**, located on the Via Quattro Fontane that leads up the hill from the Piazza. This palazzo is the home of the **National Portrait Gallery**.
- After soaking up the art, walk back almost to the piazza to a small street named Via degli Avignonesi. At the end of it you'll find a great little local place, **Trattoria Da Olimpico**. Stop here for lunch.
- Once lunch is over go back up the street to the piazza, and start up Via Veneto, the street that embodies the good life – *La Dolce Vita*. Halfway up you'll pass by the **American Embassy** on the right hand side. Stop at one of the cafés for refreshment.
- At the top of the steps, go through the massive gate, cross the street and enter the beautiful park, **Villa Borghese**. Take a leisurely stroll through the gardens to the **Galleria Borghese** that has paintings and sculptures galore.
- Follow the roads to the other entrance to the park and back to the hotel
- Dinner tonight is at **Dal Bolognese** in the Piazza del Popolo. Try their *fritto misto*, a fried mix of veggies, cheese, and meat.
- End the evening by going to the top of the **Spanish Steps** for a view over the city at night.

Day Seven

- Assuming today is a Sunday, you must visit the **Porta Portese** market that lines the Tevere every Sunday. Starting at the **Ponte Sublico**, you'll find all sorts of interesting antiques and junk here. A must visit if you're in Rome on a Sunday.
- After the market, and since it is Sunday and everything is closed (that's right, no museums, hardly any shops, etc.) except restaurants, it's time to return to the restaurant you liked best that you tried before. I always do this wherever I travel. It ensures that one of my last meals is going be great, and it makes me feel somewhat like I belong. Go to one with an outside terrace like **La Carbonara** in Campo dei Fiori.
- Return to your hotel and pack, and afterwards go for a stroll around your new neighborhood.
- End your stroll at the top of the **Spanish Steps** again. Tonight we're going to the terrace restaurant in the **Villa Hassler** for a scenic and romantic last dinner in Rome. Try their specialty *abbacchio al forno*.

4. LAND & PEOPLE

LAND

From the top of the boot to the toe, Italy is a little more than 675 miles (1,090 kilometers) long. The widest part, in the north, measures about only 355 miles (570 kilometers) from east to west. The rest of the peninsula varies in width from 100 to 150 miles (160 to 240 kilometers) making it an easily traveled country, at least side to side. In total the peninsula of Italy fills an area of about 116,000 square miles (300,400 square kilometers).

A mountainous country, Italy is dominated by two large mountain systems – the **Alps** in the north and the **Apennines** which run down the center of the peninsula. The Alps, which are the highest mountains in Europe, extend in a great curve from the northwestern coast of Italy to the point where they merge with Austria and Slovenia in the east. Just west of the port city of Genoa, the **Maritime Alps** are the beginning of the chain. Despite mighty peaks and steep-sided valleys, the Alps are pierced by modern engineering marvels of mountain passes that have allowed commerce between Italy and its northern neighbors to flow freely. These highway and railroad tunnels provide year-round access through the mountains encouraging trade, tourism and transit.

The Apennine mountain system is an eastern continuation of the Maritime Alps. It forms a long curve that makes up the backbone of the Italian peninsula. The Apennines extend across Italy in the north, follow the east coast across the central region, then turn toward the west coast, and, interrupted by the narrow Strait of Messina, continue into Sicily.

There are numerous smaller mountains in Italy, many of volcanic ancestry, most of which are thankfully extinct. But that does not mean mother nature remains dormant in Italy. Because of the volcanic nature of the peninsula, which is caused by the earth plates shifting, Italy is prone to earthquakes. In the summer of 1997 an earthquake hit Umbria and destroyed not only towns and villages but some of Giotto's precious frescoes in the cathedral in Assisi. The region was still active for months and aftershocks were felt in Rome in November of that year. I can personally attest to that since the aftershocks woke me up at 3 o'clock one November morning. There are only two active volcanoes in all of Europe and Italy has both of them, **Mount Vesuvius** near Naples and **Mount Etna** in Sicily. Maybe that has something to do with the heated and passionate Italian temperament?

PEOPLE

The Italian people are now considered to be one of the most homogeneous, in language and religion, of all the European populations. The only significant minority group are located in the region called **Trentino-Alto Adige**. These Alpine valleys of the north once made up part of the Austrian province of Tyrol, and the several hundred thousand German-speaking residents still refer to their homeland as South Tyrol. The region was incorporated into Italy after World War I, and both Italian and German are official languages in this region. Obviously, the people of the region have developed their own sense of identity - part of, but separate from, the rest of Italy.

One much smaller minority also lives in northern Italy. This group, the **Valdotains**, dwells in the region called **Valle d'Aosta** in the northwestern corner of the country, and also has two official languages, Italian and French.

About 95 percent of the Italian people speak Italian, while members of the two aforementioned groups make up the other 5%. For more than seven centuries the standard form of the language has been the one spoken in Tuscany, the region of central Italy centered around Florence. However, there are many dialects, some of which are difficult even for Italians to understand. Two of these principal dialects, those of Sicily and Sardinia, sound like a foreign language to most Italians. Because of these differences, if you have lived in Italy for a while, it is easy to discern the different accents and dialects and pinpoint where someone is from. Just like it is easy for us to figure out if someone is from New England or the South based on their accent.

But all this is just about where they live and how they speak. What are the Italians like?

Shakespeare was enamored with Italians and things Italian, as is evidenced by having many of his plays take place in Italy. And when he wrote "All the world's a stage," he definitely had Italy in mind. Filled with stunningly beautiful architecture and ancient ruins, Italy's physical landscape is a perfect backdrop for the play of Italian life. In Italy everyone is an actor, dramatically emphasizing a point with their hands, facial expressions leaving no doubt about what is being discussed and voices rising or falling based on what the scene requires.

SWITZERLAND
AUSTRIA
SLOVENIA
Bergamo
Milan
Verona
Padova
Trieste
Venice
Turin
ITALY
Ferrara
Parma
Genoa
Bologna
FRANCE
Lucca
Florence
Pisa
SAN MARINO
Ligurian Sea
Siena
Adriatic Sea
Viterbo
VATICAN CITY
ROME
Bari
Strait of Otranto
Naples
Salerno
Sardinia
Capri
Lecce
Golfo di Taranto
Tyrrhenian Sea
Mediterranean Sea
Ionian Sea
ITALY
N
Messina
Trapani
Reggio di Calabria
Palermo
Catania
Strait of Sicily
Sicily
Agrigento
Siracusa

Play in the Piazza

Italians are some of the most animated people in the world and watching them is more than half the fun of going to Italy. These people relish living and are unafraid to express themselves. There is a tense, dramatic, exciting directness about Italians which is refreshing to foreigners accustomed to Anglo-Saxon self-control. In Italy most travelers find, without even realizing it was missing, that combination of sensuality, love and sincerity that is so lacking in their own lives.

In every piazza, on every street, there is some act being played. Whether it's two neighbors quarreling, vendors extolling the virtues of their wares, a group of older ladies chatting across the street as they lean out their windows, lovers whispering hands caressing each other as they walk, a man checking his reflection in the mirror primping for all to see, there is something about the daily street scenes all over Italy that make this country seem more alive, more animated than the rest or the world. Italians really know how to enjoy the production of living; and they love to watch these everyday scenes unfold.

Seats are strategically placed in cafés to catch all that occurs. And it is easy, even for the uninitiated, to see what is transpiring a distance away because Italians are so expressive. On the faces of Italians it is easy to read joy, sorrow, hope, anger, lust, desire, relief, boredom, despair, adoration and disappointment as easily as if they were spoken aloud. When Italians visit Northern Europe, England, or America they seem lost since they seldom know what is going on, as everyone is so expressionless.

Fashion, Art & Warfare?

Virtually all Italians share a love for fashion. The Italians are some of the best dressed people in the world, and they love to prance around like peacocks displaying their finery. 'Style over substance' is an adage that well describes Italians; but they live it with such flair that it can be forgiven. Along with the finery they wear, the beauty of the Italian people is unparalleled. All manner of coloration, including the stereotypical sensual brown eyed and brown haired beauties abound. Besides fashion Italians love art. If you ask an Italian to take your photograph expect to be posed and re-posed for at least five minutes. All Italians imagine themselves to be Federico Fellini, the famous film producer. They want to get the light just right, the shading perfect and the framing ideal. They'll pose you until you're almost blue in the face, but you'll get a great picture.

They also love architecture. What happened in the United States where beautiful buildings were destroyed all over the country to erect parking lots would never happen in Italy, where you'll also never see garish strip malls or ugly suburban sprawl. For example, the McDonalds' in Italy do not stand out the way they do in America with the golden arches glowing the location for all to see. The store signs have been blended to the architecture of the building in which they are located. A balance has been found between commercialism and aesthetic appeal that has been forgotten in America.

Their love for style over substance is why Italians have always excelled in activities where appearance is paramount, like architecture, decorating, landscaping, fireworks, opera, industrial design, graphic design, fashion and cinema. It could be conjectured that because of this pursuit of such 'effeminate' pastimes, warfare has never been Italy's forté.

During the Renaissance, battles were mere window dressing. Well paid *condottieri* headed beautifully appointed companies of men, resplendent in their finest silks, carrying colorful flags bearing the emblem of the families who were paying them. Martial music was played, songs were sung, and bloodcurdling cries were bellowed. But there was not much war being made. There were limited casualties, and when blood was shed it was usually by accident. "Armies" would pursue each other back and forth for weeks in a pageantry of color and celebration until a settlement was decided by negotiation, not bloodshed. This may seem to be a ludicrous form of warfare, but it is a brilliant expression of life, and an appreciation for living.

Religion & Family

In all, the best way to describe Italians is that they are fun. They will "live while they have life to live, and love while they have love to give." But they are also very traditional in their religion. As the center of Roman Catholicism, Italy is a shining example of Christian piety, even though many of the saints they worship are only decorated pagan gods dating back to the pre-Christian era. The Pope is revered as if he truly is sitting on the right hand of God. Virtually every holiday in Italy has some religious undertones and the people perform the necessary rites and rituals associated with those holidays with vigor and enthusiasm.

Christmas is a prime example of religion's effect. In Italy it is not as garish and commercial an activity as it is in America. Religion takes precedence over mass consumption. Having a lavish dinner with family and friends is more important than going into debt to show people you love them through product purchases. Most decorations are of religious figures, not the commercial icons like Santa Claus and Rudolph.

Religion may guide the people and present a foundation for living, but the family is paramount. In a society where legal authority is weak, the law is resented and resisted (estimates place the number of people that actually pay income tax at around 20%) and the safety and welfare of each person is mainly due to the strength of the family. Family gatherings, especially over meals are common. Knowing your third cousins is not rare. And many family members live and die all in the same small neighborhoods where they were born, even in the large cities of Florence, Venice, Naples and Rome. Family traditions are maintained, strengthened and passed on. The young interact, learn from, and respect their elders. The family is the core of Italian society, strong and durable; and from it grows a healthy sense of community.

USEFUL PHRASES

If you want to take a few virtual language lessons before you go, visit the *Foreign Language for Travelers* web site at **www.travlang.com/languages**. It's helpful and fun.

General

• Excuse me, but ....

Mi scusi, ma .... (This is a good introduction to virtually any and all inquiries listed below. It is a polite way of introducing your questions.)

• Thank you

Grazie

• Please

Per favore

• If you are in trouble, yell "Help"

Aiuto (eyeyootoh)

If you are looking for something, a restaurant, a hotel, a museum, simply ask "where is ....:"

• Where is the restaurant(name of restaurant)

Dov'é il ristorante_________?

• Where is the hotel (name of hotel)

Dov'é l'hotel _________?

• Where is the museum (name of museum)

Dov'é il museo _________?

Note: *(Dov'é* is pronounced "Dove [as in the past tense of dive] -ay")

Travel-Trains

• Where is track number ...

Dov'é binnario ...

1	*uno*	11	*undici*
2	*due*	12	*dodici*
3	*tre*	13	*tredici*
4	*quatro*	14	*quatordici*

5	*cinque*	15	*quindici*
6	*sei*	16	*sédici*
7	*sette*	17	*diciassette*
8	*otto*	18	*diciotto*
9	*nove*	19	*dicianove*
10	*dieci*	20	*venti*

• Is this the train for Florence (Rome)?
E questo il treno per Firenze (Roma)?
• When does the train leave?
Quando partira il treno?
• When is the next train for Naples/Milan?
Quando e il prossimo treno per Napoli/Milano?

Travel-Cars

• Where is the next gas station?
Dov'é la prossima stazione di benzina?
• I would like some oil for my car.
Voglio un po di olio per l' automobile.
• Can you change my oil?
Puo fare un cambio dell'olio per me?
• I think I need a new oil filter.
Penso che voglio un nuovo filtro dell'olio.

Travel-Public Transport

• Where is the (name of station) metro station?
Dov'é la stazione di Metro ___________?
• Where can I buy a Metro ticket?
Dov'é posso prendere un biglietto per il Metro?
• How much is the ticket?
Quanto costa il biglietto?
• Where is the bus stop for bus number ___.
Dov'é la fermata per il bus numero ___?
• Excuse me, but I want to get off.
Mi scusi, ma voglio scendere.
• Where can I catch a taxi?
Dov'é posso prendere un tassi?

Buying Stuff!

The following you can usually get at a drug store (*Farmacia*).
• Where can I get...?
Dov'é posso prendere ...?

• toothpaste
dentifricio
• a razor
un rasoio
• some deodorant
un po di deodorante
• a comb
un pettine
• rubbers
dei profilattici
• a toothbrush
un spazzolino
• some aspirin
un po di aspirina

The following you can usually get at a *Tabacchaio*:
• stamps
francobolli
• a newspaper
un giornale
• a pen
una penna
• envelopes
buste per lettere
• some postcards
dei cartoline

The following you can usually get at an *Alimentari:*
• some mustard
un po di senape
• some mayonnaise
un po di maionese
• tomatoes
tomaté
• olive oil
olio d'oliva
• I would like ... *Voglio ...*
  • 1/4 of a pound of this salami
  un etto di questo salami
  • 1/2 of a pound of Milanese salami
  due etti di salami milanese
  • 3/4 of a pound of this cheese
  tre etti di questo formaggio

- a small piece of mozzarella
  un piccolo pezzo di mozzarrella
- a portion of that cheese
  una porzione di quel' formaggio
- a slice of ham
  una fetta (or *una trancia) di prosciutto*
- one roll
  un panino
- two/three/four rolls
  due/tre/quatro panini

• How much for the toothpaste, razor, etc?
Quante costa per il dentifrico, il rasoio, etc.
• How much for this?
Quante costa per questo?
• Excuse me, but where I can find a ...?
Mi scusi, ma dov'é un ... ?

- pharmacy
  Farmacia
- tobacconist
  Tabacchaio
- food store
  Alimentari
- bakery
  Panificio

Communications

• Where is the post office?
Dov'é l'ufficio postale?
• Where is a post box?
Dov'é una buca delle lettere
• Where is a public telephone?
Dov'é una cabina telefonica?
• May I use this telephone?
Posso usare questo telefono?

Hotel

• How much is a double for one night/two nights?
Quanto costa una doppia per una notte/due notte?
• How much is a single for one night/two nights?
Quanto costa una singola per una notte/due notte?
• Where is the Exit/Entrance?
Dov'é l'uscita/l'ingresso?

• What time is breakfast?
A che ora e prima colazione?
• Can I get another....for the room?
Posso prender un altro ... per la camera?
  • blanket
  coperta
  • pillow
  cuscino
  • bed
  letto

Miscellaneous

• Where is the bathroom?
Dov'é il cabinetto?
• What time is it?
Che oré sono?
• Sorry, I don't speak Italian.
Mi scusi, ma non parlo italiano.
• Where can I get a ticket for ...?
Dov'é posso prendere un biglietto per ...?
  • a soccer game
  una partita di calcio
  • a basketball game
  una partita di pallacanestro
  • the theater
  il teatro
  • the opera
  l'opera
• You are truly beautiful.
Tu se veramente bella (spoken to a woman informally)
lei e veramente bella (spoken to woman formally)
Tu se veramente bello (spoken to a man)
lei e veramente bello (spoken to man formally)
• Can I buy you a drink?
Posso comprarti una bevanda?
• Do you speak any English?
Parli un po d'Inglese?
• Do you want to go for a walk with me?
Voi andare a una passeggiata con me?
• Is there anyplace to go dancing nearby?
Ch'é un posto per ballara vicino?

5. A SHORT HISTORY

A short Italian history is a contradiction in terms. So much has occurred in that narrow strip of land which has affected the direction of the entire Western world, that it is difficult to succinctly describe its history in a brief outline. We've had the Etruscans, Romans, Greeks, 'Barbarian' hordes, Holy Roman Emperors, the Papacy (although not the whole time – the seat of the Catholic Church was moved to Avignon, France from 1305 until 1377), painters, sculptors, the Renaissance, the Medici family, Crusaders, Muslim invaders, French marauders, Spanish conquistadors, Anarchists, Fascists, American soldiers, Communists, Red Brigades, and much more.

What follows is an attempt at a brief outline of the major events on the Italian peninsula, concentrating mainly on the Roman Empire, since we will cover the Renaissance later. I don't claim to be an historian, only a mere *scrittore di guidi di viaggio*, so please accept this brief historical background as a basic foundation for your travel enjoyment.

ETRUSCANS

Long before Romulus and Remus were being raised by a she-wolf to become the founders of Rome, Italy was the home of a people with an already advanced civilization – the **Etruscans**. This powerful and prosperous society almost vanished from recorded history because not only were they conquered by Rome but were also devastated by marauding **Gauls**. During these conquests once from the south, the other from the north, it is assumed that most of their written history was destroyed, and little remains of it today. The **Eugubine Tablets**, the Rosetta Stone for Central Italy, are the best link we have to understanding the Etruscan language. These tablets have corresponding Umbrian language text, which evolved from the Etruscan, and a corresponding rudimentary form of Latin.

Because of the lack of preserved examples of their language, and the fact that the inscriptions on their monuments has been only partially deciphered, archaeologists have gained most of their knowledge of the

Etruscans from studying the remains of their city walls, houses, monuments, and tombs.

From their research, archaeologists have been able to ascertain that the Etruscans were a seafaring people from Asia Minor, and that as early as 1000 BCE (Before the Common Era) they had settled in Italy in the region that is today **Tuscany** and **Lazio**. An area basically from Rome's Tiber River north almost to Florence's Arno River. Their influence eventually embraced a large part of western Italy, including Rome.

As a seafaring people, the Etruscans controlled the commerce of the Tyrrhenian Sea on their western border. After losing control of Rome, they strengthened their naval power through an alliance with Carthage against Greece. In 474 BCE, their fleet was destroyed by the Greeks of Syracuse. This left them vulnerable not only to Rome, but the Gauls from the north. The Gauls overran the country from the north, and the Etruscans' strong southern fortress of **Veii** fell to Rome after a ten-year siege (396 BCE). But as was the Roman way, the Etruscans were absorbed into their society, and eventually Rome adopted many of their advanced arts, their customs, and their institutions.

THE ETRUSCAN KINGS OF EARLY ROME

When Greece was reaching the height of its prosperity, Rome was just beginning its ascent to power. Rome didn't have any plan for its climb to world domination; it just seemed to evolve. There were plenty of setbacks along the way, but everything seemed to fall into place at the right time; and the end result was that at its apex, Rome ruled most of the known world.

The early Romans kept no written records and their history is so mixed with fables and myths that historians have difficulty distinguishing truth from fiction. The old legends say that **Romulus** founded the city in 753 BCE when the settlements on the seven hills were united. But this date is probably later than the actual founding of the city. As is the case with many emerging societies, the founders are mythical figures, as was Romulus, but there is some evidence that the kings who followed him in the ancient stories actually existed.

Shortly before 600 BCE, Rome was conquered by several Etruscan princes. The Etruscans were benevolent conquerors, an attitude that Rome would itself adopt, and set about improving the native lifestyles to match their own.

The Etruscans built Rome into the center of all Latium, their southern province. Impressive public works were constructed, like the huge sewer **Cloaca Maxima**, which is still in use today. Trade also expanded and prospered, and by the end of the 6th century BCE Rome had become the largest and richest city in Italy.

THE NATIVE ROMAN POPULATION REVOLTS

But in spite of all this progress and development, the old Latin aristocracy wanted their power back from the Etruscans. **Junius Brutus** led a successful revolt around 509 BCE, which expelled the Etruscans from the city. That was when the people of Rome made themselves a **republic**.

Rome's successful thwarting of the Etruscans helped the young republic gain the confidence it needed to begin its long history of almost constant conquest. At the time Rome was only a tiny city-state, much like the city-states that were flourishing at the same time in Greece, with a population of roughly 150,000. But in a few centuries this small republic would eventually rule the known world.

ROME'S EARLY REPUBLIC

In the beginnings of early Rome, the **patricians** (Rome's aristocracy) controlled the government and ruled the **plebes** or **plebeians** (Common People). Since they were shut out from the government, their wealthy fellow citizens politically and economically oppressed the plebeians. The internal history of the republic for the next three centuries is mainly a story of how the plebeians wrested reform after reform from the patricians and gained an increasing amount of control over their existence and eventually directed the path of Roman politics.

The impetus that forced the plebes to seek their freedom was the shackle of the patrician's oppression. The wealthy patricians continued to expand their land holdings, taking the best property and increasing their herds until they monopolized the public pasturelands. They also continued the practice of lending money at ruinous interest to the small proprietors, eventually reducing the plebes to abject slavery when they could not pay.

At the same time, the population of Rome was increasing so fast that the arable land and their primitive farming methods could not support the increase in hungry mouths. Also, the burden of constant warfare fell most heavily on the plebeians, who had to leave their subsistence farms to fight the state's battles. This didn't allow them to provide for their families or even begin to pay off the debts they incurred to start farming the land.

To right these wrongs the plebeians went on what today would be called a general strike. In 494 BCE, they marched out of Rome in a body and threatened to make a new city. At the fear of losing its large labor force, the patricians agreed to cancel all debts and to release people who were in prison for debt. By 350 BCE, the plebes gained the ability to participate fully in the Republic's government.

While these important changes were taking place at home, the little city-state had been gradually extending the reach of its power. Compelled at first to fight for its very existence against its powerful neighbors (mainly the Etruscans, Aequians, and Volscians), Rome gradually fought its way into the leadership role of all the Italian peoples, called the **Latin League**. This dependence on military strength to establish then maintain their republic helped develop the patterns necessary for Rome to conquer of the world.

ROMAN CONQUEST OF ITALY

The Latin League started to develop a dislike for the growing power and arrogance of their ally and attempted to break away from its control; but Rome won the two year war that followed (340-338 BCE) and firmly established their dominance. The truce that was made between Rome and the Latin League was broken a few years later (326 BCE) by the **Samnites**, and a wild-fought struggle ensued, with a variety of interruptions, until the decisive battle of **Sentinum** (295 BCE), which made Rome supreme over all central and northern Italy.

Southern Italy, still occupied by a disunited group of Greek city-states, still remained independent. Alarmed at the spread of Roman power, the Greek cities appealed to **Pyrrhus**, king of Epirus in Greece, who heeded their warning and inflicted two telling defeats on the Roman army. He then crossed to Sicily to aid the Greek cities there in eliminating Carthaginian rule. Unfortunately this was a classic example of spreading your forces too thin and trying to fight a war on two fronts. Encouraged by the arrival of a Carthaginian fleet to combat the Greeks, Rome renewed its struggle for the Greek city-states in southern Italy, and in 275 BCE defeated Pyrrhus in the battle of **Beneventum** and a new phrase was born: a Pyrrhic victory – where you win the war but at excessive cost. Eventually, one by one the Greek cities were taken, and just like that Rome was ruler of all Italy.

KEEPING THE CONQUERED LANDS HAPPY

Rome gradually wove the lands conquered into the fabric of a single nation, contented and unified. Rome could have exploited the conquered cities of Italy for its own interests, but instead made them partners in the future success of the entire empire.

Rome also set about establishing colonies of its citizens all over Italy. Almost one sixth of all Italy was annexed and distributed among these colonizing Roman citizens. By encouraging this colonization, a common interest in the welfare of Rome spread throughout the Italian peninsula.

THE PUNIC WARS

The previous centuries of warfare had developed Rome into a nation of soldiers. The republic's only remaining rival in the western Mediterranean was the Phoenician colony of **Carthage**. While Rome obviously was the chief land power, Carthage was the established sea power of that era. They were so powerful that Carthage had a policy of sinking any trading vessel of any other city that dared to bid for a share of the rich commerce of the Mediterranean region. Rome could not abide by these restrictions, so a series of **Punic Wars** for Mediterranean supremacy began in 264 BCE.

The courage and endurance of Rome's forces were tested to the utmost in this long and devastating series of wars; but after the battle of **Zama** (202 BCE), Carthage was reduced to the position of a vassal state. In 146 BCE, during the **Third Punic War**, because Carthage was again beginning to flex its military and economic might, Rome once again savagely attacked its rival and razed the city Carthage eliminating them forever as an opposing force.

WINNING WORLD MASTERY

With the destruction of Carthage, Rome was well on its way to world domination, at least the known world at the time. Emboldened with this sudden rise to power, the new generation of Roman statesmen ignored the just policies of their successful predecessors; and they forced most of the conquered lands to be administered by governors (**proconsuls**), and did not offer these conquered people a real chance to become full Roman citizens. These foreign governors ruled like czars, and through the enormous taxes levied on the local populations, tried to amass in their one year of office enough wealth to last them a lifetime. A situation that did not ingratiate them, or Rome, to the local populations.

From these taxes, incredible amounts of gold, jewelry, and money in the form of taxes poured into Rome from all over the world, and the ancient simplicity of Roman life gave way to luxury. Morals were undermined, and vice and corruption flourished. Vast estates began to be established by buying up the small farms of the common people. And if they weren't taken over, the common peasants were too poor to compete with the hordes of slaves who were brought it to work the great plantations. One after another of the farmers either failed or were bought out, and as a result the streets of Rome grew clogged with ruined farmers, as well as with discharged soldiers and the poor from all over Italy. These people lived on state and private charity, as well as the bribes that political candidates gave them to curry their favor in the next election.

THE END OF THE ROMAN REPUBLIC

As a result of an increasing disparity in income, once again a conflict began to brew between the aristocracy (formerly the Patricians) and the vast, oppressed and poor citizens (formerly the Plebes). A number of brave men tried to step forward and right the wrongs that were occurring, but each person who did ended up assassinated for his efforts.

To try and maintain a semblance of order a law was forcibly passed that transferred supreme power from the people to the **Senate**. The aristocrats, who became Senators, however, were too corrupt and feeble to hold power, and the Roman Republic came to an end. At this time, two brilliant statesmen, **Gaius Julius Caesar** and his great-nephew **Augustus** (**Octavian**), helped save Rome by scrapping the old republican framework and remolded the tottering structure into an empire. All power was gradually concentrated in the hands of a single ruler, who was backed by the might of the Roman Legions.

TWO CENTURIES OF PEACE & PROSPERITY

With the establishment of the Empire, two centuries of profound peace ensued, the **Roman Peace** (*Pax Romana*), only broken by small frontier warfare. In the provinces men held power responsibly, because they feared the omnipotent wrath of the emperor, and in Rome literature and civilization flourished. Increasingly the Mediterranean came to resemble one great nation, with paved roads leading from the south of Italy all the way up into what are now France and Germany. After the Roman Empire crumbled, road transportation did not return to the same level of quality until well into the 19th century. Even today fragments of Roman roads and ruins still exist in Britain, aqueducts and bridges can be seen in France, Roman wells are still used in the Egyptian oases of the Sahara Desert, and Roman amphitheaters can be visited in the heart of Tunisia. All over the Mediterranean the influence of Roman remains for all to see.

After two centuries, the pursuit hedonism once again obsessed the people of Rome. The rich amused themselves by giving splendid feasts. The poor had their circuses where free bread and wine was distributed. Slave labor had degraded the once sturdy peasantry to the status of serfs or beggars, and the middle class, who once had been the backbone of the nation, had almost disappeared. A welfare mentality overcame the population. And Roman governors of the provinces once again began to concentrate on siphoning off as much money as possible during their short term of office, instead of keeping abreast of the economic and political climate.

THE FALL OF THE ROMAN EMPIRE

Political decay, economic troubles, and decadent living were sapping the strength and discipline of the Roman Empire. At this time, German 'barbarians,' who were a violent people living on the fringes of the empire and led by warrior chiefs, began to attack the edges of the empire in the 4th century CE (Common Era). These **Goths**, **Vandals**, **Lombards**, **Franks**, **Angles**, **Saxons**, and other tribes defeated unprepared Roman garrison after garrison, and sacked and pillaged the decadent and crumbling empire. In 330 CE, when the Roman emperor **Constantine** moved the capital to **Constantinople** (today's Istanbul in Turkey), the Western Roman Empire began a gradual decline. Order made way for chaos and rival governors fought over fragments of Italian territory to increase their power.

With the fall of the Western Roman Empire in CE 476, this was the beginning of the period called the **Dark Ages**. They were so called because Roman civilization and law collapse along with its artistic and engineering achievements. Order was lost, well developed distribution trade routes evaporated, people went back to the way life was like prior to Roman rule and in most cases it was a step backward in time. Coordinated agriculture was lost, the roads fell into ruin, irrigation system were not maintained, public health measures were ignored and the resulting poor hygiene set the stage for coming of the Black Plague.

What the 'barbarians' did bring with them, however, an aspect of their freedom and independence that helped shape the future of Western civilization, was their belief that the individual was important, more so than the state. In contrast, the Romans believed in the rule of the state over the people – in despotism, or the concept of a benevolent dictator. The 'barbarians' gave us a rudimentary form of personal rights, including more respect for women, government by the people for the people, and a system of law which represented the needs and wishes of the people being governed. In essence, these 'barbarians' lived under the beginnings of democracy in Europe.

AFTER THE ROMAN EMPIRE

Even **Charlemagne**, who had conquered the Lombard rulers and had himself crowned emperor of the **Holy Roman Empire** in 800 CE, could not stop the disintegration of everything the Roman Empire had built. To maintain a semblance of order, the Holy Roman Empire became a union between the Papacy and Charlemagne in which management of the empire was shared.

But Charlemagne's Holy Roman Empire fell apart after his death, only to be refounded by the Saxon **Otto I** in 962 CE, bringing Italy into a close alliance with Germany. From that time until the 1800s, the Holy Roman Empire took on many shapes, sizes, and rulers. It included at different times France, Germany, Luxembourg, the north of Italy (because the Muslims, and then the Normans had taken control of Italy south of Naples), Austria, Switzerland, and more. It had rulers from the Saxon Line, Franconian Line, Hohenstaufen Line, Luxembourg Line, and the Hapsburg Line. It may have been constantly in flux but it did last over 1,000 years in some shape or form.

While the Holy Roman Empire expanded and contracted, it eventually contracted itself outside of Italy, leaving Italy an amalgamation of warring city-states. Florence, Venice, Milan, and the Papacy became the strongest of these contending powers and they came to dominate the countryside while feudalism declined. They drew their riches from the produce of their fertile river valleys and from profits generated in commerce between the Orient and Europe. This trade flowed in through Venice, Pisa, Genoa and Naples and passed through to other European cities on its way across the Alps.

THE ITALIAN RENAISSANCE

Under the patronage of the Papacy and of the increasingly prosperous princes of the city-states, such as the **Medici** of Florence, the scholars, writers, sculptors and painters created the masterpieces of literature, art, and science that made the **Italian Renaissance** one of the most influential movements in history. In this period many splendid churches, palaces, and public buildings were built that still inspire awe in Italians and visitors alike. But at the same time as this resurgence in artistic expression, almost completely lost after the fall of the Roman Empire the dominant city states in Italy – Florence, Pisa, Siena, Venice, Perugia, Milan, the Papal States and more – were filled with social strife and political unrest.

PAWN OF STRONG NATIONS

While Italy was being torn by struggles between the local rulers and the Papacy, and among themselves, strong nations were developing elsewhere in Europe. As a result of this, Italy became an area of conquest for the other powers struggling for European supremacy. French and Spanish rivalry over Italy began in 1494. **Charles VIII of France** valiantly fought his way through the peninsula to Naples, but by 1544 **Charles I of Spain** had defeated the French three times and had become ruler of Sicily, Naples, and Milan.

For centuries the city-states of Italy remained mere pawns in other nations' massive chess games of power. Italian city-states passed from one to another of Europe's rulers through war, marriage, death, or treaty. The

Papacy was, however, usually strong enough to protect its temporal power over the areas in central Italy known as the **States of the Church**, or the **Papal States**.

SPANISH & AUSTRIAN RULE

For over 150 years (1559-1713), Spain was the dominant power in Italy. Then the **Treaty of Utrecht** (1713) ended the **War of the Spanish Succession** and established the Austrian Hapsburgs in place of the Spanish as Italy's paramount power.

As time went by the Spanish began to feel slighted by the amount of land that had been ceded to Austria, so they sought to take back their former possessions. In 1734 **Don Carlos**, son of Philip V of Spain, conquered Naples and Sicily, and ruled the area as **Charles III of Naples**.

During this time, in the 18th century, enormous wealth was held by the few while the masses lived in squalor. The peasants existed virtually without rights or defenders. In many areas they lived in abject poverty, and as a result crime rates were shockingly high despite harsh laws and punishments.

Ideas of reform coming from other nations found some response among the intellectuals and the middle class, and the concepts of liberty and equality stirring in France gained many Italian supporters. Many Italians were so blinded with these French egalitarian ideals that they offered assistance to a foreigner, **Napoleon Bonaparte**, when he began his conquest of Italy in the 1790s.

Then when Napoleon was defeated, most Italian states went back to their former sovereigns. For example, Venezia (Venice) was re-absorbed into Austrian rule, Naples and Sicily were re-absorbed into Spanish rule, and the city-states in Umbria become once again part of the Papal States. Italy remained a pawn in European politics without a political will of its own.

MOVEMENT FOR POLITICAL UNITY

Eventually hatred of foreign rule mounted, and with it grew the **Risorgimento**, or movement for political unity. Such secret societies as the Carbonari (charcoal burners, the name given from their use of charcoal burners' huts for meeting places), plotted against the Austrians, but the **Carbonari Revolts** were crushed in 1821 and again in 1831 by Austrian troops.

Then the idealistic republican leader, **Giuseppe Mazzini**, organized his revolutionary society, **Young Italy**, and called upon **Charles Albert**, king of Sardinia-Piedmont and a member of the ancient House of Savoy, to head a movement to liberate Italy. By early 1848, revolts had broken out in many regions, and constitutions had been granted to Naples, Piedmont, and Tuscany. But when Mazzini drove out the pope and set up a short-lived republic in Rome the French came to the pope's aid, and Austria quelled the revolt in the north. Despite this outside interference, the ball was rolling, and when Charles Albert abdicated his rule in Sardinia-Piedmont to his son **Victor Emmanuel II**, the stage was set for a run at independence.

Under the able leadership of the shrewd diplomat **Count Camillo di Cavour**, Victor Emmanuel's minister, Sardinia-Piedmont grew strong in resources and in alliances. Cavour was also aware that no matter how real Italian patriotic fervor was, the country would never be unified without help from abroad, so he cleverly forged an alliance with **Napoleon III** of France. Then in the spring of 1859 Austria was goaded into declaring war against Sardinia-Piedmont and France, and was defeated by the combined French and Italian forces. Italy claimed the lands of Lombardy for a united Italy, but France kept as its bounty the kingdom of Venezia.

To consolidate their power, Cavour and Victor Emmanuel lobbied the peoples of Tuscany, Modena, Parma, and Emilia who eventually voted to cast out their princes and join Sardinia-Piedmont as parts of a unified Italy. Napoleon III consented to such an arrangement, but only if Savoy and Nice voted to join France. (Politics is too complicated. I'll stick to travel writing).

GARIBALDI TO THE RESCUE

The second step toward a united Italy came the next year, when the famous soldier of fortune **Giuseppe Garibaldi** and his thousand red-shirted volunteers stormed the island of Sicily and the rest of the Kingdom of Naples on the mainland. The people everywhere hailed him as a liberator, and the hated Bourbon king was driven out.

In February 1861 **Victor Emmanuel II** was proclaimed king of Italy, and he began working closely with Garibaldi. Now only the Papal States and Venezia remained outside of the new Italian nation. Venezia joined in 1866 after Prussia defeated Austria in alliance with Italy. The Papal States and **San Marino** were now the only entities on the peninsula outside the Italian kingdom. Not yet as small and isolated as it is today, San Marino was then about the size the current region of Lazio making it a valuable prize for a unified Italy.

VATICAN CAPTURED - KINGDOM OF ITALY UNITED

Since French troops still guarded the pope's sovereignty, Victor Emmanuel, being the apt pupil of Cavour (who had died in 1861), did not want to attack the French and perhaps undo all that had been accomplished. Then, miraculously in 1870, the **Franco-Prussian War** forced France to withdraw its soldiers from Rome, at which time Italian forces immediately marched in.

Pope Pius IX, in his infinite lack of wisdom and understanding, excommunicated the invaders and withdrew behind the walls of the Vatican. There he and his successors remained 'voluntary prisoners' until the **Concordat of 1929**, or **Lateran Treaty**, between Italy and the Holy See, which recognized the temporal power of the pope as sovereign ruler over Vatican City (all 108.7 acres of it, or about 1/6 of a square mile!). The rest of the Papal States was absorbed into the new unified Italy, as was San Marino, except for the small, fortified town on top of a butte-like hill that remains independent today.

MODERN ITALY - THE BEGINNING

Staggering under a load of debt and heavy taxation, giant steps needed to still be taken for Italy to survive. Leaders of the various regions, always trying to gain an edge, were in constant disagreement - even in active conflict. At the same time citizens, used to the ultimate control of despotic rule, found it difficult to adopt the ways of parliamentary government. As a result, riots and other forms of civil disorder were the rule in the latter half of the 19th century.

Despite all of these problems, in the typical Italian mode of functioning despite complete political chaos, an army and navy were developed; railroads, ports, and schools were constructed; and a merchant marine was developed. At the same time, industrial manufacturing started to flourish as it was all over the world.

But then, in 1900, **King Umberto I** (son of Victor Emmanuel II) was assassinated by anarchists - in what was to turn out to be a string of assassinations during that time period all over Europe - and his son, **Victor Emmanuel III**, rose to the throne. Although having joined with Germany and Austria in the **Triple Alliance** in 1882, by the early 1900s Italy began to befriend France and England. With Austria's invasion of Serbia in 1914 after the assassination of Archduke Ferdinand of Austria, Italy declared its neutrality despite being Austria's ally. In April 1915, Italy signed a secret treaty with the **Allies** (Russia, France, and England), and the next month it stated that it had withdrawn from the Triple Alliance. On May 23, 1915, the king of Italy declared war on Austria.

When World War I ended in 1918, the old Austro-Hungarian Empire was broken up. Italy was granted territory formerly under Austrian rule, including "unredeemed Italy" of the Trentino in the north and the peninsula of Istria at the head of the Adriatic.

MUSSOLINI & FASCISM

The massive worldwide depression after World War I brought strikes and riots, which were fomented by anarchists, socialists, and Communists. The government of Victor Emmanuel III seemed powerless to stop bands of former servicemen lawlessly roaming the country. In these bands, **Benito Mussolini** saw his opportunity to gain power. With his gift of oratory he soon molded this rabble into enthusiastic, organized groups in many communities all over Italy, armed them, and set them to preserving the order which had been had destroyed. These bands formed the nucleus of his black-shirted **Fascist** party, whose emblem was the *fasces*, the bundle of sticks that had symbolized the authority of the Roman Empire.

On Oct. 28, 1922, the **Blackshirts**, meeting in Naples, were strong enough, well enough prepared, and willing to march on Rome and seize the government. The king, fearing civil war and his own life, refused to proclaim martial law, forced the premier to resign, and asked Mussolini to form a shared government. Within a few years Mussolini, *Il Duce* (The Leader), had reorganized the government so that the people had no voice at all. Mussolini first abolished all parties except his own Fascist party, and took from the Chamber of Deputies the power to consider any laws not proposed by him. The king remained as a figurehead because he was revered by the people and had the support of many wealthy and important families. In 1939 when Mussolini replaced the Chamber of Deputies with the Chamber of Fasces and Corporations, composed of all his henchmen, no semblance of popular rule remained.

Intimidation or violence crushed all opposition. Suspected critics of the regime were sentenced to prison by special courts or were terrorized, tortured or murdered by Blackshirt thugs. News was censored and public meetings could not be held without the government's permission. The new Fascist state was based on the doctrine that the welfare of the state is all-important and that the individual exists only for the state, owes everything to it, and has no right of protection against it. It was a return to the despotism of the later Roman Empire.

A RETURN TO THE ROMAN EMPIRE?

Mussolini, like other Italian leaders before him, longed to create a new Roman empire and to bring back Italy's lost glory. So, in 1935, with his large army and recently expanded navy, he attacked and conquered the weak, backward, and poorly defended African country of Ethiopia.

In October 1936, at Mussolini's invitation, the **Rome-Berlin Axis** was formed between Italy and Nazi Germany to oppose the power of France and England. At this time Mussolini was considered the stronger ally of the two. In April 1939, Italy invaded Albania, and which that time Italy and Germany became formal military allies.

But when Germany's program of aggression plunged it into war with England and France on September 3, 1939, Italy at first adopted the position of a non-belligerent. But on June 10, 1940, Italian forces attacked southeastern France in an invasion coordinated with German forces in the north.

DEFEAT IN WORLD WAR II

Italy lacked the military power, resources, and national will to fight a large-scale modern war. Within six months, Italian armies met defeat in Greece and North Africa. In fact a running joke during World War II was that Italian tanks had only one gear: reverse. Italy then humbly accepted the military assistance of Germany. This soon grew into complete economic and military dependence, and Italy was forced to let Germany occupy it, control its home affairs, and Mussolini became a German puppet.

The end of the war found Italy with the majority of its industry and agriculture shattered. During its occupation, the Germans had almost stripped Italy's industry bare by commandeering supplies. Italian factories, roads, docks, and entire villages were ruined by the Allied bombing raids and during the invasion. To make things worse, as the Germans retreated they had wrecked whatever industries and transportation remained.

Even with the Allies contributing substantial quantities of food, clothing, and other supplies, the people were cold, hungry, and jobless. After the war, the United Nations Relief and Rehabilitation Administration gave more aid to Italy than to any other country. Reconstruction lagged, however, because of internal political turmoil, a situation that has become something of a theme in postwar Italian politics.

POSTWAR POLITICAL CHANGES

On May 9, 1946, Victor Emmanuel III formally abdicated in favor of his son, who reigned for less than one month as **Umberto II**, because on June 2, 1946, the Italian people voted to found a republic. They then elected deputies to a Constituent Assembly to draft a new constitution.

Finally on February 10, 1947, the peace treaty between Italy and the Allies was ready to be signed. The treaty stripped Italy of its African 'empire' of Libya, Italian Somaliland, and Eritrea. The pact also ceded the Dodecanese Islands to Greece, placed Trieste under UN protection, made minor boundary changes with France, and gave about 3,000 square miles to Yugoslavia, including most of the Istrian peninsula.

Italy had to pay $360 million in reparations, and was also forced to restore independence to Ethiopia and Albania. One lone gain was that **South Tyrol**, which Austria had been forced to cede after World War I, remained with Italy; and eventually, in 1954, **Trieste** was given to Italy through a pact with Yugoslavia.

On January 1, 1948, Italy's newly formed constitution became effective. It banned the Fascist party - though today there are a number of political parties in Italy that go by another name but informally call themselves *Fascisti* - and the monarchy. Freedom of religion was guaranteed, though Catholicism remained the state religion.

But a constitution alone cannot recreate a country. Italian leaders had the double task of creating a stable parliamentary system of government while at the same time restoring the economy. (They still haven't solved the first problem.) The main economic hindrance was the poverty-stricken, agriculturally dependent south contributing little to the improving industrial economy of the north. As a result there were many riots and moments of intense civil unrest.

LAND REFORM

One of the reasons that the south of Italy was so poor was because much the lands there, as well as in Sicily and Sardinia were among the last aristocratic strongholds of large-scale landowners. The estates of these landowners covered many thousands of acres and employed only small numbers of laborers, mostly at harvest time. These landless peasants, who had no work during much of the year, lived in nearby villages and small towns and barely made ends meet all year. These people either stayed peaceful and subservient, contributed to civil unrest, or emigrated to find better employment and living conditions elsewhere.

In the early 1950s, the Italian parliament passed special land reform laws that divided large private estates into small farms and distributed them to the peasants. The new owners were given substantial government support for their first years on the land, and the previous owners received cash compensation. Thousands of new small farms were created in this way during the 1950s, and farm production, as a result of the land reform and other measures, rose quickly.

The Italian government not only invested large sums of money in land reform but at the same time also started to develop the infrastructure in the south to help the farmers. New roads were built to help carry produce to market, and new irrigation systems, needed during the long, dry summers, were constructed. Warehouses and cold storage facilities for farm products were provided, and the government also helped to introduce new crops.

CHAOS MIXED WITH STABILITY

Even with the south's new-found prosperity, Italy's economic development was mainly due to spectacular gains in industrial production in the north. But then during the mid-1960s, Italy began to suffer from severe inflation. A government austerity program to combat this trend produced a decline in profits and a lag in investments. To add insult to injury, devastating floods – the worst in 700 years which were caused by severe soil erosion – hit the country in 1966, ravaging one third of the land and causing losses of more than $1.5 billion. To make matters even worse, some of the priceless art treasures of Florence were irreparably damaged when the flood waters poured through that city.

In 1971 Italy had its largest economic recession since the country's post-World War II recovery. Strikes affected nearly every sector of the economy as Italian workers demanded social reforms. The problems of inflation, unemployment, lack of housing, and unfavorable balance of payments continued in the 1970s.

When Italy was about to pull out of its economic problems, political terrorism escalated, culminating in March 1978, when **Aldo Moro**, leader of the Christian Democratic party and former premier, was abducted in Rome by the **Red Brigades**, an extreme left-wing terrorist group. During the two months that Moro was held, Rome was like an armed camp, with military roadblocks everywhere. I was living there at that time and the memory of sub-machine guns being pointed at me still lingers. Eventually Moro was found murdered and left in the trunk of his car.

In 1980, in Italy's worst natural disaster in more than 70 years, an earthquake killed more than 3,000 persons in the Naples area. As if things could only get worse, in May 1981 a Turkish political dissident tried to kill Pope John Paul II in St. Peter's Square. Also in 1981, a corruption scandal involving hundreds of public servants who were allegedly members of a secret society erupted and brought down the government.

Economic conditions in the early 1980s were affected by growing recession and rising inflation. The Vatican Bank and the Banco Ambrosiano of Milan, Italy's biggest private banking group, were involved in a major banking scandal that forced the liquidation of Banco Ambrosiano in 1982. Two more natural disasters, an earthquake and a landslide, caused widespread damage in the regions of Perugia and Ancona in late 1982.

In 1989, another bank became involved in a scandal when it was revealed that an American branch of the Banca Nazionale del Lavoro had loaned billions of dollars to Iraq. Then severe drought occurred throughout Italy in the winter of 1989 and in Venice some canals were unusable because water levels had dropped so low. And still, into the late 1990s, the Italian government is under intense investigation for rampant corruption which includes officials taking bribes from, or actively colluding with members of the Mafia.

Despite all of this, the Italian economy continues to improve, to the point where it is one of the more successful in Europe. Throughout all of this chaos, Italy perseveres. It's almost as if without a reasonable amount of disorder, Italy could not survive.

Most recently, a separatist political party has emerged, called the **Northern League** (La Lega Nord) is attempting to create the 'federal republic of Padania' in the industrial north of Italy. Founded in 1984, the party is now gaining support and popularity because most northern Italians feel that they pay a disproportionate share of the country's taxes. Taxes which they say go to support the impoverished south and keep the bloated government functioning in Rome.

This idea of splitting Italy in two is not so far fetched when you realize that only in the last century has the peninsula been one unified country. There have always been glaring differences in culture between south and central Italy and their northern cousins. And to emphasize this point, in the last local elections, the Northern League won over 10% of the vote.

Who knows? Maybe one day you will be booking one trip to Italy and another to Padania.

6. PLANNING YOUR TRIP

BEFORE YOU GO

CLIMATE & WEATHER

The climate in Italy is as varied as the country itself, but it never seems to get too harsh. As a result any time is a good time to travel to Italy since most of the country has a Mediterranean type of climate, meaning cool, slightly rainy winters and warm, dry summers.

The summers are mild in the north, but winters there tend to be colder because these regions are in or near the Alps. The Alps do play a role in protecting the rest of Italy from cold northern winds. Because Italy is a peninsula and thus surrounded by water, the entire country never seems to get too hot except for the south and Sicily. These regions are very hot in the summer, and in the winter, wetter than normal. Winter temperatures along and near the coasts of southern Italy seldom drop to freezing in winter, and summer temperatures often reach 90 degrees F (32 degrees C) or higher.

Winter is the rainy season, when stream beds that remain empty during much of the year fill to overflowing. In Venice during this time, even a slight rain fall will cause the city to be flooded. Be aware of this when traveling there during this time. In the summer, since they are on the water, Venice can be somewhat muggy.

Rome has the mildest climate all year round, although the *sirocco* – a hot and humid red sand tinged wind blowing from North Africa – can produce stifling weather in August every other year or so. Winters are very moderate with snow being extremely rare. But it is wise to dress warmly. If you want to obtain the average temperature, temperature ranges and precipitation totals by month for Rome or other destinations in Italy visit the following website: *www.washingtonpost.com/wp-srv/weather/historical/historical.htm.*

ITALY'S FOUR SEASONS

***Spring** – Italy has an early spring. The best places to visit are Florence, around Naples and Sorrento, Sicily, and Rome.*

***Summer** – Summer can be a little hot in certain places, so to cool you down there are plenty of beach resorts along most of Italy's coast, especially in Liguria on the Italian Riviera. But the best place to go is the mountains of Tuscany or the northern regions of Lombardia, Piemonte, or Trentino Alto-Adige. This is not to say that Rome or Venice would not be pleasant, just crowded with tourists and relatively warm.*

***Autumn** – This is a pleasant time to visit Rome and other major central and southern cities, since they are less crowded and much cooler.*

***Winter** – Time for winter sports. You can find ski centers in the Alps as well as the central Apennines near Florence and Rome. Also at this time, the southern regions and Sicily are at their best.*

WHEN TO GO

Basically, anytime is good time to travel to Italy. The climate doesn't vary greatly making Italy a pleasant trip any time of year. Then again I'm biased – I spent eight wonderful years in Italy and I think it's fantastic all year. The busiest tourist season is from May to October, leaving the off-season of Spring and Autumn as the choice times to have Italy all to yourself.

I do believe though that the best time to go is the off-season, when there are less tourists around. More specifically, October and November and March and April are perfect times not only because of the weather but also because of the lack of tourists. December is also fun because there are so many festivals during the Christmas season.

Most people come during the summer making many of the most popular tourist cities like Rome, Florence and Venice over crowded. Then in August the entire country literally shuts down, since most Italians abandon the cities to vacation at the beach or in the mountains. Personally I find August a wonderful time to visit too, since the cities become sparse with people. Granted many restaurants, shops and businesses are closed during this time but the country is still as scenic and beautiful.

The summer months though packed with people in the cities are great months to come and visit the hiking trails of the Alps and Appenines. Remember to bring clothing for colder weather even though it is summer.

The sidebar above offers you a breakdown by season of the best regions to visit during those times.

WHAT TO PACK

One suitcase and a carry-on should suffice for your average ten day trip. Maybe the best advice for shoppers is to pack light and buy clothes while you're there, since there are countless clothing stores from which you can buy yourself any needed item. Also if you pack light it will be easier to transport your belongings. A suitcase with wheels is important, but since there are endless numbers of stairs even the wheels won't relieve the burden of lifting your bag every once and awhile. And even if there are no stairs, because of the uneven state of Italian pavements, and in some cases non-existent sidewalks, pulling a wheel suitcase can be cumbersome. I prefer a wheeled carry-on, but if you're the rugged type, a back pack is the best choice.

To clean your clothes you can always find a local *Tintoria* (dry cleaner) if your hotel does not supply such a service. If you want to do it yourself, it's best to look for a *Lavanderia* - coin operated laundromat - instead. Remember also to pack all your personal cosmetic items that you've grown accustomed to, since, more than likely, they're not available in Italian stores. The Italian culture just hasn't seemed to grasp the necessity of having 400 types of toothpaste, or 200 types of tampons. If you take medication remember to get the drug's generic name because name brands on medications are different all over the world.

An important item to remember, especially if you're traveling in the winter time, is an umbrella, a raincoat, and water-proof shoes. You never know when the rain will fall in the winter. You should also bring a small pack, or knapsack to carry with you on day trips. A money belt is also advised, because of pick pockets though I've never had any problems. The same can be said for handbags and purses to thwart the potential risk of purse snatchers.

But most importantly, bring a good pair of comfortable walking shoes or hiking boots. A light travel iron is not a bad idea if you cannot abide wrinkles; but a more sensible option is to pack wrinkle free clothes. And in the summer, if you want to get into most of the churches, remember to pack long pants or something to cover your legs. Tank tops and halter top type shirts are also not considered appropriate attire.

And finally, an important item to remember if you are sexually active are condoms. They can be expensive in Italy so remember to bring along your own.

PUBLIC HOLIDAYS

Offices and shops in Italy are closed on the dates below. So prepare for the eventuality of having virtually everything closed and stock up on picnic snacks, soda, whatever, because in most cities and towns there is no such thing as 24-7. The Italians take their free time seriously. To them the concept of having something open 24 hours a day, every day of the week like we do here in North America, is a little crazy.

- **January 1**, New Year's Day
- **January 6**, Epiphany
- **April 25**, Liberation Day (1945)
- **Easter Monday**
- **May 1**, Labor Day
- **August 15**, *Ferragosto* and Assumption of the Blessed Virgin (climax of Italian family holiday season. Hardly anything stays open in the big cities through the month of August)
- **November 1**, All Saints Day
- **December 8**, Immaculate Conception
- **December 25/26**, Christmas

Listed below are some dates that may be considered public holidays in different areas of Italy, so prepare for them too:

- **June 2**, Proclamation of Republic (celebrated on the following Saturday)
- **November 4**, National Unity Day (celebrated on following Saturday)

LOCAL FESTIVAL DAYS & THEIR PATRON SAINTS

Town	*Date*	*Patron Saint*
Florence	*June 24*	*St. John the Baptist*
Rome	*June 29*	*Sts. Peter and Paul*

MAKING AIRLINE RESERVATIONS

Since airfares can vary so widely it is advised to contact a reputable travel agent and stay abreast of all promotional fares advertised in the newspapers. Once you're ticketed getting there is a breeze. Just hop on the plane and 6-8 hours later you're there. Italy's two main international airports are Rome's **Fiumicino** (also known as **Leonardo da Vinci**) and Milan's **Malpensa**, which handle all incoming flights from North America and Australia.

There are other, smaller regional airports in Bologna, Florence, Pisa and Venice that accept flights from all over Europe as well as the United Kingdom, but not from North America or Australia. So, if you are only visiting the fairy tale city of Venice and want to fly almost directly there, contact your travel agent and make sure they get you on an airline, most likely British Air, that will allow for a transfer in London and a connection to Venice.

Fares are highest during the peak summer months (June through mid-September) and lowest from November through March (except during peak Christmas travel time). You can get the best fares by booking far in advance. This will also assure you a good seat. Getting a non-stop flight to Italy at the last minute is simply an impossibility during the high season. If you are concerned about having to change your schedule at the last minute, and do not want to book far in advance, look into some special **travel insurance** that will cover the cost of your ticket under such circumstances. Check with your travel agent about details and pricing since these, like ticket prices, change almost on a daily basis.

PASSPORT REGULATIONS

A visa is not required for US or Canadian citizens, or members of the European Economic Community, who are holding a valid passport, unless that person expects to stay in Italy longer than 90 days and/or study or seek employment. While in Italy, you can apply for a longer stay at any police station for an extension of an additional 90 days. You will be asked to prove that you're not seeking such an extension for study or employment, and that you have adequate means of support. Usually permission is granted almost immediately.

When staying at a hotel, you will need to produce your passport when you register; and most likely the desk clerk will need to keep your passport overnight to transcribe the relevant details for their records. Your passport will most likely be returned that same day. If not, make sure you request it since it is an Italian law that identification papers be carried at all times. Usually a native driver's license will suffice but I always carry my passport. If you are concerned about pickpockets, keep your passport in the front pocket of your pants. I keep mine in a small zip lock bag so it won't get moist with perspiration.

If you have failed to renew your passport and you need one right away try **Instant Passport**, *Tel. 800/284-2564, www.instantpassport.com*. They promise to give you 24-hour turnaround from the time they receive your passport pictures and requisite forms. They charge $100 plus overnight shipping on top of all fees associated with passport issuance.

Another company, **American Passport Express**, *Tel. 800/841-6778, www.americanpassport.com*, offers three types of service - expedited (24 hours), express (three to four business days) and regular. Prices range from $245 to $135. If you need to download passport application forms, visit the State Department web site at ***www.travel.state.gov***.

VACCINATIONS

No vaccinations are required to enter Italy, or for that matter, to re-enter the U.S., Canada, or any other European country. But some people are starting to think it may be wise, especially for Hepatitis A. One of those people is Donna Shipley, B.S.N, R.N. and President of Smart Travel, an international health service organization. She says, "Even though the perception is that Italy is safe and clean, it is still not like North America. In other words it is better to be safe than sorry. Prevention makes sense."

For information about vaccinations contact **Smart Travel**, *Tel. 800/730-3170.*

TRAVEL INSURANCE

This is the most frequently forgotten precaution in travel. Just like other insurance, this is for 'just in case' scenarios. The beauty of travel insurance is that it covers a wide variety of occurrences, such as trip cancellation or interruption, trip delay/missed connection, itinerary change, accident medical expense, sickness medical expense, baggage and baggage delay, and medical evacuation/repatriation. And to get all that for a week long trip will only cost you only $25. You'll spend more than that on the cab ride from the airport when you arrive.

For travel insurance look in your local yellow pages or contact the well-known international organization below **Travelex**, *Tel. 800/228-9792.*

REGISTRATION BY TOURISTS

This is usually taken care of within three days by the management of your hotel. If you are staying with friends or in a private home, you must register in person at the nearest police station within that three day period. Rome has a special police information office to assist tourists, and they have interpreters available: Tel. 461-950 or 486-609.

CUSTOMS REGULATIONS

Duty free entry is allowed for personal effects that will not be sold, given away, or traded while in Italy: clothing, bicycle, moped no bigger than 50cc, books, camping and household equipment, fishing tackle, one pair of skis, two tennis racquets, portable typewriter (I suppose they mean a portable computer now), record player with 10 records, tape recorder or Dictaphone, baby carriage, two still cameras with 10 rolls of film for each, one movie camera with 10 rolls of film (I suppose they mean 10 cassette tapes now), binoculars, personal jewelry, portable radio set (may be subject to small license fee), 400 cigarettes, and a quantity of cigars or pipe tobacco not to exceed 500 grams (1.1 lbs), two bottles of wine and one bottle of liquor, 4.4 lbs of coffee, 6.6 lbs of sugar, and 2.2 lbs of cocoa.

This is Italy's official list, but they are very flexible with personal items. As well they should be, since technology is changing so rapidly that items not listed last year could be a personal item for most people this year (i.e. Sony Watchmans, portable video games, etc.).

GETTING TO ITALY

FLYING TO ITALY

Alitalia is Italy's national airline. As you probably know, most international carriers have amazing service, pristine environments, serve exquisite food and overall are a joy to travel – but to be honest Alitalia is not one of them. If you want to experience the chaos of Italy at 30,000 feet, fly Alitalia. Despite all of this rhetoric, Alitalia does have the most frequent direct flights from North America to Italy, and as such they are the most convenient carrier to take to Italy.

Airlines

Below is a list of some other major carriers and their flights to Italy:

- **Alitalia**, *Tel. 800/223-5730 in US, www.alitalia.it/eng/index.html. Toll free in Italy 800/1478/65642. Address in Rome – Via Bissolati 13.* Flights from the United States, Canada, and the United Kingdom.
- **Air Canada**, *Tel. 800/776-3000; www.aircanada.com. Toll free in Italy 800/862-216. Rome address – Via C. Veneziani 58.* Flights from Canada to London or Paris, then connections on another carrier to Rome or Milan.
- **American Airlines**, *Tel. 800/433-7300; www.americanair.com. Rome Tel. 06/4274-1240, Via Sicilia 50. Italy E-mail: abtvlaa@tin.it.* Direct flights from Chicago to Milan.
- **British Airways**, *Tel. 800/247-9297; www.british-airways.com. Toll free in Italy 1478/12266. Rome address – Via Bissolati 54.* Connections through London's Heathrow to Rome, Milan, Bologna, Venice, and Palermo.
- **Delta**, *Tel. 800/221-1212; www.delta-air.com. Toll free in Italy 800/864-114. Rome address – Via Po 10.* Direct flights from New York to Rome or Milan.
- **Northwest**, *Tel. 800/2245-2525; www.nwa.com. KLM in Rome 06/652-9286.* Flights to Amsterdam connecting to KLM and onto Rome or Milan.
- **TWA**, *Tel. 800/221-2000; www.twa.com. Toll free in Italy 800/841-843. Rome address – Via Barberini 59.* Direct flights from New York's JFK to Rome or Milan.

- **United**, *Tel. 800/538-2929; www.ual.com. Rome Tel. 06/4890-4140, Via Bissolati 54.* Direct flights from Washington Dulles to Milan.
- **US Airways,** *Tel. 800/622-1015; www.ual.com. Toll free in Italy 800/870-945.* Direct flights from Philadelphia to Rome.

DISCOUNT TRAVEL AGENTS

The best way to find a travel agency for your travel to Italy is by looking in your local yellow pages; but if you want to get the same flights for less, the three organizations below offer the lowest fares available. I have had the best service and best prices from *www.lowestfare.com*, but the others are good also.

- **Fly Cheap**, *Tel. 800/FLY-CHEAP*
- **Fare Deals, Ltd.**, *Tel. 800/347-7006*
- **Lowestfare.com**, *Tel. 888/777-2222*
- **Airdeals.com**, *Tel. 888/999-2174*

In conjunction, listed below are some online travel booking services that offer great fares. Online travel searching can be cumbersome, since there is a registration process and each has a different approach to the reservation and booking process. In essence, what you learn from these services is what your travel agent goes through when they work with reservation systems like Apollo, Worldspan and System One. Also, if you shop here to find out what prices and availability are and then book your flights the regular way, from the airline or a live travel agent, these online service do not like that. Some will even terminate your registration if you shop too frequently without buying.

With that said, here are some websites:

- **Internet Travel Network**, *www.itn.net*
- **Preview Travel**, *www.previewtravel.com*
- **Expedia**, *www.expedia.com*
- **Travelocity**, *www.travelocity.com*

COURIER FLIGHTS

Acting as an air courier – whereby you accompany shipments sent by air in your cargo space in return for discounted airfare – can be one of the least expensive ways to fly. It can also be a little restrictive and inconvenient. But if you want to travel to Italy, at almost half the regular fare, being a courier is for you.

The hassles are (1) that in most cases you have to get to the courier company's offices before your flight, (2) most flights only originate from one city and that may not be the one where you are, (3) since you usually check in later than all other flyers you may not get your choice of seating,

(4) you can only use a carry-on since your cargo space is being allocated for the shipment you are accompanying, (5) your length of stay is usually only 7-10 days – no longer, and (6) courier flights don't do companion flights, which means you fly alone.

But contrary to the common impression, as a courier you usually do not even see the goods being transported and you don't need to check them through customs. Also you are not legally responsible for the shipment's contents – that's the courier company's responsibility – according to industry sources and US Customs.

All of that aside, if you are interested in saving a large chunk of change, give these services a try:

- **Halbart Express**, *Tel. 718/656-8189*
- **Now Voyager**, *Tel. 212/431-1616. Fee of $50*
- **Discount Travel International**, *Tel. 212/362-8113*
- **Airhitch**, *Tel. 212/864-2000; www.airhitch.org.* Air hitching is the least expensive but they are also the most restrictive. You really need to be very flexible, i.e. can travel at the drop of a hat.

For more information about courier flights, listed below are some books you can buy or organizations you can contact:

- **"Insiders Guide to Air Courier Bargains"** *by Kelly Monaghan. Tel. 212/569-1081.* Contact: The Intrepid Traveler, *Tel. 212/569-1081; www.intrepidtraveler.com.* Company is owned by Monaghan.
- **International Association of Air Travel Couriers**, *Tel. 561/582-8320, www.courier.org.*
- **"A Simple Guide to Courier Travel,"** *Tel. 800/344-9375*

DIPLOMATIC & CONSULAR OFFICES IN ITALY

These are the places you'll need to contact if you lose your passport or have some unfortunate brush with the law. If such situations occur, remember that the employees of these offices are merely your government's representatives in a foreign country. They are not God. They cannot do everything in the blink of an eye, but they will do their best to remedy any unfortunate situation in which you may find yourself.

Embassies & Consulates

- **Australia**, *Via Alessandria 205, Tel. 06/852-721*
- **Canadian Embassy**, *Via GB de Rossi 27, Tel. 06/445-981*
- **Great Britain**, *Via XX Settembre 80a, Tel. 06/482-5441, Website: www.grbr.it*
- **Ireland**, *Piazza di Campitelli 3, Tel. 06/697-912*
- **New Zealand**, *Via Zara 28, Tel. 06/441-7171, E-mail: nzemb.roma@flashnet.it*
- **South Africa**, *Via Tanaro 1, Tel. 06/852-541, E-mail: sae@flashnet.it*
- **United States**, *Via Veneto 199, Tel. 06/46741*

US Consulates

- **Florence** – *Lungarno Amerigo Vespucci 38. 1 50123 Firenze, Tel. 055/239-8276*

UK Consulates

- **Florence** – *Palazzo Castelbarco, Lungarno Corsini 2, 50123 Firenze, Tel. 055/21 26 94, 28 41 33 and 28 74 49*

ACCOMMODATIONS

HOTELS - WHAT TO EXPECT

Don't be surprised by hotel taxes, additional charges, and requests for payment for extras, such as air conditioning that make your bill larger than expected. Sometimes these taxes/service charges are included in room rates but you should check upon arrival or when you make your reservation. Remember to save receipts from hotels and car rentals, as 15% to 20% of the value-added taxes (VAT) on these services may be refunded if you are a non-resident. For more information, call **I.T.S. Fabry**, *Tel. 803/720-8646* or see Chapter 16, *Shopping*, Tax-Free Shopping section.

The Italian Tourist Board categorizes all of the hotels in Italy with a star rating. A five star deluxe hotel (*****) is the best, a one-star hotel (*) is the least desirable and usually the least expensive too. The term *Pensione* is in the process of being phased out, and these smaller, bed-and-breakfast type inns are being replaced with a designation of one-star (*), two-star (**), or three star (***) hotel.

MAKING RESERVATIONS

I recommend faxing the hotel(s) of your choice inquiring about availability for the dates you are interested in, as well as the rate for those dates. Faxing is preferable to calling since you can quickly and easily communicate your information, reducing any long distance telephone charges. Obviously if the hotel listed has an e-mail address, that form of communication is preferable.

Also, since most Italians who run hotels speak English, it is possible to write your fax or e-mail in English; but if you want to practice your Italian, they usually appreciate any effort at communicating in their own language. Personally, I write my requests in both English and Italian so that there is no confusion as to the information imparted.

When writing the dates you are interested in, make sure you spell out the month, since here in America we transpose the month and day in numeric dates. For example, in the US January 10, 2001 would appear numerically as 1/10/01. In Europe, it would appear as 10/01/01. See where the confusion could come in?

Expect a reply to your communication within a few days. If you do not get a reply send another message. Sometimes faxes get lost in the night shift. To book your room you will need to send the hotel a credit card number with expiration date in a reply communication. This will ensure that you show up. So if you have to cancel your trip for whatever reason, make sure you contact the hotel and cancel your room – otherwise you will be charged.

HOTEL PRICES

The prices that are listed sometimes include a range, for example L100,000-150,000. The first number in the range indicates what the price is during the off-season, the second price is the going rate during high season. If there is no range, then the hotel doesn't raise its rate for the off-season.

The high season is generally April through September, with Christmas and New Year's week thrown in. Other high seasons will include local festivals, like the **Palio** in Siena or **Calcio in Costume** in Florence. Also, the high season for the ski areas will be winter, not summer, so it is important to inquire up front about what the actual rates will be.

HOTEL PRICES, POST-JUBILEE

In the year 2000, a ***Jubilee*** *celebration year for the Catholic Church, there was a massive influx of tourists. Hotel prices rose accordingly in 2000 and may actually stay in place if people continue to pay them for 2001 and beyond. The Italians are going to try and make as much money as possible off of this Y2K situation, so be prepared for some of the prices in this book to be a little lower than what are quoted to you by the hotels. That may not be the case, but just to make sure, please confirm the cost of your room beforehand.*

HOTEL RATING SYSTEM

The star rating system that the Italian Tourist Board officially uses has little to do with the prices of the hotels, but more to do with the amenities you will find. The prices for each category will vary according to the locale, so if it's a big city, a four star will be super-expensive; if it's a small town, it will be priced like a three star in a big city.

In the ambiguous way of the Italians, nothing is ever as it seems, which means that even the amenities will be different for each star category depending on whether you are in a big city or a smaller town. But basically the list below is what the ratings mean by star category:

*****Five star, deluxe hotel**: Professional service, great restaurant, perfectly immaculate large rooms and bathrooms with air conditioning, satellite TV, mini-bar, room service, laundry service, and every convenience you could imagine to make you feel like a king or queen. Bathrooms in every room.

****Four star hotel**: professional service, most probably they have a restaurant, clean rooms not so large, air conditioning, TV (usually via satellite), mini-bar, room service, laundry service and maybe a few more North American-like amenities. Bathrooms in every room.

***Three star hotel**: a little less professional service, most probably do not have room service, should have air conditioning, TV and mini bar, but the rooms are mostly small as are their bathrooms. Some rooms in small town hotels may not have bathrooms.

Two star hotel: Usually a family run place, some not so immaculate and well taken care of as higher rated hotels. Mostly you'll only find a telephone in the room, and in big cities you'll be lucky to get air conditioning. About 50% of the rooms have either a shower/bath or water closet and sometimes not both together. Hardly any amenities, just a place to lay your head. The exception to this is in small towns, where some two stars are as well appointed as some of the best three stars.

*One star hotel**: Here you usually get a small room with a bed, sometimes you have to share the rooms with other travelers. The bathroom is usually in the hall. No air conditioning, no telephone in the room, just a room with bed. These are what used to be the low-end *pensiones*. Definitely for budget travelers.

AGRITURISMO

If you have ever wanted to work on a farm, Italy has a well organized system where you can do just that. Initially the idea behind **Agriturismo** started as a way for urban Italians to re-connect with their old towns and villages, and through that to the earth again; but every year it has grown in popularity. Traditionally you would rent rooms in family farmhouses, but some accommodations have evolved into more hotel type, bed-and-breakfast like situations with separate buildings on the farms for agriturists. Since there is such a large demand for agriturism, two separate competing bodies have published directories to assist people trying to reconnect with mother nature.

Both of the books sold by these groups are also available at selected bookstores, like the Feltrinelli Bookstores listed in this guide:

- **Agriturist**, *Via Vittorio Emanuele 89, 00186 Roma, Tel. 06/658-342. Open Monday-Friday 10:00am-noon and Tuesday, Wednesday, Thursday 3:30-5:30pm. Closed Saturday and Sunday.*
- **Turismo Verde** (Green Tourism), *Via Mariano Fortuny 20, 00196 Roma, Tel. 06/361-1051.*

MOUNTAIN REFUGES

There are a number of mountain refuges (*rifugi*) available for rent in the Alps and Apennines, many of which are run by the **Club Alpino Italiano (CAI)**. If you are a member, you can get maps and information about hiking, and all necessary information about the *rifugi*. The CAI has offices all over Italy, but there is limited centralization of resources and information, and most offices are run by volunteers and/or avid hikers. Contact the CAI offices listed below, or the local tourist office in the city nearby where you want to go hiking, for any available information.

Even if you are not a member, they are usually rather flexible about accommodating your needs. And if they are not, you can join CAI at any of their offices by simply bringing a photo of yourself and L100,000. With that you will receive a *tessera* (identification document) which is valid for discounts on all CAI merchandise and on stays in the *rifugi* for a year. You can renew by mail.

The *rifugi* are generally dormitory style and meals are available at a cost of around L25,000 per person. There are private *rifugi* which charge rates comparable to about one or two star hotel accommodations. All rifugi are usually only open from July to September and are booked well in advance.

- **CAI–Milano**, *Via Silvio Pellico 6, Tel. 02/8646-3516.*
- **CAI–Roma**, *305 Corso Vittorio Emanuelle II, 4th floor, Tel. 06/686-1011, Fax 06/6880-3424. Website: www.frascati.enea.it/cai*

RENTING VILLAS & APARTMENTS

One of the best ways to spend a vacation in Italy is in a rented villa in the country or in an apartment in the center of town. It makes you feel as if you actually are living in Italy and not just passing through. Staying in "your own place" gives your trip that little extra sense of belonging.

The best way to find a place of your own in Italy is to contact one of the agencies listed below that specialize in the rental of villas and apartments in Italy:

- **At Home Abroad, Inc.**, *405 East 58th Street, New York, NY 10022. Tel. 212/421-9165, Fax 212/752-1591.*

- **Astra Maccioni Kohane** (CUENDET), *10 Columbus Circle, Suite 1220, New York, NY 10019. Tel. 212/765-3924, Fax 212/262-0011.*
- **B&D De Vogue International, Inc.**, *250 S. Beverly Drive, Suite 203, Beverly Hills CA. Tel. 310/247 8612, 800/438-4748, Fax 310/247-9460.*
- **Better Homes and Travel**, *30 East 33rd Street, New York, NY 10016. Tel. 212/689 6608, Fax 212/679-5072.*
- **CIT Tours Corp.**, *342 Madison Ave #207, New York, NY 10173. Tel. 212/697-2100, 800/248-8687, Fax 212/697-1394*
- **Columbus Travel**, *507 Columbus Avenue, San Francisco, CA 941S3. Tel. 415/39S2322, Fax 415/3984674.*
- **Destination Italia, Inc.**, *165 Chestnut Street, Allendale, NJ 07401. Tel. 201/327-2333, Fax 201/825-2664.*
- **Europa-let, Inc.** *92 N. Main Street or P.O. Box 3537, Ashland, OR 97520. Tel. 503/482-5806, 800/4624486, Fax 503/482-0660.*
- **European Connection**, *4 Mineola Avenue, Roslyn Heights, NY 11577. Tel. 516/625-1800, 800/345 4679, Fax 516/625-1138.*
- **Four Star Living, Inc.**, *640 Fifth Avenue, New York, NY 10019. Tel. 212/518 3690, Fax 914/677-5528.*
- **Heaven on Hearth**, *44 Kittyhawk, Pittsford, NY 14534. Tel. 716/381-7625, Fax 716/381-9784.*
- **Hidden Treasure of Italy**, *934 Elmwood, Wilmette IL 60091. Tel. 708/853-1313. Fax 708/853-1340*
- **Hideaways International**, *P.O. Box 1270, Littleton, MA 01460. Tel. 508/486-8955, 800/8434433, Fax 508/486-8525.*
- **Homes International**, *Via L. Bissolati 20, 00187 Rome, Italy. Tel. 39/06/488-1800, Fax 39/06/488-1808. E-mail: homesint@tin.it.*
- **Home Tours International**, *1170 Broadway, New York, NY 10001, Tel. 212/6894851, Outside New York 800/367-4668.*
- **Interhome Inc.**, *124 Little Falls Road, Fairfield, NJ 07004. Tel. 201/882-6864, Fax 201/8051 742.*
- **International Home Rentals**, *P.O. Box 329, Middleburg, VA 22117. Tel. 703/687-3161, 800/221-9001, Fax 703/687-3352.*
- **International Services**, *P.O. Box 118, Mendham, NJ 07945. Tel. 201/545-9114, Fax; 201/543-9159.*
- **Invitation to Tuscany**, *94 Winthrop Street, Augusta, ME 04330. Tel. 207/622-0743.*
- **Italian Rentals**, *3801 Ingomar Street, N.W., Washington, D.C. 20015. Tel. 202/244-5345, Fax 202/362-0520.*
- **Italian Villa Rentals**, *P.O. Box 1145, Bellevue, Washington 98009. Tel 206/827-3964, Telex: 3794026, Fax 206/827-2323.*
- **Italy Farm Holidays**, *547 Martling Avenue, Tarrytown, NY 10591. Tel. 914/631-7880, Fax 914/631-8831.*

- **LNT Associates, Inc.**, *P.O. Box 219, Warren, Ml 48090. Tel. 313/739-2266, 800/582 4832, Fax 313/739-3312.*
- **Massimo Carli**, *Website: www.incentro.it*
- **Overseas Connection**, *31 North Harbor Drive, Sag Harbor, NY 11963. Tel. 516/725-9308, Fax 516/725-5825.*
- **Palazzo Antellesi**, *175 West 92nd Street #1GE, New York NY 10025. Tel. 212/932-3480, Fax 212/932-9039*
- **The Parker Company**, *319 Lynnway, Lynn MA 01901. Tel. 617/596-8282, Fax 617/596-3125.*
- **Prestige Villas**, *P.O. Box 1046, Southport, CT 06490. Tel. 203/254-1302. Outside Connecticut 800/336-0080, Fax 203/254-7261.*
- **Rent a Home International, Inc.**, *7200 34th Avenue. N.W. Seattle, WA 98117. Tel. 206/789-9377, 800/488-RENT, Fax 206/789-9379, Telex 40597.*
- **Rentals In Italy**, *Suzanne T. Pidduck (CUENDET), 1742 Calle Corva, Camarillo, CA 93010. Tel. 805/987-5278, 800/726-6702, Fax 805/482-7976.*
- **Rent-A-Vacation Everywhere, Inc**. (RAVE), *585 Park Avenue, Rochester, NY 14607. Tel. 716/256-0760, Fax 716/256-2676.*
- **Unusual Villa Rentals**, *Tel. 804/288-2823. Fax 804/342-9016. E-mail: johng@unusualvillarentals.com; www.unusualvillarentals.com*
- **Vacanze In Italia**, *P.O. Box 297, Falls Village, CT 06031. Tel. 413/528-6610, Fax 413/528-6222. E-mail: villrent@taconic.net. Website: www.homeabroad.com.*
- **Villas and Apartments Abroad, Ltd.**, *420 Madison Avenue. New York, NY 10017. Tel. 212/759-1025. 800/433-3021 (nationwide), 800/433-3020 (NY).*
- **Villas International**, *605 Market Street, Suite 610, San Francisco, CA 94105. Tel. 415/281-0910, 800/221-2260, Fax 415/281-0919.*

HOME EXCHANGE

*A less expensive way to have "a home of your own" in Italy is to join a **home swapping club**. These clubs have reputable members all over the world. All you'd need to do is coordinate travel plans with a family in a location you'd like to stay in Italy, and exchange houses. This type of accommodation will save you a lot of money.*

*The best one that we know is **Home Link**, PO Box, Key West FL 33041, Tel. 305/294-3720, Tel. 800/638-3841, Fax 305/294-1448.*

YOUTH HOSTELS

Youth Hostels (*ostelli per la gioventu*) provide reasonably priced accommodations, specifically for younger travelers. A membership card is needed that is associated with the youth hostel's organization, i.e. a student ID card. Advanced booking is a must during the high season since these low priced accommodations fill up fast. Hundreds of youth hostels are located all over Italy. Contact the Tourist Information office when you arrive in the city to locate them.

7. ARRIVALS & DEPARTURES

BY AIR

Most travelers will arrive at **Rome's Fiumicino** (**Leonardo da Vinci**) **Airport**, which handles most incoming flights from North America, Australia, and the United Kingdom. If you are arriving from other points in Europe you may arrive at Rome's **Ciampino** airport.

Rome's Fiumicino has a dedicated **train** to whisk you directly to the central train station (**Termini**). To get to the train station at the airport simply follow the signs (**Treno**) right after you get through customs. After you leave the arrivals building you'll see the train station about fifty feet in front of you across the street and up a ramp. The trip costs L17,000 and takes 30 minutes. The trains leave every half hour starting at 7:38am and the last train is at 10:08pm. The trains are air conditioned. Then when you arrive at **Stazione Termini** (Rome's main train station), you catch a taxi to your hotel from the taxi stand in front of the station. Or you can hop on the Metro, which is underneath the train station, or take one of the many city buses located outside the front of Stazione Termini.

If you want to spend the equivalent of a night in a hotel on a **taxi** ride from the airport, by all means do so. But you should know that this choice can sometimes take longer depending on the traffic situation in and around the airport. Your best bet is to take the train to Termini station and catch a cab from there. When returning to the airport, the trains run every half an hour and departures starting at 6:52am and ending at 9:22pm. The tracks to catch the train to the airport are 25-29.

Another option is the **Airport Connection Services**, an airport shuttle which for L33,000 per person (shared with others) will take you from the airport to your hotel and vice versa. They also offer a private Mercedes for L75,000 to perform the same service. (*Tel. 06/338-3221. Both services available 7:00am to 7:00pm. Major credit cards accepted. Must be booked at least a day in advance; closed Christmas and New Year's Day*)

There is also a **Metropolitana** service from the airport to **Stazione Tiburtina**, just outside of the center of Rome, which stops at the following stations: Ponte Galleria, Muratella, Magliana, Trastevere, Ostiense, and Tuscolana. Departures are every 20 minutes from 6:00am to 10:00pm. The trip takes about 45 minutes, and trains are air conditioned.

If you are renting a car, you can get explicit driving directions from your rental company. See the *Renting a Car* section below for more complete information. If they neglect to give you directions, make sure you get on the large road – **SS 201** – leading away from the airport to the **GRA** *(Grande Raccordo Anulare)*, which is Rome's beltway and is commonly known as the **Anulare**, going north. Get off at **SS 1** (**Via Aurelia**) and follow this road all the way into town.

If you arrive at Rome's **Ciampino** (which is really only used for flights from European counties), there are dedicated airport buses that leave for the **Anagnina Metro Station** every half an hour. They take 15 minutes to get into town. Taking a **taxi** from here also costs an arm and a leg but not nearly as much as from Fiumicino, since this airport is closer to Rome. If you rent a car, simply take **Via Appia** all the way into town. For the scenic view get on the **Via Appia Antica** a kilometer or so after passing the **GRA**.

GETTING TO & FROM THE AIRPORTS IN ROME

Rome's airport has a dedicated train to whisk you directly into town in half an hour. There are also plenty of taxis vying for your business but I would recommend taking the train. It is quick, easy, air conditioned and comfortable. And best of all the train will not cost you the equivalent of a night in a hotel. I recommend taking the train down to **Stazione Termini**, the central train station, where you can get a taxi to your hotel. For budget or more adventurous travelers, you can also hop on the Metro or a city bus to take you near your hotel.

When you are departing the country remember to have at least L15,000 (the 'L' in front of the number stands for *lire* the Italian currency) on hand to pay the airport tax.

Rome Fiumicino (Leonardo da Vinci) Airport

Direct Link. A train service is available from the airport directly to **Stazione Termini** (Rome's Central Railway Station). The trip costs L17,000 one way and takes 30 minutes. There are trains every half hour. They start operating from the airport to Termini at 7:38am and end at 10:08pm. Returning to the airport the trains also run every half hour, from track 22, but starts at 6:52am and ends at 9:22pm. Note: You can pick up a schedule for the train when you buy your tickets. This will help you plan for your departure.

Metropolitan Link. There is train service from the Airport to **Stazione Tiburtina** stopping at the following stations: Ponte Galleria, Muratella, Magliana, Trastevere, Ostiense, and Tuscolana. Departures are every 20 minutes from 6:00am to 10:00pm. Trip takes about 45 minutes. Trains are air-conditioned.

Night Time Arrivals and Departures. There is a night bus running between Fiumicino and Tiburtina station, which stops at Termini. From Fiumicino the bus leaves at 1:15am, 2:15am, 3:30am and 5:00am. From Tiburtina station to the airport the bus runs at 12:30am, 1:15am, 2:30am and 3:45am. The trip takes about half and hour.

Airport Shuttles. In the past few years a number of shuttle services have sprouted up to ferry tourists back and forth between Rome's airports and downtown. These are great options if you arrive into Fiumicino late, need a ride to Rome and don't want to pay an arm and leg to a taxi. Listed below are some of the best:

- **Airport Shuttle** – *Tel. 06/4201-4507, E-mail: airportshuttle@airportshuttle.it. Office hours 6:30am-10:30pm, 7 days a week. No credit cards. Cash only. L50,000 for one or two passengers.*
- **Airport Connection Services** – *Tel. 06/338-3221. Open 7am-7pm. L33,000 per person for shared ride; L75,000 for private car. Credit cards accepted. No extra charges for baggage.*

Rome Ciampino Airport

Bus Link – Buses leave from the airport starting at 6:00am and end at 10:30pm and will take you to the **Anagnina Metro** stop, where you can catch the subway to Termini station. The only other option is taking a taxi which can be quite expensive.

BY CAR

To get into Rome you will have to either get on or pass by the **Anulare**, Rome's beltway. If arriving from the north you will be using **Via Cassia** (which can get congested), **Via Flaminia**, **Via Salaria** or the fastest route, the **A1** *(Autostrada del Sole),* which will dump you onto the Anulare.

If arriving from the south, the fastest route is the **A2**, also referred to as the *Autostrada del Sole*. A more scenic route is along the **Via Appia**.

Sample trip lengths on the main roads:

- **Florence**: 3 1/2 hours
- **Venice**: 6 1/2 hours

BY TRAIN

When arriving by train, you will be let off at Rome's main train station, **Stazione Termini**. From here you can catch a **taxi** at the row of cabs outside the front entrance, walk down to the **Metro** and catch a train close to your destination, or hop on one of the **buses** in the main square (Piazza Cinquecento) just in front of the station.

Termini is a zoo. Packed with people from all over the world, queuing up to buy tickets, trying to cut in line to get information, and in some cases looking for unprotected belongings. So don't leave your bags unattended here or in any train station in Italy. The **Tourist Information** office is located near the train tracks *(Tel. 06/487-1270)*. You can get a good map here and make a hotel reservation. The **Railway Information** office faces the front entrance and is next to the ticket booths. If you're planning a trip, you should come here to find out when your train will be leaving. All attendants speak enough English to get by. There is a **baggage storage area** at Termini which is open from 5:15am to 12:20am. For L5,000 you can store an item there for 12 hours. There are also lockers available for L5,000 for 6 hours.

Sample trip lengths and costs for direct *(diretto)* trains:

- **Florence**: 2 1/2 hours, L45,000
- **Venice**: 5 hours, L66,000

The Italian railroad system is owned by the government and provides convenient and extensive transportation throughout the country. Train is by far the simplest, easiest, and least expensive way to get around Italy. Ferries link the principal islands with the mainland, and those that travel between southernmost Italy and Sicily carry trains as well as cars, trucks, and people. To get schedule and ticket information call the offices for the **Italian Rail Agency** (CIT) in North America, *Tel. 800/248-7245*. A great web site that contains everything you need to know about rail travel in Italy is for the Italian Rail Company (**Ferrovie dello Stato** – FS) at *www.fs-on-line.com*.

The railroad system is more extensive in north and central Italy, but main lines run along both coasts, and other routes cross the peninsula in several places. The **Simplon Tunnel**, one of the world's longest railroad tunnels, connects Italy and Switzerland. Other rail lines follow routes across the Alps between Italy and France, Austria, and Slovenia.

Taking the train is by far the most expedient, most relaxing, and by far the best way to travel throughout Italy. Trains go almost every place you'd like to visit, they are comfortable, run on time, and free you from having to drive. This efficiency of the railway system in Italy can be directly attributed to Mussolini. You may have heard the saying, "He may not have done much else, but he got the trains to arrive on time." Well, it's true.

When traveling by train, one thing to remember is that you must always stamp your ticket before boarding the train. Otherwise you may

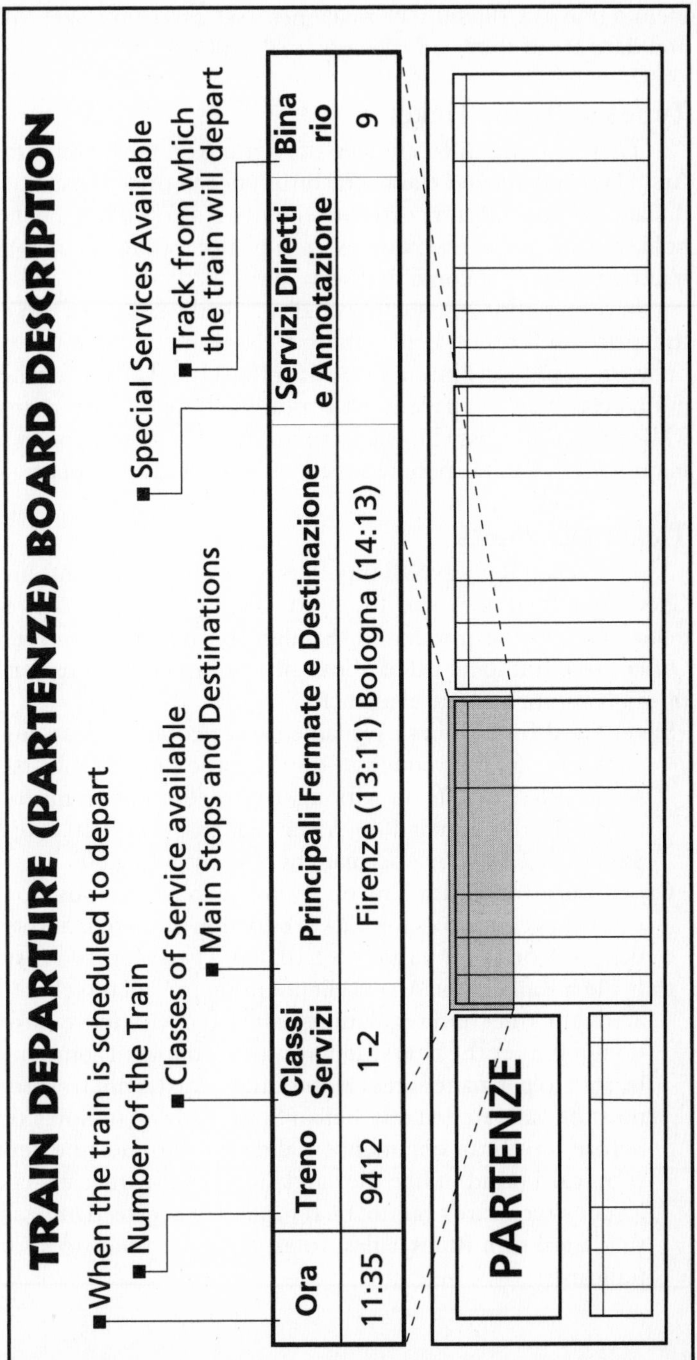
TRAIN DEPARTURE (PARTENZE) BOARD DESCRIPTION
When the train is scheduled to depart
Number of the Train
Classes of Service available
Main Stops and Destinations
Special Services Available
Track from which the train will depart
Ora
Treno
Classi Servizi
Principali Fermate e Destinazione
Servizi Diretti e Annotazione
Bina rio
11:35
9412
1-2
Firenze (13:11) Bologna (14:13)
9
PARTENZE

incur a fine of L40,000. The machines to stamp your ticket with the time and date are at the head of every track platform.

Types of Train Tickets

There are two different levels of seating on most every train in Italy: **first class** and **second class**. The difference in price is usually only a few dollars, but the difference in convenience is astounding. First class ticket holders can make reservations in advance, while second class ticket seating is on a first come first serve basis.

In conjunction, the seating quality is light-years apart. An example of the price difference between first class and second when traveling between Rome and Florence is $35 for first class, $22 for second class. But in first class you will have an air-conditioned car and separate cloth seat, while in second class you will have not A/C, and you'll be in a compartment with five other people sitting on sweat-inducing plastic seats.

Ticket Discounts

The Italian Railway System offers a variety of discounts on its tickets. Check out their web site for more details (*www.fs-on-line.com*). These tickets are can be purchased through the Italian Government Travel Offices (see numbers listed above under Driver's License section) and through authorized travel agencies.

- **Silver Card for Seniors**: Available to all people 60 years and older. It allows for a 20% reduction on the basic fare for all first class and second class tickets on national routes. For day trains for inter-city routes the discount is 40%. A one year pass costs L10,000; A two year pass costs L18,000; a permanent pass costs L24,000.
- **Green Card for Youth Travel**: Available to all persons from 12 to 26 years of age. It allows for a 20% reduction on all first and second class tickets. A one year pass costs L10,000; a two year pass costs L18,000.
- **Italy Flexi Rail Cards**: An excellent option for rail travel in Italy. There are many rules and regulations associated with these cards, but they do not hinder the bearer in any way. Example of some rules: cannot be sold to permanent residents of Italy, card is not transferable, card must be validated at any Italian State Railway station's ticket office before travel can commence, validation slip must be kept separate from card (kind of like the validation slip for travelers checks), and lost or stolen cards cannot be refunded or replaced unless bearer has validation slip. Rules, rules, rules. Here are the prices for the Flexi Railcards:

	1st Class	2nd Class
• 4 days of travel within 9 days of validity	$170	$116
• 8 days of travel within 21 days of validity	$250	$164
• 12 days of travel within 30 days of validity	$314	$210

• **Italy Rail Card** or the "BTLC Italian Tourist Ticket:" all travel and any type of train is unlimited and free, except for the special **TR450 or Eurostar** trains where a supplemental fee will be required. The time period begins on the first day of its use. Here are the prices for the Unlimited Rail Pass:

Validity	1st Class	2nd Class
8 days	$226	$152
15 days	$284	$190
21 days	$330	$220
30 days	$396	$264

EUROSTAR STYLE

A feather in the cap of the Italian rail system is the ***Eurostar trains.*** *These are very comfortable, luxurious and fast. Travel between Rome and Florence (and Venice and Florence) has been reduced to less than two hours each way. The seats on these trains are large and accommodating in both first and second class. In first class they serve you a snack with free beverage service, and offer you headphones that you can keep. A truly wonderful way to travel. So if you are going by train and want to enjoy luxury on the rails, try the Eurostar. Price is rather expensive at L110,000 (about $55) each way but well worth it.*

Types of Trains

• **Eurostar**: Top notch services and speed. Air-conditioned, comfortable seats, snacks served at your seat and head phones available for use.

• **IC-Intercity**: Both first and second class seating is available with most first class compartments air-conditioned. Dining cars are also available.

• **EC-Eurocity**: These are the trains that are used in international rail service.

• **EXPR-Expresso:** Ordinary express trains usually carry first and second class passengers. No supplemental fare and reservations are neces-

BOARDING THE RIGHT TRAIN

When taking a train in Italy the ultimate destination that is listed on the train schedule and the departure listing by the track may not be the same city or town to which you are going. To get to Pisa, for example, sometimes you have to board a train whose ultimate destination is Livorno. To make sure you're boarding the proper train, first ask the information desk in the train station when your train is leaving and which track it is leaving from, then try one of two things (or both):

***1.** Consult one of the large glass-enclosed schedules (see graphic on page 81) located in the information offices and usually at the head of the tracks. Normally they have a wildly gesturing crowd hovering around them, so you may have to squeeze your way through for a view. Match your intended departure time with the time printed on the sheet. Then check directly to the right of the time to see the list of all the destinations for the train. If the name of your destination is listed, you've found your train. Next write down the ultimate destination of the train so you can check the main board at the station that lists **partenze** (trains leaving) to see which **binnario** (track) you should board.*

***2.** If that still doesn't soothe your concerns, ask someone waiting at the track or inside the train if it is going to your destination. Ask at least two people, since I've had someone erroneously tell me a train doesn't go where I asked. It seems that these people, some of whom have been riding the same train to and from work for forty years haven't bothered to pay attention to where the train actually stops.*

*Whatever the case, to ask someone politely in Italian whether the train is going to your destination say **"Scusa, ma questo treno va a Lucca?"** ("Excuse me, but does this train go to Lucca?") Obviously substitute the underlined city name for the destination to which you wish to go. This question is asked countless times by many people, including Italians.*

*Finally, if you're standing on the platform waiting for the train to come and you suddenly see all the Italians moving away en masse, that usually means that the public address announcer just declared a track change. Ask one of the departing Italians "Has the track for the train to Lucca changed?" **(E cambiato il binnario per il treno per Lucca?)** If the answer is yes (si), either get the number and go there or simply follow them, and as you pass the board that lists the trains leaving, you'll see the change already officially noted.*

sary, but I recommend you make them. Food and drink service is available. These are the trains to take. Hardly any stops at all. Kind of like the MetroLiner Service on Amtrak between Washington DC and New York.

- **DIR-Diretto**: Semi-express trains that make plenty of stops. They often have second class seating only. During off-peak hours they are not crowded, but at peak hours they're sardine-city.
- **Locale**: These trains stop everywhere on their route and take forever, but to get to rural locations these are the only options.

VALIDATE YOUR TICKET

Whatever train you are taking, whatever type of ticket you have, remember to validate your ticket at the yellow boxes at the station by each track before you board the train. This is true for all tickets except Eurorail passes. If you do not validate your ticket, you can get fined. To validate your ticket, simply push one end into the yellow box and it will automatically date and time stamp it.

BY BICYCLE (OR HIKING)

You may think that riding a bicycle among Italian drivers would be ludicrous, but they are actually very respectful and courteous of bicyclists. Cycling is a national sport in Italy, so your reception in Italy will be more as a hero than a villain, as you can all too often be viewed in North America. And if you get tired, one benefit of the Italian train system is that many trains have bicycle cars to accommodate travelers such as us. So if you get to one location and feel like you want a breather, or if you want to make better time, you can hop on trains to your next destination.

Another way to hike or bike around Italy is with an organized tour group. Two such organizations are **Ciclismo Classico**, and **BCT Scenic Walking**. They offer magnificent tours all over Italy, from Sardinia to Tuscany, to Venice and beyond. Their guides are extremely knowledgeable and professional and speak impeccable English. And with Ciclismo you stay at fine hotels, eat fantastic food, meet wonderful people, and constantly interact with the locals – all while seeing Italy up close and personal on a bicycle. I find this to be a truly authentic way to appreciate and experience Italy.

To get more information, contact **Ciclismo Classico**, *13 Marathon Street, Arlington MA 02174; Tel. 800/866-7314 or 781/646-3377, Fax 617/641-1512, E-mail: info@ciclismoclassico.com, Web: www.ciclismoclassico.com.* **CBT Tours**, *2506 N. Clark St #150, Chicago, IL 60614. Tel. 800/736-BIKE, Fax 773/404-1833, E-mail: adventure@cbttours. Web: www.cbttours.com.*

If you are an avid hiker, and enjoy seeing a country from the perspective of the back roads or trails, contact this excellent organization, **BCT** (British Coastal Trails) **Scenic Walking**, which offers some great walking tours of Italy, England and the rest of the European continent. **BCT Scenic Tours**, *703 Palomar Airport Road, Suite 200, Carlsbad CA 92009, Tel. 800/473-1210 or 760/431-7306. Web: bctwalk.com.*

8. GETTING AROUND ROME

BY CAR

If you are thinking of driving in Rome some people would wonder if you are nuts. Unless you are from Boston and are used to aggressive driving tactics, driving a car to get around Rome is a crazy idea, considering that the public transportation system is so good and that virtually everything is within walking distance. If you want to rent a car for a day trip to the beach at Lido di Ostia or another excursion, that's another story. But even in those circumstances, you can still get to those destinations and most others by train from Stazione Termini.

So think twice about renting a car while in Rome, and if you do rent a car, beware of those automobiles with a big letter "P" taped to the rear windows or trunks. It stands for *Principinate di Patente Fresche*, meaning a newly licensed driver. They are the worst. Also beware of the cars with the words *Scuola Guida* (Driving School) on them.

Remember too that if you rent a car you'll need to buy gas, which besides being expensive can sometimes be inconvenient, because many stations in Italy are unmanned self-service and the pumps only take crisp L10,000 bills. So if you rent a car, remember to carry some of these bills at all times.

Renting a Car

Cars can be rented at **Fiumicino** or **Ciampino airports**, booked in advance by a travel agent, or rented at many offices in the city, especially at the **Stazione Termini**. Try the following places:

- **Avis**, *Information Tel. 06/41998. Their office at Termini Station is open Monday-Saturday 7:00am-8:00pm, and Sundays from 8:00am-11:00pm (Tel. 06/413-0812). Their office at Fiumicino is open every day from 7:30am-11:00pm (Tel. 06/7934-0195).*

- **Hertz**, *Customer Service 06/5429-4500. Main Office is on the Via Veneto #156. The phone number is 06/821-6881 or 06/321-6834. The office number at Fiumicino it's 06/6501-1448; at Ciampino it's 06/7934-0095. Website: www.hertz.com.*
- **National/Maggiore**, *Car reservations in Italy 1478/67067. Van Reservations in Italy 1478/48844. Website: www.maggiore .it. Fiumicino Tel. 06/ 65-010-678.*

The fees usually include the costs for towing, minor repairs, and basic insurance, but you should ask just to make sure. Also most firms require a deposit equal to the daily cost of the rental, which is usually between L200,000 and L300,000. The minimum age for rental usually is 21 and you must have had a drivers license for at least a year. Rules and regulations will vary according to company, since the concept of standard industry practices hasn't hit Italy yet.

Driver's Licenses

US, British, and Canadian driving licenses are valid in Italy, but only when accompanied by a translation. This translation is obtainable from **AAA**, the offices of the **Touring Club Italiano** in Italy, at the offices for the **Italian Government Tourist Office**, and at the Italian frontier. Even if your native driver's license is accepted, it is strongly recommended that you apply for and receive an 'International Drivers Permit,' which you can get from the Italian Government Tourist Offices listed below:

- **Touring Club Italiano**, *Via Marsala 8, 00185, Roma. Tel. 06/49 98 99*
- **Italian Government Tourist Office** – in the US: *500 N. Michigan Ave, Chicago, IL 60611, Tel. 312/644-0990; 630 Fifth Ave, Suite 1565, New York, NY 10111, Tel. 212/245-4822, Fax 212/586-9249; 360 Post Street, Suite 801, San Francisco CA 94109, Tel. 415/392-6206;* in Canada: *Store 56, Plaza 3, 3 Place Ville Marie, Montreal, Quebec, Tel. 514/866 7667. Website: www.italiantourism.com.*

TOWED CAR?

*If your car happens to have been towed, it means you parked in an illegal spot. To find out where your car is call **Vigili Urbani**, Tel. 06/ 67691, and give them the registration number, make of car and place where it was removed. They will tell you where your car has been placed, but you can only pick up your car after you have paid your fine at Via della Consolazione 4. Take your receipt with you when you retrieve your car. On Sundays the office to pay your fine is closed, but the towers are still working – so don't park illegally on Sundays.*

Parking Your Car in Rome

If you are just passing through, or you've decided to rent a car to get around Rome, you are going to have to deal with the Byzantine Roman parking system. There are spaces on the street indicated by blue lines where you can park for L2,000 per hour. This is usually only from 8am – 8pm. The tickets can be purchased at the vending machines along the sidewalks (which use coin only) or at *tabacchi* stores or newsstands. Ask for a *biglietto per parcheggio* (parking ticket). There are also some large public and private parking garages situated all around the city, where you can leave your car overnight if the hotel you are staying at does not have a garage. These public lots are located at: ParkSi in Villa Borghese, Parking Ludovisi on Via Ludovisi 60, and Parking Termini in front of the main train station.

Road Maps

If you're going to be our of Rome you are going to want adequate maps, and the only place to get really good maps is from the **Touring Club Italiano**. Your rental company will supply you something that will enable you to get the car out of their parking lot, but after that you are on your own. My recommendation to you would be to contact the **Touring Club Italiano**, *Via Marsala 8, 00185, Roma, Tel. 06/49 98 99*, well prior to your visit, or visit their store in Rome at *Via del Babuino 19-21, Tel 06/3609-5834* near the Piazza del Popolo. Here you can get all the maps they have available.

BY MOPED

If you are looking for a new experience, a different way to see Rome (or any city in Italy), try renting a moped. Walking, riding a bicycle, driving a car, taking the bus, or riding in a taxi cannot come close to the exhilaration of riding a moped.

A moped gives you freedom. A moped gives you the ability to go from one corner of Rome to another, quickly. Riding a moped makes you feel in tune with the flow of the city. With no plan, no structure, no itinerary, no boundaries, you can go from the tourist areas to a part of Rome tourists rarely see. You can find monuments and markets in Rome you would never have seen if not on a moped. It makes you feel a part of the city, and this familiarity gives you the confidence to widen your explorations.

MOPED CAUTION & RATES

*If you cannot ride a bicycle, please do not rent a moped. The concept is the same, one vehicle just goes a little faster. Also, start off renting a 50 cc (**cinquanta**), not a 125 cc (**cento venti cinque**). With more than twice the engine capacity, the 125 cc is a big difference, and in the traffic of Rome it's best to start slow. But if you insist on riding two to a moped, then a 125 cc is necessary. It's the law too. (Not that any Italians abide by it). Also you need to be at least sixteen years old to rent a moped, but you don't need a motorcycle license. Just hop on, and ride away ... but don't let Mom and Dad know about it.*

A sizable deposit (around L200,000+) is required for each moped. The deposit will increase based on the size of moped you want to rent. Your deposit can be cash in any currency, travelers checks, or on a credit card. This is standard procedure for all rental companies. Do not worry, you'll get your money back. Daily rates are between L50,000 and L80,000. Renting for a more extended period can be a better bargain. Rates should be prominently posted.

Now that I've almost convinced you to rent one, I'll counsel you to think hard about it. Traffic in Rome is like nothing you have ever seen, and as such makes riding a moped rather dangerous. Only if you feel extremely confident about your motorcycle driving abilities should you even contemplate renting a moped. This isn't the Bahamas where everyone's polite. The Romans will just as soon run you over as make way for you.

Personally, I find a moped to be the most efficient and fun way to get around Rome. They're inexpensive, quick, easy to maneuver, and practical since parking is virtually impossible for a car. But, granted, I have had my accidents. Once, as I was speeding between cars that were stopped at a light, a pedestrian walked in front of me and POW, next thing you know I'm wrapped around a pole. And then there was the time a public bus decided that he had the right of way in a circle and casually knocked me down. Anyway, only if you're *un po pazzo* or very brave should you attempt to rent a moped.

Renting a Moped

- **Bici e Baci**, *Via del Viminale 5, Tel. 06/482-8443. Website: www.romeguide.it/bicibaci/ bicibaci.html. Open 8:00am-7:00pm. All credit cards accepted.* Extensive selection of bicycles, scooter, and cars. They also organzie guided bike tours or scooter tours in English.

- **Scooters for Rent**, *Via Quattro Novembre 96, Tel. 488-5685. Open 8:30am-8:00pm, seven days a week.* A centrally located moped rental, just off the Piazza Venezia.
- **I Bike Rome di Cortessi Ferruccio**, *Viale Galappatoio, near Via Veneto. Tel. 06/322-5240. Open Monday-Saturday 9:00am-1:00pm and 4:00pm-8:00pm, and Sundays 9:00am-8:00pm.* They rent from the same underground parking garage (connecting the Piazza di Spagna Metro Stop and the Via Veneto) as does Hertz. Maybe that's why you get a 50% discount with a Hertz card.
- **St. Peter's Moto**, *Via di Porto Castello 43, Tel. 06/687-5719. Open Monday-Saturday 9:00am – 1:30pm and 3:30pm-9:30pm.*
- **Scoot-A-Long**, *Via Cavour 302, Tel. 06/678-0206. Open Monday-Saturday 9:00am-7:00pm, Sundays 10:00am-2:00pm and 4:00pm-7:00pm.*
- **Scooter Center**, *Via in Lucina 13/14. Tel. 06/687-6455. Open daily 9:00am-7:30pm. Credit cards accepted. One day L80,000. Three days L200,000.*
- **Happy Rent**, *Via Farini 3, Tel & Fax 06/481-8185. Website: www.happyrent.com.* They also have other rental locations by the Colosseum and the Spanish Steps, they rent bicycles, scooters, and cars.

BY BICYCLE

Bicycles make getting from one spot in Rome to another quicker and easier, but if you haven't been on one in awhile, trying to re-learn on the streets of Rome is not a good idea. And don't even think about having children younger than 14 try and ride around Rome unattended. Not only could they get lost very easily, but the traffic laws are so different they may not be able to adapt very well.

I've seen older teenagers fare very well, especially around the Trevi Fountain, Spanish Steps area. Letting your kids do this gives them a sense of freedom, but reinforce to them how careful they have to be.

Renting a Bicycle

Please refer to the scooter rental place above that I listed as also renting bicycles. The cost for an entire day varies from place to place, and year to year, but the latest price is around L30,000 per day and L10,000 per hour, except at the one below, which is only L25,000 a day and L8,000 per hour.

- **Bici Pincio**, *Viale di Villa Medici & Viale della Pineta, Tel. 06/678-4374.* A location in the Borghese Gardens and one near the Piazza del Popolo, this company has this side of Rome to themselves and only rents bicycles.

BY TAXI

Taxis are the best, but also the most expensive, way to get around Rome. They are everywhere so flagging one down is not a problem. And cab stands are dispersed all over the city too. The strategically placed **cab stands** that will benefit you the most as a tourist are the ones in Piazza del Popolo, Piazza della Repubblica, Piazza Venezia, and at Piazza Sonino just across the bridge in Trastevere.

Since taxis are so expensive I wouldn't rely on them as your main form of transportation. Use them as a last resort, like when you start to get tired from walking. Also have a map handy when a cabby is taking you somewhere. Since they are on a meter, they sometimes decide to take you on a little longer journey than necessary. And also watch out for the fly-by-night operators who don't have a licensed meter. They will really rip you off.

The going rate as of publication was L4,000 for the first 2/3 of a kilometer or the first minute (which usually comes first during the rush hours), then it's L600 every 1/3 of a kilometer or minute. At night you'll also pay a surcharge of L5,000, and Sundays you'll pay L2,000 extra. If you bring luggage aboard, you'll be charged L2,000 extra for each bag. In conjunction, if you go from Rome to Fiumicino you will charged L14,000 extra, Fiumicino to Rome L11,500, and between Ciampino and Rome you will be charged L10,000 extra.

Rome also has several radio taxi cooperatives: **La Capitale** *(Tel. 4994)*, **Roma Sud** *(Tel. 6645)*, **Roma** *(Tel. 3570)*, **Cosmos** *(Tel. 88177)* and **RadioTaxi Tevere** *(Tel. 4157)*. Be warned that when you call for a taxi the cab's meter starts running when it is summoned, not when it arrives to pick you up, so by the time a cab arrives at your location there will already be a substantial amount on the meter.

BY BUS

At each bus stop, called **fermata**, there are signs that list all the buses that stop there. These signs also give the streets that the buses will follow along their route so you can check your map to see if this is the bus for you. Also, on the side of the bus are listed highlights of the route for your convenience. Nighttime routes (since many of them stop at midnight) are indicated by black spaces on newer signs, and are placed at the bottom of the older signs. In conjunction the times listed on the signs indicate when the bus will pass the *fermata* so you can plan accordingly.

Riding the bus during rush hour is like becoming a sardine, complete with the odor, so try to avoid the rush hours of 8:00am to 9:00am, 12:30pm to 1:30pm, 3:30 to 4:30pm, and 7:30pm to 8:30pm. Yes, they have an added rush hour in the middle of the day because of their siesta time in the afternoon.

The bus fare costs L1,500 and lasts for 75 minutes, during which time you can transfer to any other bus, but you can only ride the Metro once. Despite the convenience and extent of the Roman bus system, which helped me get anywhere I wanted to go in Rome for a long time, since the advent of the Metro I recommend taking the underground transport as it is easier, quicker, less crowded, and more understandable.

Never board the metro or a bus without a ticket, which can be bought at any **ATAC** booth or kiosk and at tobacco shops (*tabacchi*), newsstands (*giornalaio*) and vending machines in the Metro stations. Once on board the bus remember to stamp the ticket at the rear stamp machine. If you do not have a ticket or have one and do not stamp it with the date and time, and an inspector catches you, you face an instantaneous L50,000 fine. For more information, call ATAC, *Tel. 06/4695-4444;* or ACOTRAL, *Tel. 06/ 5912-5551.*

ATAC Bus Tours

If you like the local scene, take the no-frills Giro di Roma tour on the **silver bus #110** offered by **ATAC**, the intra-city bus company *(Tel. 06/469-51)*. This three hour circuit of the city leaves from the information booth in the middle of the **Piazza Cinquecento** in front of the train station daily at 10:30am, 2:00pm, 3:00pm, 5:00pm and 6:00pm, and takes you to over 80 sites of historic and artistic significance, and stops at the most important sights like the Colosseum, Piazza Venezia, St. Peter's, and more.

Cost is only L15,000 and you can pay by credit card. To book a seat on these luxury buses with tour guides and an illustrated guide book call 06/4695-2252 between 9:00am and 7:00pm.

Bus Passes

If you are staying in Rome for an extended period of time or need to use the buses frequently, you can buy one of the following bus tickets at most newsstands, *tabacchi*, or ATAC booths by the station, and in the Metro. These tickets are:

- **Daily Ticket** *(B.I.G.): L6,000 (Valid for unlimited Metro, Bus, Trolley and Train with the Commune di Roma which includes going to Ostia but not Fiumicino Airport or Tivoli)*
- **Weekly Ticket** *(C.I.S.): L24,000 (Valid for everything under the B.I.G.)*

Lost & Found

If you misplace something on a bus, you can report the item missing at the main office, Via Volturno 65 (near the train station). But nine times out of ten I don't think you'll get it back, especially if it is an expensive item.

BY METRO

The Roman *Metropolitana* (**Metro**) has two lines (Linea A and Linea B) that intersect in the basement of Termini station. You'll find these and all other stations marked with a prominent white "M" inside a red square up on a sign outside. **Linea A** is probably the most used by the tourists since it starts near St. Peter's, and has Piazza del Popolo, Piazza di Spagna, Piazza Barberini, and Piazza della Repubblica along its route. **Linea B** comes in a close second since it takes you to the Colosseum, the Circus Maximus, and the Piramide.

HOW TO BUY A METRO TICKET

Walk down the steps into the subterranean caverns of the Roman Metro, then buy the ticket at the ever-present ticket booths or vending machines in any station. To get to the trains you stamp the ticket in a bright orange machine. The stamp received marks the start of the 75 minutes you can ride on public transportation, but only once on the Metro.

If it's late at night, the ticket booths are usually closed so you'll have to use one at the ever-present vending machines in all stations. Simply have L1,500 ready, or close to it in bills or coins. Then a touch tone screen awaits your commands. Press the upper left image on the screen to indicate to the machine you want a 75 minute ticket. Then insert your bills or coins as indicated, and presto your ticket and change (if any) will appear.

Buses used to be the way to get around Rome quickly, efficiently, and inexpensively, but now that convenience has been superseded by the Metro. But beware, the Metro can get quite crowded around **Stazione Termini** and during rush hours. Sardine-like is the best way to describe it. Besides the crush of humanity, the rides can be very pleasant. But, always be on the lookout for pickpockets. There are signs (in Italian) in the Metro and on buses warning people about them, so be prepared. The best way to do that is to put your wallet in your front pants pocket. And women, to make sure you are not the recipient of unwanted gropes on your derriere, keep your back to the wall if possible. And if you feel hands on you be sure to push them away and make a scene, otherwise it won't stop.

The Metro runs from 5:30am to 11:30pm.

Metro Lost & Found

If you misplace something on the metro, you can report the item missing at the office at the main station, Servizio Movimento delle

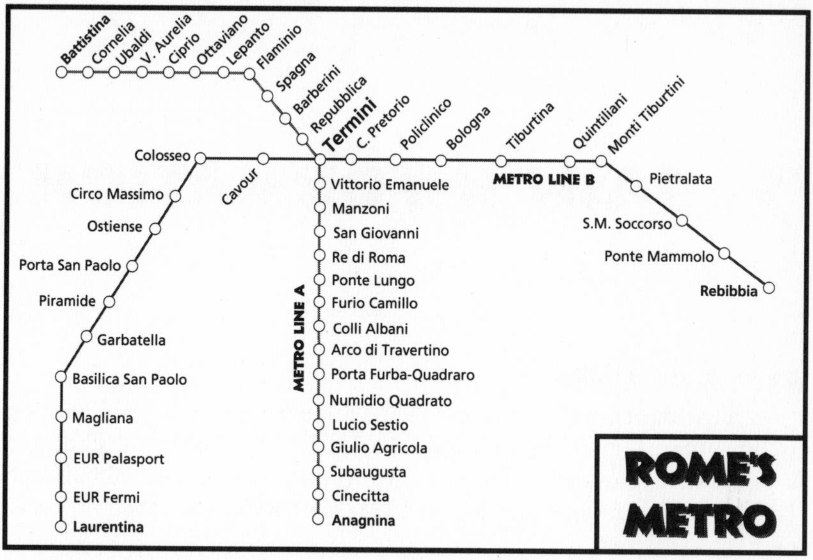

Ferrovie dello Stato *(Tel. 06/4669, ext. 7682)*. But you probably won't get it back, especially if it is an expensive item.

Take the Metro to the Beach!

If you're interested in going to the beach or visiting the ruins at Ostia Antica, take the Linea B Metro to the Magliana stop and transfer to a train that will take you there. If you only bought a bus or Metro ticket, you will have to buy an extra ticket for the train. But if you purchased the daily (B.I.G.) or weekly (C.IS.) pass you do not have to buy an extra ticket.

9. BASIC INFORMATION

ATM MACHINES

Called **Bancomat** machines, ATM's are everywhere in Italy, making it convenient for you to withdraw money directly from your checking account. One drawback is that you can only withdraw up to L500,000 each day. But the advantages of using an ATM over traditional travelers checks are easy to discern.

The ATM gives you excellent, up to date exchange rates that are better than most exchange offices. For example, when I used one a few years ago, the official exchange rate was L1,640 per dollar, I got L1,615 from the ATM and the going rate at exchange places was L1,570. Also, the transaction fee, a fixed rate of $1 to $3, is usually lower than the fees charged by exchange places. Another advantage is that you are not constrained by bank or business hours. You can access your money anytime.

Despite the advantages of ATMs I would strongly suggest bringing some travelers checks with you. Why? If there is a bank strike (and that could happen at any time in Italy), the ATMs won't be filled up with cash and you'd be left without money. And also have a credit card handy just in case.

BABYSITTERS

A list of reliable, English-speaking babysitters can be obtained through the **American Women's Association of Rome** (AWAR), *Tel. 06/482-5268.* In addition the American Embassy also has babysitter listings.

BANKING

Banks in Italy are open Monday through Friday, 8:30am to 1:30pm and from 2:45pm to 4:00pm, and are closed all day Saturday and Sunday and on national holidays. In some cities the afternoon open hour may not even exist, and in some cities, like Rome, banks may open on Saturday mornings and extend longer on Thursdays. Once again, bank hours, like business hours, vary region to region, and even city to city within the region. Check outside of banks for their posted hours of operation. Even if the bank is closed, most travelers' checks can be exchanged for Italian currency at hotels as well as shops and at the many foreign exchange offices in railway stations and at airports.

Shop around for the best exchange rate. Each bank offers a different rate and exchange fee, as do the **Casa di Cambio**, smaller exchange establishments. Sometimes the rate charged to exchange your money is a set fee, a situation that is best when you change a large amount of money. Other places charge a percentage of the total which is generally more beneficial for smaller amounts.

LOST OR STOLEN TRAVELERS CHECKS & CREDIT CARDS

The toll free numbers listed below should be called if your credit cards or traveler's checks are stolen:

***American Express**, Tel. 800/872-000 (travelers checks), Tel. 800/874-333 (credit cards)*

***Bank Americard**, Toll free in Italy 167/821-001*

***Citibank**, Tel. 06/854-561*

***Diner's Club**, Tel. 800/864-064*

***Mastercard**, Tel. 800/870-866*

***Thomas Cook/Mastercard**, Tel. 800/872-050 (traveler's checks)*

***VISA**, Tel. 800/874-155 (traveler's checks), Tel. 800/877-232 (credit cards)*

Changing Money

Besides banks, there are plenty of exchange bureaus (*casa di cambio*) around, some of which actually offer great rates and low service charges. When using these tiny, hole in the wall yet completely reputable places, if you are changing small amounts (i.e. $20) look for ones that offer a low percentage transaction fee (i.e. 1% to 2% of the amount you're exchanging). If you are changing large amounts, find one that has a reasonable set fee (i.e. L3-5,000). One such exchange place that is open until 9:00pm on weekdays and until 2:00pm on Saturdays, is in the **Stazione Termini**. But use this as a last resort since the lines are always ridiculously long, just like American Express.

Another option, if all else is closed, is to simply change your money at your hotel or any of the four star hotels that line the Via Veneto. You won't get the best rate but at least you'll have money. Some places to change your money are:

- **American Express**, *Piazza di Spagna 38, Tel. 06/67-64-1. Open weekdays 9:00am to 5:30pm, and Saturdays from 9:00am to 12:30pm.* American Express is always a great option, especially if you have their travelers checks. Remember, the lines here are long, but if you're looking for a good rate and a chance to interact with other travelers, these lines are great meeting spots.
- **Banco Nazionale del Lavoro**, *Via Veneto 11, Tel. 06/475-0421. Open 8:30am to 6:00pm Monday through Saturday.*
- **American Service Bank**, *Piazza Mignanelli 15. Open 8:30am to 6:30pm Monday through Saturday.*

Currency

The monetary unit in Italy is the **lira** (leer-ah), the plural is **lire** (leer-ay) – at least until the **Euro** goes into common circulation on January 1, 2002 (see information about the Euro below). Lira notes are issued for 1,000, 2,000, 5,000, 10,000, 50,000, and 100,000 lire. Coins come in 50, 100, 200 and 500 lira denominations. The smallest denomination is the L500 though there are no longer many in circulation. Other denominations in banknotes include L1000, L2000, L5000, L10000, L50000, and L100000. Coin denominations include L50, L100, L200, and L500.

Italy is phasing in new currency and as result you will have two, and sometimes three different versions of each of these coins and bills floating around in circulation. So be conscious of what you spend because the sizes, shapes and colors vary dramatically. Another example of Italian chaos in action. I love it.

The current rate of exchange is **US $1=2,316 lire** and this is reflected in the cost of restaurants, hotels, bars, etc. The Canadian Dollar to the lira is Can$1 =1,533 lire.

You cannot bring in any currency that totals more than 20 million lire (approximately $11,500) without declaring it at the customs office. This is also the same amount of money that can be legally exported from Italy without declaring it.

If you arrive in Italy without Italian currency, the airports have banks and monetary exchange offices *(Ufficio di Cambio)*. Remember to keep your receipts from your monetary exchanges, because at some banks, when you want to change lire back to your native currency, you will need to show proof that you first exchanged your native currency for Italian currency.

To create a pocket currency conversion chart to bring with you, simply visit this website *(www.oanda.com/converter/travel)* and follow the directions.

On January 1, 2002, the official currency for all participating members of the European Community, to which Italy belongs, is tentatively going to become the **Euro**. Already stores and restaurants are listing prices in that currency, but whether it actually becomes the official currency of the European Community remains to be seen. If it does come to pass, the Euro will appear in coin denominations of 50, 20, 10, 5, 2 and 1 cent, and bill denominations will appear in 500, 200, 100, 50, 20, 10, 5, 2, and 1 Euro.

The Euro is valued differently in relation to the US dollar as it is to the Italian lira. For example, even though one Euro is currently valued at $0.90, which would translate to L2,084, in actuality, at current exchange rates one Euro would be worth only L1,936.

US & CANADIAN EXCHANGE RATES

US DOLLAR/ITALIAN LIRE EXCHANGE RATES

US$1 = 2,316 lire

US Dollars	*$1*	*$2*	*$5*	*$10*	*$20*
Lire	*2,316*	*4,632*	*11,581*	*23,162*	*46,324*
US Dollars	*$50*	*$100*	*$200*	*$500*	*$1,000*
Lire	*115,812*	*231,625*	*463,250*	*1,158,124*	*2,316,248*

CANADIAN DOLLAR/ITALIAN LIRE EXCHANGE RATES

CDN$1 = L1,533 lire

Canadian Dollars	*$1*	*$2*	*$5*	*$10*	*$20*
Lire	*1,533*	*3,066*	*7,655*	*15,331*	*30,662*
Canadian Dollars	*$50*	*$100*	*$200*	*$500*	*$1,000*
Lire	*76,656*	*153,313*	*306,625*	*766,563*	*1,533,127*

BUSINESS HOURS

Store hours vary all over Italy, but as a rule they are open from Monday through Friday, 9:00am to 1:00pm, then re-open at 3:30 or 4:00pm to 7:30/8:00pm, and Saturdays from 9:00am to 1:00pm. In large towns, of which Rome is one, which mainly to cater to tourists, stores are open on Saturday afternoons and Sundays as well. Most stores everywhere else in Italy are closed on Sundays, and everywhere they are closed on national holidays. Don't expect to find any 24-hour convenience stores just around the corner in Italy. In Italy you need to plan ahead.

Food stores (*alimentari*) keep their own hours but generally follow the regular business hours listed above. *Alimentari* usually close at least one other day of the week besides Sunday. In most cases this day is Thursday

(*Giovedi*), but it varies region to region, and even city to city within the region. There is a sign outside each *alimentari* that you can check to see which day they are closed (*chiuso*).

Basically, you must plan on most stores being closed from 1:00pm to 4:00pm, since this is the Italian siesta time. During that time, the only places open are restaurants, and most of those close at 2:30pm or 3:00pm.

CHURCH CEREMONIES IN ENGLISH

- **All Saints' Church** (Anglican), *Via del Babuino 153b, Tel.06/3600-2171. E-mail: allsaints_roma@hotmail.com. Sunday Mass 8:30am and 10:30am (sung)*
- **Church of Jesus Christ of Latter Day Saints**, *Piazza Camaro 20, Tel. 06/827-2708.*
- **Methodist Church**, *Via del Banco di Santo Spirito 3, Tel. 06/686-8314. E-mail: iasb.trad@tiscalinet.it. 10:30 Sunday Service.*
- **Rome Baptist Church**, *Piazza San Lorenzo in Lucina 35, Tel. 06/687-6652. E-mail: rombaptist@compuserve.com. 10am Sunday worship.*
- **St. Andrews** (Scottish Presbyterian), *Via XX Settembre 7, Tel. 06/482-7627. E-mail: david.huie@flashnet.it. Sunday Service at 11:00am*
- **St. Patrick's** (English-speaking Catholic), *Via Boncompagni 31, Tel. 06/420-3121. Sunday mass at 10:00am*
- **St. Paul's within the Walls** (American Episcopal), *Via Napoli 58, Tel. 06/488-3339. E-mail: stpaul@mclink.it. Sunday Mass 8:30am and 10:30pm (sung)*
- **San Silvestro** (English-speaking Catholic), *Piazza San Silvestro 1, Tel. 06/679-7775. Sunday Mass at 10:00am and 6:00pm.*
- **Santa Susanna** (American Catholic), *Piazza San Bernardo, Tel. 06/488-2748, Website: www.santasusanna.com. Sunday Mass at 9:00am, and 10:30am. Saturdays and weekdays at 6:00pm. 11am services at Marymount International school out the Via Cassia.*
- **Synagogue**, *(no services in English) Via Lungotevere dei Cenci, Tel. 06/684-0061*

COMPUTERS IN ROME

If you decide to bring your laptop, remember to carry along a three-pronged adapter so you can plug it into the wall to recharge your batteries. You can get them at most hardware, Circuit City or Radio Shack stores in North America.

If you can't find these devices, you can order them from the **Franzus Company**, (pronounced Francis), *Murtha Industrial Park, PO Box, 142, Beacon Falls, CT 06403, Tel. 203/723-6664, Fax 203/723-6666.* They also have a free brochure, *Foreign Electricity Is No Deep Dark Secret,* which can be mailed or faxed to you.

If you forget to bring your own, most computer stores in Italy carry them too but at a much higher price. You will also need an adapter to plug in your modem cable to access your e-mails. You can get them at the same places mentioned above.

Also, when dialing out you may have to add a prefix "8" to your modem string in the software setup. Most hotels in Italy require an "8" to be dialed for you to access an outside line.

DOCTORS & DENTISTS (ENGLISH-SPEAKING)

In case of need, the **American Embassy** *(Via Vittorio Veneto 119, Tel. 06/46741)* will gladly supply you with a recommended list of English-speaking doctors and dentists. A hospital where English is spoken is **Salvator Mundi**, *Viale della Mura Gianicolensi 67, Tel. 06/588-961, Website www.smih.pcn.net, E-mail: dg.smih@pcn.net.* I had my tonsils out there and am doing fine today. Another place is the **Rome American Hospital**, *Via VE Longoni 69, Tel. 06/22551, Website: www.rah.it.* They have a physician on call 24 hours a day.

An organization that can hook you up with physicians all over the world is **Personal Physician Worldwide**. See Chapter 7, pages 85-86, for contact information. A recommended heart specialist is **Aleardo William Madden**, MD, a Fellow in the American Heart Association. For an appointment, call *06/7049-1747* (*Via Baldo degli Ubaldi 272.*)

A well-recommended dental clinic is **Bazzucchi Dental Center**, *Via I Vivanti 201. Tel 06/520-0202. E-mail: Bazzucchi@mail.wing.it. Website: www.bazzucchi.it.*

EMBASSIES & CONSULATES

- **Australia**, *Via Alessandria 205, Tel. 06/852-721*
- **Canadian Embassy**, *Via GB de Rossi 27, Tel. 06/445-981*
- **Great Britain**, *Via XX Settembre 80a, Tel. 06/482-5441, Website: www.grbr.it*
- **Ireland**, *Piazza di Campitelli 3, Tel. 06/697-912*
- **New Zealand**, *Via Zara 28, Tel. 06/441-7171, E-mail: nzemb.roma@flashnet.it*
- **South Africa**, *Via Tanaro 1, Tel. 06/852-541, E-mail: sae@flashnet.it*
- **United States**, *Via Veneto 199, Tel. 06/46741*

EMERGENCIES

The following numbers should be used in case of emergency: **113**-Police; **112** – Caribinieri (military police), **118** – Ambulance (Red Cross), and **115** – Fire. There are police and caribinieri offices in Termini station by the tracks. Other **Caribinieri** stations include: Via Mentana 6 and Piazza Venezia. Other **Polizia** stations include: Via Farini 40, Via S Vitale 15, or Piazza del Collegio Romano.

ELECTRICITY

The standard electric current in Italy is 220v, but check with your hotel before you plug in an appliance to find out what the current is, because it's not always 220v! If you want to use your blow dryer, electric razor, radio, or plug in your laptop you are going to need a hardware adapter to switch your appliance from a two-prong to a three-prong insert. These can be found at most hardware stores. Also check before you leave to see if your appliance automatically changes the voltage from 110v to 220v. If it doesn't, you will need to purchase a converter.

If you can't find these devices at your hardware store, you can order them from the **Franzus Company**, *Murtha Industrial Park, PO Box, 142, Beacon Falls, CT 06403, Tel. 203/723-6664, Fax 203/723-6666.* They also have a free brochure *Foreign Electricity Is No Deep Dark Secret* that can be mailed or faxed to you.

EXPRESS COURIERS

DHL, *Toll free in Italy 800/345-345, Fax 06/7932-0051, Via Lucrezia Romana 87a; E-mail: dhl@dhl.com, Website www.dhl.it*

UPS, *Toll free in Italy 800/822-054, Fax 06/5226-8200, Via della Magliana 329.*

FESTIVALS IN ROME

- **January 1**, Candle-lit processional in the Catacombs of Priscilla to mark the martyrdom of the early Christians.
- **January 5**, Last day of the Epiphany Fair in the Piazza Navona. A carnival celebrates the ending.
- **January 21**, *Festa di Sant'Agnese*. Two lambs are blessed then shorn. Held at Sant'Agnese Fuori le Mura.
- **March 9**, *Festa di Santa Francesca Romana*. Cars are blessed at the Piazzale del Colosseo near the church of Santa Francesca Romana.
- **March 19**, *Festa di San Giuseppe*. The statue of the saint is decorated with lamps and placed in the Trionfale Quarter, north of the Vatican. There are food stalls, sporting events and concerts.
- **April**, *Festa della Primavera* (festival of Spring). The Spanish Steps are festooned with rows upon rows of azaleas.
- **Good Friday**, The Pope leads a candlelit procession at 9:00pm in the Colosseum.
- **Easter Sunday**, Pope gives his annual blessing from his balcony at noon.
- **April 21**, Anniversary of the founding of Rome held in Piazza del Campidoglio with flag waving ceremonies and other pageantry.
- **May 1**, *Festa del Lavoro*. Public Holiday

- **First 10 days of May**, international horse show held in the Villa Borghese at Piazza di Siena.
- **May 6**, Swearing in of the new guards at the Vatican in St. Peter's square. Anniversary of the sacking of Rome in 1527.
- **Mid-May**, Antiques fair along Via dei Coronari
- **First Sunday in June**, *Festa della Repubblica* involving a military parade centered on the Via dei Fori Imperiali. It's like something you'd see in Moscow during the Cold War.
- **June 23-24**, *Festa di San Giovanni.* Held in the Piazza di Porta San Giovanni. Traditional food sold: roast baby pig and snails.
- **June 29**, *Festa di San Pietro*. Festival to Saint Peter. Very important religious ceremony for Romans.
- **July**, *Tevere Expo* involving booths and stalls displaying arts and crafts, with food and wine lined up along the Tiber. At night there are fireworks displays and folk music festivals.
- **July 4**, A picnic organized by the American community outside Rome. Need to contact the American Embassy *(06/46741)* to make reservations for the buses to take you out there.
- **Last 2 weeks in July**, *Festa de Noiantri* involving procession, other festivities, feasting and abundance of wine all in Trastevere.
- **July & August**, Open air opera performances in the Baths of Caracalla.
- **August 15**, *Ferragosto*. Midsummer holiday. Everything closes down.
- **Early September**, *Sagra dell'Uva*. A harvest festival with reduced price grapes and music provided by performers in period costumes held in the Roman Forum.
- **Last week of September**, Crafts show held in Via dell'Orso near Piazza Navona.
- **Early November**, Santa Susanna Church Bazaar. Organized by the church for the Catholic American community to raise money for the church. Great home-made pies and cookies as well as used books and clothes. Auction of more expensive items held also.
- **December 8**, Festa della Madonna Immacolata in Piazza di Spagna. Floral wreaths inlaid around the column of the Madonna and one is laid at the top by firefighters.
- **Mid-December**, Start of the Epiphany Fair in the Piazza Navona. All throughout the piazza a fair filled with food stands, candy stands, toy shops opens to the public. Lasts a week. A must see.
- **December 20-January 10**, Many churches display elaborate nativity scenes.
- **December 24**, Midnight Mass at many churches. I recommend the one at Santa Maria Maggiore.
- **December 25**, Pope gives his blessing at noon from his Balcony at St. Peter's. The entire square is packed with people.

- **December 31**, New Year's Eve. Much revelry. At the strike of midnight people start throwing old furniture out their windows into the streets, so be off the streets by that time, or else your headache from the evening's festivities will be much worse.

HEALTH CLUBS

- **Roman Sports Center**, *Via del Galoppatoio 33, Tel. 06/320-1667. Open 9:00am-10:00pm.*
- **Le Club**, *Via Igea 15, Tel. 06/307-1024. Open Monday-Friday 7:30am–7:00pm, Saturday 4:00pm-6:00pm.*

HEALTH CONCERNS

A wonderful "just in case..." option is Personal Physicians Worldwide. This organization can provide you with a list of physicians and hospitals at your destination. If you have a medical condition that may need treatment, or you just want to be safe, they can help. The Medical Director, Dr. David Abramson, will confidentially review your personal medical history. He will then contact screened and qualified physicians at your destination to see if they will agree to be available and to care for you if the need arises, while you are in their location.

This is a great service since you never know where you'll be when you need the care of a competent doctor. To find out more information, contact:

- **Personal Physicians Worldwide**, *Tel. 888/657-8114, Fax 301/718-7725.* You can e-mail either Myra Altschuler at *myra@personalphysicians.com,* or Dr. David Abramson, Medical Director at *doctors@personalphysicians.com.* Their web site home page is *http://www.personalphysicians.com.*

INTERNET ACCESS

- **Splashnet**, *Via Varese 33, Tel. 06/4938-2073.* E-mail your friend and family with Yahoo, Hotmail, AOL and others. No E-mail address? No problem. They can set you up on hotmail or Yahoo free of charge. A great place to come and stay in touch with folks at home ... and you can do your laundry at the same time. Open in the summers from 9:00am to 1:00pm and Winter from 9:00am to 10:00pm. L5,000 per half hour on line time.
- **Marco's**, *Via Varese 54. Open 10:00am to 2:00am every day.* Just down the street from Splashnet, Via Varese is turning into the Internet access point for travelers in Rome. A grungy bar type atmosphere with video games, pool tables and beverage service. Internet access costs L4,000 per half hour and L8,000 per hour.

- **Freedom Traveller**, *Via Gaeta 25, Tel. 06/478-23-862. Email: info@freedom-traveller.it. Website: www.freedom-traveller.it.* Also located nearby the other two places listed above, you get access for L5,000 for 30 minutes or less. Student discount for an hour L8,000.
- **The Netgate**, *Piazza Firenze 25, Tel 06/689-3445, Email roma.pantheon@thenetgate.it.* Also at *Borgo S. Spirito 17, Tel. 06/6813-4082, E-mail: roma.vaticano@thenetgate.it; Termini Station, Tel. 06/8740-6008, E-mail: roma.terminie@thenetgate.it.* Their website is *www.thenetgate.it.* Three locations in Rome for you to use the internet. Rates start at L3,000.

LANGUAGE STUDY

If you want to travel in Italy and actively pursue learning the language at the same time there are many different schools all over the country. But the best way to do this would be to have everything arranged for you by organizations that specifically connect students with schools in Italy. Two of the best to contact, with quite similar names, are:

- **Language Studies Abroad**, *Tel. 800/424-5522.*
- **Language Study Abroad**, *Tel. 818/242-5263.*

LAUNDRY SERVICE

- **Uondo Blu**, *Principe Amadeo 70, Tel. 06/474-4647.* Coin operated laundry open seven days a week from 8:00am to 10:00pm. If you need clean clothes, this place is inexpensive and convenient to the train station. Wash L6,000. Dry L6,000.
- **Aqua & Sapone**, *Via Montebello 66, Tel. 06/488-3209.* Self-service wash and dry L6,000 each. Open every day from 8:00am to 10:00pm. Also located near the train station but on the other side.
- **Splash LavaService**, *Via Varese 33, Tel. 06/4938-2073.* Self-service laundry with internet access (see Splashnet description below) and satellite TV to keep you occupied while you wait for your laundry. Wash and dry costs L6,000 each. Open seven days a week from 8:00am to 10:00pm.

NEWSPAPERS & MAGAZINES

At most newsstands in Italy you can find the world renowned *International Herald Tribune,* which is published jointly by The Washington Post and The New York Times and printed in Bologna. You will also be able to find a condensed version of *USA Today*. Besides these two, you can also find newspapers from all over the world at almost any newsstand.

If you want an insight into what may be going on in the English language community of the city you are visiting, simply stop into any local

English-language bookstore. There should be a list of local events posted, or itemized in a newsletter.

PAPAL AUDIENCES

General audiences with the Pope are usually held once a week (Wednesday at 11:00am) in Vatican City. To participate in a general audience, get information through the **North American College** *(Via dell'Umita 30, Tel. 06/679-0658, Fax 06/679-1448)*, the American seminary in Rome. Catholics are requested to have a letter of introduction from their parish priest. Ticket pickup is the Tuesday before the Wednesday audience.

For attendance at a Papal audience women should dress modestly, with arms and head covered, and dark or subdued colors are requested. Men are asked to wear a tie and a jacket.

At noon every Sunday, the Pope addresses the crowds gathered beneath his window in St. Peter's square. During the latter part of the summer, because of the heat in Rome, and now more so for tradition, the Pope moves to his summer residence at **Castel Gandolpho** in the Alban Hills about sixteen miles southeast of Rome. Audiences are also regularly held there.

PETS

If you're bringing your precious pooch (your dog will have to be on a leash and wear a muzzle in public in Italy) or kitty into Italy with you, you must have a veterinarian's certificate stating that your pet has been vaccinated against rabies between 20 days and 11 months before entry into Italy, and that your pet is in overall good health. The certificate must contain the breed, age, sex, and color of your pet and your name and address. This certificate will be valid only for 30 days. The specific forms that the vet needs to fill out are available at all Italian diplomatic and consular offices.

Parrots, parakeets, rabbits, and hares are also subject to health certification by a vet, and will also be examined further upon entry into Italy. Also Customs officials may require a health examination of your pet if you have just come from a tropical region or that they suspect the pet to be ill. All this means that they can do whatever they want whenever they want, so it might be wise to leave your pet at home.

PHARMACIES

Farmacia are open from 9:00am to 1:00pm and reopen from 3:30pm to 7:30pm. At nights and on Sundays and holidays, one pharmacy in each district remains open on a rotating schedule. For information, dial 192 then 1 through 5 depending on the zone (see phone book for zones) for the location of the pharmacy nearest you. Also a list of open pharmacies for holidays and Sundays is published in the Rome daily, *Il Messagero*.

POLICE

- **Pubblica Sicurezza**, *Tel. 06/4686* (for theft, lost and found, petty crimes)
- **City Police** (Vigili Urbani), *Tel. 06/67691* (for car towings)
- **Carabinieri**, *Tel. 112* (for emergencies, violent crimes, etc.)
- **Highway Police** (Polizia Stradale), *Tel. 06/557-7905* (for parking tickets, etc.)

POSTAL SERVICES (ROME & VATICAN)

You can buy stamps at local tobacconists (they are marked with a "T" outside) as well as post offices. Mailboxes are colored red, except for the international ones, which are blue. Post offices are open from 8:25am to 1:50pm on weekdays, and 8:25am to 11:50am Saturday. Some, like the one on Via Firenze, near the Economy bookstore are open until 5:00pm, Monday through Saturday. The two exceptions to this rule are: the **Main Post Office** (Piazza San Silvestro), which is open Monday through Friday from 9:00am to 6:00pm, and Saturday from 8:30am to 12:50pm; and the branch at **Stazione Termini** (*Via Terme Diocleziane 30*, near the McDonalds on the Piazza della Repubblica), which is open 8:30am-6:00pm Monday – Friday and Saturdays 8:30am – 2:00pm..

If you want to have your postcards mailed by the Vatican, with their official stamp, go to the **Vatican Post Office** (*Via di Porta Angelica 23*, close to Piaza Risorgimento) which is open 8:30am-6:00pm Monday – Friday and Saturdays 8:30am – 11:50am.

PUBLIC RESTROOMS

These are scarcer than flying pigs, but for the year 2000 more are being established all over Italy. When in need, there are always McDonalds, which have sprouted up all over Rome and Italy after they bought out the Italian burger chain *Burghy*. If no McDonalds is evident, try a well-heeled restaurant or hotel. Ask for the *servizio*, or *toilette*.

RESTAURANT HOURS

Restaurants in Italy keep rather rigid hours, which are usually 12:30pm until 2:30pm for lunch, then they close completely. The dinner hours start at either 7:30 or 8:00pm and usually run until 10:00 or 11:00pm. Some late night restaurants stay open until the early morning hours. If you are hungry when restaurants are not open you can usually find a bar/café or a little pizza rustica shop to grab a quick bite to eat.

SAFETY & STAYING OUT OF TROUBLE

Italian cities are definitely much safer than any equivalent American city. You can walk almost anywhere without fear of harm, but that doesn't mean you shouldn't play it safe. Listed below are some simple rules to follow to ensure that nothing bad occurs:

- At night, make sure the streets you are strolling along have plenty of other people. Like I said, most cities are safe, but it doesn't hurt to be cautious.
- Always have your knapsack or purse flung over the shoulder that is not directly next to the road. Why? There have been cases of Italians on motor bikes snatching purses off old ladies and in some cases dragging them a few blocks.
- Better yet, have your companion walk on the street side, while you walk on the inside of the sidewalk with the knapsack or purse.
- Better still is to buy one of those tummy wallets that goes under your shirt so no one can even be tempted to purse-snatch you.
- Always follow basic common sense. If you feel threatened, scared, or alone, retrace your steps back to a place where there are other people.

GYPSIES

You may have the misfortune of being confronted with a pack of gypsies whose only interest is to relieve you of your wallet and other valuables. These situations are rare but they do happen. Gypsies are not violent, and usually you will only encounter women and children, but they tend to swarm all around you, poke pieces of cardboard in your midsection and generally distract you to the point where they are able to pilfer your pockets, fanny packs, back packs, or knapsacks. So if you are swarmed by gypsies, do not be polite, push back if you need to, make a scene, yell, scream, start running, do anything you can to get out of their midst. Gypsies will not harm you, but if you do not act quickly you will lose your valuables.

Staying out of trouble with the law is paramount, because in Italy you are guilty until proven innocent unlike in the States where it's the other way around. And most importantly, if arrested you are not simply placed in a holding cell. The Italian officials take you directly to a maximum-security prison and lock you up. And that's where you'll stay for as long as it takes your traveling partners to figure out where you are, bribe your case to the top of the local judge's pile, and have your case heard. That whole process can sometimes take months.

So if you like your drinks strong and your nights long, remember to keep your temper in check. And don't even think about smuggling any banned substance into the country, or God forbid, buying something illicit when you're in Italy. If you are approached to buy some hashish or something else, say politely, *No Grazie* (no thank you) and walk away.

SUPERMARKETS

You can usually find all the food you need at an *alimentari*, but if you want a wider selection, there is a supermarket, **GS Supermarket** (open 9:00am–7:00pm everyday except Sunday) in the tunnel system between the Piazza di Spagna and the Via Veneto which is reached through the Metro. From the Via Veneto simply follow the signs to Spagna. From the Piazza di Spagna follow the signs to Via Veneto and you will find it.

TAXIS

Taxi service is widely available in all major cities in Italy, and a little less so in smaller cities such as Pisa or Lucca, and almost non-existent in remote towns and villages. Rates are comparable to those charged in your large American cities, which means expensive. Generally taxis locate themselves in special stands located at railway stations and main parts of the city, but many can be waved down as they cruise the streets for fares. At these taxi stands there are usually telephones that you can call directly from your hotel, but remember, in Italy, if called, the meter starts at the point of origin, so you'll be paying the cabby to come pick you up. The same goes for radio taxis if called to come pick you up.

Fares will vary from city to city, but basically when you get in the cab there will be a fixed starting charge of approximately 2,800 to 6,400 lire, and a cost per kilometer of approximately 1,000 to 1,250 lire. If you are stuck in traffic, every minute another L500 or so will be added to the fare. Some extra charges may come into play, like the **nighttime supplement** (between 10:00pm and 6:00am), a **Sunday and public holiday supplement**, as well as a **per item luggage charge**. You will also be charged for every piece of luggage. All of these vary from city to city.

On long trips, like from airports, it is advised to agree upon a price before heading out. Ask at the information booth inside each airport what the expected charge should be.

TELEPHONES & FAX

Calling Italy

Even when making local calls the area code must be used. In conjunction, before it was necessary to discard the leading zero of the area code (for example Rome's area code is 06), but now you need to use the leading zero in all area codes.

To dial Rome from the United States, first dial the international prefix, **011**, then the country code, **39**, then the city code for Rome, **06**, then the number you wish to reach.

Long Distance Calling From Italy

Most pay phones in Italy only use **phone cards** (which you can buy in denominations of L5000, L10,000 or L15,000) but some use a combination of cards and coins. You can buy phone cards at any *tabacchi* (the stores with the **T** out in front of them), newsstand, post office and some bars. You will need these cards to be able to use public pay phones

Listed below are some of the major telecommunications carriers for North America and their access numbers:

AT&T - *Tel. 172-1011* (a toll free number in Italy) to gain access to an AT&T operator (or English language prompts) for efficient service. You can bill your AT&T calling card, local phone company card, or call direct.

Canada Direct - *Tel. 172-1001* (a toll free number in Italy) and you will be connected to the Canadian telephone network with access to a bilingual operator. You can bill your *Calling Card, Call Me*™ service, your *Hello!* Phone Pass or call collect.

MCI - *Tel. 172-1022* (a toll free number in Italy) for MCI's World Phone and to use your MCI credit card or call collect. All done through English speaking MCI operators.

Sprint - *Tel. 172-1877* (a toll free number in Italy) for access to an English speaking Sprint operator who can charge your phone card or make your call collect.

An inexpensive option for international calling is to buy an international phone card (*carta telefonica internationale*) which are also sold at most *tabacchi*. You can get cards for L20,000 which have 100 minutes available on them. This translates to L200 per minute, which is about 10 cents, a steal for international calling.

Modem or Fax Usage In Italy

To connect you modem or fax to the wall you will need an adapter. These too can be bought from a hardware store or from the **Franzus Company** (see above under Electricity). Many hotels in Italy are starting to use the American standard phone plug, so this may not be a concern. When making your reservations, inquire about the type of plugs in use to insure you can communicate with home without a problem.

TIME

Italy is **six hours ahead of Eastern Standard Time** in North America, so if it's noon in New York it's 6:00pm in Rome. Daylight savings time goes into effect each year in Italy usually from the end of March to the end of September.

TIPPING

Hotels

A service charge of 15-18% is usually added to your hotel bill, but it is customary to leave a little something else, whatever you deem sufficient, but anything over L1,000-L2,000 per service rendered can be extravagant.

TIPPING AT THE RIGHT TIME

Most people tip at the end of a stay in a hotel indicating an appreciation for the services rendered. But if you want to ensure that the services rendered are exemplary, tip in the beginning of your stay. Giving on the spot tips for services rendered usually guarantees the best possible service. Slip a couple thousand lira to the person who checks you in; leave a few thousand on the bed for the maid with a note saying "Grazie" will almost always ensure service above and beyond the call of duty. A couple thousand may sound like a lot until you remember the exchange rate.

Restaurants

A service charge of around 15% is usually automatically added to all restaurant bills. But if you felt the service was good, it is customary to leave a little something. There is no set percentage, and a good rule of thumb is to leave whatever change is returned, as long as it is not above 5-10%.

The same applies in cafés and bars. For example, around two hundred lire is normal if you're standing at the counter drinking a soda, cappuccino, etc. If you have an alcoholic beverage, something to eat, etc. at the counter, the tip should be L500 or more. Leaving change in this manner is a good way to rid myself of burdensome coins.

Theater Ushers

They get L1,000 or more if the theater is very high class.

Taxis

Give the cabby 5% of the fare, otherwise they just might drive away leaving you without your luggage. (Just kidding).

Sightseeing Guide & Driver

Give L2,000 minimum per person for half-day tours, and L2,500 minimum per person for full day tours.

Service Station Attendant

Give L1,000 or more for extra service like cleaning your windshield, or giving you directions while also filling up your tank.

TOUR COMPANIES

Some of the companies that offer you a variety of tourist services and tours are listed below. Most are open Monday through Friday 9:00am-5:30pm, Saturday 9:00am-12:30pm and closed on Sundays. But besides these three, there are a number of alternatives while in Rome.

- **American Express**, *Piazza di Spagna 38, Tel. 06/676-41. For lost travelers checks the toll free in Italy is 800/872-000. For lost/stolen cards 800/874-333*
- **Carrani Tours**, *Vie V.E. Orlando 95, Tel. 06/474-2501, Fax 06/4890-3564*
- **Thomas Cook Travel**, *Piazza Barberini 21A, Tel. 06/482-80-82. Toll free number in Italy 800/004488.*

TOURIST INFORMATION & MAPS

You can buy maps and guide books at most newsstands and bookstores. This may be necessary even though the tourist offices give away free maps for the subway, buses, as well as an extensive map of the streets of Rome. Besides the tourist kiosks (see *Seeing the Sights* section), below are some sources for tourist information:

- **American Express**, *Piazza di Spagna 38, Tel. 06/676-41*
- **Rome Provincial Tourist Board** (**EPT**), *Via Parigi 5, Tel. 06/488-3748*
- **EPT Termini**, *between tracks #2 and 3, Tel. 06/487-1270*
- **EPT Fiumicino**, *just outside customs, Tel. 06/601-1255*
- **Italian Government Travel Office** (ENIT), *Via Marghera 2, Tel. 06/49711*
- **Enjoy Rome**, *Via Marghera 2, Tel. 06/446-3379 or 444-1663*
- **Centro Turistico Studentesco e Giovanile**, *66 Via Nazionale, Tel. 06/467-91*

Most of the time, especially in high season, these places will run out of tourist material, and in grand Italian fashion, nothing gets done about it. So newsstands are your only recourse. Also, the maps given out at the tourist offices and kiosks may not be as extensive as is needed when in Rome, especially if you want to use the bus system. There are maps which you can buy at newsstands which not only list the bus routes but also have an index of streets which will help you locate places of interest in Rome. The cost for these maps is anywhere from L7,000-L10,000. A bargain and a great keepsake of your trip to Rome.

WEBSITES OF INTEREST

Before you head off to Italy, I've listed some web sites below that you may find interesting or useful. Some of them are featured elsewhere in this book.

Airfare

- *www.bestfares.com*
- *www.lowestfare.com*
- *www.cheaptickets.com*
- *www.airdeals.com*
- *www.lastminutetravel.com*

Currency

- *www.oanda.com/converter/travel* – to create pocket currency conversion chart to bring with you, simply visit this website.

General Information

- *www.italiantourism.com* – website for the Italian government tourist office. Filled with lots of great information.
- *www.itwg.com* – an all-inclusive website featuring loads of useful information about Italy.
- *www.travel.it/welcome.html* – another all encompassing website produced by yet another Italian government agency.
- *www.enjoyrome.com* – offers walking tours of Rome.
- *www.mondoweb.it/livinginrome* – the complete guide to living in Rome for foreigners.

Hotels

- *www.venere.it* – you can get hotel reservations for thousands of hotels all over Italy at this site.

Language

www.travlang.com/languages – if you want to take a few virtual language lessons before you go, visit the *Foreign Language for Travelers* web site.

www.arcodidruso.com – Italian language and culture for foreigners.

Medical

- *www.personalphysicians.com* – provides you with a list of physicians and hospitals at your destination. If you have a medical condition that may need treatment, or you just want to be safe, they can help.

Passport

- *www.instantpassport.com* – this website promises to give you 24-hour turnaround from the time they receive your passport pictures and requisite forms. They charge $100 plus overnight shipping on top of all fees associated with passport issuance.
- *www.americanpassport.com* – this site offers three types of service: expedited (24 hours), express (three to four business days) and regular. Prices range from $245 to $135.
- *www.travel.state.gov* – you can download passport application forms, international travel advisories, and listings of embassies and consulates worldwide.

Weather

- *www.washingtonpost.com/wp-srv/weather/historical/historical.htm* – if you want to obtain the average temperature, temperature ranges and rain accumulation totals by month for Rome or other destinations in Italy visit this website.

WANTED IN ROME

An excellent periodical that features classified ads about accommodations, jobs, and more. Also included are the latest activities in Rome. A great resource for tourists and ex-pats alike. Cost is L1,500 and you can find it at most English language bookstores. Office located at *Via dei Delfini 17, Tel. 06/679-0190, E-mail: wantedinrome@compuserve.com, Website: www.wantedinrome.com.*

WEIGHTS & MEASURES

Italy uses the metric system, where everything is a factor of ten. This system of measurement is the simplest and easiest; even England converted their entire country some years ago; but the only country in the world to still use an antiquated system of measurement, is, you guessed it, our United States. Canada is now about half metric, half American, but that's because they're America's largest trading partner, so they have to know what we do.

The table on the next page gives you a list of weights and measures with approximate values.

WEIGHTS & MEASURES

Weights

Italy	*14 grams*	*Etto*	*Kilo*
US	*1/2 oz*	*1/4 lb*	*2 lb 2oz*

Liquid Measure

Italy	*Litro*
US	*1.065 quart*

Distance Measure

Italy	*Centimeter*	*Meter*	*Kilometer*
US	*2/5 inch*	*39 inches*	*3/5 mile*

'WHERE ROME'

This is the title of an omnipresent tourist magazine usually found in hotel rooms. In it you can find all sorts of up to date information about events in Rome, new restaurants, cafes, bars, shops etc. If you do not have one at your hotel, you can contact the publishers, *Tel. 06/578-1615*, and pick up a copy or they can tell you where to go to get one. A great resource.

WOMEN TRAVELERS

As stated in the Safety section above, Italy is a safe country, but generally women traveling alone will find themselves the recipients of unwanted attention from men. In most cases the attention you receive will be limited to whistles, stares, comments (in Italian which you will probably not understand), catcalls and the like. This may happen whether you are in groups or alone. But usually if you are with a male companion this type of unwanted attention doesn't occur.

If you choose to be alone, whether it's going for a walk, seeing a sight, or stopping for a coffee, don't expect to be alone for long. Since foreign women have a reputation for being easy, ignoring unwanted suitors won't work because they think they can charm their way into your heart and elsewhere. My suggestion is to politely tell them you are waiting for your boyfriend (*aspetto mio fidanzato*) or husband (*marito*). If that doesn't work, raise your voice, look them in the eye angrily and tell them to *lascia mi stare* (lash-ah me star-ay), which means leave you alone.

If these ploys do not work, simply walk away. If the man continues to badger you, find a local policeman for assistance, but always remain in a populated area. In the vast majority of cases there is truly nothing to fear. Most Italians just want to get lucky and when rebuffed they will go find easier prey. In conjunction, most of the attention falls into the nuisance category, but like I said in the Safety section, please use common sense. Avoid unpopulated areas, avoid walking alone on dark streets, avoid hitchhiking alone and things like that. Just be smart. Italy is much safer than America and is not even remotely as violent, but it's better to be safe than sorry.

In general too, the further south you go, the more you will be hassled. Something about the warm climate must heat the male's blood or stimulate their libido. Also in port cities women traveling alone will be pegged as targets for petty theft. So be extra careful in those types of cities.

And all over the country, when you ride public transportation you may very well be confronted with wandering hands, especially when the bus or train is crowded. To avoid this, keep your back to the wall. If someone does start to fondle your posterior or elsewhere, make a loud fuss - otherwise it will continue unabated.

YELLOW PAGES

There is an excellent **English Yellow Pages (EYP)** in Italy. It is the annual telephone directory of English-speaking professionals, organizations, services and commercial activities in Rome, Florence, Milan, Naples, Genoa and Bologna. The EYP is a well-known resource and reference source among the international community in Italy, from which you can easily find numbers for airlines and embassies, English-speaking doctors and dentists, international schools and organizations, hotels, moving companies, real estate agents, accountants, attorneys, consultants, plumbers, electricians, mechanics and much more. Listings are complete with address including zip code, phone and fax numbers, e-mail and web sites.

You can find copies at embassies, international organizations (FAO, IFAD, WWF, etc.) schools & universities, social and professional associations, English-language churches, foreign press offices, local events within the expat community and various businesses that deal directly with an international clientele. And copies of it are on sale at most international bookstores. This is a great resource for any resident or visitor to Italy.

10. FOOD & WINE

FOOD

Most Italian food is cooked with the freshest ingredients, making their dishes not only healthy but tasty and satisfying. There are many restaurants in Italy of international renown, but you shouldn't limit yourself only to the upper echelon. In most cases you can find as good a meal at a fraction of the cost at any trattoria. Also, many of the upper echelon restaurants you read about are only in business because they cater to the tourist trade. Their food is acceptable, but doesn't warrant the prices charged. I list the best restaurants in every city, where you can get a wonderful meal every time. As you will notice in each regional chapter, I feature some top-of-the-line restaurants as well as many local places, but each are well off the regular tourist path, and each offers a magnificently Italian experience for your enjoyment.

The traditional Italian meal consists of an antipasto (appetizer) and/or soup, and/or pasta and is called primo, a main course called secondo (usually meat or fish), with separately ordered side dishes of contorni (vegetables) or insalata (salad) which come either verdi (green) or mista (mixed), then dolci (dessert), which can be cheese, fruit, or gelato (ice cream). After which you then order your coffee and/or after dinner drink.

Note: Pasta is never served as an accompanying side dish with a secondo. In Italy, it is always served as a separate course. It is time to forget everything you thought you knew about "Italian" food that was learned at some run-of-the-mill restaurant chain.

Many North Americans think that there is one type of Italian food, and that's usually spaghetti and meatballs. As a result they don't know what they are missing. Region by region Italy's food has adapted itself to the culture of the people and land. In Florence you have some of the best steaks in the world, in the south the tomato-based pastas and pizzas are exquisite; in Genoa you can't miss the pesto sauce (usually garlic, pine nuts, parmiggiano and basil); and don't forget the seafood all along the coast.

GLOSSARY OF ITALIAN EATERIES

Bar *– Not the bar we have back home. This place serves espresso, cappuccino, rolls, small sandwiches, as well as sodas and alcoholic beverages. It is normal to stand at the counter or sit at a table when one is available. You have to try the* ***Medalione****, a grilled ham and cheese sandwich available at most bars. A little 'pick-me-up' in the morning is* ***Café Corretto****, coffee 'corrected' with the addition of* ***grappa*** *(Italian brandy) or Cognac.*

Gelateria *– These establishments offer gelato – ice cream – usually produced on the premises. Italian gelato is softer than American but very sweet and rich.*

Osteria *– Small tavern-like eatery that serves local wine usually in liter bottles as well as simple food and sandwiches*

Panineria *– A small sandwich bar with a wider variety than at a regular Italian bar, where a quick meal can be gotten. One thing to remember is that Italians rarely use condiments on their sandwiches. If you want mustard or such you need to ask for it.*

Pasticceria *– Small pasty shops that sell cookies, cakes, pastries, etc. Carry-out only.*

Pizzeria *– A casual restaurant specializing in pizza, but they also serve other dishes. Most have their famous brick ovens near the seating area so you can watch the pizza being prepared. There are many excellent featured pizzerias in this book.*

Pizza Rustica *– Common in central Italy. These are huge cooked rectangular pizzas displayed behind glass. This pizza has a thicker crust and more ingredients than in a regular Pizzeria. You can request as much as you want, since they usually charge by the weight, not the slice.*

Rosticceria *– A small eatery where they make excellent inexpensive roast chickens and other meats, as well as grilled and roasted vegetables, mainly potatoes. Sometimes they have baked pasta.*

Trattoria *– A less formal restaurant with many local specialties.*

Ristorante *– A more formal eating establishment, but even most of these are quite informal at times.*

Tavola Calda *– Cafeteria-style food served buffet style. They feature a variety of hot and cold dishes. Seating is available. Great places for a quick lunch.*

Listed below is a selection of the main regional specialties for Lazio, Rome's province, and the surrounding provinces of Tuscany and Umbria.

- **Toscana** – *bistecca all Fiorentina* (large T-bone steaks grilled), *arista* (roast pork), cacciucco (fish soup)

- **Lazio** – *abbacchio arrosto* (roast lamb), *porcetta* (roast pork), and pastas, including *penne all'arrabiata* (literally translated it means angry pasta; a spicy hot, garlic-laden, tomato dish; should not be missed) and *tortellini alla panna* (most of which is cheese stuffed pasta in a heavy cream sauce but sometimes it can be meat stuffed)
- **Umbria** – *Tagliatelle al tartuffo* (pasta with savory truffle sauce), and basically anything with truffles, white or black.

RESTAURANT LISTINGS IN THIS BOOK

Here's a sample listing which you'll find in this book in each of our Where to Eat sections. The number preceding the name of the restaurant tells you where to find it on the accompanying city or town map:

"**3. La Lepanto**, *Via Carlo Alberto 135, Tel. 079/979-116. Closed Mondays in the winter. All credit cards accepted. Dinner for two L140,000.*

A fine place with a quaint terrace located in the heart of the old city, but the preparation of dishes is haphazard. Sometimes it's great, other times so-so. Maybe it's because they try to do too much. The menu is extensive and seems to have everything that surf and turf could offer. I've always been pleased with the i polpi tiepido con le patate (roasted octopus in an oil and garlic sauce with roasted potatoes) and the spaghetti con gamberi e melanzane (with shrimp and eggplant). For antipasto, try the exquisite antipasto misto di pesce spada affumicato (smoked swordfish) or the insalata mista (mixed salad) with fresh vegetables from the region."

The restaurant listings indicate which credit cards are accepted by using the following phrases:

- Credit cards accepted = American Express and/or Visa or Mastercard
- All credit cards accepted = Everything imaginable is accepted, even cards you've never heard of
- No credit card accepted = Only cash or travelers checks (if a listing is left without an indication, that means that no credit cards are accepted.)

Each restaurant listing will give a ballpark price for a dinner for two in Italian lire. For example: "Dinner for two L80,000." This price represents the cost for two people who choose to eat a full meal of an antipasto, pasta dish and an entrée. In most cases you can get by with one course, which will make the actual price you will pay less than indicated. With the exchange rate at roughly $1=L2300, for this example the dollar price would be about $35 for the meal.

WINE

Italy is also famous for its wines. The experts say the reds are not robust enough, and the whites are too light, but I'm not an expert.

Personally I think Italian wines are great, one and all. Most importantly, to get a good bottle of wine, you don't have to spend a fortune. You can find some excellent wines straight out of vats in small wine stores in every city in Italy.

At any restaurant, all you'll need to order is the house wine to have a satisfying and excellent wine. (*Vino di casa*: House Wine; *Rosso*: Red; *Biancho*: White). But if you're a connoisseur, or simply want to try a wine for which a certain Italian region is known, in the sidebar above you'll find a selected list of wines and their regions (if you like red wine, try the Chianti, and if it's white you prefer, try Verdicchio or Frascati).

ITALIAN WINES BY REGION

Piemonte *– Barolo (red, dry), Barbera (red, dry), and Asti Spumanti (sweet sparkling wine)*

Lombardia *– Riesling (white, dry), Frecciarossa (rose wines)*

Trentino-Alto Adige *– Riesling (white, dry), Santa Maddalena (red, semi-dry), Cabernet (red, dry)*

Veneto *– Soave (white, dry), Valpolicella (red, dry or semi-sweet)*

Liguria *– Cinqueterre (named after a section of Liguria you must visit. Cinqueterre is five small seaside towns inaccessible by car or train, you have to walk. They're simply gorgeous.)*

Emilia Romagna *– Lambrusco (red, semi-sparkling, several kinds going from dry to sweet), Sangiovese (red, dry), Albano (white, dry or semi-sweet)*

Tuscany *– Chianti (red, dry; look for the Chianti Classico. They're the ones with a black rooster on the neck of the bottle)*

Marche *– Verdicchio (white, dry)*

Umbria *– Orvieto (white, dry)*

Lazio *– Frascati (white, dry or semi-sweet), Est Est Est (white, slightly sweet)*

Abruzzi *– Montepulciano (red, dry)*

Sardinia *– Cannonau (red, dry to semi-sweet)*

Sicily *– Etna (red and white, wide variety), Marsala (white, dry or sweet)*

Campania, Apulia, Calabria, Basilicata *– Ischia (red and white, several varieties), San Severo (red, dry)*

ORDER LIKE A NATIVE: READING AN ITALIAN MENU

Here are a few choice words to assist you when you're ordering from a menu while in Italy. Usually, the waiter should be able to assist you, but if not, this will make your dining more pleasurable. You wouldn't want to order octopus, rabbit or horse by surprise, would you?

ENGLISH	ITALIAN	ENGLISH	ITALIAN
Menu	*Lista, Carta*	Teaspoon	*Cucchiaino*
Breakfast	*Prima Colazione*	Knife	*Cotello*
Lunch	*Pranzo*	Fork	*Forchetta*
Dinner	*Cena*	Plate	*Piatto*
		Glass	Bicchiere
Cover	*Coperto*	Cup	*Tazza*
Spoon	*Cucchiao*	Napkin	*Tovagliolo*
Antipasto			
Soup	*Zuppa*	Broth	*Brodo*
Fish Soup	*Zuppa di Pesce*	Vegetable soup	*Minestrone*
Broth with beaten egg	*Stracciatella*		
Pasta			
Ravioli with meat stuffing	*Agnolotti*	Egg noodles	*Fettucine*
Large rolls of pasta	*Cannelloni*	Potato-filled, ravioli-like pasta	*Gnocchi*
Thin angel hair pasta	*Capellini*	Thin pasta	*Vermicelli*
Little hat pasta	*Capelletti*	Macaroni-like Pasta	*Penne*
Eggs	*Uova*		
soft-boiled	*al guscio*	hard boiled	*sode*
fried	*al piatto*	omelet	*frittata*
Fish	*Pesce*		
Seafood	*Frutti di mare*	Eel	*Anguilla*
Lobster	*Aragosta*	herring	*Aringa*
Squid	*Calamari*	Carp	*Carpa*
Mullet	*Cefalo*	Grouper	*Cernia*

Mussels	*Cozze/Muscoli*	Perch	*Pesce Persico*
Salmon	*Salmone*	Clams	*Vongole*
Octopus	*Polpo*	Bass	*Spigola*
Oysters	*Ostriche*	Mixed fried fish	*Fritto Misto Mare*

Meat	*Carne*		
Spring Lamb	*Abbacchio*	Lamb	*Agnello*
Rabbit	*Coniglio*	Chicken	*Pollo*
Small Pig	*Porcello*	Veal	*Vitello*
Steak	*Bistecca*	Breast	*Petto*
Pork	*Maiale*	Liver	*Fegato*
Cutlet	*Costellata*	Deer	*Cervo*
Wild Pig	*Cinghiale*	Pheasant	*Fagione*
Duck	*Anitra*	Turkey	*Tacchino*

Methods of Cooking

Roast	*Arrosto*	Boiled	*Bollito*
On the Fire/ Grilled	*Ai Ferri/ Alla Griglia*	Spit-roasted	*Al Girarrosto*
Rare	*Al Sangue*	Grilled	*Alla Griglia*
Well Done	*Ben Cotto*	Medium Rare	*Mezzo Cotto*

Miscellaneous

French fries	*Patate Fritte*	Cheese	*Formaggio*
Butter Sauce	*Salsa al burro*	Tomato and Meat Sauce	*Salsa Bolognese*
Tomato Sauce	*Salsa Napoletana*	Garlic	*Aglio*
Oil	*Olio*	Pepper	*Pepe*
Salt	*Sale*	Fruit	*Frutta*
Orange	*Arancia*	Cherries	*Ciliege*
Strawberry	*Fragola*	Lemon	*Limone*
Apple	*Mela*	Melon	*Melone*
Beer	*Birra*	Mineral Water	*Aqua Minerale*
Orange Soda	*Aranciata*	7 Up-like	*Gassatta*
Lemon Soda	*Limonata*	Juice (of)	*Succo (di)*

Wine	*Vino*		
Red	*Roso*	White	*Bianco*
House wine	*Vino di Casa*	Dry	*Secco*
Slightly Sweet	*Amabile*	Sweet	*Dolce*
Local Wine	*Vino del Paese*	Liter	*Litro*
Half Liter	*Mezzo Litro*	Quarter Liter	*Un Quarto*
A Glass	*Un Bicchiere*		

In all restaurants in Italy there used to be a universal cover charge, pane e coperto (literally "bread and cover") which was different restaurant to restaurant, and in some cases was quite expensive. **Pane e coperto** was tacked on to your bill above and beyond any tip you decided to leave; but for the Year 2000 celebrations, most of Italy has decided that foreigners would not understand what pane e coperto is so they have eliminated it. Or at least should have. If your bill has an extra L10,000 or so, that is the pane e coperto, which covers the cost of the basket of bread at your table and gives you the right to sit there.

There will also be a statement about whether service is included, **servizio incluso**, or not, **servizio non incluso**. If service is included it is usually 15% of the bill. If you felt the service was good, it is customary to leave between 5-10% more for the waiter.

Another feature on most menus are **piatti di giorno** (daily specials) and prezzo fisso (fixed price offerings.) The latter can be a good buy if you like the choices and is usually a better deal than ordering a la carte. If you have trouble reading the menu, do not hesitate to ask your waiter for assistance. Usually they will speak enough English to be able to help. And in many restaurants there are menus in a variety of different languages to help you choose the food you want.

11. BEST PLACES TO STAY

ROME

EDEN, *Via Ludovisi, 49, 00187 Roma. Tel. 06/474-3551. Fax 06/482-1584. 100 rooms all with private bath. Single L420,000-450,000; Double L600,000-750,000, Suites L1,100,000. Continental breakfast is L28,000 extra, buffet breakfast is L43,000. (Metro-Barberini or Spagna)* *****

Located west of Via Veneto in the exclusive Ludovisi section but still in the middle of everything, the Eden is but steps from the famous Via Veneto and Spanish Steps, and the Trevi Fountain is just down the street. The Eden is ideally situated for sightseeing. With a long tradition of excellent service, year after year it maintains its top-ranked exclusivity, attracting all the cognoscenti (those in the know) to its exquisite accommodations. Declared one of the *Leading Hotels of the World*, it has an ultra-sophisticated level of service and comes with amenities virtually unmatched the world over.

Some of the amenities of the Eden include the terrace restaurant, which has a spectacular view over the city. And guests and locals alike flock to this restaurant, not just because of the view but because of the excellence of Chef Enrico Derflingher. The former personal chef to the Prince and Princess of Wales, Chef Derflingher makes sure you receive food fit for royalty. And after a sumptuous meal you can work it off in their fully appointed gym that has everything from cardiovascular equipment to free weights. If you want to stay in the lap of luxury while in Rome, the Eden is the paradise you've been looking for.

LE GRAND HOTEL, *Via Vittorio Emanuele Orlando, 00185 Roma. Tel. 06/4709, Fax 06/474-7307. Single L389,000-620,000; Double L550,000-900,000; Suites L1,900,000. Extra bed costs L150,000. Breakfast L40,000. (Metro-Repubblica)* *****

Opulence knows no bounds in this extra fine hotel. Located between the Piazza della Repubblica and Piazza San Bernardo, near the American speaking church in Rome, Santa Susanna, this top-class luxury hotel has everything you'd ever need, and the prices to match. The rooms and suites are palatial, some with 16 to 17 foot ceilings, and the bathrooms have every imaginable amenity. The elegance and professional service here are refined including the hairdresser, beauty salons, and sauna. When staying here you will definitely feel like a prince or princess. Afternoon tea is served downstairs everyday at 5:00pm. They also have a very relaxing but expensive American-style bar. The Grand Hotel has recently undergone an incredible face lift and has returned to its status as a premier hotel, not just in Rome, but the entire world

VILLA HASSLER, *Piazza Trinita Dei Monti 6, 00187 Rome. Tel. 06/678-2651, Fax 06/678-9991. E:mail: hasslerroma@mclink.it. Website: http://venere.topchoice.com/roma/hassler. All credit cards accepted. 80 rooms all with bath. Single L710,000; Double L960,000-1,270,000. Suite prices on request. Continental breakfast L44,000 extra. Buffet breakfast L77,000 extra. (Metro-Spagna)* *****

The Villa Hassler may not be as opulent as the Eden, but it is just as refined and equally as elegant. In many travelers' opinions this is the best hotel in Rome, not just because of it's excellent location at the top of the Spanish Steps, but mainly because of the ultra-professional service and amazingly comfortable accommodations. Oil sheiks, movie stars, the nouveau riche, the landed gentry all have made the Hassler home, at one time or another, for over a century. They have a relaxing courtyard and an excellent (but expensive) roof garden restaurant with a superb view of the city.

These same views are shared with a number of the rooms on the upper floors facing the Spanish Steps, so remember to request one of these. Every imaginable amenity awaits you at the Hassler, and in a city filled with great restaurants, they have one of the best. So you don't even have to leave your hotel to have a first class meal. Even if you don't stay here, come to the restaurant, sample the food, and enjoy the superb view. One of the best, most famous, and ideally located hotels in Rome. If you have the means, I recommend it highly.

HOTEL BAROCCO, *Piazza Barberini 9 (entrance on Via della Purificazione 4), 00187 Roma. Tel. 06/487-2001/2/3, 487-2005, Fax 06/485-994. Email: hotelbarocco@holelbarocco.it. Website: http://www.hotelbarocco.com. 30 rooms, all with bath. Single L160,000-380,000; Double L190,000-630,000. Breakfast included. All credit cards accepted. (Metro-Barberini)* ****

There is something about small hotels that warms my heart. Maybe it's the extra attention the staff lavishes on you? Maybe it's the chance to connect more easily with fellow travelers? The Barrocco is the place for you if you're looking for an intimate and elegant four-star experience but don't want to get lost in the crowd at a larger hotel. Everything here is very refined yet comfortable and relaxed. The entrance hall is small but tastefully decorated with photos of Roman scenes. Each room is different from the other; some with two levels, others with small terraces; and all come with an electronic safe, TV, A/C and everything else befitting a four star. The bathrooms are a little small but come with hair dryer and courtesy toiletry kit. The roof terrace is a great place to get away from it all for a few hours and is especially a great location for an evening's relaxation. Centrally located with the Trevi Fountain, Spanish Steps, Via Veneto all around the corner, the Barocco is a great place to spend an entire vacation, or simply the last night of a long one. I love this quaint, intimate little hotel and I am sure you will too.

HOTEL LOCARNO, *Via della Penna 22, 00186 Rome. Tel. 06/361-0841, Fax 06/321-5249. Email: locarno@italyhotel.com. Website: www.venere.it/roma/locarno. All credit cards accepted. 38 rooms all with bath. Single L215,000; Double L330,000-460,000; Suite L490,000 and up. Breakfast L25,000. (Metro-Flaminio) ****

I know that this is only a three star, but I simply adore this hotel. Refined and elegant the Locarno will make you feel welcome and comfortable, even if they are not as opulent as the Eden or the Grand Hotel or the Hassler. Situated in an excellent part of town, near the Via del Corso and all its stores and galleries, you are also surrounded by some of Rome's best restaurants. But the real charm of the Locarno is not just its ideal location, but the hotel itself. I always feel like I have walked into the pages of F. Scott Fitzgerald's *The Great Gatsby* when I stay here. This place embodies character and oozes charm. It has a very relaxing American-style bar, spacious common areas, a small side-garden patio, and a lovely roof terrace. The rooms are tastefully decorated with all possible amenities, and the service is superb and utterly professional. Why they are still a three star is beyond me. This place is simply stupendous. If you want to stay in a great hotel, without paying five star prices, try the Locarno.

FLORENCE

HOTEL TORRE DI BELLOSGUARDO, *Via Roti Michelozzi 2, 50125 Firenze. Tel. 055/229-8145, Fax 055/229-008. 16 room all with bath. Single L250,000-290,000; Double L390,000; Suites L430,000-530,000. All credit cards accepted. *****

If you have the means, this is definitely the most memorable place to stay while in Florence. With stunning views over all of Florence, a swimming pool with a bar at which to relax, olive gardens in which to take an evening stroll, the Bellosguardo is like no other hotel in Florence.

Housed in a huge old castle that has been separated into only 16 luxury rooms, it goes without saying that the size of accommodations are quite impressive. The interior common areas with their vaulted stone ceilings and arches, as well as staircases leading off into hidden passages, all make you feel as if you've stepped back in time.

The hotel is a short distance outside of the old city walls in the middle of pristine farmland. You will find pure romance, complete peace, and soothing tranquillity all with stunning views of the city of Florence. In fact the hotel is so well thought of that they are booked solid year round, so you have to reserve well in advance. I can't say enough about the Bellosguardo, it is simply something you have to experience. Also, and most importantly, if you aren't already in love, you'll find it or rekindle it in this wonderfully majestic hideaway.

ORVIETO

LA BADIA, *1a Cat., 05019 Orvieto. Tel 0763/301-959 or 305-455. Fax 0763/305-396. All credit cards accepted. Single L250,000; Double L600,000.* ****

Umbria is Tuscany's under-appreciated cousin, quietly regal, unassuming, yet just as charming. And just over the border from Lazio, right outside the city walls of Orvieto in Umbria is this unbelievably beautiful 12th century abbey which has been converted into an incredibly beautiful hotel and restaurant. Located only an hour from Rome, here you will find one of the most unique and memorable experiences in the entire world. This historic abbey became a holiday resort for Cardinals in the 15th century, and today, through painstakingly detailed renovations, you can stay or dine in incomparable ambiance and charm.

The rooms are immense, the accommodations exemplary, the service impeccable, and the atmosphere like something out of the Middle Ages. For a fairy tale vacation this is the place to stay. Set in the lush hills and fields of Umbria, near to Rome, and just outside of the stunning town of Orvieto, this place is an ideal spot for a romantic getaway. Make sure that you eat at least once at their soon-to-be world renowned restaurant offering refined local dishes – many ingredients culled from owner Count Fiumi's farms and vineyards – in an ambiance filled with character, charm and elegance.

12. WHERE TO STAY

Hotels in Italy are strictly controlled by a government rating system that categorizes them from "no star" hotels to "four star deluxe" hotels. Each and every hotel must prominently display their official ranking for all visitors to see.

These ratings have little to do with price. They only indicate what types of facilities are available at each hotel, and even then the designation can be ambiguous. Also, the stars do not indicate what level of service you will receive, how clean the hotels are, whether management is surly or sweet. Even in hotels with the same rating, the quality of facilities can be vastly different. The stars only indicate which facilities are available. Listed below is the star ranking (see Chapter 6, *Planning Your Trip*, for more details on accommodations and ratings).

You'll find the stars listed at the end of the italicized basic information section (name of hotel, address, phone, price, cards accepted, etc.) before the review itself begins for each hotel.

*****__Five star, deluxe hotel__: Professional service, great restaurant, perfectly immaculate large rooms and bathrooms with air conditioning, satellite TV, mini-bar, room service, laundry service, and every convenience you could imagine to make you feel like a king or queen. Bathrooms in every room.

****__Four star hotel__: professional service, most probably they have a restaurant, clean rooms not so large, air conditioning, TV (maybe satellite), mini-bar, room service, laundry service and maybe a few more North American-like amenities. Bathrooms in every room.

***__Three star hotel__: a little less professional service, most probably do not have room service, should have air conditioning, TV and mini bar, but the rooms are mostly small as are their bathrooms. Some rooms may not have bathrooms.

**__Two star hotel__: Usually a family-run place, some not so clean as higher rated hotels. Mostly you'll only find a telephone in the room, and you'll be lucky to get air conditioning. About 50% of the rooms have either a shower/bath or water closet and sometimes not both together. Hardly any amenities, just a place to lay your head.

***One star hotel**: Here you usually get a small room with a bed; sometimes you have to share the room with other travelers. The bathroom is usually in the hall. No air conditioning, no telephone in the room, just a room with bed. These are what used to be the low-end pensiones. Definitely for budget travelers.

No Hotel Reservations?

If you get to Rome without a reservation and arrive at the train station, there is a free hotel finding service in the information office located at the end of **track #10** that will get you a room. There is no fee, but you usually do have to pay them for the first night's stay up front. The service calls ahead and books your room, gives you a map, and will show you how to get to your hotel. It's a great service for those who have arrived in Rome on a whim. Sometimes the lines are long, so be patient.

NEAR TERMINI STATION

1. ALBERGHO IGEA, *Via Principe Amadeo 97, 00184 Roma. Tel. 06/446-6913, Fax 06/446-6911. E-mail: Igea@venere.it. Mastercard and Visa accepted. 42 rooms, 21 doubles, 21 singles, all with shower and W/C, air conditioning, and TV. Single L120,000-170,000; Double L150,000-250,000;. Breakfast L10,000 per person. (Map A) ****

The rooms are large, clean, and with full bath facilities, air conditioning and TV in each room. The lobby is large and spacious, completely covered in white marble making it a pleasant place to relax; and the staff is friendly, knowledgeable, and professional. This is a thoroughly modern recently upgraded three star hotel that is 300 meters from the train station. Granted there's not much to do around the station, and the restaurants are better almost anywhere else in the city, but if you want a lot of amenities for a good price, near the station, stay here.

2. HOTEL RICHMOND, *Largo Corrado Ricci 36, 00184 Roma. Tel. 06/6994-1256, Fax 06/6994-4145. 13 rooms. Single L230,000; Double L340,000. Breakfast included. (Map D) ****

Not really located near the train station, but close enough, this colorful little hotel is simply fantastic. The rooms are large and incredibly accommodating. All expected three star amenities are included. And the main feature is the terrace, which has a stupendous view over the Forum, Victor Emanuel Monument and Colosseum and is the ideal place to relax in the evenings. Somewhat distant from the main tourist area by the Pantheon, Navona and the Spanish Steps, but this helps to make your stay here tranquil. Without any qualms I would highly recommend this hotel for your stay in Rome. Nearby is one of the best enoteca in Rome, *Cavour 313*, and a superb Irish pub, *Shamrock*.

3. HOTEL BRITANNIA, *Via Napoli 64, 00184 Roma. Tel. 06/488-3153, Fax 06/488-2343. E-mail:britannia@venere.it. Website: www.venere.it/home/roma/britannia/britannia.html. 32 rooms all with private baths. Air conditioning. Parking Available. All credit cards accepted. Single L200,000-335,000; Double L360,000-410,000. Breakfast included. Children up to 10 years old share parent's room for free. (Map A)* ***

Located just north of the Via Nazionale, down a small side street, this is an efficiently run hotel that offers guests every conceivable attention. The entrance hall blends into the American-style bar area and the breakfast room. The rooms are all modern with different furnishings in each. All are clean and comfortable and come with a safe, satellite TV and mini-bar. The bathrooms are also modern with hair dryers, sun lamps and courtesy toiletry kits. In the mornings, they have Italian and English language newspapers at your disposal and in the evenings chocolate on your pillow. The service is supremely courteous and professional. Situated near a Metro stop for easy access to all parts of the city.

4. DIANA, *Via Principe Amadeo 4, 00185. Tel. 475-1541, Fax 06/486-998. E-mail: Diana@venere.it. Website: www.venere.it/roma/diana/diana.html. 190 rooms all with private baths. All credit cards accepted. Single L120,000-250,000; Double L150,000-350,000. Suites L485,000. Breakfast included. Lunch or Dinner costs an extra L40,000. (Map A)* ***

Located near Stazione Termini and the opera, this is a comfortable well run three star hotel on the Principe Amadeo, a street in limbo caught between the old and the new. This is definitely an old and elegant hotel. The lobby and common areas are an eclectic mixture of marble floors and columns with subtle lighting and paintings, with two meeting rooms that can hold 30-40 people. And the restaurant is large enough to hold 300 people and the food is quite good. The room sizes vary greatly but the smallest are still very comfortable even without the mini-bar. But fear not, you still have the satellite TV.

The bathrooms are nothing special (only 30 have hair dryers) but all come with bath and shower. There is an American style bar open all the time with intimate little glass tables that seem straight out of *La Dolce Vita*. This place is comfortable and cozy, a good value for your money, and the service is exquisitely professional. Also, they have special rates for groups of 20 or more that will make your stay very cheap if you're arranging for a group. You need to call or fax for details.

5. HOTEL GALILEO, *Via Palestro 33, 00185 Roma. Tel. 06/444-1205/6/7/8, Fax 06/444-1208. Single L120-205,000; Double L160,000-295,000. All credit cards accepted. 80 rooms all with bath. Breakfast included. (Map A)* ***

There are four beautiful floors in this hidden treasure. The only drawback is that the entrance is down a driveway that leads to a garage. But once you're inside everything is transformed to cater to all your needs. They have a lovely garden terrace on the first floor where you can have your breakfast or relax at the end of the day. The prices are somewhat low for a three star, I think because of the driveway situation. A good hotel near the train station with accommodating amenities.

6. LE GRAND HOTEL, *Via Vittorio Emanuele Orlando, 00185 Roma. Tel. 06/4709, Fax 06/474-7307. Single L389,000-620,000; Double L550,000-900,000; Suites L1,900,000. Extra bed costs L150,000. Breakfast L40,000. (Map A)* *****

Located between the Piazza della Repubblica and Piazza San Bernardo, near the American speaking church in Rome, Santa Susanna, this top-class luxury hotel has everything you'd ever need, and the prices to match. There is a hairdresser service, beauty salons, and saunas. The hotel used to be located in one of the most fashionable quarters which has long since lost its chic, but that doesn't detract from the opulent ambiance of the hotel itself. The rooms and suites are palatial, some with 16 to 17 foot ceilings. You'll feel like a prince or princess when they serve you afternoon tea downstairs at 5:00pm. If tea is not your style, there's a very relaxing but expensive American-style bar. A wonderful place to stay if you are part of the world elite.

7. HOTEL GIGLIO DELL'OPERA, *Via Principe Amadeo 14, 00184 Roma. 62 rooms all with bath. Tel. 06/484-401 or 488-0219, Fax 06/487-1425. E-mail:Giglio.dell.Opera@venere.it. Website: www.venere.it/it/roma/giglio_dell_opera/. Single L300,000; Double L400,000. (Map A)* ***

Close to the opera, this hotel is a favorite with some of the performers and their hangers-on. Unfortunately I think they have realized that they attract a chic and fashionable crowd, and as a result their prices have risen proportionately. The rooms are attractive in a neo-classic style, some are more modern but all have a comparable level of comfort. Each bathroom comes with courtesy toiletry kit but is lacking a hair dryer. The lounge area is large and there is a small and intimate area that serves as a bar in the evenings, but you'd better know music to get involved in the conversations. Breakfast is served in a spartan, white, brightly-lit room off the lobby. A fun, eclectic place to stay.

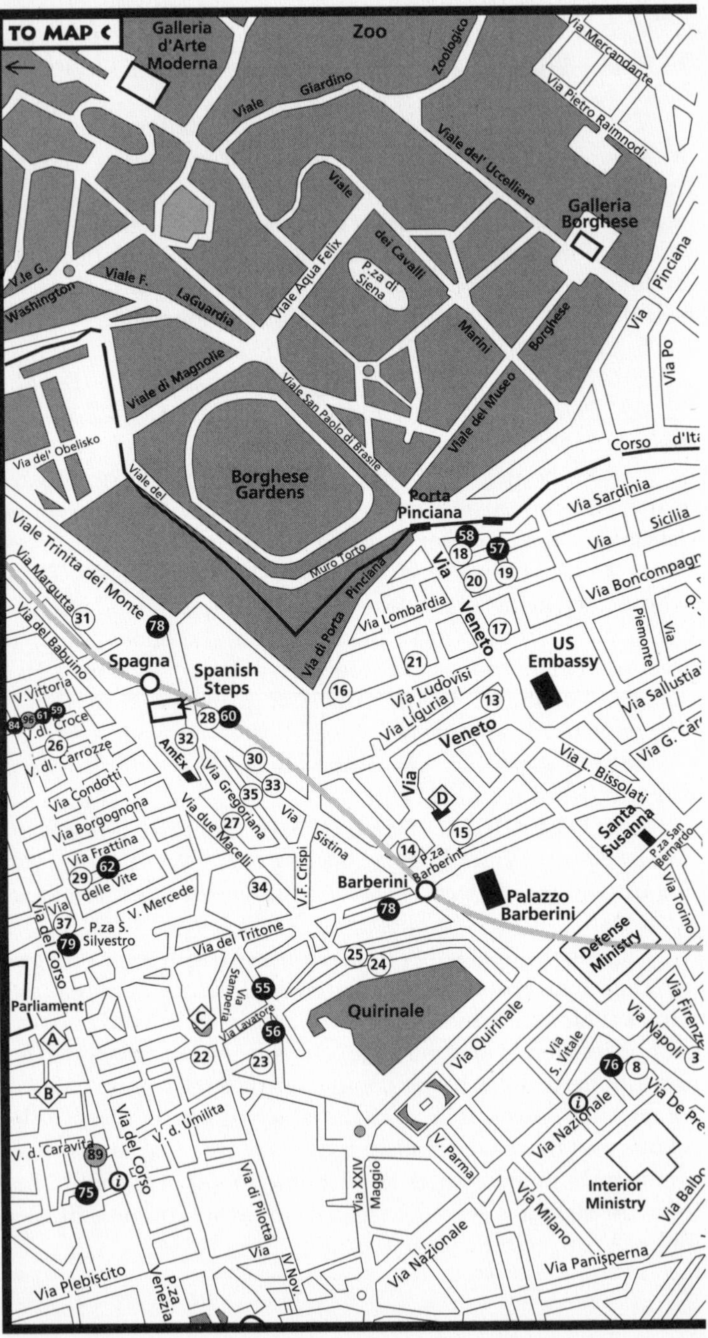

TO MAP C
Galleria d'Arte Moderna
Zoo
Viale Giardino
Zoologico
Via Mercadante
Via Pietro Raimnodi
Viale dell' Uccelliere
Galleria Borghese
Viale dei Cavalli
P.za di Siena
V.le G. Washington
Viale F. LaGuardia
Viale Aqua Felix
Marini
Borghese
Via Pinciana
Via Po
Viale di Magnolie
Viale San Paolo di Brasile
Viale del Museo
Corso d'Ita
Via del' Obelisko
Viale del Muro Torto
Borghese Gardens
Porta Pinciana
Via Sardinia
Via Sicilia
Via Boncompagni
Viale Trinita dei Monte
Via Margutta
Via del Babuino
Via di Porta Pinciana
Via Veneto
Via Lombardia
US Embassy
Piemonte
Spagna
Spanish Steps
Via Ludovisi
Via Liguria
Via Sallustia
V. Vittoria
V. dl. Croce
V. dl. Carrozze
AmEx
Via G. Car
Via L. Bissolati
Via Condotti
Via Borgognona
Via Gregoriana
Via Sistina
Via due Macelli
Via Frattina
delle Vite
Santa Susanna
P.za San Bernardo
P.za Barberini
Barberini
Palazzo Barberini
V.F. Crispi
V. Mercede
Via Torino
Via del Corso
P.za S. Silvestro
Via del Tritone
Defense Ministry
Via Stamperia
Via Lavatore
Parliament
Quirinale
Via Firenze
Via Napoli
Via Quirinale
Via S. Vitale
Via De Pre
Via Nazionale
Via del Corso
V. d. Umilita
V. d. Caravita
V. Parma
Via di Pilotta
Via XXIV Maggio
Via Milano
Interior Ministry
Via Balbo
Via IV Nov.
Via Nazionale
Via Panisperna
Via Plebiscito
P.za Venezia

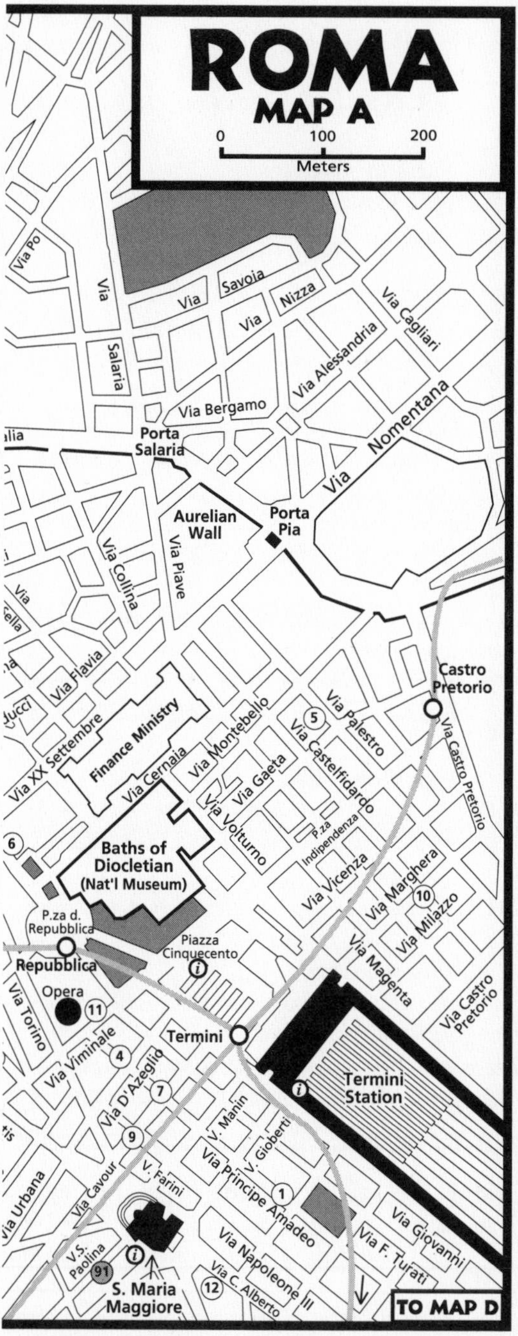

SIGHTS ◇

A. Column of Marcus Aurelius
B. Temple of Hadrian
C. Trevi Fountain
D. Church of Bones

HOTELS ○

1. Igea
3. Brittania
4. Diana
5. Galileo
6. Grand Hotel
7. Giglio dell'Opera
8. Luxor
9. Massimo d'Azeglio
10. Venezia
11. Columbia
12. Mecentate Palace
13. Ambasciatori Palace
14. Barocco
15. Bernini Bristol
16. Eden
17. Excelsior
18. Flora
19. Golden
20. Merano
21. Savoia
22. Fontana
23. Trevi
24. Julia
25. De Petris
26. Carriage
27. Doge
28. Hassler
29. Homs
30. Internazionale
31. Manfredi
32. Scalinata di Spagna
33. Lydia Venier
34. Erdarelli
35. Gregoriana
37. Parlamento

EATERIES ●

55. Al Moro
56. Al Piccolo Arancio
57. Giovanni
58. Girarrosto Toscano
59. Re degli Amici
60. Hassler
61. Otello alla Concordia
62. Le Grotte
75. Da Sabatino *(do not go here)*
76. Caffetteria Nazionale
78. Al Cafe du Jardin
79. Ciao/Spizzico
84. Enotecantina

NIGHTLIFE ●

89. Trinity College
91. Fiddler's Elbow
96. Birreria Lowenbrau

Metro Line & Stops

ⓘ Information Kiosks

TEN GREAT HOTELS IN ROME

You'll find plenty of great hotels when in Rome, but for a truly relaxing stay here is a list of my ten best to help make your stay in the Eternal City that much better.

Two star hotels

***37. HOTEL PARLAMENTO**, Via delle Convertite 5, 00186 Roma. Single without bath L130,000. Single L80,000-195,000. Double L100,000-230,000.*

***20. HOTEL PENSIONE MERANO**, Via Vittorio Veneto 155, 30 rooms 28 with bath. Single without bath L90,000-100,000; Single L110,000-130,000; Double without bath L125,000-140,000; Double L175,000-200,000.*

Three star hotels

***38. HOTEL LOCARNO**, Via della Penna 22, 38 rooms all with bath. Single L215,000; Double L330,000-460,000.*

***32. HOTEL SCALINATA DI SPAGNA**, Piazza Trinita Dei Monte 17, 15 rooms all with baths. Single L290,000-400,000; Double L480,000-580,000.*

***10. HOTEL VENEZIA**, Via Varese 18, 61 rooms all with bath. Single L175,000-250,000; Double L220,000-350,000.*

***2. HOTEL RICHMOND**, Largo Corrado Ricci 36, 00184 Roma. Tel. 06/6994-1256, Fax 06/6994-4145. 13 rooms. Single L230,000; Double L340,000.*

Four star hotels

***17. HOTEL BAROCCO**, Piazza Barberini 9 (entrance on Via della Purificazione 4), 28 rooms all with bath. Single L160,000-380,000; Double L190,000-630,000.*

***26. MECENATE PALACE HOTEL**, Via Carlo Alberto 3, 62 rooms all with bath. Single L380,000-480,000; Double L550,000-650,000.*

Five star hotels

***16. EDEN**, Via Ludovisi, 49, 100 rooms all with private bath. Single L560,000-990,000; Double L935,000-1,650,000.*

***28. VILLA HASSLER**, Piazza Trinita Dei Monti 6, 80 rooms all with bath. Single L565,000; Double L730,000-1,130,000.*

8. HOTEL LUXOR, *Via A. De Pretis 104, 00184 Roma. Tel. 06/485-420, Fax 06/481-5571. 27 rooms all with bath. Single L171,000-240,000; Double L210,000-360,000. Breakfast included. All credit cards accepted. (Map A) ****

This is a quaint little hotel off the Via Nazionale situated in three stories of a building built in the last century. The lobby is a little cramped but the proprietor and her husband will do almost anything to make you happy. The hotel has all the amenities of a three star hotel and you'll just love the classic "fin de siecle" beds and armoires. Each room is different from the other and all are quite large and accommodating. The bathrooms are comfortably sized with complimentary toiletry kit and hair dryer. There is a very small roof garden for relaxation. Centrally located, on the best local shopping street, and it is near a Metro.

9. MASSIMO D' AZEGLIO, *Via Cavour 18, 00184 Roma. Tel. 06/460-646 or 487-0270, Fax 06/482-7386. Toll free in Italy 167/860004. Toll free in the US 800/223-9832. E-mail: hb@bettojahotels.it. Website: www.bettojahotels.it. Credit cards accepted. 198 rooms, all with private baths. Single L355,000; Double 530,000. (Map A) ****

Located near Stazione Termini, this hotel first opened in 1875 and maintains its traditional manner which fills the place with old world charm. They have all the modern amenities of a four-star in Italy, but the look and feel of the place is definitely 1950s in a quaint sort of way. One of the best parts is the Cantina restaurant downstairs that looks like a wine cellar. There are lots of nooks and crannies in which to get lost. A good choice for around the train station and the opera.

10. HOTEL VENEZIA, *Via Varese 18, 00184 Roma. Tel. 06/445-7101, Fax 06/495-7687. E-mail: info@hotelvenezia.com. Website: www.hotelvenezia.com. Credit cards accepted. 61 rooms all with bath. Single L175,000-250,000; Double L220,000-350,000. Generous buffet breakfast included. (Map A) ****

This is definitely the best hotel near the Stazione Termini. For a three star the prices are quite good and the service is excellent. Located on a side street away from all the noise, you would never know that you're a block from the train station. If you are traveling alone ask for one of the single rooms on the fifth floor so you can relax and enjoy the wonderful Roman evenings on the individual balconies. Some rooms have showers to cater to North Americans; others have baths for the Asians. You can select which option you want.

The hotel caters to travelers, business customers, and visiting academics since the University is just around the corner. You'll love the 16th century altar that serves as buffet table for breakfast and bar at night, as well as the huge 16th century table in the conference room. The ever charming and hospitable owner and operator, Patrizia Diletti, will bend over backwards to make your stay pleasant This is a wonderful hotel with some of the most attentive, friendly and multi-lingual service I have encountered in the Eternal City.

11. HOTEL COLUMBIA, *Via del Viminale 15, 00184 Roma. Tel. 06/474-4289, Fax 06/474-0209. E-mail: info@hotelcolumbia.com. Website: www.hotelcolumbia.com. 45 rooms all with bath. Single L170,000-210,000; Double L220,000-280,000. (Map A) ****

Owned by the ever accommodating Patrizia Diletti, who is the proprietor of the excellent hotel Venezia listed above. This hotel has all of the positive features of the Venezia, plus a small roof garden. What makes this hotel and the Venezia stand out is the attentive and friendly service, as well as the clean and comfortable rooms. The lobby is nothing to write home about, but the rooms have all gone through a year and half renovation to fit them with all modern conveniences. And now I can say that the Columbia is a wonderful place to stay. Located by the Opera and the Via Nazionale, you are also close to the train station, and have easy access to the Metro and buses to get you anywhere you want to be when in Rome. An excellent choice when in Rome.

12. MECENATE PALACE HOTEL, *Via Carlo Alberto 3, 00187 Roma. Tel. 06/4470-2024, Fax 06/446-1354. E-mail: info@mecenatepalace.com. Website: www.mecenatepalace.com. All credit cards accepted. 62 rooms all with bath. Single L380,000-480,000; Double L550,000-650,000. Breakfast included. (Map A) *****

Attentive service, elegant accommodations, first class dining, and a spectacular view of Rome all add up to a wonderful stay. This hotel is a study in cozy elegance and is new, having only been opened in 1995. Conveniently located near the train station, it boasts its own roof garden with a wonderful view of St. Peter's in the distance and Piazza Santa Maria Maggiore nearby. Fast becoming famous for its exceptional service and beautifully appointed, welcoming rooms, the Mecentate is one of Rome's most sophisticated hotels. And what a great restaurant: the Terrazza dei Papi is fast becoming famous, not only because of chef Pasquale D'Anria's specialties, but also as a result of the splendid panorama of the city from its rooftop perch.

VIA VENETO AREA

13. AMBASCIATORI PALACE, *Via Vittorio Veneto 62, 00187 Roma. Tel. 06/47-493, Fax 06/474-3601. E-mail: ambasciatorirome@diginet.it. Website: www.hotelambasciatori.com. 142 rooms and 8 suites, all with private bath. All credit cards accepted. Single L400,000-500,000; Double L500,000-710,000; Suite L910,000. Buffet breakfast included. (Map A) ******

Virtually in the center of the Via Veneto, this hotel deserves its luxury rating since it has impeccable service, palatial rooms, and a top class restaurant La Terrazza to complement its fine ambiance. Your every need can be taken care of here: massage, evening companion, theater reservations, travel arrangements, etc. If you're looking for deluxe treatment at a deluxe price, look no further. A simply marvelous hotel on one of Rome's most fashionable streets.

14. HOTEL BAROCCO, *Piazza Barberini 9 (entrance on Via della Purificazione 4), 00187 Roma. Tel. 06/487-2001/2/3, 487-2005, Fax 06/485-994. E-mail: hotelbarocco@holelbarocco.it. 30 rooms all with bath. Single L160,000-380,000; Double L190,000-630,000. Breakfast included. All credit cards accepted. (Map A)* ****

If you're looking for an intimate and elegant four-star experience and don't want to get lost in the crowd at a larger hotel, this is the place for you. The entrance hall is tastefully decorated with photos of Roman scenes. Each room is different from the other, some with two levels, others with small terraces; and all come with an electronic safe, TV, A/C and everything else befitting a four star.

Every decoration and piece of furniture is supremely elegant. The bathrooms are a little small but come with hair dryer and courtesy toiletry kit. In the summer, breakfast is served on the roof terrace. A great location for an evening's relaxation. Centrally located with the Trevi Fountain, Spanish Steps, Via Veneto all around the corner. A great place to spend an entire vacation, or simply the last night of a long one. I love this quaint, intimate little place.

15. BERNINI BRISTOL, *Piazza Barberini 23, 00187 Roma. Tel. 06/488-3051, Fax 06/482-4266. E-mail: Bernini.Bristol@italyhotel.com. Website: www.venere.it/it/roma/bernini_bristol/. 124 rooms all with private baths. Single L280,000-520,000; Double L400,000-800,000; Jr. Suite L1,200,000. Continental breakfast buffet L45,000. VAT excluded. (Map A)* *****

The hotel is located in the Piazza Barberini at the foot of the Via Veneto facing Bernini's Triton Fountain. This is another hotel that deserves its luxury rating. Established in 1870, this hotel still retains the charm and atmosphere of that era. The entrance salon is beautifully appointed with antique furniture and lamps as well as a crystal chandelier. All rooms are elegantly furnished (each in its own style), well lit, and quite large.

The bathrooms are large and come with a phone and courtesy toiletry kit. They offer every possible convenience and comfort here and are definitely waiting on that fifth star. The suites on the top floor all have wonderful terraces with splendid views. The restaurant where you are served an abundant breakfast has a panoramic view over the rooftops of Rome. Perfectly located for shopping and sightseeing, you can get to the Spanish Steps and Trevi Fountain in minutes.

16. EDEN, *Via Ludovisi, 49, 00187 Roma. Tel. 06/474-3551, Fax 06/482-1584. 100 rooms all with private bath. Single L560,000-990,000; Double L935,000-1,650,000, Suites L1,400,000. Continental breakfast is L28,000 extra, buffet breakfast is L43,000. (Map A)* *****

The best just got more expensive, bt if you can afford it, this place is well worth it. Located west of Via Veneto in the exclusive Ludovisi section, the Eden is a long-established top-ranked, exclusive hotel. One of the *Leading Hotels of The World*, it has a sophisticated level of service and amenities virtually unmatched the world over. Located just off the crowded Via Veneto here you are in the center of it all, but it is supremely quiet too. The terrace restaurant has a spectacular view of the city and the *Villa Borghese*. Chef Enrico Derflingher is the former personal Chef to the Prince of Wales and Diane, which means you'll receive food fit for royalty. Also available is a complete gym with everything from cardiovascular equipment to free weights. The Eden is truly a paradise on earth.

17. EXCELSIOR HOTEL, *Via Vittorio Veneto 125, 00187 Roma. Tel. 06/4708, Fax 06/482-6205. All 244 doubles, 38 singles, and 45 suites have private baths. Single L360,000-620,000; Double L500,000-1,050,000, Suite L1,400,000. An extra bed costs L100,000. Continental breakfast is L30,000 extra and American breakfast is L50,000. (Map A)* *****

This superb five star hotel is located on the east side of the Via Veneto not far from the walls that lead to Villa Borghese, and right across the street from the American Embassy. All rooms and common areas are done up with ornate moldings and elegant decorations. A truly palatial experience. They have a world-renowned restaurant, La Cuppola, as well as a piano bar at night. A wonderfully elite hotel, now owned by the Westin chain which only makes it that much more elegant.

18. GRAND HOTEL FLORA, *Via Vittorio Veneto 191, 00187 Roma. Tel. 06/489-929, Fax 06/482-0359. E-mail: flora@venere.it. Website: www.venere.it/home/roma/flora/flora.html. All 8 suites and 155 rooms have private baths. All credit cards accepted. Single L385,000; Double L400,000, Suites L600,000-1,490,000. Breakfast included. (Map A)* ****

Located immediately at the top of the Via Veneto by the old Roman walls, this old-fashioned hotel has first class traditional service. The public rooms are elaborately decorated with antiques, oriental rugs, and soothingly light color schemes reminiscent of the turn of the century. The rooms are immense and some have wonderful views over the walls into the lush greenery of Villa Borghese. Try and request one of those rooms, since Borghese is beautiful at night. The bathrooms have been recently renovated and come with all modern creature comforts. This hotel offers everything you could want: location, service, and great rooms. Now owned by Marriott which has helped to upgrade the entire facility.

19. RESIDENCE GOLDEN, *Via Marche 84, 00187 Roma. Tel. 06/482-1659, E-mail: hotel.golden@tin.it. 12 of the 13 rooms have private baths. All credit cards accepted. Single without bath L70,000-100,000; Single L100,000-160,000; Double without bath L100,000-120,000; Double L150,000-280,000. (Map A) ***

An upscale pensione since it has air-conditioning, TV, phone, and mini-bar in every room. And the prices in the high season reflect the realization that they have good accommodations. The hotel is located on the first floor of an old house, on a quiet street off of the Via Veneto. The stark white breakfast room that serves the mini-buffet in the mornings doubles as the bar/lounge in the evenings. All the amenities of a three star, in a great location at the prices of an upscale two star. Clean, comfortable and well situated.

20. HOTEL PENSIONE MERANO, *Via Vittorio Veneto 155, 00198 Roma. Tel. 06/482-1796, Fax 06/482-1810. All credit cards accepted. 30 rooms 28 with bath. Single without bath L90,000-100,000; Single L110,000-130,000; Double without bath L125,000-140,000; Double L175,000-200,000. (Map A) ***

Another relatively inexpensive place to stay. Ideally located on the Via Veneto at rock bottom prices. The only reason the prices are so low is that you have to ride an elevator up to the third floor of a building to get to the hotel. The entranceway is dark but the rooms are warm and cozy. Everything is spic and span in the bathrooms, and you don't have to worry about remembering to buy your drinks for the evening, since they sell beer, soda, and water. If you want to enjoy Rome inexpensively, this is one of the best places from which to do it.

21. SAVOIA, *Via Ludovisi 15, 00187 Roma. Tel. 06/474-141, Fax 06/474-68122. 135 all with bath. All credit cards accepted. Single L200,000-850,000; Double L300,000-850,000; Suite L1,000,000. (Map A) *****

Located in the upscale Ludovisi section west of Via Veneto, this is a comfortable and well run hotel that has recently jacked up their prices astronomically. They have an excellent restaurant, offering both a la carte and a superb buffet and a lively but still relaxing bar downstairs. The service is impeccable as it should be and the decor is elaborately expensive. The rooms, even the ones that face the Via Veneto are quiet and comfortable. The location is perfect, especially if you're a spy since the hotel is almost directly across the street from the American Embassy.

TREVI FOUNTAIN AREA

22. FONTANA, *Piazza di Trevi 96, 00187 Roma. Tel. 06/678-6113, 06/679-1056. 24 rooms all with bath. Single L150,000-360,000; Double L200,000-450,000. A/C costs L30,000 extra. All credit cards accepted. (Map A) ****

The location of this hotel is great, but is not secluded or tranquil because it is in the same square as one of Rome's most famous monuments, the Trevi Fountain. You can hear the cascading waters and ever-present crowds far into the night. If you're a heavy sleeper this hotel's location is perfect, but if not try elsewhere. The rooms are sparse but comfortable and since this is a converted monastery, some rooms have been made by joining two monk's cells together. There is also a pleasant roof garden from which you can sip a drink and gaze over the rooftops of Rome.

23. HOTEL TREVI, *Vicolo del Babuccio 20/21, Tel. 06/678-9563, Fax 06/6994-1407. 29 rooms all with bath. All credit cards accepted. Single L170,000-300,000; Double L190,000-360,000. Breakfast included. (Map A)* ***

Located on a quiet side street near the Trevi Fountain, this ideal little three-star is in a wonderful location, in a beautiful palazzo, but down a side street so it is peaceful at night. Each room comes with every conceivable modern convenience. They have a roof garden, which is a great place to relax in the evenings and is where the buffet breakfast is served in good weather. But since they're just around the corner from Dunkin' Donuts you have that choice too. Though only a three-star, the prices here are rather dear, but the location and accommodations warrant them. Very professional service. An elite, upscale hotel.

24. JULIA, *Via Rasella 29, Tel. 06/488-1637, Fax 06/481-7044. 33 rooms all with bath. Single L 100,000-210,000; Double L120,000-310,000. All credit cards accepted. (Map A) ****

In the heart of Rome, on a small, tranquil little side street near the Trevi Fountain, the Julia is a hotel of great comfort and style. The entry way is small, the rooms are adequately sized, the bathrooms are relatively small and come only with showers. The singles are minuscule. The service is excellent but the main selling point is the ideal and tranquil location.

25. DE PETRIS, *Via Rasella 142, Tel. 06/481-9626. Fax 06/482-0733. 45 rooms all with bath. Single L 225,000-285,000; Double L270,000-380,000. All credit cards accepted. Breakfast included. (Map A) ****

Just across the street from the Julia, this is also in an ideal and tranquil location. Very accommodating and comfortable with all necessary three star amenities. Each room is different from the other in terms of furnishings and layout. The bathrooms are well-appointed. The breakfast is extensive and is served in a quaint room. A good choice in the heart of Rome.

PIAZZA DI SPAGNA AREA

26. HOTEL CARRIAGE, *Via delle Carrozze 36, 00187 Roma. Tel. 06/679-3312, Fax 06/678-8279. E-mail: hotelcarriage@alfanet.it. Website: www.hotelcarriage.net. All credit cards accepted. 30 rooms all with bath. Single L210,000-300,000; Double L300,000-410,000; Suite L660,000. Breakfast included. (Map A)* ***

Located near the Piazza di Spagna on a pedestrian side street, which makes it blissfully quiet. This elegant little hotel is luxuriously furnished with a variety of antiques and has a courteous and professional staff. They have a lovely roof garden terrace from which you can have your breakfast or an evening drink. There's not much of a view, but just being beyond the street level with the open sky above you has a calming effect. The rooms are not that large but are comfortable and come with every convenience such as TV, mini-bar and phone. The bathrooms are immaculately clean and have hair dryers and courtesy toiletry kit. Request one of the two rooms with tiny balconies that overlook the rooftops. A quaint, comfortable and convenient place to stay.

27. HOTEL DOGE, *Via Due Macelli 106, 00187 Roma. Tel 06/678-0038, Fax 06/679-1633. All credit cards accepted. 18 rooms all with bath. Single L110,000-180,000; Double L150,000-250,000. Breakfast included. (Map A)* **

The accommodations here are clean and spartan as well as comfortable, and you'll notice the prices are pretty good considering this is one block from the Spanish Steps. It's located on the fourth floor of an apartment building that you enter by walking through the entrance/retail show space of a local sports store, which is the reason that the prices are so low. A good value for your money in a prime location which is key since Rome is so large. Only 11 rooms, so reserve far in advance.

28. VILLA HASSLER, *Piazza Trinita Dei Monti 6, 00187 Rome. Tel. 06/678-2651, Fax 06/678-9991. E:mail: hasslerroma@mclink.it. Website: http://venere.topchoice.com/roma/hassler. All credit cards accepted. 80 rooms all with bath. Single L710,000; Double L960,000-1,270,000. Suite prices on request. Continental breakfast L44,000 extra. Buffet breakfast L77,000 extra. (Map A)* *****

In many travelers' opinions this is the best hotel in Rome. Oil sheiks, movie stars, the nouveau riche, the landed gentry all have made the Hassler home for over a century. Located at the top of the Spanish Steps, with its own garage, a relaxing courtyard restaurant in the summer, and an excellent (but expensive) roof garden restaurant with a great view of the city. Remember to request one of the nicer rooms facing the church belfry and the Spanish Steps because the view will be stupendous. Even if you don't stay here, come to the restaurant, sample the food, and enjoy the superb view. One of the best, most famous, and ideally located hotels in Rome. If you have the means, I recommend it highly.

29. HOTEL HOMS, *Via Delle Vite 71, Tel. 0/679-2976, Fax 06/678-0482. All credit cards accepted. 50 rooms 49 with bath. Single without bath L80,000-100,000; Single L140,000-170,000; Double without bath L200-290,000; Double L300,000-380,000. Breakfast included. (Map A) ****

Located on the same street as the great Tuscan restaurant Da Mario and just across from the Anglo-American bookstore, this hotel is also virtually in between the Trevi Fountain and the Spanish Steps. The hotel has a quaint, pleasant ambiance and decor and has just been upgraded from two star status. Despite the fact that some rooms do not have baths, they made the effort to improve and have been rewarded for it. Since *Via Delle Vite* is not well traveled here you will be able escape the traffic noise. The lobby area is dark, but the rooms are light and airy (though small) with simple furnishings. The bathrooms are tiny too but do have complimentary toiletry kits. There is also a wonderful terrace with great views of the rooftops of Rome, which, I believe, is the main reason this place gained its three star status.

30. HOTEL INTERNAZIONALE, *Via Sistina 79, 00187 Roma. Tel. 06/6994-1823, Fax 06/678-4764. E-mail: internazionale@venere.it. Website: www.venere.it/it/roma/internazionale. All credit cards accepted. 42 rooms all with bath. Single L320,000; Double L415,000; Extra bed L110,000. Buffet breakfast included. (Map A) ****

Written up in both *Travel & Leisure* and *Forbes* this little Roman hideaway offers old-world charm, modern comfort and super rates for its ideal location. A huge breakfast is served in an elegant salon. In all this is a wonderful hotel. Located just a stone's throw away from the top of the Spanish Steps, you can hardly find a better location. The building was erected in first century BCE, and the lobby contains artifacts from that period, which have been unearthed within the walls of the hotel during recent renovations. The rooms are accommodating and comfortable and the staff professional and very attentive. The rooms are all different from one another with a wide variety of unique decorations and furnishings, supplied by Andrea Gnecco, owner and architect. Those on the fourth floor have private terraces. The bathrooms have all the amenities of a three star including complimentary toiletry kit.

This family-owned gem is a superb hotel in an ideal location, one of my favorite choices when in Rome. But remember to request a room on a higher floor, or on the inside to avoid traffic noise at night. There is much history here, and if you want to come face to face with it, stay in room A1. A former employee witnessed a spectral monk on a donkey clip-clopping through that room only a few years back, and other eerie encounters have purported to have occurred as well!

31. HOTEL MANFREDI, *Via Margutta 61, 00187 Roma. Tel. 06/320-7676, Fax 06/320-7736. Website: www.emmeti.it/Welcome/Lazio/Roma/Alberghi/Manfredi/index.it.html. Credit cards accepted. 17 rooms all with bath. Single L280,000-380,000; Double L330,000-490,000; Triple 400,000. American style breakfast buffet included. (Map A) ****

This cozy, accommodating hotel is located near the Spanish Steps and has all the charm, service, and amenities of a four-star hotel, but it is on the third floor of a local building so they are a relegated to three star status. They even have VCRs in some rooms as well as movies to rent at the front desk for your convenience. The street they're located on is cute, extremely quiet, and home to some of Rome's best antique stores and art galleries. If you only stay here for the American style buffet breakfast of ham, eggs, cheese, fruit etc., it is worth it. A good place to stay in a great location.

32. HOTEL SCALINATA DI SPAGNA, *Piazza Trinita Dei Monte 17, Roma. 06/679-3006 and 06/679-0896, Fax 06/684-0598 All credit cards accepted. 16 rooms all with baths. Single L290,000-400,000; Double L480,000-580,000; Suite for 5 people L550,000-800,000. Breakfast included. (Map A) ****

Just across the piazza from the Hassler at the top of the Spanish Steps, this used to be a moderately priced, quaint little pensione, but once it received its three star rating the prices here have skyrocketed. Nothing much else has changed, but it is still well worth the price because of the view from their large roof terrace. The roof terrace is open in the summer months for breakfast, as well as for your own personal nightcaps in the evening. The rooms are basic, but accommodating and comfortable in three star style. This place has plenty of character and ambiance and you will simply adore the roof terrace. I highly recommend this hotel when in Rome.

33. LYDIA VENIER, *Via Sistina 42, Tel. 06/679-3815, Fax 06/679-7263. 28 rooms all with bath. Single L80,000-190,000; Double L100,000-270,000. All credit cards accepted. (Map A) ***

A small, spartan hotel, that offers few amenities except for its excellent location. The furnishings are simple and basic and the bathrooms functional with a limited courtesy toiletry set. The breakfast room is comfortable and accommodating. All in all a good budget hotel in an ideal location, but ask for a room on the inside of the building away from the street. Traffic noise can be disturbing until the wee hours.

34. ERDARELLI, *Via Due Macelli 28, Tel. 06/679-1265, Fax 06/679-0705. 28 rooms all with bath. All credit cards accepted. Single L100,000-160,000; Double L140,000-210,000. (Map A) ***

Just down from the Piazza di Spagna in a building that looks like it has seen better days on the outside but which is clean and accommodating on the inside. The singles are minuscule and the doubles functional but the real selling point for this budget two-star is its ideal location. You can get A/C for an extra L20,000 and in August this is a necessity. Nothing grand but clean and comfortable at a good price for Rome.

35. GREGORIANA, *Via Gregoriana 18, Tel. 06/679-4269. Fax 06/678-4258. 20 rooms all with bath. Single L220,000; Double L380,000. No credit cards accepted. (Map A) ****

Situated in a building on a small side street just off the top of the Spanish Steps which used to be a convent, the Gregoriana is a small hotel that is tranquil and comfortable with all possible three star amenities. The rooms are all decorated in Deco style and come with A/C and TV and a few have a small terrace. The bathrooms are small but clean and functional. Breakfast is served in the room except in warm weather when they open their little roof terrace. An intimate and comfortable place to stay while in Rome. But they do not accept credit cards so be prepared to have cash available.

36. HOTEL MARGUTTA, *Via Laurina 34, 00186 Roma. Tel. 06/322-3674, Fax 06/320-0395. All credit cards accepted. 24 rooms all with bath. Single 65,000-175,000; Double L 90,000-240,000. Breakfast included. (Map A) ***

The prices are good for the location and the star rating. And it is only a two star because there is no TV or mini-bar in the room, and no air conditioning, which is a must in August. The hotel has been totally renovated and is as modern as can be. There's a relaxing lounge area and the rooms are spacious and airy. Rooms 50 and 52 share a terrace and are very nice, and #59 is another great place to stay too. The bathrooms are micro, especially those with showers which have rather noisy screen doors. The ones with bathtubs are a little bigger and all come with phone and courtesy toiletry kit. And the location is fantastic, right between the *Piazza del Popolo* and the Spanish Steps, almost right on the super shopping street Via Del Corso. Who could ask for more? That, coupled with the excellence of the accommodations and the low prices, makes this place a definite rare gem of price/quality considerations.

37. HOTEL PARLAMENTO, *Via delle Convertite 5, 00186 Roma. Tel. 06/6992-1000, Fax 06/679-2082. All credit cards accepted. 22 rooms, 19 with bath. Single without bath L130,000. Single L80,000-195,000. Double L100,000-230,000. Breakfast included. (Map A) ***

They have added a small (read micro) elevator so you no longer have to climb the entire three flights of stairs to get to this wonderful two star. A homey atmosphere with simply furnished rooms. There is a view of the rooftops of Rome from their tiny terrace, where in the summer you are served your breakfast. In a completely renovated building, the common rooms are decorated with panoramic frescoes of Roman scenes. The rooms are all decorated differently, some have antique style furniture, and all have TVs and sound-proof windows (but if your room is on the main road, this is Rome, so noise does seep in). The bathrooms are very new and kept immaculate; some even have a phone. Most of the staff speaks English and are more than willing to help you find what you're looking for. A great price/quality option.

38. HOTEL LOCARNO, *Via della Penna 22, 00186 Rome. Tel. 06/361-0841, Fax 06/321-5249. E-mail: locarno@italyhotel.com. Website: www.venere.it/roma/locarno. All credit cards accepted. 38 rooms all with bath. Single L215,000; Double L330,000-460,000; Suite L490,000 and up. Breakfast L25,000. (Map C)* ***

I simply adore this hotel and I have no idea why it is still only a three star. Situated between the Piazza del Popolo and the Tiber River, in a nice neighborhood of stores and galleries, this hotel is wonderfully accommodating and amazingly comfortable. It has a very relaxing American-style bar, spacious common areas, a small side-garden patio, and a roof terrace where breakfast is served in good weather. The rooms are tastefully decorated with all possible three star amenities, and the service is superb and utterly professional. Why they are still a three star is beyond me, because this place is great.

There are excellent restaurants all around, *Da Bolognese* for example, which means you won't have to wander far for your gastronomic pleasures. On a side street, the Locarno offers a respite from the hectic pace of Rome. One of the best three stars Rome has to offer.

39. HOTEL VALADIER, *Via della Fontanella 15, 00187 Roma. Tel. 06/361-0592, 361-0559, 361-2344, Fax 06/320-1558. E-mail: info@hotelvaladier.com. Website: www.venere.it/roma/ valadier/valadier.html. 48 rooms and suites all with bath. Single L230,000-450,000; Double L330,000-600,000, Suite L400,000-800,000. All credit cards accepted. (Map C)* ****

The first word that comes to mind concerning this place is opulent. There is black marble everywhere and the effect is doubled by the placement of the many mirrors and shining brass fixtures. But you ain't seen nothing yet. The wood paneling here sparkles, it's so well shined. The rooms are no less ostentatious with lights, mirrors – some on the ceilings for you exotically amorous types – and the ever-present marble. The bathrooms are a little small but accommodating and have every amenity.

If you want to feel like an oil sheik who has money to burn, spend your stay in Rome here. Ideally located between the Piazza del Popolo and the Spanish Steps, you are in walking distance to many sights and shops.

BED & BREAKFASTS IN ROME

To accommodate the massive influx of tourists for the Year 2000 Jubilee celebrations, the city of Rome formalized an already existing cadre of top notch apartments, homes and villa which have been housing travelers for years, into the Bed & Breakfast Association of Rome. To find out more in information about these places visit the association's web site at ***www.bbitalia.com****, E-mail them at* ***info@bbitalia.com****, or call/fax at 06/687-7348.*

One of the best, the ***Villa Delros,*** *is located near where I used to live, about three kilometers outside the 'beltway' around Rome in a bucolic natural setting. This recently opened modern B&B has three excellent rooms to choose from, with air conditioning, a strongbox for your valuables, satellite TV, hairdryer, direct dial phone and mini-bar. They also have a swimming pool and a variety of common areas in which to relax. Excellent meals are prepared upon request and, best of all, the owner, Rosmarie Truninger Diletti, is effervescently friendly and she goes out of her way to make sure your stay is comfortable – without actually getting in the way. Multilingual and with a vibrant zest for life, she really makes your stay pleasant.*

Villa Delros*, Tel/Fax 06/33678402 or 06/33679837, E-mail: info@hotelvenezia.com (reference the Villa Delros when you E-mail). Closed December 1 to March 1. Minimum stay 3 days. Double $150 including breakfast. Dinner upon request: Large L30,000 or Small L15,000. Both are well worth it. Credit Cards not accepted. Free pickup from local public train station. Pickup at the airport $60. Pickup at Termini downtown $30.*

CENTRO STORICO

(Piazza Navona, Pantheon, Campo dei Fiori Area)

40. HOTEL CAMPO DEI FIORI, *Via del Biscione 6, 00186 Roma. Tel. 06/687-4886, Fax 06/687-6003. All credit cards accepted. Four singles with shower each L180,000; Nine Doubles with shower each L230,000, 14 doubles without shower each L180,000. Breakfast L20,000. (Map B) ***

Here you'll find another great roof terrace in Rome. The hotel is on six floors in a sliver of a building without an elevator that can make this hotel an exercise routine in and of itself. Also there's no air conditioning, which could be a problem in August. Only a few blocks away from the Trastevere area and its nightlife, here you are also in the perfect location to visit the best outdoor market in the city, the Campo dei Fiori, eat at some of the best restaurants (La Carbonara), a great bar/pub nearby (The Drunken Ship), and the best sights just around the corner. Breakfast is served in a basement dining area, but you are free to bring it to the roof with you. Ask for one of the inside rooms since the windows do not have double paned glass to cut the noise from the street.

41. HOTEL GENIO, *Via Zanardelli 28, Roma 00186. Tel 06/683-2191, 06/683-3781, Fax 06/6830-7246. Website: www.travel.it/roma/ianr. E-mail: leonardi@travel.it. Credit cards accepted. 65 rooms all with bath. Single L250,000-380,000; Double L380,000-500,000 An extra bed costs L70,000. A large breakfast buffet is included. (Map C)* ****

Located almost in the Piazza Navona here you get a great location in the Old City of Rome. Most of the guests are from Scandinavia and Germany so you may not rub elbows with any Americans while staying in this recently upgraded four star hotel. The rooms are well-appointed with tasteful paintings, Persian rugs, and cream colored wall coverings. The lobby/common areas seem a little worse for the wear but the roof garden terrace has a spectacular view. An ideal place to be served your breakfast in the morning. A great way to wake up, looking over the river and rooftops of Rome, which is the main reason it is now a four star hotel. If you choose the Genio, you have chosen well.

42. HOTEL PORTOGHESI, *Via dei Portoghesi 1, 00186 Roma. Tel. 06/686-4231, Fax 06/687-6976. E-mail: portoghesi@venere.it. Website: www.venere.it/home/roma/portoghesi/portoghesi.html. Mastercard and Visa accepted. 27 rooms all with bath. Single L280,000; Double L390,000. Jr. Suite L420,000. Suite L600,000. Extra bed L50,000. Breakfast included. (Map C)* ***

Between Piazza Navona and the Mausoleum of Augustus, nestled beside the church of Sant'Antonio, and on a narrow medieval street, this small hotel's central location is ideal. It may be not be near a Metro line but the restaurants, shops, food stores, small streets, and sights all around it make this place ideally suited for a wonderful vacation in Rome. There are a smattering of antiques all over the hotel to give the place a feeling of old world charm that matches its unique location. The rooms are small but comfortable and there is a relaxing roof garden to enjoy. A great bed and breakfast type place to stay.

43. ARENULA, *Via Santa Maria de'Calderari, 47, 00186 Roma. Tel. 06/687-9454, Fax 06/689-6188. E-mail: hotel.arenula@flashnet.it. 50 rooms all with bath. Single L120,000-180,000; Double L150,000-230,000. All credit cards accepted. Breakfast included. (Map B)* **

On the inside of an old building from the last century, in a quaint area (The Jewish Ghetto) and situated on a small street, this is a great two star. Here you have everything that a modern hotel would have with amazing charm and ambiance. On the first floor is the small entrance, TV lounge, breakfast area and ten of the rooms. On the third floor the rooms come only with shower but all have a small complimentary toiletry set. They also have A/C and TV in the rooms and have recently given each room their own bath. They are bucking for three star status but right now they are a great price/quality place to stay while in Rome.

44. ALBERGHO DEL SOLE, *Via del Biscione 76, 00186 Roma. Tel. 06/6880-6873 or 687-9446, Fax 06/689-3787. E-mail: sole@italyhotel.com. Website: www.venere.it/it/roma/sole/. 58 rooms only 24 with bath. Single without L85,000-115,000; Single L115,000-160,000. Double without L130,000-190,000; Double L160,000-220,000. No breakfast. No credit cards. (Map B) ***

A wonderful two star in a great location with two relaxing roof garden areas. Supposedly the oldest hotel in Rome, it seems its age as you enter, but the rooms are clean and comfortable. Ten rooms have TV and only 24 with private bath. Not as nice as the Hotel Campo dei Fiori just up the street, but is still a good place to stay for those on a budget, and the staff is much more accommodating than the Campo dei Fiori. Keep a look out for Cleopatra, the resident cat.

45. MARCUS, *Via del Clementino 94, Tel. 06/6830-0320, Fax 06/6830-0312. 18 rooms all with bath. Single L120,000-190,000; Double L180,000-220,000. All credit cards accepted. (Map C) ***

This small two-star is in an ideal location deep in the heart of the *centro storico* by the Pantheon. The atmosphere here is pleasant and accommodating and filled with the character of a 17th century building. The entryway is beautiful which leads to the second floor lobby. The rooms are very spacious and come with A/C (for L20,000 extra per day), and double windows to keep out noise. The bathrooms are minuscule and only have showers and some come with hair dryers. If they had a lobby on the ground floor, and added a few more amenities, this would be a three-star; but for now it is a wonderful two-star.

46. SOLE AL PANTHEON, *Piazza dell Rotunda 63, 00186 Roma. Tel. 06/78-0441, Fax 06/6994-0689. All credit cards accepted. 62 rooms all with bath. E-mail solealpantheon@italyhotel.com. Website: http://venere.it/roma/solealpantheon/. Single L420,000; Double L650,000; Jr. Suite L750,000. Breakfast L30,000. (Map C) *****

This is a place that used to be a small, well-appointed *pensione* that upgraded its rooms prior to the "star" rating system and voila: we have a fantastic four-star hotel. The clean white walls and delicate furnishings attest to its status as one of Rome's best small hotels. Most of the furniture is of the neo-classic mold leaning towards modern. Some of the rooms have a view over the *Piazza della Rotunda* and the Pantheon, which is a beautiful people watching scene, and come with soundproof windows so it's relatively quiet at night. The building has been around since 1513 so you'll be staying in history while here. The service is exquisite and everything conforms to the highest standards, making this a well-located fine little four-star hotel. For those with the means, a great place to stay.

STAY IN A CONVENT – FOR LESS

The price of a double room in Rome added onto museum fees and meals can dent anyone's wallet. Some of the best and least known places to stay, which can reduce the cost of a stay in Rome, are convents. While you may think that convents would only take women pilgrims as guests, most also welcome single men, married couples, and families with children. Couples 'traveling in sin' are usually not welcome, but some well placed pieces of jewelry can usually fool the best nun. All these convents are immaculate (no pun intended) since the nuns take pride in their work.

***Suore Teatine**, Salita Monte del Gallo 25, 00165 Roma. Tel. 06/637-4084 or 06/637-4653, Fax 06/3937-9050. L70,000 per person with full board. L60,000 with half board. L50,000 with only breakfast. Not all rooms have private bath. Curfew is 11:00pm.*

***Franciscan Sisters of the Atonement**, Via Monte del Gallo 105, 00165 Roma. Tel. 06/630-782, Fax 06/638-6149.L70,000 per person with full board. L60,000 with half board. L45,000 with only breakfast. All rooms have private bath. Curfew is 11:00pm. English spoken. Parking available. Great spacious pine-shaded garden.*

***Suore Dorotee**, Via del Gianicolo 4a, 00165 Roma. Tel. 06/6880-3349, Fax 06/6880-3311. L 80,000 full board. L70,000 half board. Some rooms have private baths. Curfew is 11:00pm. Recommended by the Vatican Tourist Information Bureau.*

***Pensione Suore Francescane**, Via Nicolo V 35, 00165 Roma. Tel. 06/3936-6531. L55,000 per person with breakfast. No private baths. No curfew. Small but lovely roof garden with views of St. Peter's. English spoken. Great location.*

***Domus Aurelia-Suore Orsoline**, Via Aurelia 218, 00165 Roma. Tel. 06/636-784, Fax 06/3937-6480. L95,000 for a double. L65,000 for a single. L120,000 for room with three beds. All rooms with private bath. Breakfast extra. 11:30pm curfew.*

***Suore Pallotini**, Viale della Mura Aurelie 7b, 00165 Roma. Tel. 06/635-697, Fax 06/635-699. L55,000 for single with breakfast. L95,000 for double without private bath. L130,000 for double with private bath. 10:00pm curfew for first night. Any night after that they give you a key.*

***Fraterna Domus**, Via di Monte Brianzo 62, 00186 Roma. Tel. 06/6880-2727, Fax 06/683-2691. L70,000 per person with full board. L60,000 with half board. L45,000 with breakfast only. Single rooms add L18,000 extra. All rooms with private bath. Curfew is 11:00pm.*

***Le Suore Di Lourdes**, Via Sistina 113, 00187 Roma. Tel. 06/474-5324, Fax 06/488-1144. L50,000 per person without bath. L55,000 per person with bath and breakfast. Curfew is 10:30pm.*

47. ALBERGHO SANTA CHIARA, *Via Santa Chiara 21, 00186 Roma. Tel. 06/687-2979, Fax 06/687-3144. E-mail: info@albergosanta.chiara.com. Website- www.albergosantachiara.com. All credit cards accepted. 96 rooms all with bath. Single L350,000-385,000; Double L320,000-430,000. Suite L430,000-710,000. Breakfast included. (Map C) ****

A three star that should be a four star, and their prices reflect that. This is a supremely elegant hotel in the heart of Rome near the Pantheon. Once you enter the lobby you feel as if you've been whisked away to a palace. Everything is marble, buffed to a high polish, and the ceilings reach to the sky. The rooms are all tastefully decorated and the ones on the top floors get great breezes, if you don't want to use your air conditioning, and some have small balconies. There is also a tranquil inside terrace area, the service is impeccable and the breakfast buffet huge. This place is great. If you want four star accommodations for a three star price, stay here.

TRASTEVERE

48. HOTEL TRASTEVERE, *Via Luciano Manara 24/25, 00153 Roma. Tel. 06/58-14-713, Fax 06/58-81-016. 30 rooms all with bath. All credit cards accepted. Single L120,000-160,000; Double L130,000-190,000. (Map B) ***

Located in the heart of Trastevere, one of the city's oldest and most distinctive neighborhoods, here you will be surrounded by locals and far from the thundering herd of tourists. The Roma Trastevere train station is only 700 meters away, which means you should get the local train from the airport and not the one that goes directly to Termini. The rooms are all spacious and accommodating, though simply furnished. If you want to stay in local atmosphere of Trastevere, this is the best option.

13. WHERE TO EAT

Before I guide you to the wonderful restaurants Rome has awaiting you, please take some time to refer to the augmented, Rome-specific version of Chapter 10, *Food & Wine*. For Map A locations, see pages 120-121.

ROMAN CUISINE

"Italian Food" is definitely a misnomer, because each region of Italy has its own special dishes, and in most cases so do each province and locality. As a rule, Roman cooking is not elegantly refined and is considered rustic. The food is basic, unpretentious, yet exquisitely enjoyable. Authentic Roman dishes today are often based on simple ingredients such as tomatoes, garlic, hot pepper, and parmesan cheese and the results are magnificent. If you are bold try some favorite Roman dishes like brains, tripe, oxtail, and pig's snout. If not treat yourself to the omnipresent pasta and grilled meats.

Besides these staples, Romans enjoy a harvest of seafood from the shores just 15 miles from their city; and as a result they prepare excellent grilled seafood dishes, the famous *spaghetti alla vongole verace* (spicy clam sauce), as well as other pastas brimming with this harvest from the sea. The Roman countryside provides exquisite fresh greens and vegetables, which arrive daily at the city's open air markets. Also in never-ending supply are the local cheeses like *pecorino*, made from sheep's milk, and plump *mozzarella* balls, generally made from the milk of water buffaloes.

The Jewish ghetto has made a lasting impression on Roman cuisine. The most memorable dish to come from there is the *carciofo alla giudia*, a small artichoke flattened and fried. What I'm trying to say is that it is very difficult not to eat well in any one of Rome's 5,000-plus restaurants. But what I have supplied you with here are some of the best in and around your hotel choices.

Lunch hour is usually from 12:30pm to 2:30pm, and dinner from 7:30pm to 10:00pm, but is usually served at 8:30pm. So enjoy your meal and remember to take your time. Meals are supposed to be savored, not rushed through.

Traditional Roman Fare

You don't have to have a traditional meal complete with all the courses listed below, but in some restaurants it is considered bad form not to. Most Italians accept the fact that we seem to like to rush through our meals, even if they don't understand it, so don't feel embarrassed if all you order is a pasta dish or an entrée with a salad or appetizer.

But if you do want to order the traditional way the Italians do, you will spend a lot of time over dinner. Meals consists of an *antipasto* (appetizer) and/or soup and/or pasta and is called **primo**; a main course is **secondo** (usually meat or fish) with separately ordered side dishes of *contorni* (vegetables) or *insalata* (salad) which come either *verdi* (green) or *mista* (mixed); then **dolci** (dessert), which can be cheese, fruit, or *gelato* (ice-cream) – after which you order your coffee and/or after-dinner drink.

Note: Pasta is never served as an accompanying side dish with a secondo and especially never on the same plate. It is always served as a separate course. It is time to forget everything you thought you knew about "Italian" food that was learned at some run-of-the-mill restaurant chain. In Italy your are going to have well-prepared food served the proper way!

Antipasto – Appetizer

- **Bruschetta** – Garlic bread brushed with olive oil
- **Antipasto Misto** – Mixed appetizer plate. Differs from restaurant to restaurant
- **Tomate, Mozzarella ed olio** – Tomato and mozzarella slices covered in olive oil with a hint of basil

Primo Piatto – First Course

Pasta

- **Spaghetti alla carbonara** – Spaghetti tossed with bacon, garlic, peppers, grated cheese, and a raw beaten egg
- **Bucatini all'amatriciana** –Thin tubes of pasta with red pepper, bacon, and pecorino cheese
- **Penne all'arrabbiata** – Literally means angry pasta. It is short ribbed pasta tubes with a hot and spicy tomato base, garlic and parsley sauce (this is my favorite, but if your stomach can't handle spicy food, steer clear of this delicacy)
- **Fettucine al burro** – Fettucine with butter and parmesan
- **Spaghetti alla puttanesca** – Literally translated it means whore's spaghetti! So named because the ingredients, peppers, tomato, black olives and garlic are so basic that prostitutes could quickly create a meal between tricks.

Zuppa - Soup

- **Stracciatella** – a light egg-drop soup
- **Pasta e ceci** – a filling pasta and chick pea soup
- **Zuppa di telline** – soup made from tiny clams

Secondo Piatto - Entrée

Carne - Meat

- **Abbacchio** – Milk-fed baby lamb. Can be grilled (*alla griglia*), sautéed in a sauce of rosemary, garlic, onions, tomatoes, and white wine (*alla cacciatore*), or roasted (*al forno*)
- **Saltimbocca alla Romana** – Veal fillets that are covered in sage and prosciutto and cooked in butter and white wine
- **Pollo alla cacciatore** – Same dish as the lamb above but replaced with chicken
- **Pollo alla Romana** – Chicken stewed with yellow and red bell peppers
- **Pollo al diavolo** – So called because the chicken is split open and grilled over an open fire and flattened by a weight placed on top of it. I guess it's what Romans think hell would be like.
- **Fritto misto** – a selection of mixed deep-fried meats and seasonal vegetables
- **Lombata di vitello** – Grilled veal chop
- **Porchetta** – Tender suckling pork roasted with herbs
- **Maile arrosto can patate** – Roasted pork with exquisite roast potatoes

Pesce - Fish

- **Sogliola alla griglia** – Thin sole lightly grilled
- **Ciriole** – Small tender eels dredged from the Tiber

Contorno - Vegetable

- **Carciofi alla giuda** – Jewish-style artichokes, pressed flat and fried. Usually served with an anchovy garlic sauce.
- **Peperonata** – Stewed red and yellow bell peppers
- **Patate arrosto** – Roasted potatoes that usually come with a grilled meats but can be ordered separately.
- **Insalata Mista** – Mixed salad. You have to prepare your own olive oil and vinegar dressing. American's thirst for countless types of salad dressings hasn't hit Italy yet.

Wines

Frascati is a white wine intimately tied to Rome since it is grown in the hills around the eternal city. Frascati vineyards are located in the region called Castelli where the Roman patricians and popes built their luxurious villas to spend the shot summer months. On top of that tie, both Pope Innocent X and Clement X celebrated their elections with the pleasantly pagan gesture of having the fountains of Rome gush with Frascati. From then on Romans have bonded with their local wine.

Over time Frascati has become more refined and in some cases can be considered to be of very high quality. Traditionally the grapes of Frascati were supported by tall trees, instead of cultivated on poles or columns. Only recently have the Frascati vines been pruned and managed closer to the earth out of the shade of large trees. This allows the direct rays of the sun to ripen them better creating a greater concentration of sugars, which in turn allows for a more complete alcohol fermentation.

Once maligned but now respected, a good Frascati is a pale yellow and has a fresh, light, balanced flavor that will complement any fish dish, or a cream or tomato-based pasta sauce. Most Frascati wines are soft, well-rounded and simple whites that most anyone can appreciate. They do well in countering the aggressive flavors of the Roman food.

In most restaurants you can also get better known wines such as Chianti, Orvieto, Verdicchio, Pinto Grigio, and Barolo, but the best bet if you're not a wine expert is to simply try the *vino da casa* (house wine) of the restaurants you visit. You will find this to be not only less expensive but just as enjoyable as a more expensive bottle.

The house wine, which is generally Frascati if white and full-bodied, robust and Tuscan if red, can usually be ordered in liters *(un litro)*, halves *(mezzo litro)*, or quarters *(quarto do un litro)*.

Sambuca liqueur

You have to try **Sambuca**, an anise-flavored after-dinner drink, usually served with an odd number of coffee beans (to serve it with an even number is bad luck). It's called *Sambuca con mosce*, Sambuca with flies, because if you blur your vision a little the beans do look a little like flies floating in the milky liqueur. When sipping this small drink get one of the beans in your mouth and chew on it. The bitter taste compliments the sweetness of the liqueur perfectly. The best brand of Sambuca is **Molinari**, and the next is **Romana**, which is better known in the States because of the company's aggressive marketing campaign.

Limoncello

The latest after-dinner drink to rage across Italy is **Limoncello**. This tasty lemon flavored high octane drink can be bought commercially, but many establishments make their own. That's right, Limoncello is mostly made prohibition-style. One place that makes some of the best is La Buca di Ripetta. But they'll only serve it to you if they consider you 'worthy' of such a special drink, lovingly created, and sparingly served.

WHERE TO GET YOUR WINE TO TAKE HOME

The most complete and best located store to buy your duty free wine quota (three liters per person) is **Buccone** *(Via di Ripetta 19-20, Tel/Fax 06/361-2154) near the Piazza del Popolo. The walls of these two storefronts are lined from floor to ceiling with bottles from every different region in Italy, as well as other countries. Extensive does not do this place justice. The prices here are comparable with duty free at the airport and you get a much better selection. The prices for Sambuca and Limoncello are better at the airport, but get your wine here.*

REVIEWS EXPLAINED

The reviews below are arranged first according to establishment – first **ristorante/trattorie/pizzerie**, then **spuntini veloci** (italian fast food), then **enoteche** (wine bars), and finally **gelateria** (ice cream shops) and **pasticcerie** (pastry shops). Within the first section the eating establishments are separated into specific areas in Rome. Each entry mentions a price that reflects dinner for two, if two people order two dishes apiece (i.e., a pasta and a meat for one person and an antipasto and a fish dish for the other, etc.) exclusive of wine. Obviously, if you only choose to eat one dish per sitting, which we Americans are apt to do, the actual price for your meal will be significantly less than what is indicated in this guide.

RISTORANTE, TRATTORIE & PIZZERIE

As mentioned in the augmented *Food & Wine* section in Chapter 10, **ristorante**, **trattorie** and **pizzerie** are all traditional italian eateries. The ristorante are more formal, trattorie are more rustic and pizzerie usually serve only pizza's and other baked goods. But all the places listed here will offer you an excellent meal, quality service and an authentically Roman dining experience.

TRASTEVERE

This is the perfect place for exploring the way Romans actually live. **Trastevere** literally means "across the river," and this separation has allowed the area to remain virtually untouched by the advances of time. Until recently it was one of the poorest sections of Rome, but now it is starting to become gentrified, though these changes have not altered Trastevere's charm. You'll find interesting shops and boutiques, and plenty of excellent restaurants among the small narrow streets and *piazzetta* (small squares). The maze of streets is a fun place to wander and wonder where you're going to end up.

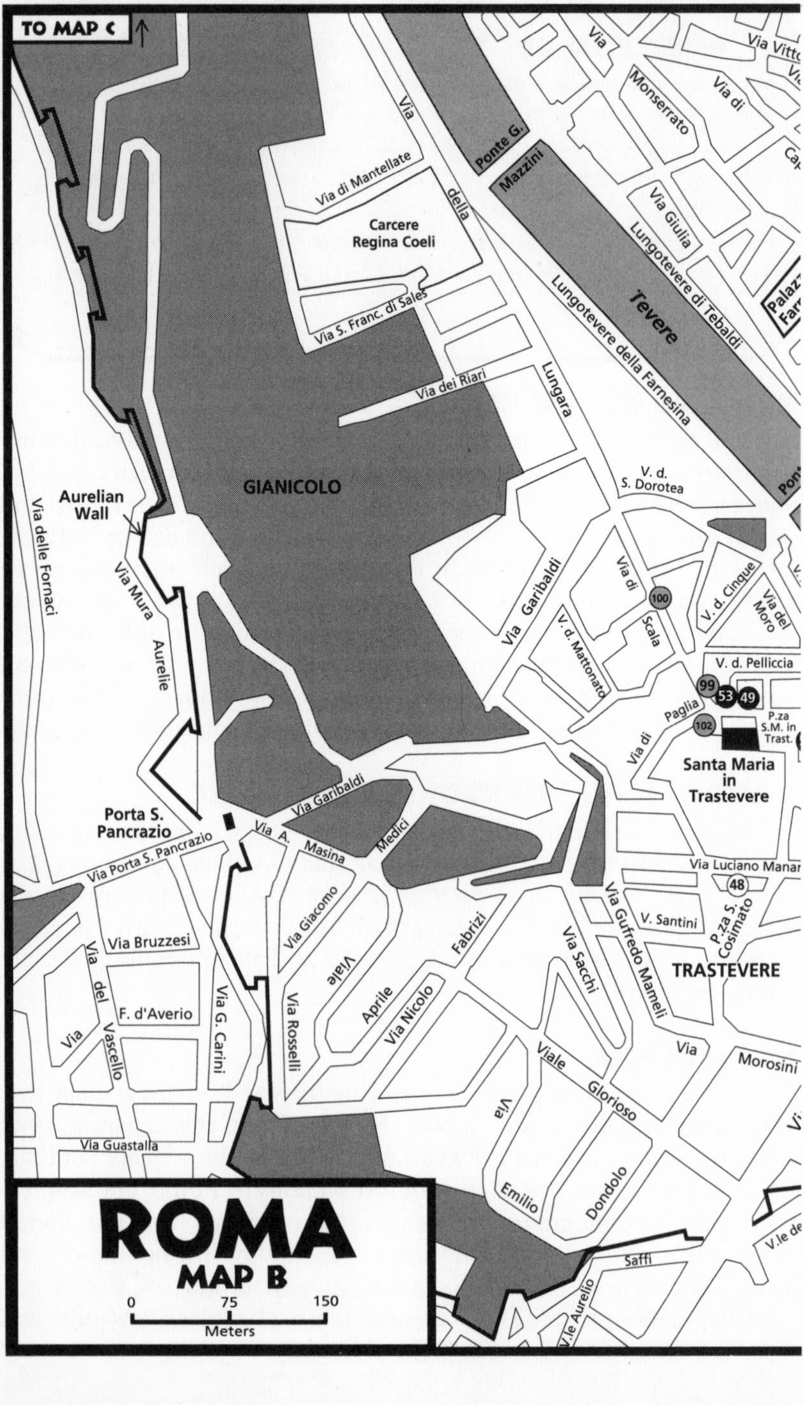
TO MAP C
Via
Monserrato
Via di
Via Vitto
Ponte G.
Mazzini
Via di Mantellate
della
Carcere
Regina Coeli
Via Giulia
Lungotevere di Tebaldi
Tevere
Palazz
Farn
Via S. Franc. di Sales
Lungotevere della Farnesina
Via dei Riari
Lungara
V. d.
S. Dorotea
GIANICOLO
Aurelian
Wall
Via delle Fornaci
Via Mura
Aurelie
Via Garibaldi
Via di
Scala
V. d. Mattonato
V. d. Cinque
Via del
Moro
V. d. Pelliccia
99
53
49
100
102
Via di
Paglia
P.za
S.M. in
Trast.
Santa Maria
in
Trastevere
Porta S.
Pancrazio
Via Porta S. Pancrazio
Via Garibaldi
Via A. Masina
Medici
Via Luciano Manar
48
V. Santini
P.za S. Cosimato
TRASTEVERE
Via Giacomo
Viale
Fabrizi
Via Sacchi
Via Gufredo Mameli
Via Bruzzesi
Via del Vascello
F. d'Averio
Via G. Carini
Via Rosselli
Aprile
Via Nicolo
Via
Morosini
Viale Glorioso
Via
Emilio
Dondolo
Via Guastalla
ROMA
MAP B
0
75
150
Meters
Saffi
V.le Aurelio
V.le de

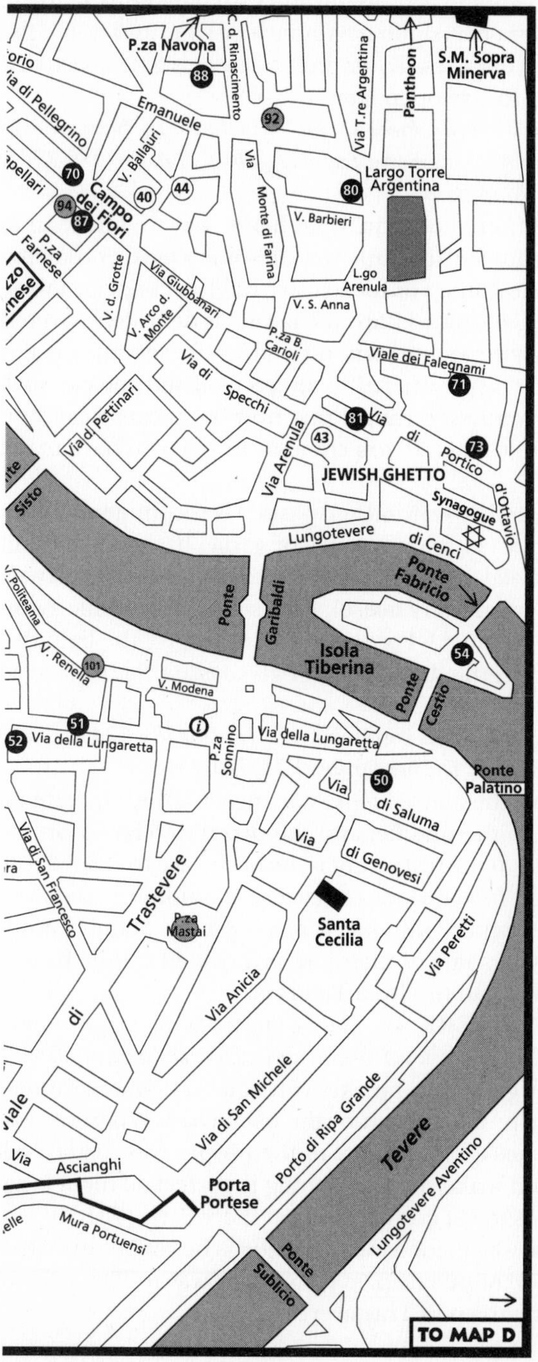

HOTELS ○

40. Campo dei Fiori
43. Arenula
44. Del Sole
48. Trastevere

EATERIES ●

49. La Canonica
50. Camparone
51. Gino in Trastevere
52. Sabatini I
53. La Tana de Noantri
54. Sora Lella
70. La Carbonara
71. Hostaria Guilia
73. Vecchia Roma
80. Brek
81. Anacleto Bleve
87. Vineria Reggio
88. Cul de Sac

NIGHTLIFE ●

92. John Bull Pub
94. Drunken Ship
99. Ombre Rosse
100. La Scala
101. Accademia
102. Artu Cafe

ⓘ Information Kiosks

This area offers some of the best dining and casual nightlife in town. Here you can sit in a piazza bar, sipping Sambuca or wine and watch the life of Rome pass before your eyes. To accommodate this type of activity, many stores have begun to stay open later.

49. LA CANONICA, *Vicolo dei Piede 13, just off of the Piazza Santa Maria in Trastevere. Closed Mondays. Major credit cards accepted. Tel. 06/580-3845. Dinner for two L80,000. (Map B)*

In the capital of the Catholic world, what better way to dine than in a de-consecrated chapel transformed into one of Rome's most entrancing restaurants? Located near Rome's only exclusive English language movie theater, Il Pasquino, La Canonica's Baroque facade is delicately covered with vines and flowers. In the summer months tables are set outside. For me, the best place to sit is inside where it is always cool and you can soak in the atmosphere of a renovated chapel that now has meats, kegs, and bottles hanging from the ceiling. If you come to Rome, you have to eat here.

The menu is dominated by seafood and pasta. My recommendations: *spaghetti alla vongole verace* (spicy clam sauce of garlic, basil, oil, and hot peppers) or the *spaghetti alla carbonara* (a light cream sauce, covered with ham, peas, and grated parmesan cheese), or a simply incredible *penne all'arrabiata* (spicy tomato sauce). For the main course, try the light fish dish of *sogliola alla griglia* (grilled sole). The *grigliato misto di pesce* (mixed grilled fish) is also good.

50. CAMPARONE, *Piazza in Piscinula 47. Tel 06/581-6249. Closed Mondays. Credit cards accepted. Dinner for two L75,000. (Map B)*

This restaurant owns the entire block, starting with the bar/café on the left, the restaurant in the middle, and the pizzeria/birreria on the right. The outside seating at the restaurant is the best place to enjoy a true Trastevere evening. Their food includes an excellent rendition of *ossobuco alla Romana* which they prepare with *fungi* (mushrooms). Mainly known for their grilled meats and some of their pastas. Located off the beaten path near the Tiber River and the Isola Tiberina.

51. GINO IN TRASTEVERE, *Via Della Lungaretta 85, 00153 Roma. Tel. 06/580-3403. 06/580-6226. Closed Wednesdays. Dinner for two L80,000.*

The spacious and bright interior makes you want to sit outside under their awning on the side or in the front by the main road. Wherever you end up the food will be exceptional. One of the proprietors, Paulo, will greet you at the door and make sure everything is perfect all night long. Since it's popular it tends to get crowded, so get there early (7ish) or late (10ish) otherwise you may be in for a wait. But later is better because then you can watch the parade of people pass by on their way to Piazza Santa Maria and a night on the town in Trastevere.

They have an extensive fish and meat menu: try the *sogliola alla griglia* (grilled sole), or the *saltimbocca alla Romana* (veal shanks in sauce and spices) for seconds. Your primo piatto has to be one of their great Roman pasta dishes like *arrabiatta* (tomato-based with garlic and peppers), or *vongole verace* (clams in a spicy oil, garlic, and basil sauce). Or if the desire for pizza hits you, it's great here.

52. SABATINI I, *Piazza Santa Maria in Trastevere 13, Tel. 06/581-8307 (outside seating) or 06/581-2026 (inside seating with an entrance on side). Closed Wednesdays, and two weeks in August. No credit cards accepted. Very expensive. At least L100,000 for dinner. (Map B)*

Besides the excellent fish dishes here, you can soak up the Trastevere life-style, especially in summer when outside seating is available. At night the floodlights keep the church at the opposite end of the piazza aglow. Try the *spaghetti alle cozze* (mussels), *zuppa di pesce*, the *spiedino misto di pesce al forno* (mixed grilled fish), and the grilled sole (*sogliola alla griglia*). If you want to see the fish grilled go to the very back of the restaurant and there they'll be roasting over an open fire, scales and all. (The waiter will de-bone, de-head and de-tail either at your table or by the fire). The inside is cozy and comfortable and they have singers walking through the tables serenading the customers, which is nice if you like that sort of thing.

ROME'S BEST EATERIES

You'll find plenty of good eateries in Rome, but for a truly great meal every time, here is my list of favorites.

49. LA CANONICA, *Vicolo dei Piedi 13, Dinner for two L80,000.*

56. AL PICCOLO ARANCIO, *Vicolo Scandberg 112, Dinner for two L90,000.*

61. OTELLO ALLA CONCORDIA, *Via Della Croce 81, Dinner for two L80,000*

62. PIZZERIA LE GROTTE, *Via delle Vite 37, Dinner for two L70,000.*

63. PIZZERIA LA CAPRICCIOSA, *Largo dei Lombardi 8 Dinner for two L75,000.*

68. LA BUCA DI RIPETTA, *Via di Ripetta 36, Dinner for two L70,000.*

70. LA CARBONARA, *Campo dei Fiori 23, Dinner for two L90,000.*

84. ENOTECANTINA, *Via del Croce 76, Meal for two L55,000.*

85. VINI E BUFFET, *Piazza della Torretta 60, Meal for two L50,000.*

86. CAVOUR 313, *Via Cavour 313. Meal for two L50,000.*

88. CUL DE SAC, *Piazza di Pasquino 73, Meal for two L50,000.*

53. LA TANA DE NOANTRI, *Via della Paglia 1-2-3, 00158 Roma. Tel. 06/580-6404 or 06/589-6575. Credit cards accepted. Closed Tuesdays. Dinner for two L75,000. (Map B)*

Located past Piazza Santa Maria and past the tables laid out for La Canonica, this superb restaurant has rather boring seating inside, but oh so wonderful places outside in the Piazza di San Egidio at night. Here you can sit under awnings and savor dish after dish of succulently seasoned Roman specialties. Great atmosphere and great food.

I've had the *pizza con salsiccia* (with sausage) as a primo, then moved onto the *braccioline di abbacchio* (literally translated it means "little arm of lamb"). My partner had the *tortellini alla crema con funghi* (cheese or meat stuffed tortellini with cream sauce and mushrooms). Even though we were too full to go on, we lingered over a bottle of white wine then ordered some *spaghetti alla carbonara* to close out the night. It was a real feast in a great atmosphere.

54. SORA LELLA, *Via di Ponte Quattro Capi 16, Tel. 06/686-1601. Closed Sundays. Credit cards accepted. Dinner for two L120,000. (Map B)*

A wonderful little local place magically situated on the Isola Tibertina in the middle of the Tiber River, you'll find great local atmosphere and wonderful food. Family-run for generations, they prepare real *cucina romana* (Roman cooking) here. There are only two rooms that can seat maybe 45 people. Try their *gnocchi alla amatriciana* (dumplings in a red pepper, bacon and pecorino cheese sauce) or the *spaghetti al tonno* (with a tuna sauce). For seconds their *abbacchio* (lamb) is some of the best in Rome. It may seem expensive but the food and exclusive atmosphere justifies the cost.

TREVI FOUNTAIN AREA

The **Trevi Fountain** is the place where you toss a coin at Neptune's feet for a guarantee that you will one day return to Rome. It is an impressive 18th century baroque statue that dominates the square it is in. In fact, it seems too large for so small a space, especially at night when it is lit up by floodlights. All around Trevi are shoe stores and small *pizzerie* and is one of the most popular spots in Rome.

55. AL MORO, *Vicolo delle Bollette 13 (off Via del Lavatore), Tel. 06/678-3495. Closed Sundays and the entire month of August. No credit cards accepted. Dinner for two L110,000. (Map A)*

The food is excellent in the Roman style, the ingredients are all fresh and of the highest quality, but the prices are a little high, and since this a popular eating establishment you'll need to make reservations. I swear the *spaghetti al moro* (a light carbonara sauce with cheese, egg, bacon, and red pepper flakes) is the best pasta dish I have ever tasted. They make an excellent *all'arrabbiata* (hot and spicy sauce) too. I also enjoyed the *scampi alla moro* (broiled shrimp). Other excellent dishes are the *abbacchio romanesco al forno con patate* (roasted lamb with superb roasted potatoes with a sprinkle of rosemary).

The inside front room is dominated by a large picture of Moro himself, long since passed away. The other two rooms have wine bottles surrounding the walls above the tables and are relatively roomy. If you want to sit outside you'll be crowded against a wall on a lightly traveled little *via*. I recommend the inside seating.

56. AL PICCOLO ARANCIO, *Vicolo Scandberg 112, Tel. 06/678-6139. Closed Mondays. Credit cards accepted. Dinner for two L90,000. (Map A)*

Located on a dark side street near the Trevi fountain you would walk right past if you did not know this place existed. Great food served either at the few tables outside, or in the boisterous inside rooms. Excellent pastas, great meat dishes, wonderful service. An ideal choice when in Rome.

VIA VENETO AREA

The **Via Veneto** was backdrop for the 1959 film *La Dolce Vita*. It used to be the chic gathering place for international movie stars but now it's simply an expensive place to stay, shop, and eat. Yet is still retains a lot of character. The area is hectic and thoroughly Roman, filled with shopping opportunities, offices, and only a few sights like the **Baths of Diocletian**.

57. GIOVANNI, *Via Marche 64, Tel. 06/482-1834. Closed Saturdays and the entire month of August. Credit cards accepted. Dinner for two L150,000. (Map A)*

Close to the hustle and bustle of the Via Veneto is this good restaurant with an Adriatic flair. The owners are from Ancona and they serve fresh fish brought in from there. The soups in their restaurant are also very good, so if you've had your fill of pasta, come here and try the seafood and soups. I really like the *calamaretti ai ferri* (small shrimp cooked over an open flame). The house white from the Verdicchio region is quite good.

58. GIRARROSTO TOSCANO, *Via Campania 29, Tel. 06/493-759. Closed Wednesdays. No credit cards accepted. Dinner for two L120,000. (Map A)*

Located in the cellar of a huge building facing onto the Aurelian Wall, this is a first-class restaurant that accepts orders until 1am. An ideal place to come back to after a night of revelry if you have a lingering hunger. The food is mainly veal and beef grilled on a spit over an open wood fired oven. Prior to the meal you can indulge in melon, *prosciutto di Parma* and *ovoline* (small mozzarella cheeses). The servings are large and so are the prices, and befitting its location near the Via Veneto the service is excellent.

Beside the food you'll enjoy the rustic atmosphere, with hams hanging in the entrance way along with a table filled with fresh produce.

In the dining area bottles of wine line the walls above the tables, and the wood paneling adds to the peasant appeal at princely prices.

PIAZZA DI SPAGNA AREA

Around the **Piazza di Spagna** is where it all happens in Rome. You have the best shops, great restaurants, and beautiful buildings. Stately *palazzos* lining the streets look like an ideal place to live, but today much of the housing has been replaced by offices, shops, boutiques, or restaurants. Only the lucky few can afford an apartment in this location.

This area is home to the **Spanish Steps**, which gets its name from the Piazza, which gets its name from the Spanish Embassy to the Holy See that used to sit on the site. The area was adopted by British travelers in the 18th and 19th centuries, because it was not yet a popular location. The British presence is still here in the form of Babbington's Tea Rooms, an expensive but satisfying establishment in the piazza; as well as a plaque commemorating the house where Keats died in 1821. The area used to be called *il ghetto degli Inglesi* – the English ghetto.

At the beginning of Spring, the steps are laden with banks of flowers that make the whole area look like a garden. Even though you are not suppose to sit and relax on the steps anymore (a rule in place since 1996), you'll find others doing it. So sit a spell and watch the world walk by.

59. RE DEGLI AMICI, *Via della Croce 33b, Tel. 06/679-5380 or 678-2555. Credit cards accepted. Closed Mondays and the last three weeks in June. (Map A)*

This *trattoria* close to the Spanish Steps has been serving traditional Roman food for years. If you don't want a full meal their antipasto bar will more than suffice, and after 7:30pm, you can get one of their excellent pizzas. My favorite is the one named after the restaurant, made with sausage, mozzarella, oregano and tomatoes. The pasta dishes here are also something that shouldn't be missed. Try any of the Roman specialties: *carbonara*, *amatriciana*, or *arrabiata*.

60. HASSLER, *Piazza Trinita dei Monti 6, Tel. 06/678-2651. Credit cards accepted. Open 7 days a week. Dinner for two L120,000. (Map A)*

If you have the money to spend, the view down the Spanish Steps and over the rooftops of Rome from the glassed-in and air-conditioned terrace is worth every penny. You can pick out the Castel Sant'Angelo, the Jewish Ghetto's synagogue, the Pantheon, and the Quirinale Palace from the terrace. The food used to be passable, but now the Italian and Continental menu has begun to sparkle. The multilingual waiters will tell you that the *abbacchio al forno* is excellent, and I'd agree. There are many fine dishes on the menu, so you can order anything, but remember it's expensive.

61. OTELLO ALLA CONCORDIA, *Via Della Croce 81. Tel. 06/679-1178. No credit cards accepted. Closed Sundays. Dinner for two L80,000. (Map A)*

This is a family-run, small trattoria set off the main road, Via della Croce. It's location used to render it unnoticed, but now it seems to be crowded all the time. And with good reason – the food is excellent. You enter through a tiny entrance then a small shady garden to get to the restaurant. They have now made the garden eating area enclosed in removable glass, so people can eat out here all year round. In the summer it's especially nice.

On the inside the walls are filled with countless oil paintings, many received as trade for a good meal by a struggling artist. The prices are perfect and the food is simple, basic, and good. I loved the *abbacchio arrosto can patate* (roast lamb with grilled potatoes). The pasta dishes are not that good, which is strange for Rome, but if you stick with the meat dishes and vegetables you'll have a great meal. They open at 7:30pm. Make sure you get here early (or make reservations) or else you'll have a wait. The help is surly, but in a congenial Roman way.

62. PIZZERIA LE GROTTE, *Via delle Vite 37. No telephone. Credit cards accepted. Dinner for two L70,000. (Map A)*

This place has superb atmosphere and exquisite food. They are known for their excellent antipasto bar and superb pizza. I've had the *spaghetti alla vongole verace* (spicy clam sauce) and the *pollo arrosto* (spit roasted chicken) and loved them both. The food is down-to-earth peasant style in the true Roman fashion, and mixes well with the rustic ambiance. While dining here you really do feel as if you are in a series of caves (grotte). When in Rome make sure you eat here not only for the food, but the excellent atmosphere as well.

63. PIZZERIA LA CAPRICCIOSA, *Largo dei Lombardi 8 just off of the Via Del Corso. Tel. 06/6794027 & 6794706. Open lunch and dinner (until 1 am). Closed Tuesdays. Credit cards accepted but frowned upon. Dinner for two L75,000. (Map A)*

Don't be fooled by the name. This is no ordinary pizzeria. It is a large, wonderfully authentic Italian restaurant with over 50 tables inside. At night and on weekends, the restaurant expands outside into the Largo dei Lombardi. The best place to dine is outside, because inside the nickname for this place could be La Cucaracha. In a convenient location directly in the middle of Rome's premier shopping area, Via del Corso, this is a good place to stop in after an evening of shopping. But remember to bring cash, because La Capricciosa doesn't like to accept credit cards.

They have a large selection of antipasto with all sorts of prepared vegetables, ham, salami, and mozzarella. Mainly a pasta and pizza restaurant (pizza served only in the evenings), they also serve great meat and vegetable platters. Their best pizza is the gargantuan *pizza capricciosa*, one with everything, Italian style. They also make all of the Roman pasta staples perfectly: *arrabbiata, amatriciana*, and *vongole*. One pasta dish that is a little different but really good is the *spaghetti al burro con funghi* (with butter and mushrooms). Or try the *mezzo pollo al diavolo* (half chicken cooked on the grill) if you're in the mood for poultry.

64. ARANCIO D'ORO, *Via Monte d'Oro 17, Tel. 06/686-5026. Credit cards accepted. Closed Mondays. Dinner for two L90,000. (Map C)*

Refine, elegant and not frequented by tourists. This is gem of a restaurant hidden down a small side street, with a small sign and curtains hindering the view inside so people who do not know of it walk right on by. Tuesdays and Thursday are fresh fish days. Excellent food, great service, wonderful atmosphere. Come here when in Rome.

65. DA ALFREDO ALL'ANGOLETO, *Piazza Rondanini 51, Tel. 06/686-8019, 06/686-1203. Credit cards accepted. Closed Mondays and August 11-15. Dinner for two L100,000. (Map C)*

A vibrant and noisy trattoria specializing in fish for many years. Try to resist the lure of the innumerable, mouth-watering *antipasti* or you won't have room for the superbly fresh fish, the enormous Mediterranean prawns, or the still live lobsters in the display case awaiting your cooking instructions. This tentatively can be called the best seafood restaurant in Rome so if you want some come here. Mushrooms are another Alfredo specialty from late summer to late autumn. I recommend you try any of their seafood dishes, roast meats, or pastas.

There is outside seating on the small piazza as well as air-conditioned inside seating. The decor is simple, with wine bottles lining the shelves set above the tables. Come here for great food and wonderful atmosphere.

66. ALFREDO ALLA SCROFA, *Via della Scrofa 104, Tel. 06/654-0163. Closed Tuesdays. Credit cards accepted. Dinner for two L110,000. (Map C)*

There are photographs of the very rich and famous literally papering the walls. The restaurant has been in business for over half a century and was even frequented by Douglas Fairbanks and Mary Pickford which should give you an idea of what the prices are like now. All the pasta dishes are superb, especially *fettucine al triplo burro* (a rich artery clogging concoction made with triple butter sauce). The wine list is excellent and so are their house variations. If you like music with your meal, there is a strolling guitarist inside. One of *the* places to be seen in Rome.

67. DAL BOLOGNESE, *Piazza del Popolo 1-2, Tel. 361-1426., 06/322-2799. Closed Mondays and Sunday evenings, and August 9-25. Credit cards accepted. Dinner for two L85,000. (Map C)*

The cooking is Bolognese in style, which some claim is the best in Italy. Why? Because of the *parmigiano reggiano* cheese and the *prosciutto di parma*, as well as their affinity for pastas that use one or both of these ingredients. They have a menu in English to help you search through their great dishes. The *fritto misto alla bolognese,* which includes fried cheeses, meats and vegetables, is great. The *misto di paste* (mixed pasta and sauces) was filling enough for two. By ordering this dish you get to sample a variety of dishes while only ordering one. They have outside seating, perfect for people watching, but the intimacy of their inside rooms decorated with a fine collection of modern paintings appeals to me more. Also inside, you don't have to breathe exhaust fumes while you eat.

68. LA BUCA DI RIPETTA, *Via di Ripetta 36, Tel. 06/678-9528. Closed Mondays and the whole month of August. No credit cards accepted. Dinner for two L70,000. (Map C)*

This is a very small, friendly local trattoria, where you must arrive early if you have not made a reservation. Immensely popular for its food, reasonable prices, and festive atmosphere. Also, the jovial *padrone* is in constant attendance. The food is basic, straightforward Roman fare. Try the *lasagna al forno, saltimbocca alla romana,* or the *ossobuco di vitello*. They take their food seriously, so if you want to eat the Roman way with course after course, this is the place to do it. The restaurant is only one tiny room, its high walls covered with cooking and farming paraphernalia like enormous bellows, great copper pans, etc. Reservations are needed. When in Rome, you simply must dine here.

69. OSTERIA DEL TEMPO PERSO, *Via dell'Oca 43, Tel. 06/322-4841 or 322-0947. All credit cards accepted. Dinner for two L65,000. (Map C)*

Great rustic, succulent Roman fare, a stone's throw away from the Piazza del Popolo - and at great prices too. The restaurant has a small outside seating area enclosed by planters in which you can eat your meals on wooden tables. There is also some seating inside, but in the summer, the terrace is the best place to be. This *osteria* is not haute cuisine, but every dish is excellent. They have the largest selection of pastas, pizzas and meat dishes I have seen anywhere in Italy, so if you can't find something you like here, you don't like to eat.

Come here for the Roman specialties such as *spaghetti alla carbonara, penne all'arrabiata,* or *bucatini all'amatriciana*; or really treat yourself and sample the super-fantastic *tagliatelle ai funghi porcini* (with porcini mushrooms) with the most succulent sauce you can find anywhere. For seconds, the *abbacchio arrosto con patate* (lamb with rosemary potatoes) is exquisite as is the *vitello arrosto con patate* (veal with rosemary potatoes). Mimmo, the head waiter, is perfectly attentive, and since he was married to an American he speaks good English. While in Rome, definitely try this place. I did not put it on the top ten list, but it is number ten and a half.

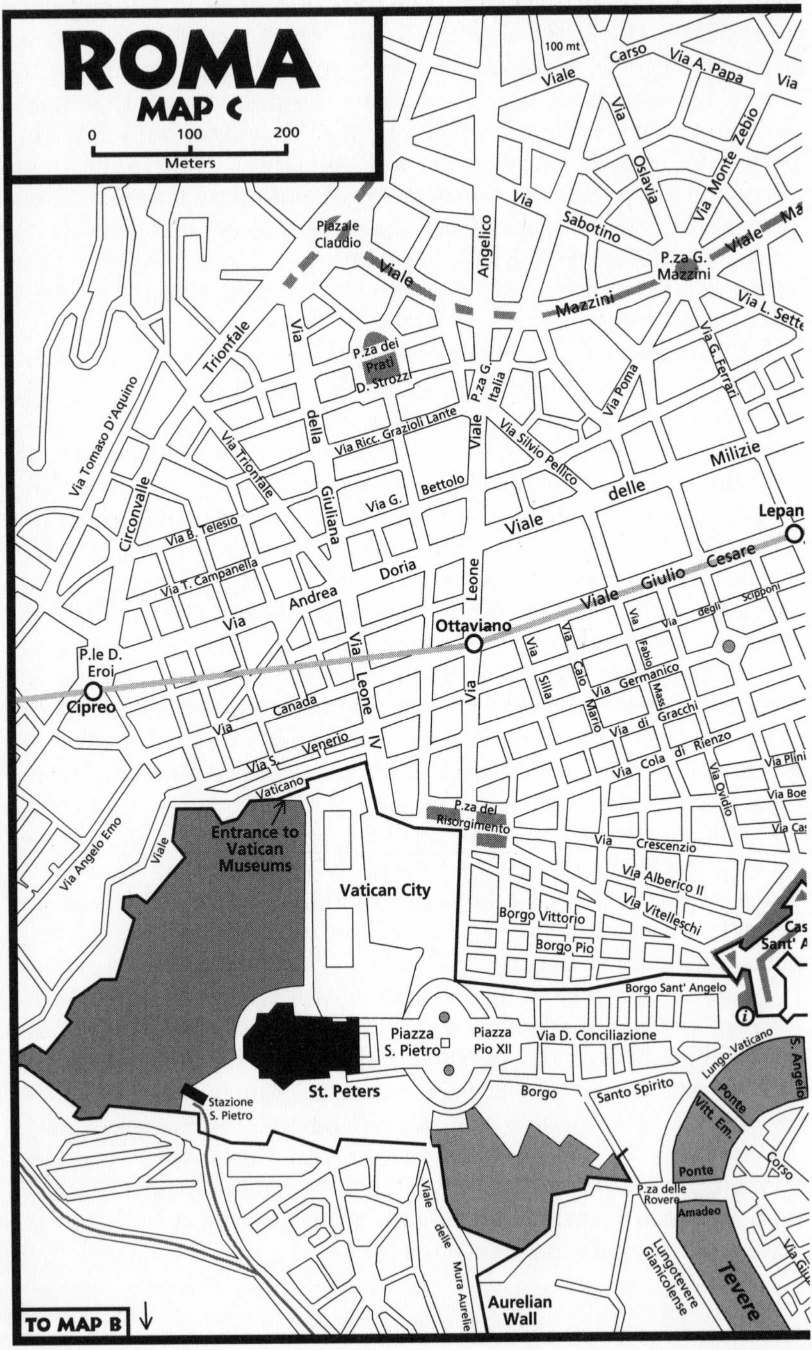
ROMA
MAP C
0
100
200
Meters
100 mt
Carso
Via A. Papa
Via
Viale
Via
Oslavia
Via Monte Zebio
Via
Sabotino
Piazzale Claudio
Angelico
P.za G. Mazzini
Viale
Viale
Mazzini
Via L. Sette
Trionfale
Via
P.za dei Prati D. Strozzi
P.za G. Italia
Via G. Ferrari
Via Poma
Via Tomaso D'Aquino
della
Via Ricc. Grazioli Lante
Viale
Via Silvio Pellico
Via Trionfale
Milizie
Circonvalle
Giuliana
Via G.
Bettolo
delle
Via B. Telesio
Viale
Lepan
Via T. Campanella
Doria
Leone
Viale
Giulio
Cesare
Andrea
Via
Via
Via degli Scipponi
Via
Ottaviano
Via
Fabio
P.le D. Eroi
Via
Leone
Via
Silla
Caio
Mario
Via Germanico
Massi
Cipreo
Canada
Via
Via di Gracchi
Via
Venerio
IV
Via Cola di Rienzo
Via Plini
Via S.
Via Ovidio
Via Boe
Vaticano
P.za del Risorgimento
Via Cas
Entrance to Vatican Museums
Via
Crescenzio
Via Angelo Emo
Viale
Via Alberico II
Vatican City
Via Vitelleschi
Borgo Vittorio
Cas
Sant' A
Borgo Pio
Borgo Sant' Angelo
Piazza S. Pietro
Piazza Pio XII
Via D. Conciliazione
Lungo. Vaticano
S. Angelo
St. Peters
Borgo
Santo Spirito
Ponte
Stazione S. Pietro
Vitt. Em.
Corso
Ponte
Viale
P.za delle Rovere
Amadeo
delle
Mura Aurelie
Lungotevere Gianicolense
Via Giu
Tevere
Aurelian Wall
TO MAP B

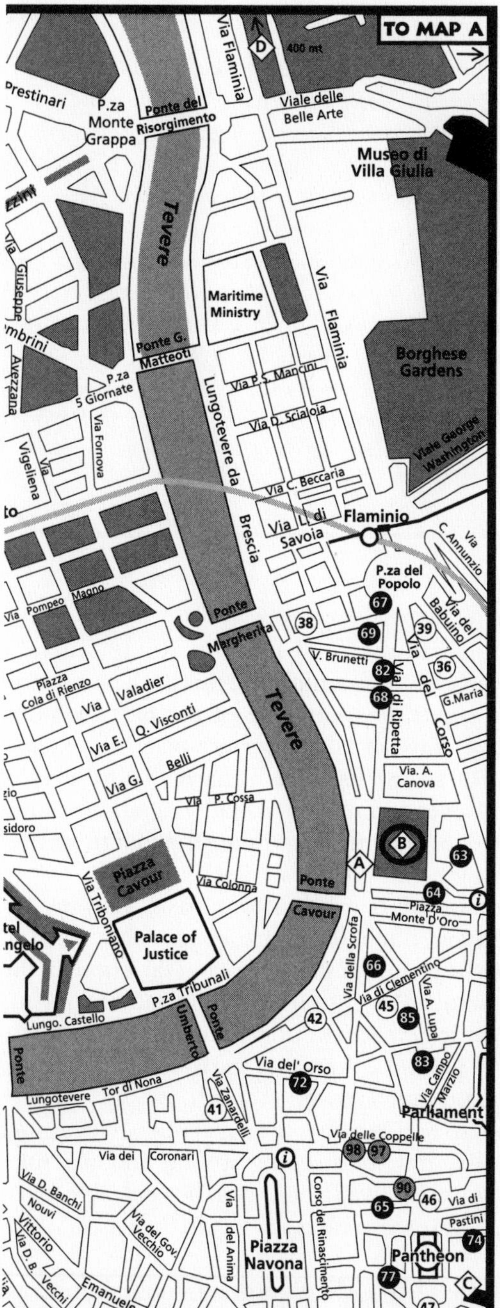

SIGHTS ◇

A. Tomb of Augustus
B. Mausoleum of Augustus
C. Santa Maria Sopra Minerva
D. Ponte Milvio

HOTELS ○

36. Margutta
38. Locarno
39. Valadier
41. Genio
42. Portoghesi
45. Markus
46. Sole Al Pantheon
47. Santa Chiara

EATERIES ●

63. La Capricciosa
64. Arancio d'Oro
65. Da Alfredo all'Angoletto
66. Alfredo alla Scrofa
67. Dal Bolognese
68. Buca di Ripetta
69. Osteria al Tempo Perso
72. Orso "80"
74. La Sacrestia
77. La Caffetteria
82. Buccone
83. Al Parlamento Achilli
85. Vini e Buffet
88. Cul de Sac

NIGHTLIFE ●

90. Black Duke
97. Ned Kelly's
98. Oliphant

Metro Line & Stops

ⓘ Information Kiosks

AMERICAN PIE

If you are looking for an oasis of Americana in Rome, there are now plenty of places to satisfy this craving. ***McDonalds,*** *which only ten years ago was a rarity in the eternal city, now number over twenty. Another bastion of Americana, which I never thought would succeed in Italy,* ***Dunkin' Donuts,*** *is flourishing with one store at the Trevi Fountain (Via S. Vincenzo 1) and another in the main hall of Termini Station (Tel. 06/785-1987, E-mail: g.cont@iol.it, Website: www.dunkin'donuts.com). And if you're looking for something a little more upscale but still completely American, there is now a* ***Planet Hollywood*** *(Via del Tritone 118, Tel. 06/4282-8012) near the Piazza Barberini, and a* ***Hard Rock Cafe*** *(Via Veneto 62a, Tel. 06/420-3051) right across the street from the American Embassy. Also available is* ***T-Bone Station*** *(Via F. Crispi 29/31, Tel. 06/6787-650, Website: www.tbone.it) which is a quality American-style steakhouse.*

CENTRO STORICO

Piazza Navona, Pantheon and Campo dei Fiori Area

The **centro storico** is the old medieval heart of Rome. Literally translated centro storico means 'historic center' and this is where you will find many of Rome's main sights, as well some of the best nightlife, restaurants and cafes. **Piazza Navona** is the perfect place to explore Rome's tapestry of history. The square itself has a charm that makes you want to come back over and over again. It is like a living architectural gallery, with its baroque churches and buildings lining the square and the immense statues standing majestic in the square itself.

On a hot day, the fountains here are a visitor's oasis, allowing for needed foot soaking refreshment. But before you take your shoes off and relax your sore feet, stroll to the center of the piazza and take note of the magnificence of Bernini's **Fontana Dei Quattro Fiumi** (Fountain of Four Rivers). You'll also find great ice cream, wonderful cafes, good restaurants as well as fire-eaters, painters, jugglers, caricaturists, tourists, rampaging Italian children, and much more.

And from mid-December to mid-January, the square becomes a giant Christmas market with booths and stalls selling stuffed animals, toys, handicrafts, and candy that looks like coal. Since it is the central focus of the holiday season there are also some great toy stores in the piazza which I loved to visit as a kid.

Another focal point of the area is the **Pantheon**, built almost two thousand years ago by Consul Marcus Agrippa as a pantheistic temple, hence its name. The city's population was centered in this area during the Middle Ages, and except for the disappearance of a large fish market, the area has remained virtually unchanged.

The area is completed by the **Campo dei Fiori** (literally translated this means "field of flowers") which has a produce and flower market every morning except Sundays. The entire centro storico is genuinely picturesque and intriguing, with a maze of interconnecting narrow streets and *piazzetta* (small squares); and evokes a feeling of what Rome was once like many eons ago, with the centuries-old buildings and the peddlers, carts, and small stores lining the narrow streets.

70. LA CARBONARA, *Campo dei Fiori 23, Tel. 06/654-783. Credit cards accepted. Closed Tuesdays. Dinner for two L90,000. (Map B)*

Located in the best piazza for atmosphere, and the food's not bad either. As could be expected, *pasta alla carbonara* is the house specialty so give that a try here. Here it is prepared to perfection with *rigatoni* in a rich peppery sauce of egg, cheese, and bacon. They also make the best *spaghetti alla vongole verace* (spicy clam sauce) I've ever had anywhere. The *fritto misto* (lightly fried mixed vegetables and cheese) is excellent since most of the produce comes in directly from the *mercato* in the square. The market can be a problem at early lunch since there are still discarded veggies on the ground where the tables should be. There's no smell, but the sight isn't too appetizing. As always, I loved the *abbacchio alla griglia* (roast baby lamb) and the roasted potatoes.

71. HOSTARIA GUILIA, *Via della Barchetta 19, Tel. 06/6880-6466. Dinner for two L65,000. (Map B)*

They have a beautiful arched interior with brown tiled floors that emits all the character of Rome. The dishes are basic but great Roman fare too, like the *penne all'arrabbiata* or the *spaghetti alla vongole*. Besides the pasta they have fresh fish and grilled meats. These guys are off the beaten track and their prices are great. Give them a try if you're in the neighborhood.

72. ORSO "80," *Via dell'Orso 33, Tel. 06/656-4904. Credit cards accepted. Closed Mondays. Dinner for two L85,000. (Map C)*

This is a fine Roman restaurant, a place to come for some classic pasta dishes, good fresh fish, and juicy meats. They bake their breads on-site in their red-brick pizza oven. Basically this is a restaurant with a little bit of everything for everybody. Pasta, pizza, fish, grilled meats, home-made breads, extensive antipasto, etc. I really like the Roman favorite *spaghetti alla carbonara* as well as the *abbacchio alla griglia* (grilled baby lamb). The place always seems to be crowded even though it's large, so try to get here early. Located near Piazza Navona, Pantheon, and Campo dei Fiori making it ideally situated.

73. VECCHIA ROMA, *Piazza di Campitelli 18, Tel. 06/656-4604. No credit cards accepted. Closed Wednesdays. Dinner for two L85,000. (Map B)*

The setting of the piazza with its Baroque church and three beautiful palazzos makes your meal worthwhile, even if the buildings are covered in grime. This menu changes constantly, but the basics are the wide variety of antipasto (which could be a meal in itself), as well as *agnello* (lamb) and *capretto* (goat) or their grilled artichokes. You have to try the artichoke, since this is the Jewish ghetto and the dish is a local favorite.

74. LA SACRESTIA, *Via del Seminario 89, Tel. 06/679-7581. Closed Wednesdays. No credit cards accepted. Dinner for two L85,000. (Map C)*

Close to the Pantheon, this restaurant has over 200 places for seating, and offers good food at reasonable prices. The decorations leave much to be desired, especially the garish ceiling and fruit-clustered grotto. Come for their pizzas, served both during the day and at night, an unusual offering for an Italian restaurant. They also serve good cuts of grilled meat, and the pasta is typically Roman also, which naturally makes it good.

75. DA SABATINO, *Piazza S. Ignazio 169, Tel. 06/67.97.821. (Map A)*

Do not eat here. Not only have I been rudely received here, but fellow travellers I have conferred with have confirmed that this place despises tourists. I have never, ever experienced such rude, belligerent behavior in my life. And it is not a theme they are trying to present. This is not a game. They honestly do no care for tourists. They will take your money, gladly, but they will give you bad, late, rude and despicable service.

Sadly, this place is located in one of the most beautiful piazza's in Rome. But do not be swayed by the attractive setting. The waiters' behavior will make your meal and the time you spend here ugly.

SPUNTINI VELOCI

In the middle of a shopping spree or tourist frenzy stop in one of these places for a light meal or a filling snack. Called *Spuntini Veloci*, these are Italian-style fast food places where you can get cold and hot entrees, baked pasta and boiled pasta, excellent meat choices, salads and more. All fast, all good, all at reasonable prices. Come to these places if you want to satisfy your hunger quickly, with authentic Italian food, but do not want to reduce yourself to going to (ugh) McDonalds.

76. CAFFETTERIA NAZIONALE, *Via Nazionale 26/27, Tel. 06/4899-1716. Closed Sundays and in August. Hours 7am–10pm. Meal for two L40,000. (Map A)*

A classic cafeteria-style food place with all modern flourishes. Plenty of traditional choices here like boiled and baked pastas, as well as appetizing and fast quiches, tarts, sandwiches (*panini* or *tramezzini*). This place is packed for lunch, but all day long locals and tourists drop in to grab a bite since it is very close to *Termini* train station.

77. LA CAFETTERIA, *Piazza di Pietra 65, Tel. 06/679-8147. Closed in August and Sundays in July. Hours 7am-9pm. Meal for two L50,000. (Map C)*

Near the Pantheon this upscale, regal and traditional little cafeteria serves up scrumptious breakfast, lunch and dinner. You can find some of the best quick and healthy food in the city here, at a good price. Always a little crowded, but if you want quick eats in a relaxing ambiance in the old historic center this is the place to come.

78. CIAMPINI AL CAFÉ DU JARDIN, *Viale Trinita dei Monti, Tel. 06/678-5678. Closed Wednesdays and all of March. Hours 8am-7pm. Summer hours 8am-1am. Meal for two L40,000. (Map A)*

In a fantastic location near the Villa Borghese, Villa Medici and the top of the Spanish Steps this frenzied and always full local place is perfect for hungry tourists and locals alike. A combination cafeteria, ice cream parlor and restaurant, here you'll find many choices, both hot and cold, and you can get some excellent ice cream for dessert.

79. CIAO/SPIZZICO, *Via del Corso 181, Tel. 06/678-9135. Hours 7am-midnight. Fridays until 1:30am. Saturdays until 2:00am. Meal for two L40,000. (Map A)*

Located on the hippest, happiningest shopping street in Rome, almost right next door to the great department store La Rinascente, this place will satisfy your hunger quickly for breakfast, lunch, dinner, as well as a late night snack when you stumble back from the disco. Your choices are many from pastas, to meat, salads, cheese or fruit. Service is fast, and many of the first course pasta dishes are created right in front of your eyes. The portions are large and the ingredients fresh and tasty and the prices are reasonable. This place is an Italian-style food court with all sorts of choices.

80. BREK, *Largo di Torre Argentina 1, Tel. 06/6821-0353. Open 12-3:30pm and 6:30-11:00pm. Meal for two L40,000. (Map B)*

An Italian-style fast food place, which is all over the country. They have just opened this location in Rome. There is restaurant seating upstairs, café fare downstairs, all quick, all convenient, and all very tasty. Located near the Pantheon, Campo dei Fiori and Navona this is a good place to come and grab a quick bite in the middle of the day.

ENOTECHE

Wine bars (*enoteche*) have existed in Italy since the beginning of grape cultivation, but in the past have usually been dark, dingy affairs populated by older men, playing cards at rickety tables, slurping hearty local vintages from chipped mismatched glasses. Most of those places are gone, and have been replaced with newer, more upscale, ambient, fern-filled establishments such as those listed below. These places offer some excellent vintages from all over the Italian peninsula and the world. Usually open mid-day until the wee hours of the morning, with a break in the afternoon, *enoteche* are an upscale place for Italians to go for lunch, an early meal, a light dinner or just for a quiet evening out. These places offer excellent light food such as salads, sandwiches, crepes, quiches, and salami and cheese plates.

81. ENOTECA ANACLETO BLEVE, *Via S. Maria del Pianto 9a, Tel. 06/686-5970. Meal for two L50,000. (Map B)*

Located at the entrance to the Jewish quarter, just off the Via Arenula this place has one of the best selections of wines in all of Rome. Lunch is served in the side room and is an exquisite buffet, with hot plates prepared quickly, as well as typical local artesian cheeses and salamis, all accompanied by their superb vintages served by the glass. Wonderfully courteous service. A superb option when near the Campo dei Fiori. It's hard to find especially since their sign is upside down and backwards.

82. BUCCONE, *Via di Ripetta 19, Tel. 06/361-2154. Lunch served everyday, dinner only Thursday-Saturday. Meal for two L50,000. (Map C)*

A great enotecha in Rome, not only because of the offerings by the glass but also the bottled selection you can choose from. Mentioned in a sidebar in this book as the best place to buy wine to bring home, Buccone also stands on its own as a place to come in and grab a tasty, light and healthy snack and a glass of wine at either their counter serving area or side room. An excellent choice for wine lovers, in a fun local area near the main shopping street of Via Del Corso.

83. ENOTECA AL PARLAMENTO ACHILLI, *Via dei Prefetti 15, Tel. 06/687-3446. (Map C)*

Located in the centro storico near the Parlamento, here you can find ample supplies of bottles for sale, as well as glasses of their vintages offered at their counter top serving area. You can get some small snacks to go with your glass of wine. There are also cognacs and liqueurs for sale as well as chocolates, candies, jams and other boutique food items. To be complete they need a small seating area, but many locals come in for a quick glass of wine and wander out.

84. ENOTECANTINA, *Via del Croce 76, Tel. 679-0896. Closed Sundays. Meal for two L55,000. All credit cards accepted. (Map A)*

Opened in 1860, until a few years ago this was an old-fashioned wine store selling local vintages directly from large vats. You would walk past the huge wooden doors and into the cool, dark, and damp store lined with shelf upon shelf of wine and olive oil, and it would seem as if centuries had been erased. Now it's a fern-filled wine bar with wooden stools with ceramic seats, and ample seating. Light meals and snacks of all sorts are served here, and wine by the glass. A great place to stop in a perfect location.

85. VINI E BUFFET, *Piazza della Torretta 60, Tel 06/687-1445. Open 12:30pm-2:30pm and 7:30pm to midnight. Closed Sundays. Meal for two L50,000. (Map C)*

Set on a tiny side streets, near the Parliament building, just off the Via del Corso, this little wine shop and café is a breath of fresh air. It is a simply fantastic place to grab a light lunch (sandwiches, crepes, salads, etc.) and some great wine. My favorite wine bar in Rome because it evokes an ambiance of time past. The rustic and charming setting is authentically Roman and offers a unique dining experience. This is my favorite enotecha in Rome.

86. CAVOUR 313, *Via Cavour 313, Tel. 06/678-5496. Open 12:30pm-2:30pm and 7:30pm-12:30am. Closed Sundays. Meal for two L50,000. (Map D)*

Wow. What a great wine bar. Rustic and down-to-earth atmosphere. Superb light and healthy local food, prepared fresh. If you happen by the Colosseum or Forum, you simply must stop here for lunch, an afternoon snack or a light dinner. An excellent menu of local salamis, cheeses, sandwiches, salads and much more, all accompanied by a varied and extensive wine list. My second favorite place to Vini e Buffet above.

87. VINERIA REGGIO, *Campo dei Fiori 15, Tel. 06/6880-3268. Open 12:30pm - 2:30pm and 7:30pm - 2:00am. Closed Sundays. Meal for two L50,000. (Map B)*

An ideal location, in the same piazza as the bar, The Drunken Ship, and the excellent restaurant La Carbonara, this is a wine bar and late night spot for fun too. The seating outside is great on a warm day, and when it's not, you'll mostly only find places at the bar since seating inside is very limited. An adequate menu and wine list, what really makes this place is their location in the Campo dei Fiori.

88. CUL DE SAC, *Piazza di Pasquino 73, Tel. 06/6880-1094. Open 12:30pm-3:30pm and 7:00pm-12:30am. Closed Mondays for lunch. Meal for two L50,000. (Map B&C)*

This intimate winebar with outdoor tables set up in nice weather has over 1,400 Italian and foreign vintages for you to sample. This place has been around since the 1970s and serves up hot and cold light meals as well as dessert and ice cream. Quick informal service and a stunning ambiance, especially inside among the bottles lining the walls and at the marble topped tables.

GELATERIE

Gelato, or what we would call ice cream, is a combination of whole milk, eggs, sugar, and natural flavoring – or fresh fruit and sugar in the fruit flavors. It is a less firmly frozen, softer, more intensely flavored and colored creation than what we know as ice cream here in North America. The best fruit *gelato* is made from crushed fresh ripe seasonal fruit. The best milk-based *gelato* is flavored with all-natural ingredients and has a silky consistency. They will all melt faster than ice cream does, so be prepared for that on a hot summer day.

Besides *gelato* there are also three different types of frozen concoctions savored by the Italians:

Semifreddo, which means "half cold," and refers to any of a variety of chilled or partially frozen desserts including cake, whipped ice cream. It vaguely resembles a mousse, which is what the chocolate flavor is called.

Sorbetto is basically a fruit sorbet and has become popular in many Italian restaurants as a separator between the fish and meat courses to act as a palate cleanser. It also makes a wonderful dessert.

Granita is frozen flavored ice water. It usually, but not always, comes in lemon, orange or coffee flavors. Besides homemade varieties, you can find some excellent packaged granitas sold from coolers at most cafes. This is my favorite.

Some gelato shops for you to try include:

SAN CRISPINO, *Via della Panetteria 42, Tel. 06/679-3924. Open Noon to 12:30am Mondays, Wednesdays, Thursdays and Sundays; and Noon to 1:30am Fridays and Saturdays. Closed Tuesdays.*

Easily the best *gelateria* in Rome. Located near the Trevi Fountain, here you can find any flavor imaginable, and whether its creamy or fruity, all are made from scratch. All ingredients are natural, without preservative so you cannot choose by color, since the *nocciola* (hazelnut) looks like vanilla, the *pistacchio* looks like chocolate, and the *Stracciatella* (chocolate chip) looks like mud. There are no cones, only cups priced at L3,000, L4,000 and L6,000 which are filled to overflowing every time. Or you can get your favorites packed for take-out in styrofoam tubs. You simply must come here when you are in Rome.

CREMERIA MONTEFORTE, *Via della Rotonda 22*, Tel. 06/686-7720. Closed Mondays.

The ice cream in this minuscule little local *gelateria* is some of the best in the entire city. Since there's not much room, grab a cone or a cup here and wander out and sit by the Pantheon. All natural ingredients. Great ice cream.

TRE SCALINI, *Piazza Navona 28, Tel. 06/6880-1996. Closed Wednesdays.*

A staple in Rome for many years, here you can grab a cone and eat in the piazza, or sit at a table outside and watch the world go by. Very upscale and very pricey, but this is place is world renowned as a great *gelateria* in Rome.

PALAZZO DEL FREDDO, *Via Principe Eugenio 65/67, Tel. 06/466-4740, Closed Mondays. Open noon-11pm. Sundays 10am – Midnight.*

A famous, traditional gelateria near the train station that has been in existence since 1924. The ice creams and sorbets are all made with the finest ingredients and maintain a traditional quality and character unfazed by any new trends. You can sample cones and cups of their exquisite ice creams either outside on their patio, inside at the bar or in their own interior courtyard. Rather out of the way. Come here only if you are staying by the train station.

ALBERTO PICA, *Via della Segiola 12, Tel. 06/6880-6153. Closed Sunday mornings. Holiday August 15-30. Hours 8am to 2am.*

You will be overwhelmed with the choices here, especially the creative concoctions, and all are made with all natural, organic ingredients. Located just off of the Via Arenula, a stones throw from the Campo dei Fiori, this place is open late to satisfy your ice cream cravings after you have been bar hopping into the wee hours.

PASTICCERIE

Rome is filled with some incredible pastry shops. Listed below are the best, but stop in any *pasticceria* you pass and you will not be disappointed. The Romans make superb pastries.

VALZANI, *Via del Moro 37b, Tel. 06/580-3792. Closed Tuesday and in Spring also Mondays.*

One of the last truly traditional *pasticcerie Romane* where you can find all sorts of classic pastries. Located in a small fragrant little shop, here you can grab a cup of coffee, select a delectable morsel and be transported to culinary heaven. Located in Trastevere, just across the Ponte Sisto from Campo dei Fiori, this is a superb place to savor an authentic Roman pastry. This is my favorite pastry shop in Rome.

LA DELIZIOSA, *Vicolo Savelli 50, Tel. 06/6880-3155. Closed Tuesdays.*

The name of this place says it all – *Deliziosa* means Delicious. One of the best pastry shops in the city, here you can find all sorts of filled pastries, crumbly, spongy, thick, gooey, heavy, light, some creatively concocted, others made from traditional recipes, but all incredibly delicious. When in Rome, if you're hungering for a pastry, come here.

LA DOLCEROMA, *Via dei Portico d'Ottavia 20b, Tel. 06/689-2196. Closed Sunday afternoons and Mondays.*

Here you will find exquisite Austrian and American style pastries made by Stefano Ceccarelli and which are famous city wide. All sorts of pastries abound in this wonderful little shop including strudels and tarts all covered in rich abundance of chocolate, marzipan, fruit preserves and anything else that is delectable and attractive. You can also find cherry, lemon and pecan pies and chocolate chip cookies, a rarity in Italy. So if you have a craving for them, come here.

IL FORNO DEL GHETTO, *Via del Portico d'Ottavia 2, Tel. 06/687-8637. Closed Saturdays.*

In this small store located in the heart of the Jewish quarter in Rome, you can sample the creations of three generations of pastry makers. Traditional Italian and Jewish-Roman pies and pastries abound, filled with fruit, covered in chocolate and begging to be eaten. My favorite is the tasty cheese cake. In the mornings you can sample their home-made breakfast creations.

L'ANTICO FORNO, *Via della Scrofa 33, Tel. 06/686-5405. Closed Sundays.*

Right next door to Volpetti, the great alimentari mentioned earlier, here you can get all sorts of tasty pastries as well as excellent pizza by the slice. Everything is made in-house in the their extensive back room, so it is all fresh and oh-so-tasty.

14. SEEING THE SIGHTS

For the Jubilee year, Rome has introduced nine **tourist information kiosks**, which are run by multilingual staff from 9:00am-6:00pm every day. At the locations below, you can get excellent maps of Rome, wonderful color brochures of the local museums and tons of information about virtually anything to do in Rome. After the year 2000, these places will still be open, dispensing similar information though not as extensive. They will also act as ticket booths for theatrical performances, museums, special events and sporting events. You should make a point of stopping at one of these kiosks when you first arrive in Rome:

- **Termini Train Station**, *Tel. 06/4890-6300. Open 8:00am-9:00pm daily*
- **Termini**, *Piazza Cinquecento, Tel. 06/4782-5194*
- **Castel S. Angelo**, *Piazza Pia, Tel. 06/6880-9707*
- **Imperial Forums**, *Piazza Tempio della Pace, Tel. 06/6992-4307*
- **Piazza di Spagna**, *Largo Goldoni, Tel. 06/6813-6061*
- **Piazza Navona**, *Piazza Cinque Lune, Tel. 06/6880-9240*
- **Via Nazionale**, *Palazzo delle Esposizioni, Tel. 06/4782-4525*
- **Trastevere**, *Piazza Sonnino, Tel. 06/5833-3457*
- **San Giovanni**, *Piazza S. Giovanni in Laterano, Tel. 06/7720-3535*

The chief difficulty most visitors find is that there is so much to see in this huge historic city. With even a month's worth of concentrated touring, you'd only scratch the surface. If your time is limited, consider a sightseeing tour or series of tours by bus. This way you can be sure to see at least the greatest sights in Rome and its environs. There are a variety of tours available through **Appian Line** (*Piazza dell'Esquilino 6, Tel. 06/487-861*), **Carrani** (*Via Vittorio E. Orlando 95, Tel. 06/474-2501*), **Green Line** (*Via Farini 5, Tel. 06/483-787*), and **Vastours** (*Via Pienmonte 34, Tel. 06/481-4309*). One of the best is **Stop 'n' Go Bus Tours** *(Tel. 06/321-7054)* which stops at a number of different sights in Rome and also offers half day trips to Tivoli and Ostia Antica and a full day trip to Cervetri and Tarquinia.

If you want a personalized tour of Rome, by licensed tour guides, that can also be arranged through the following organization: **Centro Guide Roma**, *Via S. Maria delle Fornaci 8, Tel. 06/639-0409, Fax 06/630-601*, **Centro Assistenza Servizi Turistici**, *Via Cavour 184, Tel. 06/482-5698*, **Italian Language and Culture for Foreigners**, *Via Tunisi 4, Tel. 06/3975-0984; www.arcodidruso.com; E-mail: cultura@arcodisdruso.com*, or **Walking Tours of Rome**, *Via Varese 39, Tel. 06/644-51-843, Fax 06/4450-734; www.enjoyrome.com*.

TEN MUST-SEE SIGHTS IN ROME

The Vatican Museums alone can take you an entire day to work through, so don't believe that you can do all of these places justice in a few short days. Also, when you visit Piazza Navona, Piazza di Spagna, and Trevi Fountain, you will get a different experience depending on the time of day you go. At night each of these places livens up with Italians of all ages strolling, chatting, sipping wine, strumming guitars, while during the day they may only be swarmed by tourists. Take your time – don't do too much, and don't rush through. Take your time, be Italian and savor the experience. These ten could easily last you a week.

Sistine Chapel *– Site of Michelangelo's magnificent frescoed ceiling and walls.*

Vatican Museums *– Everything you could imagine including Egyptian, Greek & Roman artifacts, as well as the best collection of paintings and sculptures anywhere in the world.*

St. Peter's *– The world's largest cathedral, exquisitely decorated.*

Castel Sant'Angelo *– The fortress that used to protect the Vatican, now houses a wonderful armaments museum.*

Imperial and Roman Forums *– The center of ancient Roman life. A great place for people of all ages to explore.*

Capitoline Museum on the Campidoglio *– The second best museum in Rome, with many fine sculptures and paintings.*

Piazza Navona *– In what used to be the place for naval gladiatorial battles is now a lively piazza filled with wonderful fountains, churches, and palazzi as well as good cafés and restaurants.*

Piazza di Spagna *– Walk to the top and get a great view of the city. Sit by the fountain during siesta and enjoy Rome as it passes you by.*

Trevi Fountain *– One of the most beautiful fountains in Italy. At night, when lit up it is a magnificent sight.*

Saint Paul's Outside the Walls *– Location of many buried Saints, some fine sculptures and mosaics. Walls ringed with portraits of all the popes.*

A map of Rome (which you can get at any newsstand, but be sure to get one with the bus routes listed), some walking shoes, and a spirit of adventure are all you need to explore the innumerable *piazzas*, churches, galleries, parks, and fountains of this unique city. If you want the most up to date information about what is happening in Rome, whether a museum exhibit, performing arts festival, or simply what is going on in the local American community, pick up a copy of *Wanted in Rome* (L1,500) at any newsstand. This is the resource for the ex-pat community to know exactly what's going on in Rome.

If you saunter through the narrow streets of old Rome, behind the **Piazza Navona**, for example, or along the **Via Giulia** or near the **Pantheon**, you'll get many unexpected and revealing glimpses of flower hung balconies, inner courtyards, and fountains. Here, perhaps more than in the impressive ruins of antiquity, you will get a little of the feeling of this city where civilizations have been built on the ruins of the previous ones for centuries. Rome is an ancient city whose vitality seems to be renewed perpetually by each new generation.

In addition to the sights map on pages 166-167, I have listed some sights on the previous city maps in this book; they can be found on the following pages:

- **Map A**: pages 120-121
- **Map B**: pages 144-145
- **Map C**: pages 154-155
- **Map D**: pages 168-169

ANCIENT ROME

THE IMPERIAL FORUMS

Via IV Novembre 94. Admission L5,000. Tel. 06/679-0048. Open 9:00am-8:00pm and in the summers on Saturday until midnight. Metro-Colosseo.

The **Imperial Forums** were built in the last days of the Republic, when the Roman Forum became inadequate to accommodate the ever-increasing population, and the emperors needed space to celebrate their own magnificence. These forums were used as meeting places for Romans to exchange views, as lively street markets, or as places where official announcements could be proclaimed to the populace. The first was built by Julius Caesar, and those that followed were created by Augustus, Vespasian, Domitian, Trajan, Nerva, and Hadrian.

After the fall of the Roman Empire, these places of great import fell into disrepair; by the time of the Middle Ages and the Renaissance all that was left are the ruins we see today. Gradually, over the centuries, these

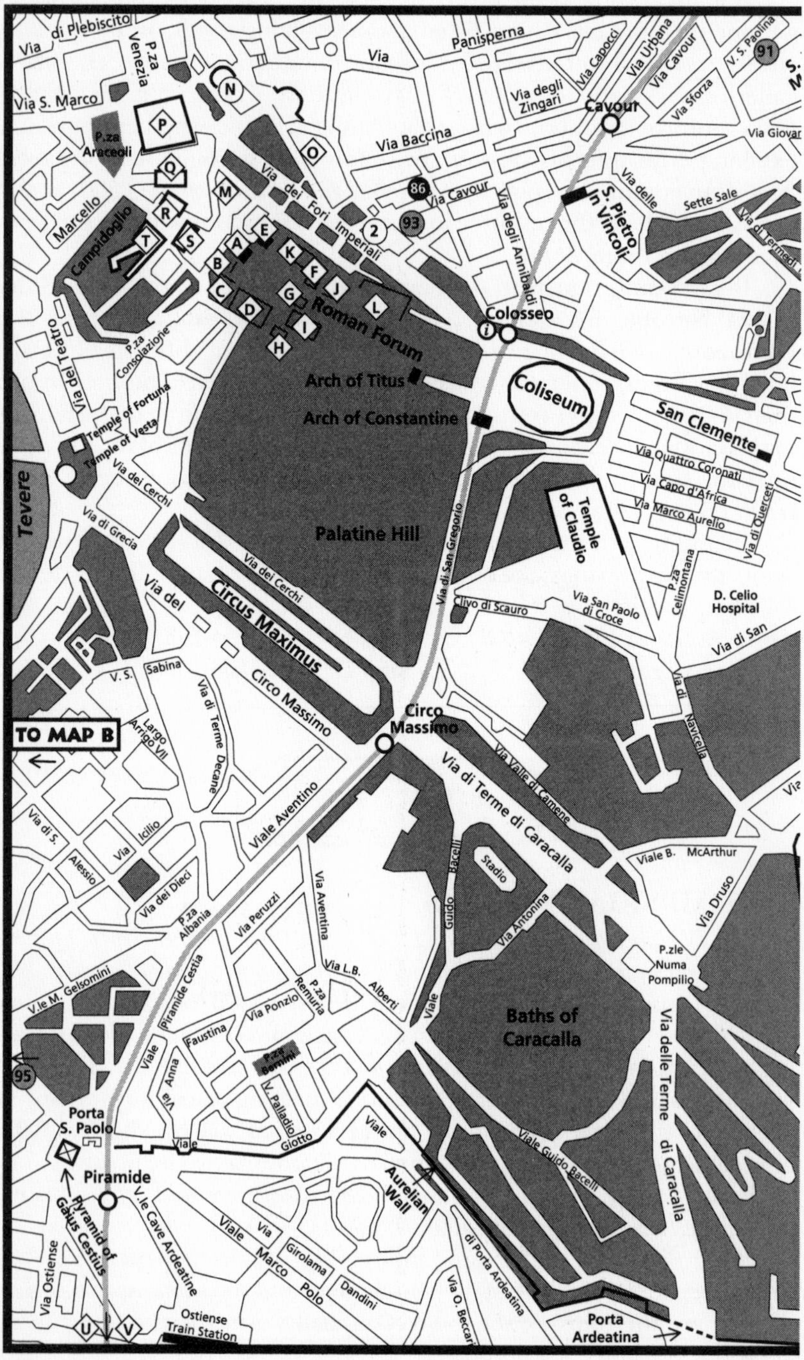

Via di Plebiscito
P.za Venezia
Via S. Marco
P.za Araceoli
Marcello
Campidoglio
Via Panisperna
Via degli Zingari
Via Baccina
Via Capocci
Via Urbana
Via Cavour
V. S. Paolina
Via Sforza
Cavour
Via Giovan
Via dei Fori Imperiali
Via Cavour
Via degli Annibaldi
S. Pietro In Vincoli
Via delle Sette Sale
Via di Termedi
Roman Forum
Colosseo
Arch of Titus
Arch of Constantine
Coliseum
San Clemente
Via del Teatro
P.za Consolazione
Temple of Fortuna
Temple of Vesta
Tevere
Via dei Cerchi
Via di Grecia
Via Quattro Coronati
Via Capo d'Africa
Via Marco Aurelio
Via di Querceti
Temple of Claudio
Palatine Hill
Via di San Gregorio
Via dei Cerchi
Circus Maximus
Via del
Clivo di Scauro
Via San Paolo di Croce
P.za Celimontana
D. Celio Hospital
Via di San
V. S. Sabina
Via di Terme Decane
Circo Massimo
Largo Arrigo VII
TO MAP B
Circo Massimo
Via Valle di Camene
Via di Terme di Caracalla
Via di Navicella
Via di S. Alessio
Via Icilio
Viale Aventino
Via dei Dieci
P.za Albania
Via Aventina
Via Peruzzi
Guido Bacelli
Stadio
Viale B. McArthur
Via Druso
Via Antonina
P.zle Numa Pompilio
V.le M. Gelsomini
Piramide Cestia
Via L.B. Alberti
P.za Remuria
Via Ponzio
Faustina
P.za Bernini
Viale
Baths of Caracalla
Via delle Terme di Caracalla
Viale Anna
Via
V. Palladio
Viale Giotto
Porta S. Paolo
Piramide
Pyramid of Gaius Cestius
V.le Cave Ardeatine
Aurelian Wall
Viale Guido Bacelli
Viale Marco Polo
Via Girolama
Dandini
di Porta Ardeatina
Via O. Beccari
Via Ostiense
Ostiense Train Station
Porta Ardeatina

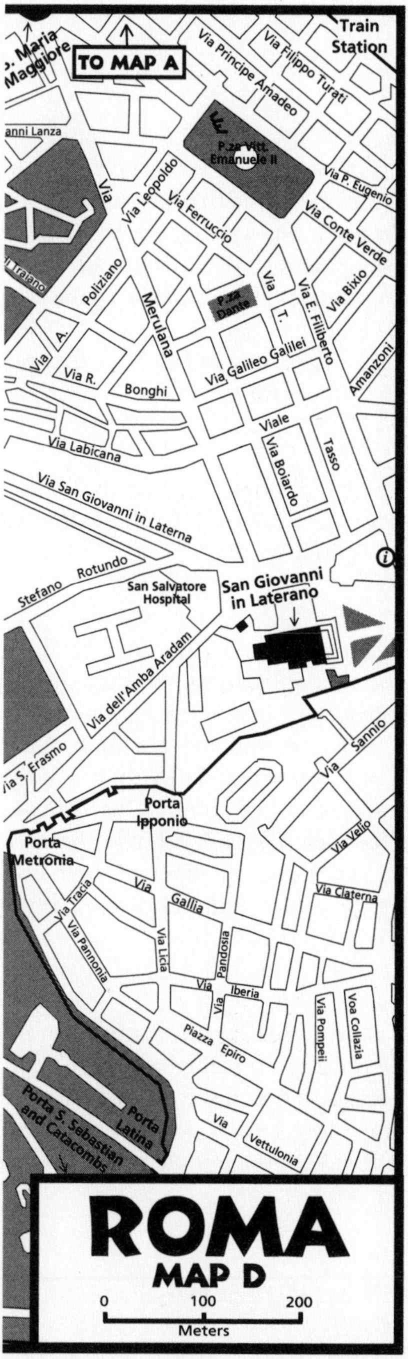

SIGHTS ◇

A. Arch of Septimus Severus
B. Rostra
C. Temple of Saturn
D. Basilica Giulia
E. Curia (Senate House)
F. Temple of Anthony & Foustina
G. Temple of Caesar
H. Temple of Castor & Pollux
I. House of the Vestal Virgins
J. Temple of Romulus
K. Basilica Emilia
L. Basilica of Maxentius
& Constantine
M. Caesar's Forum
N. Trajan's Fourm/Column/Market
O. Augustus' Forum
P. Vitt. Emanuele II Monument
Q. S.M. d'Araceoli
R. Capitoline Museum
S. Senatorial Palace
T. Conservatorio
U. St Paul's Outside the Walls
Metro - San Paolo
V. Museo della Civilta Romana
Metro - EUR Palasport or Fermi

HOTELS ○

2. Richmond

EATERIES ●

86. Cavour 313

NIGHTLIFE ◉

91. Fiddler's Elbow
93. Shamrock
95. Radio Londra

Metro Line & Stops

ⓘ Information Kiosks

monumental ruins became covered with soil until they began to be excavated in 1924.

Trajan's Forum

Located well below current street level, this is the most grandiose of the Forums of the imperial age and reflects the emperor's eclectic taste in art and architecture. Here you can see one of the finest monuments in these Imperial Forums, **Trajan's Column**, built to honor the Victories of Trajan in 113 CE. It is over 30 meters high and is covered with a series of spiral reliefs depicting the military exploits of the Emperor against the Dacins in the 1st century CE.

At the summit of this large column is a statue of St. Peter that was placed there by Pope Sixtus V in the 17th century.

Trajan's Market

This is a large and imposing set of buildings attached to Trajan's Forum, where people gathered and goods were sold. In the vast semicircle is where the merchants displayed their wares.

Forum of Caesar

Located to the right of the Via dei Fori Imperiali (the road itself was built in 1932 on the site of a far more ancient road to more adequately display the monuments of ancient Rome), this was the earliest of the Imperial Forums. It was begun in 54 BCE to commemorate the Battle of Pharsalus, and finished in 44 BCE. Trajan redesigned many parts of this Forum to meet his needs in 113 CE and celebrate some of his victories.

For example, Trajan added the **Basilica Argentaria** (Silver Basilica) that was a meeting place for bankers and money changers. Originally a bronze statue of Julius Caesar stood in the center of this Forum; currently it is located in the Campidoglio.

Forum of Augustus

Built around the time of Christ's birth, this Forum commemorates the deaths of Brutus and Cassius (the traitors who allied against Caesar) at the Battle of Philippi in 42 BCE. Here you'll find some remains of the **Temple of Mars**, the god of war, including a high podium and some trabeated (horizontal) columns. To the side of the temple you'll find the remains of two triumphal arches and two porticos.

Basilica of Maxentius & Constantine

This large building was begun by Maxentius between 306-312 CE and eventually completed by Constantine. It was used as a court of law and a money exchange, as were all Roman basilicas. It faces the Colosseum and is one of the best preserved of the buildings in the Imperial Forums. In its prime, the building was 100 meters long and 76 meters wide and divided into three arched naves, most of which remains to this day.

REALLY SEEING THE SIGHTS

*If you are interested in seeing the Eternal City from a bird's eye view, **Umbria Fly** offers airborne tours of Rome. You will take home some memorable photos from this tour! Each 20 minute flight offers the best views of Rome for only L100,000 per adult and L50,000 per child accompanied by an adult. For more information on how to get to the Urbe Airport (Via Salaria 825) and times of departures each day, call 06/8864-1441.*

THE COLOSSEUM

Piazza del Colosseo. Admission L8,000. Hours in the summer 9:00am-7:00pm. In the winter 9:00am-5:00pm. Buses 11, 27, 81, 85, 87. Metro-Colosseo.

The **Colosseum** (*Flavian Amphitheater*) remains the most memorable monument surviving from ancient Rome. Its construction began in 72 CE by Vespasian on the site of the Stagnum Neronis, an artificial lake built by Emperor Nero near his house on the adjacent Oppian Hill for his pleasure. The Colosseum was eventually dedicated by Titus in 80 CE. It is recorded that at the building's opening ceremony, which lasted three months, over 500 exotic beasts and many hundreds of gladiators were slain in the arena. These types of spectacles lasted until 405 CE, when they were abolished. The building was severely damaged by an earthquake in the fifth century CE and since then it has been used as a fortress and as a supply source for construction material for Vatican buildings.

What we see today is nothing compared to what the building used to look like. In its prime it was covered with marble, and each portico was filled with a marble statue of some important Roman. The Colosseum used to be fully elliptical and could hold over 50,000 people. Each of the three tiers is supported by a different set of columns: Doric for the base, Ionic for the middle and Corinthian for the top. Inside, the first tier of seats was reserved for the knights and tribunes, the second tier for citizens, and the third tier for the lower classes. The Emperor, Senators, Government Officials and Vestal Virgins sat on marble thrones on a raised platform that went around the entire arena.

Inside the arena we can see vestiges of the subterranean passages that were used to transport the wild beasts. Human-powered elevators were employed to get the animals up to the Colosseum floor. At times the arena was flooded to allow for the performance of mock naval battles. Unremarkable architecturally, the Colosseum is still an engineering marvel to admire. A great site for kids to explore.

ARCH OF CONSTANTINE

Piazza Colosseo. Buses 11, 27, 81, 85, 87. Metro-Colosseo.

Located near the Colosseum, this monument was built in 312 CE to commemorate the Emperor's victory over Maxentius at the Ponte Milvio (the oldest standing bridge in Rome) and is comprised of three archways. This is the largest and best preserved triumphal arch in Rome. The attic is not continuous but is broken into three parts corresponding to the placement of the arches. Even though this is the Arch of Constantine, the attic panels are from a monument to Marcus Aurelius. On one side of the attic the bas-reliefs represent Marcus Aurelius in his battle with the Dacians, and on the opposite side there are episodes of deeds by Marcus Aurelius and Constantine. On the lower areas there are bas-reliefs from earlier arches of Trajan and Hadrian.

THE ROMAN FORUM, PALATINE HILL & NEARBY SIGHTS

Largo Romolo e Remo 1. Tel. 06/699-0110. Admission L12,000. Open 9:00am-8:00pm and in the summers on Saturday until midnight. Buses 11, 27, 85, 97, 181, 186, 718, and 719. Metro-Colosseo.

The best way to get an overall view of the **Roman Forum** is to descend from the Piazza del Campidoglio by way of the Via del Campidoglio, which is to the right of the Senatorial Palace. You get a clear view of the Forums in the front, with the Colosseum in the background, and the Palatine Hill on the right. The entrance is some distance down the *Via dei Fori Imperiali*. You can also enter from the Via di San Gregario near the Colosseum.

The Roman Forum lies between the Palatine and Quirinale hills and was first a burial ground for the early settlers of both locations. Later the area became the center for the religious, commercial and political activities of the early settlers. The surrounding area was greatly expanded in the Imperial era when Roman emperors began building self-contained *Fora* in their own honor. The entire area has been decimated by war, used as a quarry for other buildings in Rome, and has been haphazardly excavated, but is still a wonder to behold. A great site for kids to explore.

In the Roman Forum you'll find the following sights and more:

Arch of Septimus Severus

Built in 203 CE to celebrate the tenth anniversary of the Emperor Septimus Severus' reign. This triumphal arch is constructed with two lower archways flanking a larger central one and is the one of the finest and most imposing structures remaining from ancient Rome. Over the side arches are bas-reliefs depicting scenes from victorious battles fought by the Emperor over the Parthians and the Mesopotamians.

In 1988, in pure Italian fashion, one half of the arch was cleaned to allow citizens to decide whether the complete structure should be cleaned. By 1998 they decided how they wanted it and were finally getting around to cleaning the other half. In a few years it will be covered in pollution grime again.

Rostra

Located directly to the left of the Arch of Septimus Severus, this building was decorated with the beaks of ships captured by the Romans at Antium in 338 BCE. It was the meeting place for Roman orators. In front of it is the **Column of Phocas**, erected in honor of the Eastern Emperor of the Roman Empire in 608 CE. The column was the last monument to be erected in the Forum.

Temple of Saturn

Built in 497 BCE, it was restored with eight ionic columns in the 3rd century CE. In the temple's basement was the Treasury of State.

Basilica Giulia

Started in 54 BCE by Julius Caesar and completed by Augustus, it was destroyed by fire and restored by Diocletian in 284 CE. The building served as a large law court.

Basilica Emilia

Located to the right of the entrance to the Forum, it was erected in 179 BCE, and because of the ravages of fire, destruction by "barbarian hordes" and neglect, little remains today. Together with the Basilica Giulia, it was one of the largest buildings in Rome and was used by money-changers and other business people.

The Curia

Founded by Tullus Hostilius and built between 80 BCE and 44 BCE, this was the house of the Senate, the government of Rome in the Republican period, and the puppet government during the empire. It was once covered with exquisite marble but is today a combination of stucco and brick. The structure was rebuilt after a fire in 283 CE, and converted into a church in the seventh century CE. The interior is still a large plain hall, with marble steps that were used as the senator's seats. Take time to go inside and sit where the Roman Senators used to.

Temple of Anthony & Faustina

Built by Antonius Pius in honor of his wife Faustina, the temple was later converted to a church in the 11th century, **San Lorenzo in Miranda**. All that remains of the original Roman temple are the ten monolithic columns that are 17 meters high, and an elegant frieze. The baroque facade is from the 1600s.

Temple of Caesar

Near the Arch of Augustus and past the Temple of Castor and Pollux you'll find the Temple of Caesar, built in 42 BCE by Octavius. It was on this site that Caesar's body was cremated.

Temple of Castor & Pollux

Built in 484 BCE and restored by Hadrian and Tiberius. The three Corinthian columns in the podium are from that period of restoration. It was originally built to pay homage to the Gods Castor and Pollux who, according to legend, aided the Romans against their enemies.

House of the Vestal Virgins

This is where the vestal virgins lived who dedicated themselves to maintaining the sacred fires in the nearby **Temple of Vesta**. A portico of two stories adorned with statues of the Vestals surrounded an open court that was decorated with flower beds and three cisterns. In the court you can still see the remains of some of the statues and the pedestals on which they sat.

Arch of Titus

Erected to commemorate the victories of Vespasian and Titus after they conquered Jerusalem. The arch contains bas-reliefs of the Emperor and of soldiers carrying away the spoils of Jerusalem. One of the most imposing structures remaining from ancient Rome and a pilgrimage site for every Jewish tourist to the city.

Temple of Romulus

Built by the Emperor Maxentius who dedicated it to his deified son Romulus. A circular building that was converted to a church in the sixth century.

The Palatine Hill

This is one of the seven hills of Rome and was the residence of the Roman emperors during the Golden Age as well as the Imperial Period. It was here, in 754 BCE, that Romulus is said to have founded the city of Rome. But actual records and not just myth have indicated that settlement was actually established in the 9th century BCE. Aristocratic families also resided here, leaving behind wonderful architectural relics most of which have been excavated today, making the Palatine Hill one of the must-see places when you tour the Forum. It is also a wonderful respite from the hectic pace of Rome, filled with lush greenery and plenty of shade; it's a great place to have a picnic or go on a relaxing walk through history.

Here you'll find the baths of Septimus Severus, the Stadium of Domitian, the Farnese Gardens, the House of Livia, the Flavia Palace, the House of Augustana, and more. Many of the ruins are under excavation and as such are only occasionally accessible for foot traffic, but all can be viewed.

BATHS OF CARACALLA

Via Terme di Caracalla, Tel. 06/575-8626. Admission L8,000. Hours Monday–Saturday 9:00am until one hour before dark. Mondays and Holidays 9:00am–1:00pm. Buses 90, 90b, 118. Metro-Circo Massimo.

Built in 217 CE by the Emperor Caracalla, these baths were second in size only to the Baths of Diocletian. They were used until the sixth century when they were destroyed by Gothic invaders, and today it takes quite an imagination to reconstruct the building mentally. The baths were once rich with marble and statues and decorated with stucco and mosaic work. All that is left are the weathered remains of the massive brick structure which offers an insight into the scale of the baths, but doesn't offer a glimpse of their beauty. Today, on cool summer evenings, opera performances are held among the ruins of the **Calidarium**, the circular vapor bath area.

BATHS OF DIOCLETIAN

Viale E de Nicola. Open 9:00am-2:00pm, Holidats only until 1:00pm. Buses 57, 64, 65, 75, 170, 492, and 910. Metro-Repubblica.

These were the most extensive baths of their times in which more than 3,000 bathers could be accommodated at one time. They were built by Maximilian and Diocletian from 196–306 CE. Today the **National Museum** is located within their walls, as is the **Church of Santa Maria Degli Angeli**.

CAMPIDOGLIO

Piazza del Campidoglio 1. Open 9:00am-7:00pm. Closed Mondays. L10,000. Buses 94, 95, 713, 716. Metro-Colosseo.

The Capitoline Hill is one of the seven hills of Rome. It forms the northwest boundary of the Forum and today is home to the **Capitoline Museum, Senatorial Palace**, the **Palace of the Conservatori**, the **Church**

of Santa Maria D'Aracoeli (formerly the Temple of Juno Moneta), and the bronze **statue of Marcus Aurelius**. The Palazzo di Senatori (Senatorial Palace) was finished in the beginning of the 14th century; the statue was placed there in 1528, and the piazza along with the other two buildings were completed in 1570. These last three structures as well as the stairs leading up to them were based on a design developed by Michelangelo, who died in 1564 not seeing his plan completed.

The **Capitoline Museums** were founded by the Popes Clement XII and Benedict XIV and house some exquisite works (see Capitoline Museum in the *Museums* section below).

To ascend the hill, take either the steep stairway that leads to the church, the winding ramp of the Via delle Tre Pile, or from between the two of these by way of the monumental stairs, Cordonate, which were designed by Michelangelo. At the entrance to these stairs you'll find two imposing Egyptian lions and at the top you'll find the statues of Castor and Pollux.

The church of Santa Maria D'Aracoeli was originally a pagan temple then was converted for use as a Christian church. In the 12th century it was given its present form with a colonnade of mismatched ancient columns, stolen from a nearby Roman ruin, and a wide nave. The enormous set of stairs in front are one of the church's main features.

You must visit the museums on this hill, since they are second in magnificence only to the Vatican Museums, and certain exhibits are even better. Also, having your picture taken in front of the large pieces of Constantine's statue is a wonderful memento.

CIRCUS MAXIMUS

Via del Circo Massimo. Buses 15, 90, 90b, 94. Metro-Circo Massimo.

This circus (race-track) was established on the flat lands to the south of the fortified Palatine Hill. It was erected in 309 CE by the Emperor Maxentius in honor of his deified son Romulus, whose temple is nearby. Then in Imperial times it was expanded, destroyed, enlarged and used as a quarry until little is left of the original marble.

But today its shape is clearly visible underneath the contoured grass and earth, and some of the original seats remain at the turning circle of the southwestern end. The slight hump running through the center marks the location of the *spina*, around which the chariots, and at times runners, would race. In its prime the Circo Massimo could hold between 150,000-200,000 spectators, more than most modern stadiums.

CATACOMBS

Saint Callistus (Via Appia Antica 110, Tel. 06/513-6725. Closed Wednesday.)

San Sebastian (Via Appia Antica 132, Tel. 06/788-7035. Closed Thursday.)

Santa Domitilla (Via di Sette Chiese 282, Tel. 06/511-0342. Closed Tuesday.)

Entrance for each L10,000. Hours for each 8:30am-12:00pm and 2:30pm-5:00pm

Buses 118 and 218.

Located next door to one another on and around the Via Appia Antica south of the city, these tombs were originally an ancient Roman necropolis. They were then used by the early Christians as a meeting place as well as one of worship, and were finally a haven for them from prosecution. Here you can visit the **crypts of the Popes**, the crypt of Saint Cecilia, the crypt of Pope Eusebius, as well as frescoes dating back to the 3rd century CE. All three are an eerie reminder of the time before Christianity dominated the Western world. A time when Christians were actually the ones being persecuted instead of doing the persecuting. A great site for kids to explore.

ALTAR & MAUSOLEUM OF AUGUSTUS

Piazza Augosto Imperatore. Altar open 9:00am-2:00pm. You need to call to gain access to the mausoleum, Tel. 06/6710-3819. Closed Sundays. Buses 81, 90, 119, 926. Metro-Spagna.

This is an excellently preserved altar built from 13-9 BCE. Reconstructed and housed in this glass building in 1938 by Mussolini to glorify Italy's past, this marble structure is essentially a wall with a doorway that encloses the raised altar itself. The carved friezes on the walls were created by Greek masons imported to Rome.

The mausoleum of Augustus is the circular structure nearby overrun with grass and shrubs. It used to be a series of intricate passageways where niches of urns filled with funeral ashes were located, and it used to be topped with a large statue of Augustus. It has been used as a fort, a bull ring, a theater and a concert hall. In 1938 when the museum of Augustus was dedicated inside, the medieval buildings surrounding the mausoleum were razed and the present piazza was built, creating a rather stagnant, overly modern backdrop to this historic site.

PYRAMID OF GAIUS CESTIUS

Piazzale Ostiense. Buses 13, 23, 57, 95, 716. Metro-Piramide.

Built in 12 BCE as a tomb for the Praetor Gaius Cestius, this structure is a prime example of the influence that Egypt and its religion had on ancient Rome. During early Rome a cult of Egyptology was one of the largest of the pagan religions. Built of brick and rock and covered with limestone, this is one of the more striking structures left from ancient Rome and as such is a great photo op, one that my family has been coming back to since the '50s.

If you are out here in the mornings, other than Sunday, make a point of heading to the **Testaccio market** in Piazza Testaccio. A wonderfully authentic local market. If you're out here at night, or in the evenings, the Testaccio section is the place to be for nightlife in Rome. Rome's best discos are located here, and there are number of restaurants from which to choose.

PONTE MILVIO

Via Flaminia/Piazza Cardinale Consalvi. Take the 225 bus to Piazza Mancini and walk to Piazza Cardinale Consalvi, or take the 201 bus from Piazza Mancini.

Located north of the Aurelian and Servian walls, the Ponte Milvio was the first Roman bridge over the Tiber and was built in 109 CE. This bridge was the location of much military activity throughout Italian history, including one battle that helped establish Christianity as the world's dominant religion. Here in 312 CE the Christian Emperor Constantine defeated forces led by Maxentius who was then thrown into the river to perish after his defeat.

The current bridge has been destroyed and rebuilt countless times but retains its original form. It was last destroyed in 1849 when Garibaldi's troops blew it up to prevent the advance of the French army. In 1985 it was closed to vehicular traffic for restoration and remains a pedestrian bridge today.

AURELIAN WALL

Built from 272-279 CE, this wall is a testament to the faded glory of the Roman Empire. Built to protect Rome from an incursion of Germanic tribes, one of the best places to witness its protective shield is at the top of the Via Veneto at the **Porta Pinciana**. The walls enclosed not only the old city of Rome but also included land outside of the developed areas.

Today the walls extend to the Baths of Caracalla in the south, Piazza del Popolo in the north, Trastevere and Saint Peter's in the west, and the University and Stazione Termini in the East. They have a total length of about 12 miles; the walls of concrete rubble encased in brick are almost 12 feet thick and 25 feet high. In some places their height is 50 feet after extensions made in 309-12 and 402-3 CE. There is a parapet running across the top and there are 380 square towers interspersed along its length. These towers are a distance of two arrow shots apart, which was one hundred ancient Roman feet or just under 30 meters, which strangely enough is about 100 modern American feet.

There were 18 main roads where gates were built, many of which have been rebuilt to accommodate different defense strategies throughout the ages; most recently they were adapted for the onslaught of automobile traffic. The ones that are the best preserved with most of their Roman features are the **Porta San Sebastiano** (take bus 188 from San Giovanni in Laterano), **Porta Asinara** (next to Porta San Giovanni) and the **Porta Toscolana** (behind the train station).

COLUMN OF MARCUS AURELIUS

Piazza Colonna. Buses 56, 60, 62, 85. Metro-Barberini.

Carved between 180 and 196 CE, this column is a continuous spiral of sculptures celebrating Marcus Aurelius' military victories. It used to be surrounded by buildings from its own era, but only the ruins of the Temple of Hadrian in the wall of the *Borsa* remain (see description below). Statues of Marcus Aurelius and his wife used to adorn the top of the column, but they were replaced by St. Paul in the 16th century. Today this piazza has been made another of Rome's car-free zones, since the citizens of this city, as well as other cities in Europe, are realizing that automobiles may enhance individual transportation possibilities, but they drastically eliminate community livability.

TEMPLE OF HADRIAN

Piazza di Pietra. Buses 56, 60, 62, 85. Metro-Barberini.

Located near Piazza Colonna and the Via del Corso, this is a fantastic example of architectural pastiche, where structures from different eras are molded and blended together into one building. In this case, one wall of the modern Roman Stock Exchange (*Borsa*) has eleven Corinthian columns that remain from the temple dedicated by Antonius Pius to his father Hadrian in 145 CE. This is a great place for photos of how Rome's history is woven together with the present. Also note the path that runs in front of this sight, which leads to the Trevi Fountain and the Pantheon, as well as the exhibit sign describing what the significance of this sight is. By building this pathway and erecting these signs, as if these sights were actually exhibits in museums, Rome has decided to forgo being a museum in spirit and has started to make itself one in fact.

CHRISTIAN ROME

CASTEL SANT'ANGELO

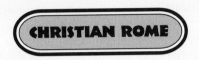

Lungotevere Castello 50, Tel. 06/687-5036. Admission L10,000. Open 9:00am–7:00pm. Closed the second and fourth Tuesdays of the month. Last entrance time is 1 hour before closing. Buses 23, 34, 64, 280, 982. Metro-Lepanto.

Also known as the **Mausoleum of Hadrian** since it was built for Hadrian and his successors, for eighty years it was used as a funeral monument where the ashes of the Roman emperors were stored. As the papacy began to establish itself near the tomb of St. Peter's during the Middle Ages, the structure was converted into a fortress for the Popes. During that period the bulky battlements and other military fortifications were added. A covered walkway leads from Saint Peter's to the Castel Sant'Angelo and, because of the volatile political situation in Italy for many centuries, this walkway was used more than once to protect the Pope. Since then it has been used as a residence for popes and princes, as a prison, and as a military barracks.

On the summit of the building is the statue of an angel (hence the name of the castle), and rumor has it that in 590 CE, Gregory the Great saw a vision with an avenging angel sheathing its sword at the summit of the castle. He took this to mean the plague that had ravaged Rome was over. To commemorate this event he placed an angel on top of the building. Today the castle houses a museum with one of the best collections ever assembled of armaments from the Stone Age to the present day. There are also some nondescript art exhibits and luxuriously preserved Papal apartments. A must-see when in Rome. A great site for kids to explore.

SAINT PETER'S

Piazza San Pietro. Hours 8:00am–6:00pm, but only until 5:00pm in the winter. Tel. 06/6988-4466. Buses 19, 62, 64, or 492. Metro-Ottaviano.

Located in the monumental square **Piazza San Pietro**, Saint Peter's is a masterpiece created by **Bernini** between 1655 and 1667, and is the largest church in the world. The square itself is oval and 240 meters at its largest diameter. It is composed of 284 massive marble columns, and 88 pilasters forming three galleries 15 meters wide. Surrounding the square, above the oval structure are 140 statues of saints.

In the center of the square is an obelisk 25.5 meters high with four bronze lions at its base, all of which were brought from Heliopolis during the reign of Caligula (circa 40 CE) and which originally stood in the circus

PROPER ATTIRE AT MUSEUMS & CHURCHES

When you're visiting most museums and monuments in Italy, follow these necessary rules: ***Women:*** *wear either long pants or a long skirt or dress, and a top with sleeves.* ***Men:*** *wear long pants and no tank tops.*

Both men and women will be denied entry to St. Peter's, and to many other sights as well, if you are wearing shorts or short skirts and/or a revealing top!

of Nero. It was placed here in 1586. Below the monument you can see the points of the compass and the names of the winds. Around this obelisk during the Christmas season a life-sized crèche is erected, and since 1980 has become a site that many Italians come to admire during that season. If in Italy during this time, come out and pay a visit, especially at night, when it is all lit up.

To reach Saint Peter's you must pass the obelisk and walk up a gradual incline. The church rises on the site where Saint Peter is buried. The early Christians erected a small oratory on the site of the tomb, but that was destroyed in 326 when Constantine the Great erected the first Basilica on this site. Over the centuries the church began to expand and became incongruously and lavishly decorated, so that by 1452 Nicholas V decided to make it more uniform. He commissioned Bernardo Rossellino to design a new structure. When the Pope died three years late this work was interrupted, but in 1506 Pope Julius II, with the assistance of Bramante, continued the work on a grander scale.

Bramante died in 1514 before his work could be finished. His successor was Raphael, and when he died four years later, Baldassare Peruzzi and Antonio de Sangallo the Younger took over the responsibility jointly. Work was interrupted by the sack of Rome in 1527, then again in 1536 when Peruzzi died. When Sangallo died in 1546, the project was taken over and modified by the 72-year old **Michelangelo**. Before he died eight years later, he had modified Bramante's plan for the dome and we are blessed with his pointed Florentine version today. After he died, the plans he made for St. Peter's were more or less adhered to by his successors Vignola, Pizzo Ligorio, Giacomo dell Porta, Domenico Fontana, and finally Carlo Maderno, who designed the facade according to his plan. On November 1, 1626, **Urbano VIII** dedicated the Basilica as we know it today.

The Facade

Rounding off, the **facade** is 115 meters long and 45 meters high, and is approached by a gradually sloping grand staircase. At the sides of this

FREE ENGLISH-LANGUAGE TOURS OF ST. PETER'S

One of the best ways to see St. Peter's and one of the least known is on an ***English-language tour*** *of the basilica by trained volunteer guides. Available seven days a week, Monday-Saturday at 3:00pm and Sundays at 2:30pm, the tour lasts an hour and a half and offers an in-depth historical and religious perspective of this magnificent church. The tours start at the information desk to the right as you enter the portico of St. Peter's. For more information, call 06/6972. To coordinate your day, go to the Vatican museums in the morning, have a light lunch, get here for the tour about half an hour early, and enjoy a stimulating and fact-filled afternoon.*

staircase are the statues of **Saint Peter** (by De Fabis) and **Saint Paul** (by Adamo Tadolini). On the balustrade, held up by eight Corinthian columns and four pilasters, are the colossal statues of the Savior and St. John the Baptist surrounded by the Apostles, excluding Saint Peter.

There are nine balconies, and from the central one the Pope gives his Christmas and Easter benedictions. There are five doors from which to enter the church, but today only the large central one is used.

The Interior

The church is more than 15,000 square meters in area, 211 meters long and 46 meters high. There are 229 marble columns: 533 of travertine, 16 of bronze, 90 of stucco, and 44 altars. On the floor of the central nave you'll find lines drawn identifying where other churches in the world would fit if placed in Saint Peter's. Kids love to explore this aspect of the basilica.

Also on the floor, near the front entrance, is a disk of red porphyry indicating the spot where **Charlemagne** was crowned Holy Roman Emperor by Leo III on Christmas Day in 800 CE. To the right of this, in the first chapel, is the world famous *Pieta* created by Michelangelo when he was only 24, in the year 1498. In the niches of the pilasters that support the arches are statues of the founders of many religious orders. In the last one on the right you'll find the seated bronze statue of Saint Peter. The statue's foot has been rubbed by so many people for good luck that it has almost disappeared.

Just past the statue is the grand **cupola** created by Michelangelo. One of the most amazing architectural wonders of all times, it is held up by four colossal spires which lead to a number of open chapels. Under the cupola, above the high altar rises the famous **Baldacchino** (or Grand Canopy) made by Bernini. It's made from bronze taken mainly from the roof of the

THE SWISS GUARDS

The world's smallest and perhaps most colorful army, The Swiss Guards were formed in 1506 by Pope Julius II as the papal protectors and remain so today. You can often see them in their trademark blue, red and yellow tunics, purported to have been designed by Michelangelo himself, with a plumed Spanish Conquistadorial helmet sitting jauntily on their heads. For routine work, the guards dress down to their more modern blue uniforms and berets.

This tiny force is all that is left of the papal military corps that medieval popes commanded to exert worldly power over much of the Italian peninsula, a power that has been reduced to the 108 acres of the Vatican City. Most of the guards' work is purely ceremonial, but their main task is much like that of the Secret Service in the U.S., except the Swiss Guards' protectee is the pope, not the president.

New recruits are sworn in annually on May 6, the anniversary of a 1527 battle in Rome in which 147 Swiss Guards were killed defending Pope Clement VIII from troops of the Holy Roman Emperor Charles V. To become a Swiss Guard one must be Roman Catholic of Swiss nationality, be under the age of 30, stand at least 5 feet 8 inches tall and be willing to learn Italian.

Pantheon. In front of the altar is the **Chapel of Confessions** made by Maderno, around which are 95 perpetually lit lamps illuminating the **Tomb of Saint Peter's**. In front of the shrine is the kneeling **Statue of Pius VI** made by Canova in 1822.

Throughout the rest of the Basilica you'll find a variety of superb statues and monuments (including the magnificent *Pieta* by Michelangelo), many tombs of Popes, and a wealth of chapels, not the least of which is the **Gregorian Chapel** designed by Michelangelo and executed by Giacomo della Porta. It is rich in marbles, stuccos, and mosaics, all put together in the creative Venetian style by Madonna del Soccorso in the 12th century.

If you grow tired of the many beautiful works of art and wish to get a bird's eye view of everything, you can ascend into Michelangelo's Cupola either by stairs (537 of them) or by elevator. If you come to Saint Peter's, you should do this. Kids of all age love it.

VATICAN CITY

Piazza San Pietro. Buses 19, 62, 64, or 492. Metro-Ottaviano. The city is generally inaccessible except for official business, but you can look into gardens from the cupola of St. Peter's.

Vatican City sits on the right bank of the Tiber river, in the foothills of the Monte Mario and Gianicolo section of Rome. In ancient Rome this was the site of the Gardens of Nero and the main circus where thousands of Christians were martyred. Saint Peter met his fate here around 67 CE. Today it is the world center for the Catholic Church, rich in priceless art, antiques, and spiritual guidance.

The Vatican (officially referred to as **The Holy See**) is a completely autonomous state within the Italian Republic and has its own radio station, railway, newspaper, stamps, money, and diplomatic representatives in major capitals. Though it doesn't have an army, the **Swiss Guards**, who are volunteers from the Swiss armed forces, guard the Vatican day and night.

PIAZZAS, FOUNTAINS, MONUMENTS, PALAZZI & GARDENS

PIAZZA NAVONA

Buses 70, 81, 87, 90.

The piazza is on the site of a stadium built by Domitian in 86 CE that he used for mock naval battles, other gladiatorial contests, as well as horse races. The stadium's north entrance has been excavated and you can see the stone arch of the entrance outside of the Piazza Navona toward the Tiber on the south side of the Piazza di Tor Sanguigna. Located some 20 feet below the current street level, this is an intimate glance at how much sediment has built up in Rome over the past 2,000 years.

After the Roman era the piazza was lined with small squatters' homes which followed the tiers of the stadium, but because of its wide open space it soon became a prime spot for large palazzi. Today the style of the piazza is richly Baroque, featuring works by two great masters, **Bernini** and **Borromini**. Located in the middle of the square is Bernini's fantastic **Fontana Dei Quattro Fiumi** (Fountain of Four Rivers), sculpted from 1647-51. The four figures supporting the large obelisk (a Bernini trademark) represent the four major rivers known at the time: the Danube, the Ganges, the Nile, and the Plata Rivers. The idea behind the representation of the statues is that the Catholic church reigns triumphant over the world.

Besides the statue's obvious beauty and meaning, Bernini has hidden a subtle treasure in this piece. When visiting Rome, notice the figure representing the Nile shielding its eyes. Some historians interpret the position of the figure's hand blocking its view of the facade of the church it is facing, **Santa Agnese in Agone**, as a statement of revulsion. This church was designed by Bernini's rival at the time, Borromini, and Bernini, as the story is told, playfully showed his disdain for his rival's design through the sculpted disgust in his statue. Others claim the revulsion comes from the fact that the church, built as a family chapel for Pope Innocent X's Palazzo Doria Pamphili, is located on the site of an old neighborhood brothel. Maybe both are true?

To the south of the piazza is the **Statue of Il Moro** (actually a replica) created by Bernini from 1652-54. To the north is a basin with a 19th century **Statue of Neptune** struggling with a sea monster.

To savor the artistic and architectural beauty, as well as the vibrant nightlife of the piazza, choose a table at one of the local bars or cafés and sample some excellent Roman *gelato* (ice cream), grab a coffee, or have a meal and watch the people go by. Navona has been one of Rome's many gathering spots for people of all ages since the early 18th century. You'll find local art vendors, caricaturists, hippies selling string bracelets, and much more. This is the place to come for ice cream in Rome, and Tre Scalini is the most famous *gelateria*. The piazza is also home to a fun Christmas fair that lasts from mid-December to mid-January. Filled with booths and performers, it is much like an old fashioned carnival that kids of all age love. Another feature of Navona that kids will love is that it contains two of Rome's best toy stores. This is a place you cannot miss if you come to Rome.

PIAZZA DI SPAGNA & THE SPANISH STEPS

Buses 52, 53, 56, 58, 60, 61, 62, 71, 81. Metro-Spagna.

This is one of the most beautiful and visited spots in Rome. It is named after the old Spanish Embassy to the Holy See that used to stand on the site. The 137 steps are officially called the *Scalinata della Trinita dei Monti*, and are named for the church which they lead to at the top. But most people just call them the **Spanish Steps**. The fountain in the middle of the piazza is known as the **Barcaccia** and was designed in 1628 by Pietro Bernini in commemoration of the big flood of 1598. To the right is the column of the **Immaculate Conception** erected in 1865 by Pius IX. The Spanish Steps were built in the 17th century. Besides being the location of fine works of art and architecture, it is also a favorite meeting spot for Italians of all ages.

CAMPO DEI FIORI

Campo dei Fiori. Buses 46, 62, 64, 65, 70.

This is a typically Roman piazza that hosts a lively flower and food market every morning until 1:00pm. Here you'll find the cries of the vendors blending with the bargaining of the customers. Though there are now some vendors specifically catering to the tacky souvenir needs of tourists, the majority of the stands are for the locals, and the majority of the visitors are the same. A perfect place to see and smell the vibrant local beauty and bounty of Rome.

The campo used to be a square where heretics were burned at the stake and criminals were hanged. The monument in the middle is in memory of Giordano Bruno, a famous philosopher who was burned here in 1600.

The campo is also a great place to come at night, because it is home to a great restaurant, **La Carbonara**, that serves the best *spaghetti alla vongole verace* I've ever had, and a great American-style bar, **The Drunken Ship**. It is also an active local shopping area. So if you're looking for intriguing and original items, or rare antiques, wander through the back streets around this piazza, Piazza Navona and the Pantheon.

TREVI FOUNTAIN

Piazza di Trevi. Buses 52, 53, 56, 58, 60, 61, 62, 71, 81. Metro-Barberini.

Another meeting place for Italians in the evenings. You'll always find an impromptu guitar solo being performed as well as wine being savored by many. A great place to hang out in the evenings and make new friends. This is the largest and most impressive of the famous fountains in Rome and is truly spectacular when it is lit up at night. Commissioned by Clement XII, it was built by Nicola Salvi in 1762 from a design he borrowed from Bernini and takes up an entire wall of the Palazzo Poli built in 1730. In the central niche you see Neptune on his chariot drawn by marine horses preceded by two tritons. In the left niche you see the statue representing Abundance, and to the right Health. The four statues up top depict the seasons and the crest is of the family of Clement XII, Corsini.

There is an ancient custom, legend, or myth, that says that all those who throw a coin into the fountain are destined to return to Rome. So turn your back to the fountain and throw a coin over your left shoulder with your right hand into the fountain and fate will carry you back. That is if you can get close enough. In the summer, and especially at night, this place is packed wall to wall with people. Also, please don't try and recreate Anita Ekberg's scene in the film *La Dolce Vita* when she waded through the fountain to taunt Marcello Mastroiani. It is completely illegal to walk in the fountain, and the authorities enforce this regulation severely. If they didn't, the local kids would all swim in and collect the coins thrown by tourists.

PANTHEON

Piazza della Rotonda. Tel. 06/6830-0230. Open Monday-Saturday 9:00am-6:30pm, Sundays 9:00am-1:00pm. At 10:00am on Sundays is a mass. Tel. 06/6830-0230. Buses 70, 81, 87, 90.

Located in a vibrant piazza, the **Pantheon** is one of the most famous and best preserved monuments of ancient Rome. Besides the architectural beauty, the entrance area to the Pantheon is by far the coolest place in Rome during the heat wave of August. So if you want to relax in cool comfort in the middle of a hot day, park yourself just in front of the entrance under the portico.

First constructed by Agrippa in 27 BCE, it was restored after a fire in 80 CE and returned to its original rotunda shape by the Emperor Hadrian. In 609 CE, it was dedicated as a Christian Church and called Santa Maria Rotunda. In the Middle Ages it served as a fortress. In 1620 the building's bronze ceiling was removed and melted into the cannons for Castel Sant'Angelo and used for Bernini's Baldacchino (Grand Canopy) in Saint Peter's that marks the site of the saint's tomb.

But during all this pillage the Pantheon was never left to ruin. It always remained in use and thoroughly maintained. The building is made up of red and gray Egyptian granite. Each of the sixteen columns is 12.5 meters high and is composed of a single block.

You enter the building by way of the cool and comfortable portal area and the original bronze door. As you enter it is impossible not to feel the perfect symmetry of space and harmony of its architectural lines. This feeling is somewhat lessened by the fact that the Roman authorities have placed a ticket booth inside along with a small souvenir stand each of which detracts from the perfection of the structure. Sad. Nonetheless you will still be awed by the marvelous dome (diameter 43 meters) with the hole in the middle through which rain cascades during moments of inclement weather.

There are three niches in the building, two of which contain tombs: the tomb of **Victor Emmanuel II** (died 1878), one of Italy's few war heroes, and the tombs of **Umberto I** (died 1900) and **Queen Margherita** (died 1926), and in another niche the tomb of renowned artist **Raphael Sanzio** (died 1520).

Around the Pantheon are a number of wonderful and famous cafes, restaurants and shops. It is a meeting place for locals and tourists alike and is a fun area to enjoy any time day or night.

THE BORGHESE GARDENS

Buses 95, 490, 495, 910. Metro-Spagna.

The most picturesque park in Rome, complete with bike and jogging paths (you can rent bikes in the park), a lake where you can rent boats, a wonderful museum – **Galleria Borghese** – lush vegetation, expansive grass fields, the Roman **zoological park**, a large riding ring, and more.

This is the perfect place to come and relax in the middle of a hard day of touring. Sundays fill the park with families, couples and groups of people biking, jogging, walking their dogs, playing soccer, strolling or simply relaxing in Rome's largest green space. Small food stands are interspersed in the park offering refreshments and snacks.

The gardens are a great sanctuary just outside the ancient walls of Rome. If you only want an afternoon's respite from the sights of the city, or you're tired of spending time in your hotel room during the siesta hours, escape to these luscious and spacious gardens.

To get to the gardens is simple enough: either exit the old walls of Rome through the gates at the Piazza del Popolo or at the top of the Via Veneto. From the Piazza del Popolo exit, the gardens will be on your right through the iron gates just across the busy Piazzale Flaminio. Once you enter you will be on the Viale Washington. Anywhere to the left of you, after a few hundred meters, will be prime park land. From the Via Veneto exit, cross the major thoroughfare in front of you and you're in the Borghese. From here stroll to your right and you will instantly find a pleasant area to picnic or take a small nap for the afternoon.

Borghese Gardens is home to Rome's **zoo** (but I would not recommend visiting it since the accommodations for the animals is criminal), several museums (including Galleria Borghese and the Galleria Arte Moderna), playing fields for *calcio*, a small lake, an amphitheater, and many wooded enclaves to have a wonderfully secluded picnic. Make sure you keep an eye for those heated Italian couples if you have kids in tow.

Galleria Borghese

One of Rome's finest museums is in the Borghese Gardens, the **Galleria Borghese**. For those of you who entered the Gardens from Piazza del Popolo, it will be a long hike up the Viale Washington to the lake, and around it to the Viale Dell'Uccelleria (the zoo will be on your left) which leads directly to the Galleria Borghese.

From the Via Veneto it is not quite as long. From where you first entered the gardens, there is a road, Viale Del Museo Borghese, on your right. Take this all the way to the Galleria.

The Galleria Borghese was built by Dutch architect Hans van Santes during the 1820's. It houses a large number of rare masterpieces from many disciplines and countries. There are classical works of Greeks and Romans, along with 16th and 17th century paintings by such notables as Raphael, Titian, Caravaggio, and Antonella da Messina. Sculptures are also featured with works by Lorenzo Bernini, Pietro Bernini, and Houndon. A must see when in Rome.

For more details, see the Galleria Borghese description below under *Museums.*

VITTORIO EMANUELE II MONUMENT

Piazza Vittorio Emanuele. Buses 70, 81, 87, 90.

A monument to the first king of Italy who died in 1878. Work started in 1885 but was not finished until 1910. It is an inflated version of the Temple of Fortune on the hillside at Praenestina. To all in Rome it is affectionately called "The Wedding Cake," since its shape and white marble make it look eerily like a larger version of one. The monument is also home to the tomb of the unknown soldier.

ISOLA TIBERINA

Buses 44, 75, 170, 710, 718, 719.

Halfway across the river going towards Trastevere, this island used to be a dumping ground for dead and sick slaves. At that time, the 3rd century BCE, there was a cult of healing *(aesculapius)* located here. Currently half the island is taken up by a hospital showing that traditions do live on. The church on the island, **San Bartolomeo** was built in the 12th century, and was substantially altered in the seventeenth. One of the bridges to the mainland, **Ponte Fabricio**, is the oldest in Rome. A fun place to explore with wide walkways around the island and along the river. If you have kids, keep them in tow because there are no railings.

PONTE FABRICIO (DEI QUATTRO CAPI)

There is some debate as to whether this is the oldest span in Rome still in use, or the Ponte Milvio. The actual first bridge in Rome the, **Pons Aemilius**, an arch of which is still visible south of the Isola Tiberina, and was washed away in 1598 and never rebuilt. This is a good place to cross the Tiber going towards Trastevere after you've been exploring the Jewish Ghetto and the Sinagoga.

PALAZZO BARBERINI

Via delle Quattro Fontane, 13. Tel. 06/482-4184. Admission L10,000. Hours 9:00am–9:00pm Tuesday-Friday, until midnight on Saturdays, until 8:00pm on Sundays. Closed Mondays. Buses 95, 490, 495, 910. Metro-Barberini.

Located just off the Piazza Barberini on the Via Quattro Fontane, this baroque palace was started by Carlo Maderno in 1623 with the help of Borromini and was finished in 1633 by Bernini. When the entrance was rearranged to the south from the northeast in 1864, the baroque iron gates were designed, built and installed by Francesco Azzuri.

One wing of the palace is the site of the **Galleria Nazionale d'Arte Antica**. Besides the wonderful architecture which is impossible to miss, the gallery has many wonderful paintings such as *Marriage of St. Catherine* by Sodoma, *Portrait of a Lady* by Piero di Cossimo, and *Rape of the Sabines* by Sodoma. A wonderful little museum, and a great place to visit in the evenings since it stays open so late.

PALAZZO FARNESE

Piazza Farnese. Buses 23, 65, 70, or 280.

This palace represents one of the high points of Renaissance architecture. It was started in 1514 by Antonio da Sangallo the Younger for Cardinal Alessandro Farnese (later Pope Pius III), and was continued by Michelangelo who added the large window, the molding on the facade, the third floor of the court, and the sides. It was finally finished by Giacomo della Porta. As well as being an architectural wonder, there is a first floor gallery of frescoes depicting mythological subjects by the painters Carracci, Domenichino, and Reni.

The palace became the French Embassy in 1625 and remains so today. As such it is not open to the public unless you get written permission from the French government.

ROMAN NEIGHBORHOODS

PIAZZA DEL POPOLO

Buses 90, 119. Metro-Flaminio.

This impressive piazza is the base of the ascent to the **Pincio**, a relaxing area of Rome where you can get some great views of the city. It was consolidated as a piazza in 1538 during the Renaissance, and today has been made another car-free zone in the city of Rome. Citizens of this city, as well as other cities in Europe, are realizing that automobiles may enhance individual transportation possibilities, but they drastically eliminate livability. In 1589, the **Egyptian Obelisk** which is 24 meters high and came from Egypt during the time of Ramses II in the 8th century BCE, was moved from the Circus Maximus and erected in the middle of the square. The present layout was designed by G. Valadier at the beginning of the 19th century and is decorated on its sides with two semi-cycles of flowers and statues. During this re-design the obelisk was placed in a new fountain with the present sculpted lions.

There are two symmetrical baroque churches at the south end of the piazza flanking the intersection of the Via del Corso. These two churches,

Santa Maria dei Miracoli (1678) – also called Santa Maria del Popolo – and **Santa Maria in Monesanto** (1675) both have picturesque cupolas that were begun by C. Rainaldi and finished by Bernini and Carlo Fontana respectively.

EERIE ROMAN TRIVIA

There is a movie theater directly next to Santa Maria dei Miracoli that played the first-run release of the "Exorcist" when it came out in the 1970's. During the first showing of the film, the cross on the top of the church dislodged itself from its perch and shattered itself directly in front of the movie theater. No one was hurt but all of Italy was shocked. This is a true story.

VIA VENETO

Buses 52, 53, 56, 58. Metro-Barberini.

Definitely the most famous and most fashionable street in Rome. It used to be the center of all artistic activities as well as the meeting place for the jet set, but it doesn't quite have the same allure it used to. Nonetheless, it's still a great place to wander since it is flanked by wonderful hotels, stores, and cafés.

At the bottom of the street is the **Piazza Barberini**, where you'll find the graceful **Fontana delle Api** (Fountain of the Bees) as well as the more famous **Fontana del Tritone**, both designed and sculpted by Bernini. Both sculptures were created to celebrate the Barberini family and their new palace just up the Via delle Quattro Fontane. Up the Via Veneto a little ways from the Piazza Barberini is the grandiose **Palazzo Margherita**, built by G. Koch in 1890 and is now the home of the American Embassy. You'll recognize it by the armed guards and the American flag flying out front.

CHURCH OF BONES

Right at the bottom of the Via Veneto you will find the famous 'Church of Bones,' **Santa Maria della Concezione**. In the **Cappucin crypt** of the church there is a macabre arrangement of the bones of over 4,000 skeletons of ancient friars who were exhumed and decoratively placed on the walls. The reason this display exists is that a law was passed many centuries ago which decreed that no graveyards or burial grounds could exist inside the walls of Rome. Rather than part with the remains of their brothers by re-burying them in a cemetery outside the walls, the Cappucin brothers exhumed the fraternal remains and decorated the crypt with them. I guarantee that you'll never see a sight like this anywhere else.

VIA APPIA ANTICA

Buses 118 and 218.

The most celebrated of all Roman roads was begun by Appius Claudius Caecus in 312 BCE. The road has been preserved in its original character as have the original monuments. At first it was the chief line of communication between Rome and Southern Italy, Greece, and the eastern possessions of the Roman Empire. Now it is a well traveled picturesque road to the country and the famous Roman/Christian **catacombs.**

TRASTEVERE

Buses 44, 75, 170, 710, 718, 719.

This is the perfect place to immerse yourself in Roman life. **Trastevere** literally means "across the river" and this separation has allowed the area to remain virtually untouched by the advances of time. Until recently it was one of the poorest sections of Rome, but now it is starting to become gentrified. Yet these changes have not altered Trastevere's charm. You'll find interesting shops and boutiques, and plenty of excellent restaurants among the small narrow streets and *piazzette* (small squares). The maze of streets is a fun place to wander and wonder where you're going to end up.

During the month of July the *Trasteverini* express their feeling of separation from the rest of Rome with their summertime festival called **Noiantri**, meaning "we the others," in which they mix wine-induced revelry with religious celebration in a party of true bacchanalian proportions. *Trasteverini* cling to their roots of selling clothing and furnishings to make ends meet by continuing to hold the **Porta Portese** flea market on Sundays. The market and event are true Trastevere even though the area has been gentrified for decades.

This area offers some of the best dining and casual nightlife in town. Here you can sit in a piazza bar sipping Sambuca or wine and watch the life of Rome pass before your eyes. To accommodate this type of activity many stores have begun to stay open later. Trastevere is a great place to enjoy for a day or even more, because it is the way Rome used to be.

JEWISH GHETTO

Buses 780, 774, 717.

Long before any Pope reigned in Rome, another religion thrived here: Judaism. The ancient Jewish quarter is a peaceful, tiny riverside neighborhood with narrow curving street and ocher apartment buildings. It looks much like any other section of Rome until closer inspection reveals Kosher food signs, men in skullcaps and spray painted stars of David. Technically the Ghetto ceased to exist in 1846 when its walls were torn down, but the neighborhood that retains its name remains home to Europe's oldest and proudest Jewish community.

The history of the Jews in Rome dates back to 161 BCE when Judas Maccabaeus sent ambassadors to Rome to seek protection against the Syrians. Over time many traders followed these emissaries and a Jewish community sprouted. After Rome colonized and eventually conquered the Land of Israel culminating in 70 CE with the fall of Jerusalem and the destruction of its Temple (an event etched in stone on the Arch of Titus), over a short time as many 40,000 Jews settled in Rome. They contributed in all aspects of Roman society and they and their religion were accepted as different but equal. But that was before Christianity became the religion of the state, at which point discrimination against the Jews became widespread.

In the 13th century, for instance, the Catholic Church ordered Jews to wear a distinctive sign on their clothing: a yellow circle for men and two blue stripes for women. Anti-Semitism continued to grow to the point where in 1556, Pope Paul IV confined all Jews to this small poor section of the city and closed it in with high walls. This was not the first virtual imprisonment of its kind, because the Venetians did the same thing to its Jewish population four decades earlier. In Venice the Jews were forced to live on the site of an old cannon foundry, or *getto*. The name stuck and has since evolved to mean any section of a city that is composed of one type of activity (e.g., an Office Ghetto), or is inhabited by one group of people, usually underprivileged.

Today there are only about 400 Jews living in this quaint little neighborhood that harbors so many memories. And because of those memories the Ghetto is still the meeting place for the Jews of Rome. To find out more about this neighborhood stop in the **Jewish Museum** in the **Sinagoga** *(Lungotevere de Cenci, Tel. 06/684-0061, Fax 06/6840-0684; open 9:00am-6:30pm Tuesday-Friday, until 8:00pm on Sundays and also from 9:00pm-midnight on Saturdays in the summer)*. Inside you will find a plan of the original ghetto, as well as artifacts from the 17th century Jewish community.

Besides learning about the history of the ghetto, you can find some of Rome's truly great restaurants here along with many ancient Roman buildings, arches, and columns completely incorporated into modern day buildings. It seems as if a number of structures have been better preserved in this area. Maybe it is because the locals did not have the resources to tear them down and replace them. Whatever the situation, visit the Ghetto and feel history come alive.

GIANICOLO

Piazza Garibaldi. Bus 41.

Offering one of the best panoramas of Rome, the **Gianicolo Hill** is located between Trastevere and the Vatican, across the river from the old city of Rome. At the terrace of the Piazza Garibaldi, you'll find the equestrian statue of Giuseppe Garibaldi, as well as a panoramic photo, with accompanying titles for all the domes and buildings of note, of the scene laid out in front of you This is a perfect photo opportunity. The walk may be a little tiring but the view is calming and serene.

CHURCHES

SAINT PAUL'S OUTSIDE THE WALLS

Via Ostiense. Church open 7:00am–6:00pm. Cloisters Open 9:00am–1:00pm and 3:00pm–6:00pm. Metro-San Paolo.

Located a short distance beyond the Porta Paolo, **St. Paul's Outside the Walls** (San Paolo Fuori le Mura) is the fourth of the patriarchal basilicas in Rome. It is second only in size to St. Peter's and sits above the tomb of St. Paul. It was built by Constantine in 314 CE and then enlarged by Valentinian in 386 CE and later by Theodosius. It was finally completed by Honorius, his son.

In 1823, the church was almost completely destroyed by a terrible fire and many of its great works of art were lost. Immediately afterward, its renovation began and today it seems as magnificent as ever. (So much so that every time my family returns to Rome, whoever is left lines up just inside to the left of the entrance to the *quadroportici* with its 150 granite columns and get our picture taken with the palm trees in the background. We've been doing this since the 1950's and in that time the palms have grown from stubby bushes into gigantic trees.) With the beautiful garden surrounded by the great rows of columns, the palms growing in the center, the gigantic statue of St. Paul, and the facade with mosaics of four prophets (Isaiah, Jeremaih, Ezekial, and Daniel), just getting inside this church is a visual treat.

The interior is 120 meters long and has four rows of columns and five naves. The columns in the central nave are Corinthian that can be identified by their splendidly ornate capitals. The walls contain Medallion Portraits of the Popes from Saint Peter to Pius XI. On the High Altar still sits the ancient Gothic tabernacle of Arnolfo di Cambio (13th century) that was saved from the fire in 1823. Saint Paul rests beneath the altar in the confessional. The mosaic in the apse, with its dominating figure of Christ, was created by artists from the Republic of San Marino in 1220.

To the left of the apse is the **Chapel of St. Stephen**, with the large statue of the saint created by R. Rainaldi, and the **Chapel of the Crucifix** created by Carlo Maderno. This chapel contains the crucifix which is said to have spoken to Saint Bridget in 1370. Also here is St. Ignatius de Loyola, who took the formal vows that established the Jesuits as a religious order. To the right of the apse is the **Chapel of San Lorenzo** and the **Chapel of Saint Benedict** with its 12 columns. One other place of note in the church are the cloisters that contain fragments of ancient inscriptions and sarcophagi from the early Christian era.

SANTA MARIA SOPRA MINERVA

Piazza della Minerva (behind the Pantheon). Hours 7:00am–7:00pm. Buses 70, 81, 87, 90.

Built on the pagan ruins of a temple to Minerva (hence the name) this must-see church was begun in 1280 by the Dominican Order which also commissioned the beautiful Santa Maria Novella in Florence. With their wide Gothic vaulted nave and aisles, the two churches are much alike in design. The facade was created during the Renaissance by Meo del Caprino in 1453.

In this expansive church, you can find many tombs of famous personages of the 15th through the 16th centuries as well as beautiful paintings, sculptures, frescoes and bas relief work. Saint Catherine of Siena, who died in Rome in 1380, rests at the high altar. To the left of the altar is the statue of *Christ Carrying the Cross* created by Michelangelo in 1521. The bronze drapes were added later for modesty. If you compare this work to the one to the right of the altar, *John the Baptist* by Obici, you can easily see why Michelangelo is considered such a master. His statue looks like it could come to life, while Obicis is just carved out of stone.

Behind the altar are the tombs of Pope Clement VII and Leo X which were created by the Florentine sculptor Baccio Bandanelli. In the Sacristy is a chapel covered with frescoes by Antoniazzo Romano, brought here in 1637 from the house where Catherine of Siena died.

In front of the church is a wonderful sculpture designed by Bernini and carved by Ercole Ferrata called *Il Pulcino* of an elephant with an obelisk on his back.

SAN PIETRO IN VINCOLI

Piazza di San Pietro in Vincoli. Hours 7:00am–12:30pm and 3:30pm–6:00pm. Metro-Cavour.

Located only a few blocks from the Colosseum, this church was founded in 442 by the Empress Eudoxia as a shrine dedicated to preserving the chains with which Herod bound St. Peter in Jerusalem. These chains are in a crypt under the main altar.

THE MASTERS IN ROME

Listed here are where you can find some of the works of the Masters of Italian art:

***Michelangelo** – Sistine Chapel, Statue of Moses (San Pietro in Vincoli), Pieta (St. Peter's), Dome of St. Peter's, Christ Carrying the Cross (SM Sopra Minerva), Campidoglio square and steps.*

***Bernini** – The Ecstasy of Santa Teresa (SM della Vittoria, Via XX Settembre 17), Ecstasy of Beata Ludovica Albertoni (S. Francesco a Ripa, P.za S. Fracesco d'Assisi), the Baldacchino (St. Peter's), the Throne (St. Peter's), the Tomb of Pope Alexander VII (St. Peter's) the square and colonade of St. Peter's, Fountain of the Four Rivers (Piazza Navona), San Andrea al Quirinale, Elephant Obelisk (outside of SM Sopra Minerva), Ponte San Angelo.*

***Caravaggio** – Painting of Saints Peter and Paul (SM del Popolo), Madonna dei Pellegrini (SanAgostino, Via della Scrofa 80), The Life of St. Matthew (three paintings in S. Luigi dei Fracesi), and a number of works, including Young Girl with Basket of Fruit, and The Sick Bacchus (which is a self-portrait) in the Borghese Gallery.*

***Raphael** – Numerous works, including Lady of the Unicorn and Deposition in the Borghese Gallery, Chigi Chapel (SM del Popolo), La Fornarina (Palazzo Barberini), Cherub holding a Festoon (Academy of San Luca), Double Portrait (Doria Pamphili Gallery), The Prophet Isaiah (Sant'Agostino), the Loggia di Psiche (Villa Farnesina), and a number of works, including the School of Athens, in the Vatican Museums.*

But the reason to come to this church is the tomb of Julius II. Not really the tomb itself, because the great patron of the arts Julius is actually interred in St. Peter's, but come for the unforgettable seated figure of *Moses*. Created by the master himself, Michelangelo, this statue captures the powerful personification of justice and law of the Old Testament.

In fact, Moses appears as if he is ready to leap to his feet and pass judgment on you as you stand there admiring him. You can almost see the cloth covering his legs, or the long beard covering his face move in the breeze. Flanking Moses are equally exquisite statues of *Leah* and *Rachel* also done by Michelangelo. Everything else was carved by his pupils. Because of this one work, this church is definitely worth your time.

SANTA MARIA MAGGIORE

Piazza di Santa Maria Maggiore. Tel. 06/483-195. Hours 8:00am–7:00pm. Buses 4, 9, 16, 27, 714, 715. Metro-Termini.

Like St. Paul's Outside the Walls, St. Peter's, and St. John Lateran, this is one of the four patriarchal basilicas of Rome. Its name derives from the fact that it is the largest church (*maggiore*) in Rome dedicated to the Madonna (*maria*). The facade, originally built in the 12th century, was redone in the 18th century to include the two canon's houses flanking the church. It is a simple two story facade and as such is nothing magnificent to look at, and as result, if you are not going out of your way to come here, many people simply amble on by.

But the interior, in all its 86 meters of splendor, is interesting and inspiring mainly because of the 5th-century mosaics, definitely the best in Rome, its frescoes, and multi-colored marble. On the right wall of the **Papal Altar** is the funeral monument to Sixtus V and on the left wall the monument to Pius V, both created by Fontana with excellent bas-reliefs. Opposite this chapel is the **Borghese Chapel**, so called since the sepulchral vaults of the wealthy Borghese family lie beneath it. Here you'll view the beautiful bas-relief monumental tombs to Paul V and Clement VIII on its left and right walls. Towards the west end of the church is the **Sforza Chapel** with its intricately designed vault. Pius VI's eerie crypt is below and in front of the main altar.

SAN GIOVANNI IN LATERANO

Piazza San Giovanni in Laterano 4, Tel. 06/7720-7991. Hours Bapistery: 6:00am–12:30pm and 4:00–7:00pm; Cloisters 9:00am-5:00pm. Buses 16, 85, 87, and 650. Metro-San Giovanni.

Another of the great basilicas of Rome. Most people don't realize that this church is the cathedral of Rome as well as the whole Catholic world, and not St. Peter's. Established on land donated by Constantine in 312 CE, that first building has long been replaced by many reconstructions, fires, sackings and earthquakes over the centuries. Today, the simple and monumental facade of the church, created by Allessandro Galiliei in 1735, is topped by fourteen colossal statues of Christ, the Apostles, and saints. It rises on the site of the ancient palace of Plautinus Lateranus (hence the name), one of the noble families of Rome many eons ago.

To get inside, you must pass through the bronze door that used to be attached to the old Roman Senate house. The interior of the church, laid out in the form of a Latin cross, has five naves filled with historical and artistic objects. In total it is 150 meters long, while the **central nave** is 87 meters long. This central nave is flanked by 12 spires from which appear 12 statues of the Apostles from the 18th century. The wooden ceiling and the marble flooring are from the 15th century.

The most beautiful artistic aspect of the church is the vast transept, which is richly decorated with marbles and frescoes portraying the *Leggenda Aurea* of Constantine. One piece of historical interest is the wooden table, on which it is said that Saint Peter served mass, which you'll find in the **Papal Altar**.

SAN CLEMENTE

Via di San Giovanni Laterano. Admission L4,000 (to the lower church). Hours to visit the basement 9:00am–1:00pm. Not on Sundays. Catch bus 65. Metro-San Giovanni.

Located between the Colosseum and St. John Lateran is this hidden gem of a church, **San Clemente**. One of the better preserved medieval churches in Rome, it was originally built in the fifth century. The Normans destroyed it in 1084 but it was reconstructed in 1108 by Pachal II. Today when you enter you are in what is called the **Upper Church**, a simple and basic basilica divided by two rows of columns. Above the altar are some intricately inlaid 12th century mosaics.

The thrill of this church is that you can descend a set of stairs to the **Lower Church**, which was discovered in 1857, and immediately you have left the Middle Ages and are now in subterranean passages that housed an early Christian place of worship, from the days when Christians had to practice their religion below ground for fear of persecution.

Even further below that are the remains of a temple dedicated to Mithraic, a religion that practised in the 4th century CE known for their barbaric blood rites. Brought to Rome from Asia Minor in 67 BCE by soldiers of Rome's Legions, this pagan religion became entrenched in the military because of its bonds of violence, fidelity, loyalty and secrecy. Before the Roman Legions adopted it, Mithraic was the religion of Alexander the Great's army.

This is a must see church while in Rome. They also have a bucolic little porticoed garden, where you can relax, with a spritzing fountain in the center.

SANTA CECILIA IN TRASTEVERE

Via Anicia. Hours 10:00am–noon and 4:00pm–6:00pm. Buses 181, 280, 44, 75, 717, 170, 23, 65.

Normally visitors don't go to Trastevere to visit churches. Instead they are attracted by the more secular delights of this part of Rome. But if you're interested in beautiful churches, **Santa Cecilia** is one to visit in Trastevere; the other is Santa Maria.

Santa Cecilia was founded in the fifth century and had a make-over in the ninth century as well as the 16th. A baroque door leads to a picturesque court, beyond which is a baroque facade, with a mosaic frieze above the portico, and a beautiful bell tower erected in the 12th century. There are several important works of art to be found in the church, not the least of which is the expressive statue of Santa Cecilia by Stefano

Maderno. It represents the body of the saint in the exact position it was found when the tomb was opened in 1559.

Another place of interest to visit on the church grounds is the Roman house where Santa Cecilia suffered her martyrdom by being exposed to hot vapors. There are two rooms preserved, one of them the bath where she died. It still has the pipes and large bronze cauldron for heating water. A great church to visit, not just for the art, but also for the history.

SANTA MARIA IN TRASTEVERE

Piazza Santa Maria in Trastevere 1. Hours 7:00am–7:00pm. Mass at 9:00am, 10:30am, noon, and 6:00pm. Buses 181, 280, 44, 75, 717, 170, 23, 65.

A small church in Trastevere, in a piazza of the same name that is frequented by many locals and tourists alike, making the church one of the most visited. Around this church are some of the best restaurants and cafés in all of Rome, a popular English language theater, a handsome 17th century fountain where hippies hang out, and the Palace of San Calisto.

This was one of Rome's earliest churches and the first to be dedicated to the Virgin Mary. It was built in the 4th century and remodeled between 1130-1143. It is best known for its prized mosaics, especially the 12th and 13th century representation of the Madonna which adorns the facade of the church. The Romanesque bell-tower was built in the 12th century. The interior is of three naves separated by columns purloined from ancient Roman temples.

On the vault you'll find exquisite mosaics depicting the Cross, emblems of the Evangelists, and Christ and the Madonna enthroned among the Saints (created by Domenichino in 1140). Lower down, the mosaics of Pietro Cavallini done in 1291 portray, in six panels, the life of the Virgin.

MUSEUMS

CAPITOLINE MUSEUM

Piazza del Campidoglio 1. Tel. 06/6710-2071, Admission L10,000. Hours 9:00am-7:00pm. Closed Mondays. Buses 44, 46, 56, 57, 90, 90, 94, 186, 710, 713, 718, 719. Entrance L10,000.

The **Capitoline Museum** is actually two museums, the **Capitoline** and the **Palazzo dei Conservatori**. The Capitoline Museum is the perfect place to come to see what ancient Romans looked like. Unlike Greek sculpture, which glorified the subject, Roman sculpture captured every realistic characteristic and flaw. There are rooms full of portrait busts dating back to the republic and imperial Rome, where you have many individuals of significance immortalized here, whether they were short, fat, thin, ugly. Here they remain, warts and all. Because of these very real depictions of actual Romans, and many other more famous sculptures, this museum ranks only second in importance to the Vatican collections.

Besides the busts, you'll find a variety of celebrated pieces from antiquity including *Dying Gaul*, *Cupid and Psyche*, the *Faun*, and the nude and voluptuous *Capitoline Venice*. Then in the **Room of the Doves** you'll find two wonderful mosaics that were taken from Hadrian's Villa many centuries ago. One mosaic is of the doves drinking from a basin, and the other is of the masks of comedy and tragedy. Besides these items in the interior, the exterior itself was designed by none other than the master himself, Michelangelo.

The **Palace of the Conservatori** is actually three museums in one, the **Museum of the Conservatori**, the **New Museum**, and the **Pinocoteca Capitolina**. It too was also constructed by a design from Michelangelo. What draws me to them, as well as most people young at heart, are the largest stone head, hand and foot you're ever likely to see. A great place to take a few pictures. These pieces are fragments from a huge seated statue of Constantine.

You could wander here among the many ancient Roman and Greek sculptures and paintings but remember to see the famous *Boy with a Thorn*, a graceful Greek sculpture of a boy pulling a thorn out of his foot, the *She-Wolf of the Capitol*, an Etruscan work of Romulus and Remus being suckled by the mythical wolf of Rome, the death mask bust of Michelangelo, the marble *Medusa* head by Bernini, the celebrated painting *St. Sebastian* by Guido Reni that shows the saint with arrows shot into his body, and the famous Caravaggio work, *St. John the Baptist*.

NATIONAL MUSEUM - MUSEO DELLE TERME

Baths of Diocletian, Viale delle Terme. Admission L2,000. Hours 9:00am–2:00pm. Holidays until 1:00pm. Closed Mondays. Buses 57, 64, 65, 75, 170, 492, 910. Metro-Repubblica.

If you like ancient sculpture you'll enjoy this collection of classical Greek and Roman works, as well as some early Christian sarcophagi and other bas-relief work. Located in the **Baths of Diocletian**, which are something to see in and of themselves, this museum is easily accessible since it is located near the train station and right across from the Repubblica Metro stop. Since there are so many fine works here, you should spend a good half day perusing the items, but remember to start with the best, which are located in the *Hall of Masterpieces*. Here you'll find the *Pugilist*, a bronze work of a seated boxer, and the *Discobolus*, a partial sculpture of a discus thrower celebrated for its amazing muscle development.

At the turn of the century this collection was graced with the Ludovisi assembled, collected by Cardinal Ludovico Ludovisi and a number of Roman princes. The most inspiring of these many fine works of art is the celebrated *Dying Gaul and His Wife*, a colossal sculpture from Pergamon created in the third century BCE. The collection also contains the famous Ludovisi throne, created in the 5th century BCE and which is adorned with fine Greek bas-reliefs.

Another must-see in the museum is the *Great Cloister*, a perfectly square space surrounded by an arcade of one hundred Doric columns. It is one of the most beautiful architectural spaces in Rome, which is saying something. Rumor has it that it was designed and built by Michelangelo in 1565, which may be the case, but since he was so busy many experts believe that it is actually the work of one of his more famous, and possibly intimate pupils, Jacopo del Duca. Another great museum to see in Rome.

ROME THE MUSEUM

For years Rome has been considered a museum in and of itself, but finally the city fathers have made it official. Rome's sights still stand out for all to see, but now Rome has constructed a pathway between many of the major sights in the centro storico area (including Trevi Fountain and the Pantheon) with an official sign, like you would find in an exhibit in a museum, describing the history and significance of each sight – in Italian, English, and Braile.

GALLERIA BORGHESE

Villa Borghese, Piazza dell'Uccelliera 5. Tel. 06/632-8101. Admission L12,000. Hours 9:00am–9:00pm, until midnight on Saturdays, only until 8:00pm on Sundays. Closed Mondays. Entrance is only available in two hour increments starting at 9am. Closed Mondays. Buses 95, 490, 495, 910. Metro-Spagna.

Located in the most picturesque public park in Rome, and housed in a beautiful villa constructed in the 17th century, the ground floor contains the sculpture collection, which would be considered without peer if not for the fact that it is located in Rome where there are a number of other superb collections. The sculptures are just the appetizer because the main draw of this museum is the beauty of the gallery of paintings on the first floor.

But before you abandon the sculptures, take note of the reclining *Pauline Borghese*, created by Antonio Canova in 1805. She was the sister of Napoleon, and was married off to one of the wealthiest families in the world at the time to ensure peace and prosperity. She looks quite enticing posing half naked on a lounge chair. Another work not to miss is *David and the Slingshot* by Bernini in 1619. It is a self-portrait of the sculptor. Other works by Bernini are spotlighted and intermixed with ancient Roman statuary.

On the first floor there are many great paintings, especially the *Madonna and Child* by Bellini, *Young Lady with a Unicorn* by Raphael, *Madonna with Saints* by Lotto, and some wonderful works by Caravaggio. If you are in Rome, you have to visit this museum. Advanced booking is suggested from *www.ticketeria.it,* otherwise you may not gain access since there are a limited number of spaces available. There is a gift shop and snack bar in the basement area where you pick up your reserved tickets. You will also have to relinquish your handbags, camera, umbrellas, etc., for safekeeping at the basement baggage area.

MUSEUM OF VILLA GIULIA

Piazza di Villa Giulia 9. Tel. 06/332-6571. Admission L10,000. Hours 9:00am–6:30pm Tues-Fri, Sundays until 8:00pm and Saturdays in the summer open also from 9:00pm-midnight. Closed Mondays. Buses 19b or 30b. Metro-Flaminio.

Located in the Palazzo di Villa Giulia, built in 1533 by Julius III, and situated amid the Borghese Gardens, this incredible archaeological museum contains 34 rooms of ancient sculptures, sarcophagi, bas-reliefs, and more, mainly focusing on the Etruscan civilization. Items of interest include the statues created in the 5th century BCE of a *Centaur,* and *Man on a Marine Monster;* Etruscan clay sculptures of *Apollo, Hercules with a Deer,* and *Goddess with Child;* objects from the Necropoli at Cervetri including a terra-cotta work of *Amazons with Horses* created in the 6th century BCE and a sarcophagus of a "married couple," a masterpiece of Etruscan sculpture from the 6th century BCE.

PALAZZO ALTEMPS

Museo Nazionale Romano, Piazza Sant'Appolinare 44, Tel. 06/683-3759. Open 9:00am-9:00pm Tues-Thurs and until midnight every other day except Monday when it is closed. Entry L10,000.

A must see museum while in Rome. Located just outside the Piazza Navona, this little museum has an elegant collection of sculptures and paintings, but best of all it is a respite from the frenetic pace of Rome. Tranquility abounds in this peaceful museum that is an architectural curiosity in and of itself. Besides the excellent pieces inside, the building itself offers a glimpse into what life was like many years ago in Rome. The inner courtyard is mesmerizing and the private chapel an oasis of calm.

ART COPIES MADE TO ORDER

Have you ever wanted to own a Michelangelo, or a Raphael, or a Caravaggio? Well, now's your chance. If you want an exact, painstakingly painted copy, all done perfectly legal, contact ***Studio d'Arte*** *(Via F Crispi 24a, Tel. 06/4741-644). Though copies, these are works of art in and of themselves, and will be expensive. These are not prints. So if you are seriously interested, give them a call, and stop by their showroom to see the paintings they have in stock, or arrange to have your favorite painting – whether it is a scene from Michelangelo's Sistine Chapel or Caravaggio's Drunken Bacchus – re-done just for you.*

Though it does not have as many pieces as the Vatican or the Campidoglio, here you will able to savor each piece without having to fight the crowds at those other places.

VATICAN MUSEUMS

Viale Vaticano. Tel. 06/6988-4466. Admission L13,000. From November to the first half of March and the second half of June through August open 8:45am-12:45pm. From the second half of March to the first half of June and September and October open 8:45am to 3:45pm. Closed most Sundays and all major religious holidays like Christmas and Easter. The last Sunday of every month in January, February, April, May, July, Aug., September, October, November and December are open and the entrance is free. Buses 19, 23, 32, 45, 51, 81, 492, 907, and 991. Metro-Ottaviano.

The Vatican Museums keep rather short hours, so make a point of getting here early since the lines are very long. There are a number of self-guided tape cassette tours available that take you through different sections of the Vatican Museums. Touring the museums is almost like an amusement park ride, except the sights you see are amazing works of art. These are the best way to get an insight into the many splendid works you are witnessing.

Pinacoteca Vaticana

A wonderful collection of masterpieces from many periods, covering many styles all the way from primitive to modern paintings. Here you can find paintings by Giotto (who was the great innovator of Italian painting, since prior to his work Italian paintings had been Byzantine in style), many works by Raphael, the famous *Brussels Tapestries* with episodes from the Acts of the Apostles created by Pieter van Aelsten in 1516 from sketches by Raphael, and countless paintings of the Madonna, Virgin, Mother and Child, etc.

Pius Clementine Museum

Known mainly as a sculpture museum, it was founded by Pius VI and Clement XIV. You can also find mosaic work and sarcophagi from the 2nd, 3rd and 4th centuries. One mosaic in particular is worth noting, the *Battle between the Greeks and the Centaurs,* created in the first century CE. The bronze statue of Hercules and the **Hall of the Muses** that contain statues of the Muses and the patrons of the arts are also worth noting. Here you can also find many busts of illustrious Romans including Caracalla, Trajan, Octavian and more.

In the **Octagonal Court** are some of the most important and the beautiful statues in the history of Western art, especially the *Cabinet of the Laocoon.* This statue portrays the revenge of the gods on a Trojan priest, Laocoon, who had invoked the wrath of the gods by warning his countrymen not to admit the Trojan horse. In revenge the gods sent two enormous serpents out of the sea to destroy Laocoon and his two sons.

Chiaramonti Museum

Founded by Pope Pius VII, whose family name was Chiaramonti, this museum includes a collection of over 5,000 Pagan and Christian works. Here you can find Roman Sarcophagi, *Silenus Nursing the Infant Bacchus,* busts of Caesar, the Statue of Demosthenes, the famous *Statue of the Nile* with the 16 boys representing the 16 cubits of the annual rise of the Nile, as well as a magnificent Roman chariot recreated in marble by the sculptor Franzone in 1788.

Etruscan Museum

If you can't make it to any of the Necropoli around Rome, at least come here and see the relics of a civilization that preceded Ancient Rome. Founded in 1837 by Gregory XVI, it contains objects excavated in the Southern part of Etruria from 1828-1836, as well as pieces from later excavations around Rome. Here you'll find an Etruscan tomb from Cervetri, as well as bronzes, gold objects, glass work, candelabra, necklaces, rings, funeral urns, amphora and much more.

Egyptian Museum

If you can't make it to Cairo to see their splendid exhibit of material excavated from a variety of Egyptian tombs, stop in here. Created by Gregory XVI in 1839, this museum contains a valuable documentary of the art and civilization of ancient Egypt.

There are sarcophagi, reproductions of portraits of famous Egyptian personalities, works by Roman artists who were inspired by Egyptian art, a collection of wooden mummy cases and funeral steles, mummies of animals, a collection of papyri with hieroglyphics, and much more.

Library of the Vatican

Founded through the efforts and collections of many Popes, this museum contains many documents and incunabula. Today the library contains over 500,000 volumes, 60,000 ancient manuscripts, and 7,000 incunabuli. My favorite are the precious manuscripts, especially the *Codex Vaticanus B* or the 4th century Bible in Greek.

Appartamento Borgia

Named after Pope Alexander VI, whose family name was Borgia, since he designed and lived in these lavish surroundings. (What about that vow of poverty?) From the furnishings to the paintings to the frescoes of Isis and Osiris on the ceiling, this little "museum" is worth a look.

Sistine Chapel

This is the private chapel of the popes famous for some of the most wonderful masterpieces ever created, many by **Michelangelo** himself. He started painting the ceiling of the chapel in 1508 and it took him four years to finish it. On the ceiling you'll find scenes from the Bible, among them the *Creation*, where God comes near Adam, who is lying down, and with a simple touch of his hand imparts the magic spark of life. You can also see the *Separation of Light and Darkness*, the *Creation of the Sun and Moon*, *Creation of Trees and Plants*, *Creation of Adam*, *Creation of Eve*, *The Fall and the Expulsion from Paradise*, the *Sacrifice of Noah and his Family* and the *Deluge*.

On the wall behind the altar is the great fresco of the *Last Judgment* by Michelangelo. It occupies the entire area (20 meters by 10 meters) and was commissioned by Clement VII. Michelangelo was past 60 when he started the project in 1535. He completed it seven years later in 1542. Michelangelo painted people he didn't like into situations with evil connotation in this fresco. The figure of Midas, with asses' ears, is the likeness of the Master of Ceremonies of Paul III, who first suggested that other painters cover Michelangelo's nude figures.

This covering was eventually done by order of Pius IV, who had Daniele da Volterra drape the most prominent figures with painted cloth. These changes were left in when the entire chapel underwent its marvelous transformation a few years back, bringing out the vibrant colors of the original frescoes that had been covered by centuries of dirt and soot.

Rooms of Raphael

Initially these rooms were decorated with the works of many artists of the 15th century, but because Pope Julius II loved the work of Raphael so much, he had the other paintings destroyed, and commissioned Raphael to paint the entire room himself. He did so spending the rest of his life in the task. Not nearly as stupendous as the Sistine Chapel work by Michelangelo, but it still is one of the world's masterpieces.

Chapel of Nicholas V

Decorated with frescoes from 1448-1451 by Giovanni da Fiesole. The works represent scenes from the life of Saint Stephan in the upper portion and Saint Lawrence in the lower.

The Loggia of Raphael

Divided into 13 arcades with 48 scenes from the Old and New Testaments, these were executed from the designs of Raphael by his students, Giulo Romano, Perin del Vaga, and F. Penni. The most outstanding to see are the *Creation of the World, Creation of Eve, The Deluge, Jacob's Dream, Moses Receiving the Tablets of Law, King David,* and the *Birth of Jesus.*

Grotte Vaticano

Not to be confused with the Tombe dei Papi, which you can enter towards the back of St. Peter's and see a few papal tombs, the Vatican caves seem to be a well-kept secret even though they've been around for some time. You need special permission to enter them, and if you haven't made plans prior to your arrival it is quite difficult to gain access at short notice. To gain permission you need to contact the **North American College** in Rome *(Via dell'Umita 30, Tel. 06/672-256 or 678-9184).* The entrance to the Grotte is to the left of the basilica of St. Peter's where the Swiss Guards are posted. The Grotte were dug out of the stratum between the floor of the actual cathedral and the previous Basilica of Constantine. This layer was first excavated during the Renaissance. After passing fragments of inscriptions and mosaic compositions, tombstones, and sarcophagi, you descend a steep staircase to get to the Lower Grottos, also called the **Grotte Vecchie** (the Old Grottos).

Here you'll find pagan and Christian Necropoli dating from the 2nd and 3rd century. The Grotte are divided into three naves separated by massive pilasters that support the floor of St. Peter's above. Along the walls are numerous tombs of popes and altars adorned with mosaics and sculptures. At the altar is the entrance to the **Grotte Nuove** (New Grottos), with their frescoed walls, marble statues, and bas-reliefs.

MUSEO DELLA CIVILTA ROMANA

Piazza G Agnelli 10, Tel. 06/592-6041. Open 9:00am – 7:00pm. Holidays only until 1:30pm. Closed Mondays. Metro-EUR Palasport (Marconi) or Fermi.

If you've always wanted to see a scale model of ancient Rome, you have to visit this museum. In it you'll find a perfect replica of Rome during the height of empire in the 4th century BCE. This piece is an exquisitely detailed plastic model that brings ancient Rome to life. It really helps to bring some sense to the ruins that now litter the center of Rome. Even if you are not a museum person, this exhibit is well worth seeing. Ideal for kids of all ages.

The rest of the museum contains little original material, and is made up of plaster casts of Roman artifacts. The museum is located in the section of Rome called **EUR** (Esposizione Universale di Roma), which was built as an exposition site for an event that was to take place in 1941. It is a perfect example of grandiose fascist architecture and its attempt to intimidate through size. Built with Mussolini's guidance halfway between Rome and its old port of Ostia, it was an attempt to reclaim some of Rome's glory and add to its grandeur. EUR has none of the human feel of the rest of Rome, since it is in essence an urban office park with a connected residential ghetto eerily similar to American suburbs, but with a little more style.

MUSEO TIPOLOGICO NAZIONALE DEL PRESEPIO

Via Tor de' Conti 31a, Tel. 06/679-6146. Open 5:00-8:00pm (weedays) and 10:00am-1:00pm & 5:00-8:00pm holidays. L5,000.

This museum exhibits creches and individual statuettes for creches (over 3,000) from all over the world, made from all kinds of materials. Each of these nativity scenes and figurines help illuminate for us the way in which Christmas is celebrated worldwide. If you are an afficionado of creches, as is my mother, you simply must make a point of visiting this great little museum.

MUSEO INTERNAZIONALE DEL CINEMA E DELLO SPETTACOLO

Via Bettone 1, Tel. 06/370-0266, Fax 06/3973-3297.

This museum contains film making equipment, costumes used in movies, a film library of over 5,000 mostly rare and unique films, a photographic library with over 2 million photos from 1850 onward, and a comprehensive video cassette library. If you are a videophile you will simply love this museum. But you need to book in advance to get in. There are no regular hours. Call or fax and request a time and date to be introduced to this small but informative museum of film.

PICCOLO MUSEO DELLE ANIME DEL PURGATORIO

Lungotevere Prati 12, inside the Chiesa del Sacro Cuore del Suffragio. Open every day 7:30-11:30am and 4:30-7:30pm.

This has got to be the wierdest museum in Rome. It is the museum for the souls in purgatory and used to be called the Christian Afterlife

Museum. There are supposedly records of souls in purgatory expressing their displeasure of where they are by impacting the physical world, such as a burnt handprint that appears on a missal, which suddenly appeared there during mass one day.

MUSEO STORICO NAZIONALE DELL'ARTE SANITARIA

Lungotevere in Sassia, Tel. 06/68351. Open Mon., Wed. & Fri. 9:30am-1:30pm.

Located in the interior of a hospital founded by Pope Innocent III in 1198, the museum holds pieces, surgical instruments, apothecary cases, wax models, apothecary pots, a laboratory and an extensive library that are precious records of the history of medicine and how it has been practised over the ages. If you think doctors are a bunch of quacks today, wait until you see what they worked with and believed years ago.

GALLERIA COMUNALE D'ARTE MODERNA

Via Reggio Emilia 54, Tel. 06/884-4930. L5,000. Open everyday from 10:00am-9:00pm. Holidays and Sundays 9:00am-2:00pm. E-mail: GalleriaModerna@comune. roma.it. Metro B – Policlinico.

Situated in the old Peroni brewery, whose renovated open spaces make for a perfect backdrop for this superb gallery of modern art. A working museum with laboratories as well as exhibit space, multimedia rooms, bookshops and also displays of the recent history of the building when it used to cater to the more 'spiritual' interests of the citizens of Rome. If you want a change of pace, or simply a taste of something different, stop by this brand new, just opened gallery of modern art in Rome. Nearby, in another section of the Peroni Brewery, is a Coin department store, so you can satisfy some consumer needs while here too.

LITERARY ROME

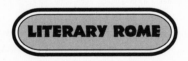

For centuries Rome has been luring artists from all over the world to be inspired by its charms. Here you can explore the city with the realization that Virgil, Robert and Elizabeth Browning, Hans Christian Anderson, Henry James, Lord Byron, Mark Twain, Goethe and more all traced the same steps you are taking.

If you are interested in following almost exactly in these famous writers' footsteps, read on, for we are going to trace for you the paths taken, the places stayed and the restaurants/cafés frequented by *literati* of times gone by.

The perfect place to start is the **Piazza di Spagna**. In the 18th and 19th century this piazza was literally (no pun intended) the end of the line for many traveling coaches entering the city. Near the western end of the piazza, the **Via delle Carrozze** (Carriage Road) reminds us that this is where these great coaches tied up at the end of their long journeys. More often than not, travelers would make their homes in and around this area.

At *Piazza di Spagna #23*, you'll find **Babbington's Tea Rooms** (see above, *Where to Eat*) where Byron, Keats, Shelley, and Tobias Smollett all shared at one time or another some afternoon tea. Across the piazza, *at #26*, is the **Keats/Shelley Memorial** where Keats spent the three months before his death in 1821 at the age of 25. The memorial contains some of Keats' manuscripts, letters and memorabilia, as well as relics from Shelley and other British writers. Keats and Shelley still reside in Rome, in the **Protestant Cemetery** near the metro stop Piramide. Located at *Via Ciao Cestio 6*, it is open all day, but visitors must ring the bell for admittance. Next, at *#66* in the piazza, the grand poet George Gordon (Lord) Byron took lodging in 1817 and performed work on *Child Harolde's Pilgrimage*.

From here, you can explore the **Via Condotti**, Rome's center for high level consumerism. **Caffe Greco**, at *#86*, is where, in its double row of interconnecting rooms, you could have found Goethe, Hans Christian Anderson or Mark Twain sipping an aperitif and other drinks that were a little stronger than can be found at Babbington's. In 1861, one of the upper rooms was also the lodging for Hans Christian Anderson of *Ugly Duckling* fame. A little further along, at *#11 Via Condotti*, poet Alfred Lord Tennyson and writer William Thackeray made their home when they visited Rome.

Just off the Via Condotti, at *Via Bocca di Leone #14*, is the **Hotel d'Inghlitera** where Mark Twain scratched many pages for *Innocents Abroad* in 1867 and where Henry James initially stayed during his forays into the Eternal City. Later on, James would reside at the **Hotel Plaza** at *Via del Corso 126* where he began his work *From a Roman Notebook*, which described his exploration of the city, its culture, history, and expatriate social activities.

Further down the Corso, at *#20*, is where the German poet Goethe made his home from 1786 to 1788. Here he penned his immortal travel diary *Italian Journey*. Goethe's old house now contains a small museum of photographs, prints, journals, books, and other material relating to the poet's travels in Italy.

At *Bocca di Leone, #43*, you'll see where Robert and Elizabeth Browning lived in 1853. This is where Robert got the inspiration for his epic poem *The Ring and the Book*, a tragic tale of the murder of the Comparini family and their daughter Pompilia (who had lived on the Via Bocca di Leone in 1698), by Pompilia's husband, Count Franchescini.

Another famous writer who resided in Rome was the magnificent Charles Dickens, who wrote part of his *Pictures From Italy* at *Via del Babuino #9*. If you get a chance, try and read this book, since it brings the Rome of that time to life as vividly as he brought London to life in his many other books.

'NERO'S GOLDEN HOUSE' OPEN AGAIN!

After 15 years of additional excavations, the **Domus Aurea** *is once again open to public viewing. Known as Nero's Golden House, the Domus Aurea was Nero's palace that he had built after the great fire of 64 CE destroyed his first abode, not to mention a great deal of Rome. Nero appropriated a huge amount of land in much of central Rome and had the greatest craftsmen of the day work on the structure, and a number of innovations were introduced thatplayed a part in inspiring early Renaissance painters, sculptors, and architects. But Nero only lived in the palace a few short years, after which most of it was abandoned and much of the grounds given back to the people of Rome.*

You can view eight rooms today, all underground, and admire the vaulted ceilings, extant pieces of frescoes and stone reliefs, beautiful floor mosaics, and pieces of broken sculpture here and there. It's a magnificent building, and well worth the sight if you are in the neighborhood of the Colosseum and have the time. Be sure and get the audio guide, since you will be accompanied by someone who is only there to show you from room to room . You have to call in advance and make a reservation, since only small groups are allowed at a time.

Directions: same as for the Colosseum – Buses 11, 27, 81, 85, 87. Metro-Colosseo. Hours: 9am to 8pm summer; 9am to 5pm winter; closed on Tuesdays. Admission L12,000. Tel. 06/399-67700. When you get off the bus or metro, look for the public gardens across the street from the Colosseum (Calle Oppio Gardens). The street entrance is on Viale della Domus Aurea.

15. NIGHTLIFE & ENTERTAINMENT

Rome is filled with many discos, pubs, and *birrerias* (bars) where you can spend your evening hours having wild and raucous times. If that's what you want to do, I've compiled a list of the best places to go. But if you want to do like most of the Romans do for evening and nightly entertainment, seat yourself at a bar/café or restaurant, savor your meal or a few drinks and revel in the beauty that is Rome. Lingering in the evening air while recalling the day's events or planning tomorrow's is a great way to relax, slow down your pace of living, and adapt to the culture.

Anyway, there are a few great places in Rome where you can become part of the culture. The best is in **Trastevere** at one of the little open air cafés where you can either stay all night sipping a few glasses of wine, or visit after you've had your dinner in one of the restaurants around the piazza (see Trastevere, *Where to Eat*). This is definitely *the* best place to go for a night out in Rome.

Another is **Campo dei Fiori**, which also has many cafés and restaurants where you can sit while you watch the life of Rome amble past. Three other great nightspots are the **Piazza Navona**, around the **Pantheon**, and around the **Trevi Fountain** where you can admire the fine sculpture, the beautiful people, and the many different life forms that comprise the streetlife of Rome.

But if this sedate, appreciative, slow-paced lifestyle is not for you, by all means try one of the following. I found them all perfect for letting off some steam.

Map references for the nightlife entries are as follows: numbers 89, 91, and 96 are on map A (pages 120-121); numbers 92, 94, 99, 100, 101 and 102 are on map B (pages 144-145); numbers 90, 97, and 98 are on map C (pages 154-155); and numbers 93 and 95 are on map D (pages 168-169).

IRISH-STYLE PUBS

89. TRINITY COLLEGE IRISH PUB, *Via del Collegio Romano 6, Tel. 06/678-64-72. E-mail: trinity-pub@flashnet.it. Website: www.trinity-rome.com. Open 7:30am to 3:00pm and 8:00pm to 2:00am. Credit cards accepted. (Map A)*

This is more of a place to come for a good meal and a few pints rather than a watering hole in which to drink the night away. The menu comes complete with pub fare such as sandwiches, Shepherd's Pie, salads, hamburgers, hot dogs, french fries and more, as well as an extensive and excellent Roman menu. The atmosphere and ambiance are impeccably upper crust. A great place to come for an intimate meal or some early evening drinks and relax over one of the many complimentary newspapers in a variety of languages. Another plus to this place is that in the summer, the air conditioning is cranked, so it's the perfect spot to escape the heat of Rome. An upscale crowd hangs out here.

WHEN IN ROME ... DO AS THE IRISH DO!

When you think of Rome, you picture magnificent monuments, savory food, wonderful wine, flavorful gelato, and most importantly romantic moons hovering over picturesque piazzas stirring long forgotten passions. To that list you can add Irish pubs and cold Guinness on draught, because everywhere you look in the Old City of Rome you'll find quaint, authentic Irish-style pubs, jam packed with customers, the majority of whom are Italian. From Campo dei Fiori, to the Pantheon, to Via del Corso, to Trastevere and beyond, stopping in a local pub for lunch or a pint in the evening has become a facet of daily life in Rome.

Only a few years ago there were but a small number of seedy, vaguely pub-style bars, mainly catering to the foreign population. Today you can find authentic Irish-style pubs everywhere, filled to capacity with Italians enjoying the time honored Anglo-Saxon tradition of bellying up to the bar and throwing down a few pints.

Just as we in the States have adopted coffee bars into our culture, so have the Italians incorporated Irish-style pubs into the fabric of their everyday lives. Cheers.

90. THE BLACK DUKE, *Via della Maddelena 29, Tel. 06/6830-0381. Open for lunch in the summers. Open until 2:00am all year long, every day. (Map C)*

Located near the Pantheon there is outside seating bordered by large shrubs that separate you from the street. You can also sit inside in the large downstairs dining and bar area that seats 120 people. The air circulation is not that great so non-smokers beware...even in the small area designated for your use, breathing can be quite difficult. Here you can savor a full menu of authentic pub grub in the traditional dark and dinghy (yet clean and comfortable) English/Irish pub setting of dark wood decor and furnishings. More of an upscale crowd.

91. THE FIDDLERS ELBOW, *Via dell'Olmata 43, Tel. 487-2110. Open 7 days a week 5:00pm -1:15am. (Maps A&D)*

Rome's oldest authentic pub, which has knock-offs in Florence and Venice, this place has a slightly run-down feel but that gives it a truly Irish flavor. Located near the Piazza Santa Maria Maggiore, you'll get a taste of home here but no real food. Only snacks like potato chips, peanuts and salami sticks are served. A little off the beaten path, unless you are staying near the Train Station, this is not really a place to go out of your way to visit. Mixed crowd.

92. THE JOHN BULL PUB, *Corso Vittorio Emanuele II 107a, Tel. 06/687-1537. Open 12:00pm to 2:00am. (Map B)*

The English John Bull company's version of what the Irish Guinness is promoting all over the world: authentic pub experience in which to sell their beer. There is wood, brass, glass, and mirrors, and English knick-knacks everywhere. Totally British, including the friendly service. Ideally located near Piazza Navona, The Pantheon and Campo dei Fiori on the main street Vittorio Emanuele, this is a fun place to come for a few drinks or their extensive antipasto spread at happy hour. Besides that you can muster up some sandwiches, salads, or other basic pub food for around L5,000.

93. SHAMROCK IRISH PUB, *Via del Colosseo 1/c, Tel. 06/679-1729. Open noon to 2:00am. (Map D)*

A truly authentic Irish pub, complete with two dart boards in the back. The place to play darts in Rome. Located near the Colosseum, the superb small hotel, Hotel Richmond and the great enoteca on Via Cavour, Cavour 313. If you are looking for great pub food, cold beer, a fun crowd, stop in here in the evenings, or in the middle of the day whilst touring.

BARS & DISCOS

94. THE DRUNKEN SHIP, *Campo dei Fiori 20/21, Tel. 06/683-00-535. Open 1:00pm-2:00am. Some days (the schedule changes ... this is Italy, remember), they don't open until 6:00pm. Happy Hour 6:00-9:00pm. (Map B)*

The best bar in the best location in Rome. American owner Regan Smith has created a wild and raucous American style bar in one of Rome's oldest piazzas. Loud music, rowdy crowd, great drinks, draft beer and bilingual and beautiful waitresses. The crowd is mainly Italian with a sprinkling of foreign students and travelers. All adventurous and fun.

You'll love the Jello shots and adorable English speaking waitresses and bartenders. The decor is dark wood and the whole place has a slight tilt to it befitting, I suppose, a drunken ship. This is the place to come for a pint or two in the early evenings as well as the best place to party the night away. They have specials every night to keep you coming back for more. A younger crowd hangs out here.

95. RADIO LONDRA, *Via di Monte Testaccio, 65B. Tel. 06/575-0044. Open Monday-Friday 9:00pm to 3:00am, and Saturdays until 4:00am. All credit cards accepted. (Map D)*

This place is totally insane, and crowded, and loud, and completely out of this world. You have segments of all parts of society here, making for a complete viewing pleasure. If the goings-on inside the inferno gets too hot, you can always sojourn to one of the tables on the terrace. A great place to meet other single people, not necessarily tourists. The interior is complete with an 18th century vaulted ceiling and 1940s style decor. They offer live music Tuesday through Friday. Food specialties are house pizza and grilled steaks. Located in the recently trendy Testaccio section of town by the Piramide Metro stop, around here you will find most of Rome's dance clubs and hot night spots.

96. BIRRERIA LOWENBRAU MUNCHEN, *Via delle Croce 21, Tel. 06/679-5569. Open 11:00am-11:00pm. All credit cards accepted. (Map A)*

You can eat here if the need for Viennese cuisine creeps up on your stomach (you'll find plenty of German tourists here enjoying the staples from their homeland), but I find it's a perfect place to have the best German beer on tap. It's a festive place to throw down a few pints with your travel partners. They serve their large beers in glass boots which adds to the charm of this *birreria*. In conjunction you're in one of the best nighttime areas in Rome, around the Piazza di Spagna, where you can go for a casual stroll before or after your drinking adventure.

97. NED KELLY'S AUSTRALIAN PUB, *Via delle Coppelle 15, Tel. 06/685-2220. Open 6:30pm to 2:00am week days and 3:00pm on weekends. Lunch open Monday-Friday 12:30-3:30. (Map C)*

A small hole in the wall place that is the unofficial rugby and darts bar in Rome. One board is to the right as you walk in and there is league play in the winter. There are four owners, two of which do most of the bar work. David, the lone American, helps draw some local foreign students and Tony, the manager of the local rugby club, brings in the Italian rugby community. This mix of fifty-fifty Italian/foreigners makes for a fun place in the evenings. Then at lunch from 12:30pm to 3:00pm, they have one of Rome's best salad bars. Located a stone's throw from the sports bar Oliphant.

98. OLIPHANT TEX MEX RESTAURANT, *Via delle Coppelle 31/32, Tel. 06/686-14-16. Open 11:00am to 2:00pm. Happy hour 6:00-8:00pm. (Map C)*

Besides the Tex Mex menu, this place is also a really great sports bar – if you're into that. TVs are everywhere in the bar area and there's an American flag fluttering in the middle of the restaurant, a crew boat hanging from the wall, a cut-out of Michael Jordan by the bar, surfboards precariously placed everywhere, and other athletic memorabilia thrown in for that authentic sports bar feel. The menu is super-extensive, complete with nachos (L5,000), quesadilla (L14,000), BBQ back ribs (L25,000), burgers (L13,500) and hot dogs (L15,000). A great place to watch the game and escape back into where you came from for a while.

99. OMBRE ROSSE, *Piazza Sant'Egidio 12, Tel. 06/588-4155. Hours 7am-2am. (Map B)*

Wonderful service from morning 'til the wee hours. Strange for a late night place to open so early, but they are, and their breakfasts are excellent. There are all kinds of wines, as well as beer on tap in this oasis of calm in the frenzy of late night Trastevere. Inside or out, here you'll be able to grab a quick bite to eat and a superb glass of wine. One of my favorites.

100. LA SCALA, *Piazza della Scala 60, Tel. 06/580-3763. Closed in August. Hours 7pm-2am. (Map B)*

Divided into five rooms, each with a different theme, this is a great late night place in Trastevere. There are plenty of courses to sample, including the *Vecchia America* (a steak with chili and french fries), the *Mexico e Mexico* (ossobucco, rice, chili and french fries), as well as many pizzas. An excellent late night place with food, music, dancing, and little corners for couples to cuddle in. The patio is a little 'foo-foo' but inside its more fun.

101. ACCADEMIA, *Vicolo della Renella 88/90, Tel. 06/589-6321. Open 6:30pm-2:00am. (Map B)*

With two big rooms and a grand terrace, this place has enough space for everyone. There's live music, great food and fun times. A good place to come for a late night drink or a romantic small dinner in one of the upstairs rooms with a view over the rooftops of Rome.

102. ARTU CAFÉ, *Largo MD Fumasoni Biondi 5, Tel. 06/588-0398. Closed Mondays. Open 6:00pm-2:00am. (Map B)*

Inside you'll find a comfortable entry room with a few tables, a fireplace leading to a cozy bar area, then from there you have a back room where the hip locals hang out. This place has a great feel, an extensive snack menu, an adequate wine list, and friendly wait staff. It's one of my favorite places to come for a late night after dinner drink when I'm in Trastevere.

CAFES/BARS

The cafes and bars of Rome are where the locals gather. These places are the heart and soul of the city, and if you want to grab drink or a snack at some of the most authentic, try any of these listed here. Regular bar hours vary, but most are open early (6am) for breakfast, and close late (around 10pm). Come here for a truly authentic Roman experience.

TEICHNER, *Piazza San Lorenzo in Lucina 17, Tel 06/687-1683. Closed Sundays. Open 8am–midnight.*

A classic cafe in a calm and relaxing piazza amid the chaos of Rome. The best place to grab a cup of coffee or gelato in Rome. You can get all sorts of snack to nibble on as well as foodstuffs to bring home with you from the small store inside. Just off the main shopping street, Via del Corso, this is a perfect place to stop for a break. And if the tables are all full, there are also two other cafes to choose from in this, my favorite relaxing piazza in Rome.

BABINGTON'S TEA ROOMS, *23 Piazza di Spagna, Tel. 06/678-6027. Credit cards accepted. Closed Thursdays.*

Really a place to grab a spot of tea, except in the mornings when they serve massive breakfasts of scones, shepherd's pie, and other British culinary delights (if there is such a thing). This ancient café, with its heavy furniture, musty decor, and creaky floors has been serving customers for several centuries. The service is out of the 18th century, but the prices are from the 21st. Expect a cup of tea to cost over $5.

DOLCE VITA, *Piazza Navona 70a, Tel. 06/6880-6221. Closed Mondays.*

Located in one of the best piazzas in the world, Piazza Navona, whether seated inside, but preferably out, you will have an authentic Italian café experience at this time honored locale. The patio area has a view over the entire piazza, the church by Borromini, and the fountain of the rivers by Bernini; and is the perfect spot to grab a coffee or an after dinner drink and watch the Romans walk by.

ROSATI, *Piazza del Popolo 5, Tel. 06/322-5859.*

Since 1922 this historic café has opened its doors on one of the most animated piazzas in Rome, Piazza del Popolo. Since traffic has been lessened in the piazza, sitting outside is not such a noxious affair, and is a great place to watch Romans and tourists alike cavort. Inside the elegant atmosphere remains as hospitable as ever. The breakfast *cornetti* are exquisite, as are many of their pies, pastries, sandwiches and snacks, all made in house.

SANT'EUSTACHIO, *Piazza Sant'Eustachio 82, Tel. 06/686-1309. Closed Mondays.*

Opened in 1938 this place has been a favorite of the *centro storico* around the Pantheon, especially at night, and mainly in the summers. The attraction has remained the same – great coffee and wonderful ambiance.

You can also get all sorts of sweets, snacks and drinks. A perfect spot to take a break from touring and sample an authentic piece of the Roman way of life.

TAZZA D'ORO, *Via degli Orfani 84, Tel. 06/679-2768. Closed Sundays.*

In an historic location near the Pantheon, and maintaining a bustling ambiance out of the 1940s, this place is perfect for a mid-day or early evening coffee and snack. It's a wonderful slice of another era. Snacks, ice creams, liqueurs, pastries, and other goodies are also served. I recommend at least one cup of coffee here, just to savor the atmosphere. You can also buy their coffee to bring back with you.

CAFÉ GRECO, *Via Condotti 86, Tel. 06/678-5474. Closed Sundays. Open 8am to midnight.*

This places has been here since 1740 and has been a stop on the grand tour of Rome since then. A unique and elegant café where you can get all sorts of drinks, snacks and pastries. Expensive, but worth at least one stop just to be a part of the history.

OPERA

If you are in Rome from December to June, the traditional opera season, have the proper attire (suits for men, dresses for women), and a taste for something out of the ordinary, try the spectacle of the opera:

TEATRO DELL'OPERA, *Piazza D. Gigli 1, 00184 Roma. Tel. 06/481-601, Fax 06/488-1253.*

MOVIES IN ENGLISH

ALCATRAZ, *Via Cardinal Merry del Val, Tel 06/588-0099. Mondays only.*

GREENWICH, *Via G. Bodoni 59, Tel. 06/574-5825. Mondays only.*

Nuovo Sacher, Largo Ascianghi 1, Tel. 06/581-8116. Mondays and Tuesdays only.

PASQUINO, *Piazza San Egideo, Tel. 06/580-3622. Three screens. Daily films in Enlgish.*

QUIRINETTA, *Via M. Minghetti 4, Tel. 06/679-0012. Original Language films daily.*

16. SHOPPING

Store hours are usually Monday through Friday 9:00am to 1:00pm, 3:30/4:00pm to 7:30/8:00pm, and Saturday 9:00am to 1:00pm. In major cities like Rome, shops will also open in the afternoons on Saturday, but everywhere in Italy they will be closed on Sunday. This may vary in Milan and/or Turin, where sometimes the lunch break is shorter so shops can close earlier.

The big Italian chain stores are **La Rinascente**, **Coin**, **UPIM**, and **STANDA**. In some Coin, UPIM, and STANDA, you will also find supermarkets filled with all manner of Italian delectables. At the end of this chapter I'll make some suggestions about what you could buy at a local Italian *Supermercato* or *Alimentari* (smaller food store) to bring home with you so you can make a fine Italian meal with authentic ingredients!

Besides food and clothing, Italy has a wide variety of handicrafts. Any one of Italy's crafts would be a perfect memento of your stay. Works in alabaster and marble can be readily found in and around Florence, Milan, and Venice. Wood carvings are the specialty of many of the cities in the south, such as Palermo and Messina. Beautiful glasswork is at its best in and around Venice and Pisa. Embroidery and lace work can be found all over Italy, and rugs from Sardinia rival those of most other European countries. Sardinia is also known for its straw bags, hats, and mats, as is Florence.

Exquisite gold and silver jewelry is a specialty of Florence, where, on the Ponte Vecchio, you'll find shop after shop of jewelry stores. In other parts of Tuscany you can find hand-wrought iron work as well as beautiful tiles.

And finally, the main fashion centers in Italy are, of course, Milan, Florence and Rome, with Florence specializing in shoes and gloves, and Milan and Rome everything else. You will find plenty of everything in Rome, long recognized as one of the world's great shopping meccas.

TAX-FREE SHOPPING

Italian law entitles all non-European Union residents to a **VAT (IVA) tax refund** with a minimum purchase exceeding L300,000. Ask for an invoice (*fattura* in Italian) or a Tax-Free Check when completing a purchase. Upon departure from Italy, purchased goods must be shown to a customs agent at the airport or border station and a customs stamp must be obtained no later than three months after the date of purchase. The stamped invoice must be returned to the store or the VAT Refund Companies Office in Italy no later than four months after the date of purchase.

Direct refunds at the airport or the border are only offered by **Tax-Free for Tourists**. You will usually see their signs in most upscale stores. Shop at them if you want instant refunds when you leave Italy.

GET YOUR TAX REBATE ON PURCHASES

If you acquire products at the same merchant in excess of L300,000 (about $180), you can claim an ***IVA*** *(purchase tax)* ***rebate****. You must ask the vendor for the proper receipt* ***(il ricetto per il IVA per favore)****, have the receipt stamped at Italian customs, then mail no later than 90 days after the date of the receipt back to the vendor. The vendor will then send you the IVA rebate. I know it's complicated, but if you spend a fair chunk of money in Italy on clothing or other items, this is a good way to get some money back.*

LITTLE ITALIAN STORES

Since there are no 24-hour pharmacies or convenience stores that carry everything under the sun like we have in North America, shopping for the basic necessities can be a little confusing, but exciting. Listed below are specific types of shops and what you can find in them:

Cartoleria

Shopping at a *cartoleria* brings you face to face with Italian make-work programs, since most are not self-service. Some products you can pick out what you want, others you will have to enlist a stockboy/girl to help you get it. But you don't bring the products up to the register. In most cases you will have the cost of your purchases tabulated for you by the stockperson. You bring this receipt and your desired products up to the register, where another person rings them up for you.

pen	*penna*
pencil	*mattita*
notebook	*quaderno*

paper	*carta*
envelope	*borsa per una lettera*
binder	*classificatore*
calendar	*calandra*
wrapping paper	*carta da regalo*

Alimentari

When shopping at an *alimentari* some products are self-service and some have to be prepared for you. Most meats, cheeses and breads are not pre-packaged and therefore you will have to talk to someone behind a glass counter to get you what you want. Other goods, like mustard and water, are self-service. When ordering meats, cheeses or breads, you will get the products and the receipt for the products from the person behind the counter. Bring the receipt and all your other products to the cashier where you pay.

mustard	*senape*
mayonnaise	*maionese*
tomatoes	*tomaté*
olive oil	*olio d'oliva*
salami	*salame* (the best types are *Milanese* or *Ungherese*)
cheese	*formaggio*
mineral water	*aqua minerale*
wine (red/white)	*vino (rosso/bianco)*
beer	*birra*
potato chips	*patate fritte*
cookies	*biscotti*
roll	*panino*
bread	*pane*
butter	*burro*

Sometimes *alimentari* do not have bread. If that is the case you'll need to find a *panificio* (bakery). Same type of service here as in an *alimentari*.

Farmacia

Shopping in a pharmacy is full service. You do not have access to anything. If you want anything you have to ask the pharmacist or his/her assistant.

toothpaste	*dentifricio*
razor	*rasoio*
deodorant	*deodorante*
comb	*pettine*
rubbers	*profilattici*

toothbrush	*spazzolino*
aspirin	*aspirina*
tampon	*tampone*

Tabacchaio

Most everything but the tobacco products and stamps are self-service in a *tabacchaio*.

stamps	*francobolli*
newspaper	*giornale*
pen	*penna*
envelopes	*buste per lettere*
postcards	*cartoline*
cigars	*sigaro*
cigarettes	*sigarette*
cigarette paper	*cartina*
pipe tobacco	*tabacco da pipa*
matches	*fiammiferi*
lottery ticket	*biglietto di lotteria*
lighter	*accendino*

SIZES

The chart below is a comparison guide between US and Italian sizes. Many sizes are not standardized, so you will need to try everything on anyway. Generally if you are above 6'2" and weigh over 200 pounds you may have trouble finding clothing in Italy because the Italians just are not big people. The following conversions should help you out in your shopping quest:

WOMEN'S CLOTHING SIZES

US	2	4	6	8	10	12	14	16
Italy	36	38	40	42	44	46	48	50

Continued

	18	20	24
	52	54	56

WOMEN'S SHOE SIZES

US	5 1/2	6 1/2	7	7 1/2	8	8 1/2	9	10
Italy	35	36	37	38	38 1/2	39	40	41

WOMEN'S HOSIERY SIZES

US	Petite	Small	Medium	Large
Italy	I	II	III	IV

MEN'S SUITES, OVERCOATS, SWEATERS, & PAJAMAS

US	34	36	38	40	42	44	46	48
Italy	44	46	48	50	52	54	56	58

MEN'S SHIRTS

US	14	14 1/2	15	15 1/2	16	16 1/2	17	17 1/2
Italy	36	37	38	39	40	41	42	43

MEN'S SHOES

US	6	6 1/2	7	7 1/2	8	8 1/2	9	9 1/2
Italy	30	40	40 1/2	41	41 1/2	42	42 1/2	43

Continued

	10	10 1/2	11-11 1/2
	43 1/2	44-44 1/2	45

MEN'S HATS

US	6 7/8	7	7 1/8	7 1/4	7 3/8	7 1/2	7 5/8	7 3/4
Italy	55	56	57	58	59	60	61	62

CHILDREN'S SIZES

US	1	2	3	4	5	6	7	8
Italy	35	40	45	50	55	60	65	70

Continued

	9	10	11	12	13	14
	75	80	85	90	95	100

CHILDREN'S SHOES

US	4	5	6	7	8	9	10	10 1/2
Italy	21	21	22	23	24	25	26	27

Continued

	11	12	13
	28	29	30

KEY SHOPPING & BARGAINING PHRASES

Italian	**English**
Quanto costa?	How Much is This?
E Troppo	That's too much
No Grazie	No thank you
Voglio paggare meno	I want to pay less
Che lai questo pui grande?	Do have this in a bigger size?
..... *pui piccolo*	..... in a smaller size
..... *in nero*	..... in black
..... *in bianco*	..... in white
..... *in roso*	..... in red
..... *in verde*	..... in green

ITALIAN SOCCER ATTIRE & TICKETS

If you or someone you know is a soccer nut, there a re plenty of places to get a jersey, hat, or scarf while in Rome, but three of the best are listed here. ***Soccer Point*** *(Via Daniele Manin 41, Via Principe Amedeo 44, Tel. 06/4890-3132) has two store near the train station, and* ***Goal*** *(Via Tomacelli 11, Tel. 06/687-6159) has a store just off the Via del Corso. These two stores carry stuff for teams from all over the world but especially for Italian teams.*

But my favorite shop is the ***AS Roma Store*** *(Piazza Colnna 360, Tel 06/678-5614, www.asromastore.it), where you can get anything and everything from my favorite team. You can also get tickets for Roma games here at their* ***ticket office*** *(Tel. 06/6920-0642, infoline Tel. 06/506-0165, seats Tel. 06/506-0200, www.asromacalcio.it). Outside of games vendors will be selling everything from key rings to official soccer jerseys, all at a lower price than you will find in the above stores.*

WHEN TO BARGAIN

In all stores, even the smallest shops, bargaining is not accepted, just like here in North America. But you can bargain at any street vending location, even if they have placed a sign indicating the price. Don't be afraid to bargain, otherwise you'll end up spending more than you (ahem) 'bargained' for.

Most Italian vendors see foreigners as easy marks to make a few more lire because they know it is not in our culture to bargain, while in theirs it is a way of life.

The best way to bargain, if the street vendor doesn't speak English, is by writing your request on a piece of paper. This keeps it subdued in case you're embarrassed about haggling over money. Basically while in Italy try to let go of that cultural bias. Anyway, you and the vendor will probably pass the paper back and forth a few times changing the numbers before a price is finally agreed upon. And of course, the Italian vendor will be waving his arms about, jabbering away, most probably describing how you're trying to rip him off, all in an effort to get you to pay a higher price. Remember, this is all done in fun – so enjoy it.

BRINGING PURCHASES THROUGH CUSTOMS

You can bring back to the US $400 worth of goods duty free. On the next $1,000 worth of purchases you will be assessed a flat 10% fee. These products must be with you when you go through customs.

You can mail products duty free, providing the total value of each package sent is not more than $50 *and* no one person is receiving more than one package a day. Also, each package sent must be stamped "Unsolicited Gift" and the amount paid and the contents of the package must be displayed. They'll be able to tell you all this again at the post office.

What you cannot bring back to North America are any fruits, vegetables, and in most cases meats (because of mad-cow disease), even if they're for your consumption alone, and even if they are vacuum sealed. Customs has to do this to prevent any potential parasites from entering our country. Unfortunately, this means all those great salamis you bought at those quaint outdoor food markets and had on one of your picnics will not be let back into North America. Most cheeses are fine to bring back, especially the hard cheeses like *Parmigiano Reggiano* and *Pecorino*.

ITALIAN DEPARTMENT STORES

It's always fun to go to supermarkets and department stores in other countries to see what the natives enjoy. Even if you don't buy anything, it's still fun to browse. Both STANDA and UPIM are designed for the Italian on a budget, while Rinascente is a little more chic.

***STANDA**, Viale di Trastevere 60 and Via Cola di Rienzo 173.*

Italy's largest food market, the perfect place to find that food product to bring back to the States with you. Since most of their stuff is vacuum sealed and pre-packaged you should not have any problems with customs. STANDA also has a large selection of housewares and clothing. This is the combined K Mart and Safeway of Italy, with slightly better quality products.

***UPIM**, Via Nazionale 111, Piazza Santa Maria Maggiore and Via del Tritone 172.*

This department store is just like STANDA, except without the food.

***LA RINASCENTE**, Piazza Colonna and Piazza Fiume.*

This is much more upscale than the other two and has about the same prices as boutiques. Very chic shopping.

Because the very best of Italian design and craftsmanship are conveniently located all over Rome, this city is one of the finest shopping places in the world. You can find beautiful items made from the very best material, and as such this is not the place to look around for cut-price bargains. Leather and silk goods predominate, but Rome is also an important location for jewelry, antiques and general top of the line *pret-a-porter* (ready to wear) fashion.

The main shopping area is near the Spanish Steps and is a network of small and large streets featuring the famous **Via Condotti**. The shopping area boundaries extend over to **Via della Croce** in the north to **Via Frattina** in the south, and **Via del Corso** in the west to **Piazza di Spagna** in the east.

Romans, like most Italians, prefer to shop in boutiques, and the Via Condotti area has these quaint little shops selling everything from shirts to gloves. This specialization originated from the village craft shops of old, and generally ensures top quality and personal service. In Italy, **department stores** are the exception rather than the rule, but in this shopping area there are some that warrant a look, like **La Rinascente**, **STANDA**, **UPIM**, and **Coin** (see sidebar on previous page).

To get instant respect, you may have to dress the part here in Italy. It's not like in the malls back home where it doesn't matter how you dress; here in Rome the wealthier you look the better assistance you'll get. Unfortunately as tourists we usually leave our best attire back home, but try the best you can. Shorts and tank tops usually will get you no respect at all, particularly if you're shopping on the Via Condotti and Via Borgognona. This holds true, and I can vouch for this personally, if you're shopping on some of the parallel streets like Via Frattina, some of the little cross-streets, and even in Piazza di Spagna or Via del Babuino.

SHOPPING STREETS

Top of the Line Shopping *– Via Condotti, Via Borgognona, Via Bocca di Leone*

Mid-Range Fashion *– Via Nazionale, Via del Corso, Via Cola di Rienzo, Via del Tritone, and Via Giubbonari*

Antiques *– Via del Babuino, Via Giulia, Via dei Coronari, around Piazza Navona*

Inexpensive Shoes *– Fontana di Trevi area*

Leather Goods and Apparel *– Via due Macelli, Via Francesco Crispi*

Straw and Wicker Products *– Via dei Deiari, Via del Teatro Valle*

Other shopping districts are less formal, and many of these are worth investigating if you have time, because in these locations is where you'll find some real bargains. **Via del Tritone** and the streets around the **Trevi Fountain**, **Via Cola di Rienzo** across the Tiber and north of the Vatican, **Piazza San Lorenzo** in Lucina and the streets around **Piazza Campo dei Fiori** are all areas where you will find less expensive leather bags and shoes. **Via Veneto** also has more of an international flavor, but boy, is it expensive.

Besides these areas, Rome also has many colorful street markets offering a vast selection of top quality fruit, flowers, vegetables, prosciutto, salami, cheeses, meat and fish, as well as cheap and inexpensive clothes. Because of this proliferation of small shops and markets, and the Italian penchant for shopping in them, there are few large department stores or supermarkets in the city center.

Bargaining is an accepted practice in clothes markets, but elsewhere transactions are conducted in a more roundabout way. At food stalls, cheeses and other weighed items have *prezzi fissi* (fixed prices), and in nearly all clothes shops, you can try asking for a *sconto* (discount). Reasons for meriting a *sconto* may be numerous - buying two articles at once is a good example - but if you are bold you will ask for a *sconto* for no good reason at all, and will usually get one. This practice applies to all but the very grandest of shops. Try it in hotels too.

Surprisingly few shopkeepers speak English, but in the larger shops there is usually one person on hand who understands enough to be able to help you. Try to get your shopping done in the morning hours, when the stores are not so busy. At night, traditionally when Italians shop, it is so crowded it is difficult to get assistance.

HIGH FASHION, EXCLUSIVE SERVICE

If you're looking for high-end fashion accessories and top of the line service, look no further than Shigeo Amino's two stores in Rome, ***Avriga****. You'll find the best of the best, all at duty-free prices. One store is near the Trevi Fountain (Via del Lavatore 46-47, Tel. 06/678-7875) and another is almost directly across from the American Catholic Church in Rome, Santa Susanna's (Via XX Settembre 122, Tel. 06/481-5616).*

ANTIQUES

Today, the typical Roman antique can be either a precious Roman artifact or pieces in the baroque and neoclassical style. There are also many French and English antiques masquerading as Italian. One thing that they all have in common is that they are extremely expensive.

Some good antique shops in Rome can be found in the **Via del Babuino** and the **Via Margutta**. Other shops can be found on the **Via dei Coronari**, and the **Via Giulia**. And don't forget to check out the **Porta Portese** Sunday market *(open 6:30am–2:30pm)*. You'll find some interesting antiques there, but not too many.

But the best area to visit to find antiques is the area of the old city of Rome, the *centro storico* from Piazza Navona to the tip of the peninsula that points towards St. Peter's. There are also some excellent stores on the other side of Via Vittorio Emanuele, around the Campo dei Fiori in that same area.

OUTDOOR MARKETS

Many natives buy their vegetables, fruits, flowers, meats and cheeses from one of the many street markets held daily all over the city. Stalls of inexpensive clothing are also available, and I advise you not to miss the opportunity to wander through one in the mornings, since they are usually closed in the afternoons.

Here are some of the better markets, most of which are open from 7:00am and close at 2:00pm, Monday through Saturday:

CAMPO DEI FIORI, *Piazza Campo dei Fiori. Closed afternoons and Mondays.*

Rome's oldest and definitely best market held in the cobblestone square in the center of Rome's old medieval city. You can buy flowers (the name Campo dei Fiori means fields of flowers), fruits and vegetables, all delicately presented under makeshift awnings or giant umbrellas. Also available are hardware products, clothing and more. Surrounding the square are some *Alimentari* and *Panneterie* where you can pick up cold cuts, cheeses, and bread for picnics.

PORTA PORTESE, *Ponte Sublico. Open 6:30am–2:30pm, Sundays only.*

This flea market stretches along the Tiber from Ponte Sublico (where the Porta Portese is) in the north to the Ponte Testaccio in the south. That's roughly south of the center of Trastevere along the river. It is not even on most maps, but tell a cab driver where you're going and he'll know, since it is truly a Roman institution where anything and everything under the sun is sold: from live rabbits to stolen antiques to trendy clothes to kitchen items and all sorts of odds and ends. The clothes and accessories are inexpensive but are not of the highest quality, as befits most flea markets. Not many tourists venture here, but it's safe (though beware of pickpockets), and if you like flea markets, it is a whole lot of fun. A great place to come and get Italian soccer jerseys, hats and scarves. And it goes without saying that you have to bargain.

TESTACCIO, *Piazza Testaccio, Metro – Piramide. Closed Sundays.*

An authentic Roman covered market in the newly gentrified section of Rome. This market is in an old working class section of Rome, which was indelibly transformed into the grid pattern that exists today at the end of the 19th century. This neighborhood is named after the earthenware jugs (*testae*) which were discarded here. Today it is home to one of Rome's best local markets. Come here for the atmosphere and leave with baskets of fruit and vegetables.

PIAZZA VITTORIO EMANUELE, *Metro – Termini. Closed Sundays.*

Located 5 minutes from the south of Termini station is an excellent fresh fruit market which circles the Piazza Vittorio Emanuele. Ideally situated if you are staying by the train station, or want to grab something quick before you get on the train. A wonderfully authentic local market.

ANTIQUES & COLLECTIBLES UNDERGROUND FLEA MARKET, *Via Fr. Crispi, Tel. 06/3600-5345, L3,000. Open First Saturday (5:00-8:00pm) and Sunday (10:30am-7:30pm) of every month. Saturdays.*

Though technically not an outside market, which means it should not be under this heading, this is a fantastic flea market that should be visited if you are in Rome on the First Saturday and Sunday of every month. Located in an underground parking garage near the Via Veneto and the Spanish Steps, you can find all sorts of interesting knick-knacks here that would be impossible to find anywhere else.

ENGLISH-LANGUAGE BOOKSTORES

ANGLO-AMERICAN BOOKSTORE, *Via delle Vite 102. Tel. 06/679-5222. Credit cards accepted. Monday–Friday 9:00am–1:00pm, and 3:30pm–7:30pm. Saturdays 9:00am–1:00pm.*

Located between the Spanish Steps and the Trevi Fountain, this bookstore caters to all manner of bibliophiles and computer nerds too. As well as a full selection of travel books, paperbacks, history books, etc. They have a multimedia computer center too.

THE CORNER BOOKSHOP, *Via del Moro 48, Tel. 06/583-6942. Credit cards accepted. Open Mondays 3:30pm–7:30pm, Tuesday–Sunday 10:00am–1:00pm and 3:30pm–7:30pm.*

Located in Trastevere, just over the Ponte Sisto, this place is owned by the very knowledgeable, helpful, and friendly Claire Hammond,and features English-language titles exclusively. They're stocked with hardbacks, paperbacks in non-fiction, fiction, general interest and more. Also a great place to meet other ex-pats or fellow travelers.

ECONOMY BOOKSTORE AND VIDEO CENTER, *Via Torino 136, Tel. 06/474-6877. Website: www.booksitaly.com. Credit cards accepted. Mondays 3:00pm–7:30pm, Tuesday–Saturday 10:00am–1:00pm and 3:30pm–7:30pm.*

This mainstay of the English-speaking community for the past three decades buys and sells secondhand English language paperbacks and have an excellent selection of both new and used books, including everything from fiction to non-fiction, children's, science fiction, best sellers and mysteries. They also carry a complete range of guidebooks on Rome and Italy.

THE ENGLISH BOOKSHOP, *Via di Ripetta 248, Tel. 06/320-3301. Credit cards accepted. Open Mon-Sat 9:00am – 7:00pm.*

The newest English language bookshop in Rome, just off the Piazza del Popolo and parallel to the Via del Corso. In this ideal location, you will find all sorts of great titles.

FELTRINELLI INTERNATIONAL, *Via VE Orlando 78, Tel. 06/484-4430. Website: www.feltrinelli.com. Credit cards accepted. Open Mon-Sat 9:00am – 7:00pm.*

Feltrinelli's is one of Italy's best and biggest bookstore chains, and in this location, next door to one of their regular bookstores, is one specifically dedicated to books in languages other than Italian. They have an extensive section in the English language. Located near the Termini, Via Veneto, and by the American Catholic Church in Rome, Santa Susanna.

LIBRERIA 4 FONTANE, *Via Quattro Fontane 20a, Tel. 06/481-4484. Credit cards accepted. Open Mon-Sat 9:00am – 7:00pm.*

All sorts of English and American titles available in this small shop up from the Piazza Barberini.

THE LION BOOKSHOP, *Via dei Gresci 36, Tel. 06/3265-4007. Credit cards accepted. Open Mon-Sat 9:00am – 7:00pm.*

A wide selection of fiction, science fiction and new releases from London and New York in this mainstay of the ex-pat community in Rome.

THE OPEN DOOR BOOKSHOP, *Via della Lungarette 25, Tel. 06/589-6578. Credit cards accepted. Open Mon-Sat 9:00am – 7:00pm.*

A small, intimate little shop that carries a number of titles.

NEWSPAPERS

The *International Herald Tribune* is published jointly by the Washington Post and The New York Times and printed in Bologna for distribution throughout Italy. They have an insert specifically for Italy. You can also find a condensed version of *USA Today*. There used to be the local English-language paper for Rome, *The Daily American*, but that perished years ago. You can also find newspapers from all over the world, in any language, at almost any newsstand.

AUTHENTIC ITALIAN FOOD STORES

As mentioned above in outdoor markets, the best places to get your fresh fruit, cheese, salami, ham, turkey, and bread for a picnic would be at any of the markets mentioned above in the section under *Outdoor Markets*. But if you are looking for something special, listed below are some food stores and shops where you can find some excellent authentic food products and unique gift items.

Alimentari & Gastronomie

Italy is a land of fine food, all made from the best ingredients and crafted with care by local artisans who learned their trade through time-honored traditions of excellence. And the place to find these tasty traditional foodstuffs is in small local *alimentari* and *gastronomie*. Listed below are some of the best, from which you can bring back something tasty to remember Italy. But also these places are great just to stop and savor the sights and smells or Rome. If you cannot make it to one of those listed below, stop in any local food store you run across and you will find many tantalizing gifts or ingredients to take home with you. These places are usually open 9am -12:30pm and 4pm-7pm.

LA CORTE, *Via della Gatta 1, Tel. 06/678-3842. Closed Saturday afternoons.*

Smoked fish, salmon, pate of smoked fish, and all sorts of meats, olives, prepared and packaged food fill up this quaint and colorful little store near the Piazza Venezia and the great chocolate store *Moriando & Gariglio*.

ANTICA SALUMIERIA, *Piazza della Rotonda 4, Tel. 06/687-5989. Closed Thursday afternoons and Saturday afternoons in the summer.*

Located in the same piazza as the Pantheon, the entry display is always tantalizing whether with smoked fish, mushrooms and truffles and an assortment of many different typically Italian food products. Here you can also find all sorts of cheese, salamis, olive oils, and packaged goods.

IL SALUMIERE DI GIUSEPPE CIAVATTA, *Via del Lavatore 31, Tel. 06/679-2935. Closed Thursday afternoons and Saturday afternoons in the summer.*

An excellent variety of local, artesian foods as well as local and European cheeses, salamis, pates, wine and olive oil. Located near the Trevi fountain, this small store is easily accessible during your tourist wanderings.

VOLPETTI ALLA SCROFA, *Via della Scrofa 31/32, Tel. 06/686-1940. Closed Sundays and Tuesday afternoons.*

One of the most famous and in my opinion, by far the best *gastronomie* in the center of town. They have an ample supply of cheeses and salamis, as well as local and foreign delicacies like caviar, sauces, salmon, mushrooms and truffles. There is also an excellent *rosticceria* inside with an inviting buffet of quick dishes like *pasta al forno* (baked pasta), *gnocchi* (on

Thursdays), *pollo arrosto* (juicy roasted chicken ... you have to try this), and a variety of *verdure* (green veggies) and *contorni* (vegetable side dishes). A great place to come for a quick bite and to load up on gift food items.

ANTICA NORCINERIA, *Via della Scrofa 100, Tel. 06/6880-1074.*

Almost directly across the street from Volpetti this place has a much better selection of salamis, and also carry bread. More of a locals shop because they also serve choice cuts of meat, here you can find all sorts of regional salamis as well as a number of gift items.

LATTICINI, *Via Collina 16, Tel. 06/474-1784. Closed Sundays.*

By far the best cheese store in Rome. They have all kinds of different cheeses to choose from and offer excellent advice, shrink wrapping service (*sotto vuoto*) which will keep your choices fresh if you want to bring them back with you. A little out of the way, but well worth the trip if you are looking for some exotic cheeses and great prices.

F.LLI CARILLI, *Via Torre Argentina 11, Tel. 06/6880-3789.*

Located close to the Pantheon and Campo and Piazza Navona, this place is a wonderful local alimentari run by two brothers. You can find all sorts of pastas, cheeses, meats and more here. Ideally located with friendly service.

SALUMERIA, *Via della Croce 43, Tel. 06/679-1228.*

They are more than their sign suggests since they carry all sorts of cheeses, sauces, pastas, focacci – and not just salami. Well located near the Spanish Steps, this a great local store though a bit pricey because of its location.

Cioccolaterie

Listed below are some artisan chocolate stores where you can get some tasty morsels to snack on or to bring back as gifts. The chocolate is all made in house and all lovingly selected, packed and wrapped while you wait. A wonderful experience and great chocolate at each.

MORIANDO & GARIGLIO, *Via del Pie di Marmo, Tel. 06/699-0856. Closed Sundays, August, and Saturdays in July.*

A gem of a chocolate store in the ambiance, presentation, flavor and price. This place came to Rome in 1886 bringing with it a grand tradition of chocolate making from the Alps. Still a family business they use nothing but the best chocolates and mix their ingredients in the traditional ways. In all there are 80 varieties of chocolate covered sweets to choose from. Located behind the Pantheon this place is perfectly situated for you to stop in while touring. This is my favorite chocolate store in Rome.

LA BOTTEGA DEL CIOCCOLATO, *Via Leonina 82, Tel. 06/482-1473. Closed Sundays.*

This chocolate store located near the Colosseum needs to be mentioned even though it is a bit out of the way. There are over 50 types of chocolate candies for sale, all made in-house, all made from only the best cacao from Brazil. Here you'll find delicious white chocolate concoctions as well as the sublimely rich *superamaro* 80 percent pure chocolate candies. The owner, Maurizio Proietti is a second generation chocolate artisan, and his creations will make your soul sing.

PUYRICARD, *Via delle Carrozze 26, Tel. 06/6929-1932. Closed Sundays.*

A transplanted French chocolate maker has made its home on one of Rome's best shopping streets near the Spanish Steps. Placed here with the intent of luring in the many female shoppers, they have been successful in doing just that. With 92 varieties to choose from, and many awards for excellence to their name, you can find something to satisfy even the most discerning palate. Whether you want something with Grand Marnier, with nuts, or simply a glob of dark chocolate, Puyricard is the place to come. You can also get items gift wrapped to bring home with you. Everything here is rather pricey, but well worth it.

INTERESTING LITTLE SHOPS

Rome is filled with all sorts of funky little shops and exotic clothing boutiques, all stuffed with so many different types of products that after shopping here a day at the mall will seem boring. Three of the most interesting little shops where you can find all sorts of interesting gifts or keepsakes are listed below.

TERECOTTE PERSIANE, *Via Napoli 92, Tel. 06/488-3886, Open 10:00am–1:30pm and 3:30pm–8:00pm.*

Come here for an eclectic mix of terra cotta figures, tiles, masks, planters and post boxes. Located in a small courtyard just down from the American church in Rome, Santa Susanna's, the place is filled with everything terra-cotta you can imagine. Even if you don't want to buy, come and browse. The prices are rather high, so do not be afraid to bargain.

L'IMPRONTA, *Via del Teatro Valle 53, Tel. 06/686-7821.*

For the most amazing, intricate and colorful prints of the piazzas, monuments, and buildings of Rome, in all shapes and sizes, framed or unframed, visit this wonderful little shop. It's an adventure to find this place since it is tucked away on a tiny side street between the Pantheon and Piazza Navona; but once you get here you will not be disappointed.

AI MONESTARI, *Corso Rinascimento 72, Tel 06/6880-2783. Closed Thursday afternoons. In the summer closed Saturday afternoons.*

Located just outside the Piazza Navonna, this tiny shop is filled with soaps, jams, pates, olive oils, wines, all made by men of the cloth. Hence the name of the place – *Ai Monestari* means 'of the monastery.' These monk-made products are all made with the best ingredients, have ever so quaint packaging and make perfect keepsakes or gifts.

CHIMERA, *Via del Seminario 121, Tel. 06/679-2126; open Mon. 3:15pm-7:30pm, Tuesday-Thursday 10:30am-7:00pm; Friday 10:30am-5:30pm; Mondays and Saturdays 1:00-7:00pm; closed Sundays.*

This consignment shop/antique store specializes in collector's items and objects like paintings, drawings, porcelain, silver, jewelry, art, coins, and much more. A short walk from the Pantheon, located in the basement of a 16th century palazzo, this is where Rome's well-heeled pawn their family heirlooms so they can continue living the life of luxury. An antique shop of the utmost tradition and discretion, this is a fun place to visit when you are around the Pantheon.

FEFE ALDO, *Via della Stelletta 20b, Tel. 06/6880-3585. Open 8:00am - 8:00pm.*

A small store near the Pantheon that is an outlet for handmade stationery crafts, journals, address books, and artisan book binding products. Here you can find all of the same stuff that is in the far more upscale and expensive Il Papiro (see below). The stores a mess, since it is really a small warehouse, but if you take the time to look through what they have you will find some real gems at great prices.

IL PAPIRO, *Via del Pantheon 50, Tel 06/679-5597, E-mail info@ilpapirofirenze.it, Website www.ilpapirofirenze.it.*

This is but one site of three surrounding the Pantheon. Here you can get all sorts of unique stationery gift items like journals, pens, blotters, cards, wrapping paper and more. They started in Florence but have now firmly established themselves here in Rome. A great store, but look at Fefe Aldo and Daniela Rosati (see below) for similar items at a lower price.

DANIELA ROSATI, *Via della Stelletta 27, Tel. 06/6880-2053. Open 9am-7pm.*

Just down the street from Fefe Aldo, this place is a quaint little shop that makes boxes, all sorts and sizes of boxes. The place is a little cluttered since it is a small artisan factory but come here and price boxes before you go to either Il Papiro or Fefe Aldo. The prices here are better.

PELLICANO, *Via del Seminario 93, Tel. 06/6994-2199.*

If you have ever wanted a tailormade tie (*cravatta su misura*), this is the place to come. They can usually do it in 10 days, but if you ask they will rush an order for you. A small intimate little store with reams of silk waiting for you. And the prices are the same as Brooks Brothers back home. High quality attentive service at a reasonable price.

BONORA , *Via dei Prefetti, 44, Tel. 06/73593. Closed Sundays. Hours Monday-Saturday 9:30am–1:00pm and 3:30pm–7:30pm. In winter open only Monday afternoons. In summer open only Sat mornings.*

And now that you have your tailormade tie, you can stroll over to this elegantly refined little store by the Parliament building to have a pair of shoes tailormade. Sorry, only men's shoes. And once again the prices are incredibly reasonable. The same as you would pay for a pair of regular shoes at Brooks Brothers.

GUSTO, *Piazza Augusto Imperatore 9, Tel. 06/322-6273.*

This is by far the most extensive and complete kitchenware store I have seen in Rome. It is also an enoteca and restaurant, but I suggest you come here to find that unique gift for the kitchen. Not that the food isn't good here ... but boy is the line long. Gusto is now the hippest place to grab a bite downtown.

POIGNEE, *Via Capo le Case 34, Tel. 06/679-0158, Fax 06/678-9382, E-mail: poignee@surfingontheweb.it, Website: www.poignee.com.*

An incredibly unique urban artifacts store where you can pick up antique brass door handles, shelf handles, locks, and so much more. In this store you can find basically everything you have ever imagined needing to complete that restoration project you have been putting aside so you can find that one special item. Check out their website to see what I mean.

CARTOLERIA PANTHEON, *Via della Rotunda 15, Tel. 06687-5313.*

Here you will find articles of wonderful design and high quality such as note cards, photo albums, stationary, telephone books, schedulers, and many other items which would be perfect as inexpensive and completely unique gifts.

PINEIDER, *Via Fontanella di Borghese 22, Tel 06/6830-8014. Also located at Via due Macelli 68, Tel. 06/678-9013.*

Two locations for this superb little stationary store that carries much more than that. Here you'll find all sorts of funky pens, schedulers, note cards, notebooks with creative designs, pencil cases, back packs. Another one of my favorites since both are so easily accessible.

GALLERIA SAN CARLO, *Via del Corso 114-116, Tel. 06/679-0571.*

This is a really cool toy store on Rome's best shopping street, the Via del Corso. Here you can find dolls, doll houses, toy cars/buses/planes, models, backgammon boards, chess sets, stuffed animals and a whole lot more. Two slender hallways display the items in glass cases. Find something you like and ask one of the attendants to get it for you. A great place for gifts for kids of all ages.

17. CULTURE & ARTS

FROM ETRUSCANS TO THE RENAISSANCE

Italy is perhaps best known for its great contributions to painting and sculpture; and many art lovers have described the country as one vast museum. Italy gave birth to such world renowned artists as Giotto, Donatello, Raphael, Michelangelo, Leonardo da Vinci, and Botticelli, who are revered the world over.

The oldest works of art in Italy are those of the **Etruscans**, and they date back to the 9th century BCE. This mysterious society's main cities and art centers were in the middle of the peninsula, between Rome and Florence, mainly in the province now know as Tuscany (the region was named after them ... Etruscans ... Tuscany). In Tarquinia, Volterra, Cerveteri, and Veio, the Etruscans have left behind magnificent temples, sculptures, and bronzes as well as other fascinating testimonies to their presence. The best museum collections of Etruscan art can be found in Rome's **Etruscan Museum**, Florence's **Archaeological Museum**, the **Bologna Municipal Museum**, and the **Municipal Museum of Volterra**.

Italy is also known for being a repository of ancient Greek art. During the time of the Etruscans, the Greeks established colonies in the south of modern-day Italy as well as Sicily. Magnificent ruins of temples exist today in some of these ancient Greek colonies: **Syracuse**, **Agrigento**, and **Taormina** in Sicily; and **Paestu** and **Coma** in Campania. There are good collections of Hellenic art in the **National Museum of Naples**, and in the museums in Palermo, Syracuse, Reggio Calabria, Paestum, and Taranto.

After the Greeks and Etruscans, the Roman Empire left its lasting impression all over Italy. There are still roads, bridges, aqueducts, arches, and theaters built by the Romans still in use today, some of which are over 2,000 years old. The most extensive excavations of ancient Roman ruins have been made at the **Forum** in Rome, at **Ostia** near Rome by the beach, and at **Pompeii** and **Herculaneum** – the cities that the volcanic **Mount Vesuvios** buried. For a first-hand, up-front feel of what life was like in the Roman Empire, don't miss these sites.

After the fall of the Roman Empire, the Byzantine Empire ruled many parts of the southern and eastern regions of Italy. This period left behind many churches, with their glorious mosaics, like those of the 6th century in Ravenna near the east coast; as well as the morbid but powerful **catacombs** outside of Rome.

Then after the Dark Ages, when the Roman Empire's progress reverted back to tribalism, the Renaissance came. This artistic period, meaning "rebirth," began in Italy in the 14th century and lasted for two hundred years. The Renaissance left us an extensive array of churches, palaces, paintings, statues, and beautiful city squares in almost every city of Italy. The main cities of Florence, Rome, Venice, Milan, and Naples have most of the treasures and beauty of this period, but smaller towns like Ferrara and Rimini also have their share. The best museums for viewing Renaissance art are the **Uffizzi Gallery** and **Pitti Palace** in Florence, as well as the **Vatican** and **Borghese Galleries** (in the Borghese Gardens just outside the walls) in Rome.

After the Renaissance, **baroque art** became fashionable. And Rome, more than any other Italian city, contains a dazzling array of churches, paintings, and statues recalling the splendor of such famous artists as Bernini, Borromini, and Caravaggio of the late 16th and 17th centuries.

RENAISSANCE PAINTING

In Italy (with France and Germany soon following suit) during the 14th and 15th centuries, the Renaissance was a period of exploration, invention, and discovery. Mariners from all over Europe set sail in search of new lands. Scientists like **Leonardo da Vinci** studied the mysteries of the world and the heavens. Artists found the human body to be a marvel of mechanics and beauty (but had to secretly study it, as Michelangelo did, lest the Church condemn them for heresy). This was undoubtedly one of Italy's most exciting periods in the history of artistic and scientific advancement.

Many consider the birthplace of Renaissance art to be Florence. It seemed to start with a young painter named **Masaccio**, who began introducing many bold new ideas into his painting. He made his paintings vibrantly interesting by drawing each person completely different from another, as well as making each person as realistic as possible. In conjunction with his ability to express the human form, Masaccio used combinations of colors to give the impression of space and dimension in his landscapes. Now every art student studies how brown makes objects appear closer, and blue makes them appear as if they in the distance.

Paolo Uccello, another Florentine, worked at the same time as Masaccio. A mathematician as well as an artist, he expanded on the mechanical and scientific issues of painting rather than on the human and psychological ones.

One of his paintings, *The Battle of San Romano*, circa 1457, celebrated the victory of Florence over Siena some 25 years earlier, and is a brilliant study in **perspective**. His depiction of objects, men, and horses all help to accentuate the sense of real perspective he was trying to achieve. One technique he used, which is now part of any good art school's curriculum, is **foreshortening**. In the left foreground of *The Battle of San Romano* is a fallen soldier with his feet facing the front of the picture. To give this figure a proper perspective, Uccello had to shorten the perceived length of the body, an extremely difficult task, and one not usually seen in other artists' previous works. In conjunction, Uccello drew roads, fields, etc., going back into the painting towards the horizon, to give the impression of distance. Now these are all well used and rather pedestrian artistic techniques, but back then they revolutionized the art world.

But most definitely three of the most influential Renaissance artists were **Raphael**, **Leonardo da Vinci**, and **Michelangelo**. Raphael was mainly known for his paintings of the Madonna and Child, from which our conceptual image of the Mother of Jesus is largely based. All of his paintings reflect a harmony that leaves the viewer with a warm and positive feeling of contentment.

Leonardo da Vinci is most well known for his *Mona Lisa*, painted in Tuscany in 1505-06 and now hanging in the Louvre, but he was also a versatile architect and scientist as well. Leonardo studied botany, geology, zoology, hydraulics, military engineering, anatomy, perspective, optics, and physiology. You name it, he did it – the original Renaissance Man!

Another versatile artist of the Italian Renaissance, and definitely its most popular then and now – he was always being commissioned to paint or sculpt all the wealthy people's portraits – was Michelangelo Buonarroti. Although he considered himself chiefly a sculptor – he trained as a young boy to become a stone carver – he left us equally great works as a painter and architect. As a painter he created the huge **Sistine Chapel** frescoes, encompassing more than 10,000 square feet in area. As an architect he helped complete the designs for **St. Peter's**, where his world renowned statue, *La Pieta*, currently resides.

RENAISSANCE SCULPTURE

Besides painting and architecture, **Michelangelo Buonarroti** was also the pre-eminent sculptor of the Renaissance. By the age of 26 he had carved *La Pieta*, his amazing version of Virgin Mary supporting the dead Christ on her knees; and was in the process of carving the huge and heroic marble *David*. He also created the memorable **Medici tombs** in the

Chapel of San Lorenzo, Florence. His greatest but lesser known work is his majestic *Moses* designed for the tomb of Pope Julius II, which can be viewed at the basilica of **San Pietro in Vincoli** in Rome.

Even though Michelangelo was commissioned to create many works by the Popes themselves, he had learned his amazing knowledge of the human anatomy by dissecting cadavers in his home town of Florence as a young man, a crime punishable by death and/or excommunication at the time.

During the Renaissance there were many other sculptors of note, but Michelangelo was truly the best. One of the others was **Lorenzo Ghiberti**, who died a few years before Michelangelo was born. For 29 years he labored to produce ten bronze panels, depicting Biblical episodes, for the doors of the Baptistery of Florence. Michelangelo was said to have been inspired to become a great artist because of these beautiful bronze doors.

MUSIC

Italy also has a great tradition in music. Even today, Italian folk music has made a resurgence, mainly because of the theme song for the *Godfather* movie series. Can't you just hear it playing in your head right now?

Besides folk music and Gregorian chants, Italy is known for its opera. If you are an opera fan you cannot miss taking a tour of the world famous **La Scala** in Milan. Getting a ticket to a performance is another matter. But have no fear, if your appetite cannot be sated without the shrill explosion of an *aria* there are other famous opera houses in Italy: **The Opera** in Rome, **The San Carlos** in Naples, **La Fenice** in Venice, **The Reggio** in Turin, **The Communale** in Bologna, **The Petruzzelli** in Bari, **The Communale** in Genoa, and **Massimo Bellini** in Catania (see addresses and phone numbers below).

These are also many opera festivals all over Italy virtually year-round.

Italian Opera

Italian opera began in the 16th century. Over time such composers as Gioacchino Rossini, Gaetano Donizetti, and Vincenzo Bellini created **bel canto** opera – opera that prizes beautiful singing above all else. The best singers were indulged with *arias* that gave them ample opportunity for a prominent display of their vocal resources of range and agility.

Rossini, who reigned as Italy's foremost composer of the early 19th century, was a master of both melody and stage effects. Success came easily, and while still in his teens he composed the first of a string of 32 operas that he completed by the age of 30. Many of these are comic operas, a genre in which Rossini excelled, and his masterpieces in this form are still performed and admired today. Among them is one you probably recognize, *The Barber of Seville* (1816).

Rossini's immediate successor as Italy's leading operatic composer was **Donizetti**, who composed more than 70 works in the genre. A less refined composer than Rossini, Donizetti left his finest work in comic operas, including *Don Pasquale* (1843) and *Lucia di Lammermoor* (1835).

Although he lived for a shorter time than either Rossini or Donizetti and enjoyed a far briefer career, **Bellini** wrote music that many believe surpassed theirs in refinement. Among the finest of his ten operas are *La Sonnambula* (The Sleepwalker, 1831), *Norma* (1831), and *I Puritani* (The Puritans, 1835), all of which blend acute dramatic perceptions with florid virtuosity.

From these roots came Italy's greatest opera composers of all times, **Puccini** and **Verdi**. Giacomo Puccini lived from 1858-1924 and composed twelve operas in all. Considered by many to be a close second to Verdi in skill of composition, Puccini's music remains alive in the popular mind because of enduring works like *Madame Butterfly* and *La Boheme*. Even though Puccini was the fifth generation of musicians in his family, he was mainly influenced to pursue his career after hearing Verdi's *Aida*.

Giuseppe Verdi lived from 1813-1901, and is best known for his operas *Rigoletto* (1851), *Il Trovatore* and *La Traviata* (both 1853), and what could be the grandest opera of them all, *Aida* (1871). Verdi composed his thirtieth and last opera *Falstaff* at the age of 79. Since he mainly composed out of Milan and many of his operas opened at La Scala opera house in that city, today a **Verdi museum** has been established there to honor his work.

Opera, Music, Drama, & Ballet Festivals

As the birthplace of opera, Italy offers visitors a variety of choices during the operatic seasons, which are almost year-round. In the summer months there are wonderful open-air operas presented at the **Terme di Caracalla** (Baths of Caracalla) in the center of Rome near the main train station from July to August, at the **Arena** in Verona from July to August, and at the **Arena Sferisterio** in Macerata in July. In general the opera season lasts from December to June.

Two of the most spectacular festivals for Italian performing arts are the **Maggio Musicale Fiorentino** with opera, concerts, ballet, and drama performances in Florence from May to June, and the **Festival of Two Worlds** with opera, concerts, ballet, drama performances and art exhibits in Spoleto from mid-June to mid-July.

Other events in or near Rome, include:

- **Perugia**, mid-July to late July: Umbria Jazz Festival. Italy's top jazz festival
- **Rome**, June through August: concerts in the Basilica Maxentius
- **Siena**, August: musical weeks

CONTACT INFO FOR MAJOR OPERA HOUSES

***Teatro dell'Opera**, Piazza D. Gigli 1, 00184 Roma. Tel. 060/481-601, Fax 060/488-1253*

***Teatro Communale**, Corso Italia 16, 50123 Firenze. Tel. 055/211-158 or 2729236, Fax 055/277-9410*

If you wish to obtain tickets to opera performances, concerts, ballet, and other performances you can either write directly to the theater in question or ask your travel agent to obtain the ticket for you. Currently there is no agency in the US authorized to sell concert and/or opera tickets, so this is the only way. When you are in Italy, your hotel should be able to assist you in obtaining tickets for performances in their city.

REGIONAL & NATIONAL FOLK FESTIVALS

Despite the encroachment of the modern world, the traditional festivals and their accompanying costumes and folk music have survived surprisingly well all over Italy. In many cases they have been successfully woven into the pattern of modern life so as to seem quite normal. Despite all possible modern influences these festivals (both secular and religious) have preserved their distinctive character.

Two of the most famous, the secular festivals of the **Palio** in Siena and **Calcio in Costume** in Florence give foreigners a glimpse into the past customs and way of life of medieval Italians. Both of these festivals pit different sections of their respective cities against each other to see who can earn bragging rights for the year. In Siena, a heated horse race takes place in a crowded city square. In Florence the Piazza della Signorina is turned into a veritable battleground when a game that is a cross between boxing, soccer, rugby, and martial arts is played. And what is most impressive of all in these festivals, besides the competition, is the fact that all participants dress in colorful period garb making each city appear to come alive with the past.

Since Italy is the home of the Catholic church, religious festivals also play a large part in Italian life. Particularly interesting are the processions on the occasion of **Corpus Christi**, **Assumption**, and **Holy Week**. In Italy, holiday times such as Easter and Christmas have not lost their religious intent as they have in most other places, and commercialism takes a back seat to the Almighty. This also means that tradition has not made way for consumerism, allowing us to experience a rich display of costumes, statues, parades, masses and more that evoke a simpler, more peaceful time.

The items below marked by an asterisk are festivals you simply cannot miss; if you can do so, plan your trip around them.

JANUARY

- **New Year's Day**, *Rome*: Candle-lit processional in the Catacombs of Priscilla to mark the martyrdom of the early Christians
- **January 5**, **Rome*: Last day of the Epiphany Fair in the Piazza Navona. All throughout the piazza a fair filled with food stands, candy stands, toy shops opens to the public. Lasts a week. A must see if you are in Rome for the holidays.

FEBRUARY/MARCH

- **Both Months**: **Venice*: Carnival in Venice with costume sand masks, with street mimes, music, and fireworks. A fun time.
- **19 March**, *Many places*: San Giuseppe (St. Joseph's day)

MARCH/APRIL

During March or April, *Rome* celebrates the Festa della Primavera (Spring Festival).

- **Palm Sunday**, *Many places, particularly Rome and Florence*: Blessings of palms, with procession
- **Wednesday before Easter**, *Many places, particularly Rome*: Mercoledi Santo (lamentations, Miserere)
- **Thursday Before Good Friday**, *Many places, particularly Rome and Florence*: Washing of the Feet, burial of the sacraments
- **Good Friday**, *Many places, particularly Rome and Florence*: Adoration of the Cross. *Taranto*: Procession of the Mysteries (Solemn procession with many beautiful period costumes).
- **Easter Saturday**, *Many places, particularly Rome and Florence*: Lighting of the Sacred Fire
- **Easter Day**, *Rome*: Papal blessing; *Florence:* Scopplo dei Carro ("Explosion of the Cart" – A pyramid of fireworks is set off in the Cathedral square to commemorate the victorious return of the first Crusade.

MAY

- **1 May**, **Florence*: Calcio in Costume (historical ball game – A Must See; Can't Miss This One)
- **During May**, *Florence*: Maggio Musicale (Music festival of May)
- **May 26**, *Rome*: San Filippo Neri
- **Ascension**, *Florence*: Festival of the Crickets. A lot of fun. You get to take home a cricket in a small cage. I loved this festival as a kid.
- **Corpus Christi**, *Many places, particularly Orvieto (Umbria)*: Processions

JUNE

- **First Sunday in June**, **Either Pisa, Genoa, Venice, or the Amalfi Coast:* Regatta of the maritime republics. Each year the four former maritime republics of Italy meet to battle for supremacy at sea. The friendly contest takes the form of a historic regatta in which longboats representing each of the republics race for first prize: respect. Site changes between the four cities/regions each year.
- **Mid-June**, *Many places*: Corpus Domini (Ascension processions)
- **June 23-24**, *Rome*: Vigilia di San Giovanni Battista (St. John's Eve, fireworks, eating of snails, song competition)
- **June 29**, *Rome*: Santi Pietro e Paulo (feast of Saints Peter and Paul); *Genoa*: "Palio Marinaro dei Rioni." Rowing race in ancient costumes.

JULY

- **July 2**, **Siena (Tuscany)*: Palio delle Contrade (horse race, historical parade). Also held on August 16th.
- **July 19-26**, *Rome*: Festa de' Noantri folklore festival of old Rome in Trastevere, Rome's oldest habitable section, which includes a colorful procession, folk dances, songs, carnival floats, and fireworks. Everybody gets real worked up for this. A must see.

AUGUST

- **15 August**, *Many places*: Assumption (processions and fireworks)
- **16 August**, *Siena (Tuscany)*: Palio delle Contrade (horse-races and processions in medieval costume)

SEPTEMBER/OCTOBER

- **September 7**, *Florence*: Riticolone (nocturnal festival with lanterns)

NOVEMBER/DECEMBER

- **November 22**, *Many places*: Santa Cecilia (St. Cecilia's day)
- **December 25**, *Rome*: Papal blessing
- **Mid-December to mid-January**, *Many places*: Christmas crib (Nativity Scenes)
- **Mid-December**, *Rome* – Nativity Scene and Huge Christmas Tree in St. Peter's Square

CRAFTS

Hundreds of thousands of skillful Italian artisans are the heirs to a 2,000-year tradition of craftsmanship. Their products – fashioned of leather, gold, silver, glass, and silk – are widely sought by tourists who flock to Florence, Rome, Milan, and Venice. Cameos made from seashells, an ancient Italian art form, are as popular today as they were in the days of the Roman Empire. The work of Italian artists and artisans is also exported for sale in the great department stores of France, Germany, the United Kingdom, and the United States.

Italian clothing designers are world famous, especially for precise tailoring, unusual knits, and the imaginative use of fur and leather.

The best place to see Italian artisans at work is in the glass blowing factories of Venice. There you'll be amazed at how easily they can manipulate molten balls into some of the most delicate, colorful, and beautiful pieces you've ever seen. Each chapter in this book highlights specific traditional crafts by region.

LITERATURE

Perhaps Italy's most famous author/poet is **Dante Aligheri**, who wrote the *Divine Comedy*, in which he describes his own dream-journey through Hell *(l'Inferno)* Purgatory *(Purgatorio)*, and Paradise *(Paradiso)*. At the time it was extremely controversial, since it is a poem about free will and how man can damn or save his soul as he chooses, which was contrary to church teachings. Even today it sparks controversy since it seems apparent that Dante's description of Purgatory is actually describing the life we all lead on earth, and shows his belief in reincarnation.

SHAKESPEARE'S ITALY

The Immortal Bard chose Italy as the setting for a number of his best-known masterpieces: ***Othello*** *takes place in part in Venice, and features both honorable and conniving Venetians;* ***Two Gentlemen from Verona*** *and* ***Romeo & Juliet*** *take place in Verona (the latter was pretty much lifted from Luigi da Porto's identical story, and today you can visit Juliet's House in Verona);* ***The Merchant of Venice*** *of course takes place in Venice;* ***The Taming of the Shrew*** *concerns the doings of rich Paduans, Pisans, and Veronans; about half of* ***A Winter's Tale*** *takes part in Sicily; all of* ***Much Ado About Nothing*** *takes place in Sicily; and finally,* ***All's Well That Ends Well*** *has one part set in Florence.*

Ancient Rome and the ageless themes of power, love, and intrigue also held great allure for Shakespeare: pick up ***Julius Caesar, Titus Andronicus, Troilius & Cressida,*** *or* ***Coriolanus*** *for some light reading about the tragic nature of the men and women who made the Roman Empire the world's first superpower!*

Two other notable Italian writers (you should remember these for quality cocktail party conversation) are **Petrarch**, famous for his sonnets to Laura, a beautiful girl from Avignon who died quite young, and is known as the "First of the Romantics;" and **Boccaccio**, the Robin Williams of his time, except he wrote, not performed, his famous *Decameron*, a charming and sometimes ribald series of short stories told by ten young people in a span of ten days. He was sort of like the Chaucer of Italy.

Among contemporary Italian writers, **Umberto Eco** stands out on his own. You may know two of his books that have been translated into English: *The Name of the Rose* and the more recent *Foucault's Pendulum*. If you are looking for complex, insightful, intriguing, and intellectual reading, Eco's your man. Last but not least, one Italian writer whom children all over the world should know is **Calo Collodi**, who wrote *Pinnochio*.

18. SPORTS & RECREATION

There are many different sporting activities to participate in and around Rome, since the city is only 15 miles from the beach and 65 miles from great skiing country. Below is a list of possible activities:

AMUSEMENT PARK

There is a permanent amusement park, **Luna Park**, in EUR on the outskirts of Rome and accessible by Metro. To get there take the Metropolitana on Linea B to the EUR stop. EUR stands for *Esposizione Universale Romana*, a grandiose project sponsored by Mussolini as a permanent exhibition to the glory of Rome. The park is to your left as you enter EUR along the Via Cristoforo Colombo. The rides are simple but the atmosphere is fun and rather old style carnival-like.

BICYCLING

Reckless Roman drivers can make biking on the city streets dangerous if you're not careful, and especially if you're a young North American used to the defensive drivers in the States and Canada. But if you are interested in riding a bicycle you can rent them at many different locations (see *Getting Around Town*) and take them for a trip through the **Borghese Gardens** (see *Seeing the Sights*, above) or along the city streets. I find it easy and manageable but I ride a bike a lot back home. So if you don't ride a bicycle normally I would advise against trying to do so here in Rome. This is not the Bahamas.

BOATING

Rowboats can be rented at the **Giardino del Lago** in the Villa Borghese. You can also rent dinghies at **Lido di Ostia** (see *Excursions & Day Trips* in the next chapter).

BOWLING

There are two good bowling alleys *(bocciodromi)* in Rome, but unless you have your own car, both of these places are far outside of the old walls of the city and thus rather difficult to get to except by taxi:

- **Bowling Brunswick**, *Lungotevere dell' Aqua Acetosa, Tel. 0348/229-0139. Website: www.brunswick.it. E-mail: brunswick@brunswick,it.*
- **Bowling Team Alley**, *Viale Regina Margherita 181, Tel. 06/8555-1184.*

GOLF

There are a variety of 18 hole and 9 hole courses all around Rome:

- **L'Eucalyptus Circolo del Golf**, *Via della Cogna 3/5, 04011 Aprilla. Tel. 06/926-252, Fax 06/926-8502.* Located 30 km from Rome, this is an 18 hole par 72 course that is 6,372 meters long. It is open all year except on Tuesdays. They also have a small executive course, driving range, pro shop, tennis courts, swimming pool, guest quarters, and a restaurant/bar.
- **Golf Club Torvalaianica**, *Via Enna 30, 00040 Marina di Ardea. Tel. 06/913-3250, Fax 06/913-3592.* Located 25 km from Rome, this is a 9 hole par 31 course that is 2,208 meters long. It is open all year except Mondays. They have a driving range as well as a restaurant/bar.
- **Golf Club Castel Gandolpho**, *Via Santo Spirito 13, 00040 Castel Gandolpho. Tel. 06/931-2301, Fax 06/931-2244.* This is an 18 hole par 72 course near the Pope's summer residence that is 5,855 meters long. It's open all year except on Mondays. They have a driving range, carts, pro shop, swimming pool, and a restaurant/bar.
- **Circolo del Golf di Fioranello**, *Via della Falcognana 61, 00134 Roma. Tel. 06/713-8080 or 731-2213, Fax 06/713-8212.* Located 17 km from the center of Rome, this is an 18 hole par 70 course that is 5,417 meters long. It is open all year except for Wednesdays. They also have a driving range, pro shop, swimming pool, and a bar/restaurant.
- **Macro Simone Golf Club**, *Via di Marco Simone, 00012 Guidonia. Tel. 0774/370-469, Fax 0774/370-476.* Located 17 km from Rome, this is an 18 hole par 72 course that is 6,360 meters long. It is open all year except for Tuesdays. They also have an 18 hole executive course, driving range, pro shop, swimming pool, tennis courts, massage room, sauna, gymnasium, and an excellent restaurant and bar.
- **Golf Club Parco de' Medici**, *Viale Parco de' Medici 20, 00148 Roma. Tel. 06/655-33477, Fax 06/655-3344.* Located 10 km outside of the city center, this is an 18 hole par 72 course that is 5,827 meters long. It is open all year except on Tuesdays. They also have a driving range, swimming pool, tennis courts, and a restaurant/bar. This is the course most accessible and nearest the city center.

- **Circolo del Golf di Roma – Aqua Santa**, *Via Appia Nuova 716 or Via Dell'Aquasanta 3, Roma 00178, Tel. 06/780-3407, Fax 06/7834-6219.* Located 11 km from Rome, this is an 18 hole par 71 course that is 5,825 meters long. It is open all year except on Mondays. They have a driving range, putting green, swimming pool, and a restaurant/bar.
- **Olgiata**, *Largo Olgiata 15, Roma 00123, Tel. 06/378-9141. Fax 06/378-9968.* Located 19 km from the center of Rome, in a housing development similar to many golf courses in the U.S. At Olgiata there is an 18 hole par 72 course that is 6,396 meters long and a 9 hole par 34 course that is 2,968 meters long. The course is open all year except on Mondays. They have a driving range, pro shop, swimming pool and a bar/restaurant.

RIVER TRIPS ON THE TIBER

In July and August you can take a river trip through central Rome. The trips are organized by the **Tourvisa Boat Trips on the Tiber**, *Via Marghera 32, Tel. 06/446-3481.*

SWIMMING

The best nearby beach is at **Lido di Ostia**, less than an hour west-northwest of Rome. The beaches are clean and large, and they have plenty of *cabanas* to rent where you can change your clothes. There are also some excellent seafood restaurants where you can leisurely eat, sip wine, and enjoy the beautiful Italian summers.

Listed below are available swimming pools in Rome which you can pay to use:

- **Cavalieri Hilton**, *Via Cadiolo 101, Tel 06/3509-2950*
- **Piscina del Rose EUR**, *Viale America 20, Tel. 06/592-6717*
- **Roman Sports Center**, *Via Galoppatoio 33, Tel. 06321-8096*

TENNIS

The following public courts require reservations and there are hourly fees charged:

- **Circolo Montecitorio**, *Via Campi Sportivi 5, Tel. 06/875-275*
- **EUR**, *Viale dell'Artigianato 2, Tel. 06/592-4693*
- **Foro Italico**, *Tel. 06/361-9021*
- **Tennis Belle Arti**, *Via Flaminia 158, Tel. 06/360-0602*

19. EXCURSIONS FROM ROME

I've planned some fun excursions for you: **Tivoli Gardens**, **Castel Gandolfo**, **Frascati**, **Ostia Antica** and **Cervetri**. Please see the separate sections for **Florence**, **Siena**, **Orvieto**, and **Pompeii** & **Herculaneum** even though each of them can be accessed as a day long excursion from Rome.

EXPLORING BEYOND ROME

Whether you wish to explore outside of Rome for a day, a weekend or longer, ***Elegant Etruria*** *is a great travel organization to use. They help find the best accommodations, offer sightseeing tours, and make your travel easier and worry-free. So if you want to explore the best of the little hill towns around Rome and want someone else to make all the arrangements for you, contact Mary Jane Cryan at Elegant Etruria.*

Elegant Etruria*, Palazzo Pieri Piatti, Vetralla (VT) 01019 Italia, Tel. 0761/485008, Fax 0761/485002, E-mail: macryan@tin.it, Website: www.dbws.com/Etruria/Home.htm.*

TIVOLI GARDENS

Tivoli has about 45,000 inhabitants, and is situated on the **Aniene**, a tributary of the Tiber, overlooking Rome from its place on the **Sabine Hills**. This town is where the wealthy ancient Romans built their magnificent summer villas, and the three main attractions are **Villa Adriana** (Hadrian's Villa), **Villa d'Este**, and **Villa Gregoriana**.

The **Villa Adriana's** main attraction is its huge grounds, where you and lizards can bask in the sun. There are plenty of secluded spots to relax or enjoy a picnic on the grass. The building itself was begun in 125 CE and completed 10 years later, and was at the time the largest and most impressive villa in the Roman Empire. From his travels **Hadrian**, an

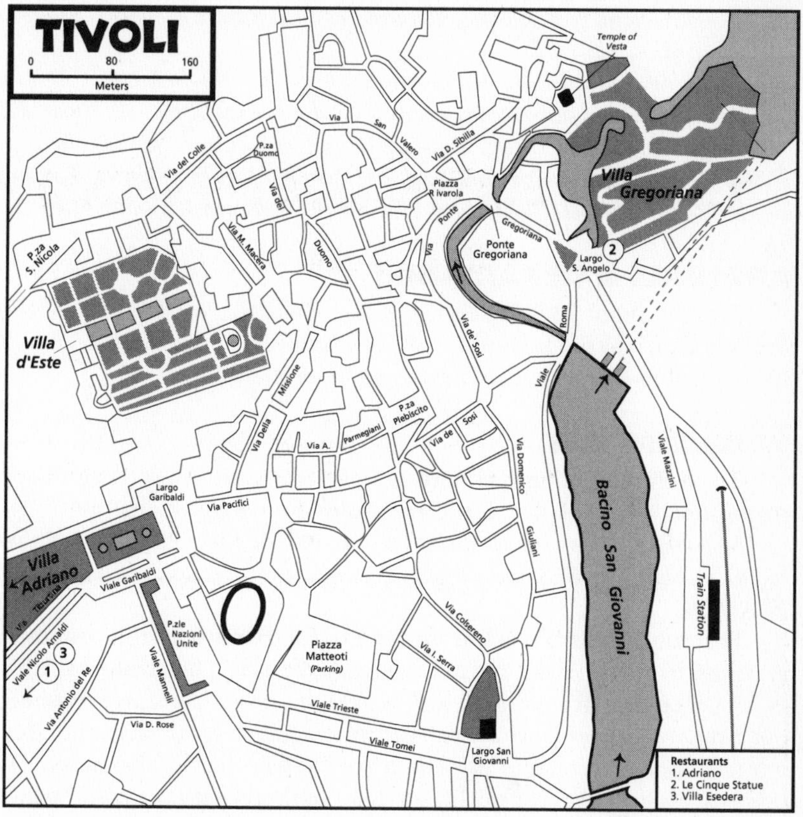

accomplished architect, found ideas that he recreated in his palace. The idea for the **Poikile**, the massive colonnade through which you enter the villa, came from Athens. And the **Serapeum** and **Canal of Canopus** were based on the Temple of Serapis near Alexandria, Egypt.

The **Villa D'Este's** main draw are its many wonderful fountains. The villa itself was built on the site of a Benedictine convent in the mid-16th century. The **Owl Fountain** and **Organ Fountain** are especially beautiful, as is the secluded pathway of the **Terrace of the Hundred Fountains**. If you make it out to Tivoli, these gardens and their fountains cannot be missed, especially at night during the months of May through September when they are floodlit. They are simply spectacular then.

The **Villa Gregoriana** is known for the **Grande Cascata** (the Great Fall), which is a result of Gregory XVI diverting the river in the last century to avoid flooding. The park around the cascade has smaller ones as well as grottoes. This is the least interesting of the three villas.

The addresses and hours of the three villas are:

- **Villa Adriana**, *Bivio Villa Adriana, 3.5 miles southwest of Tivoli. Open*

Tuesday–Sunday, 9:30am–1 hour before sunset. Closed Mondays. Small fee required.

- **Villa d'Este**, *Viale delle Centro Fontane. Open Tuesday–Sunday, 9:30am to 1.5 hours before sunset. May–September also open 9:00pm–11:30pm with the garden floodlit. Closed Mondays. Small fee required. Sundays free.*
- **Villa Gregoriana**, *Largo Sant'Angelo. Open Tuesday–Sunday 9:30am to 1 hour before sunset. Closed Mondays. Small fee required. Sundays free.*

ARRIVALS & DEPARTURES

Tivoli is about 23 miles east of Rome. Take the Via Tiburtina (SS5). The Villa Adriana lies to the right about 3.5 miles before the town. By train from Stazione Termini, the trip takes about 40 minutes.

WHERE TO EAT

Tivoli simply abounds with restaurants, many offering a magnificent panoramic view of Rome. Here are some of my suggestions.

1. ADRIANO, *(near Hadrian's Villa), Via di Villa Adriana 194, Tel. 0774/529-174. Closed Sunday nights. All credit cards accepted. Dinner for two L130,000.*

Basically at the front of the entrance to Hadrian's Villa, this restaurant attached to a hotel has a beautiful garden terrace. They make excellent *crostini di verdure* (fried dough with vegetables inside), *raviolini primavera con ricotta e spinaci* (ravioli with spring vegetables, spinach and fresh ricotta), *tagliata di coniglio alle erbette* (rabbit with herbs) and more. The prices are a little rich for my blood, but the food keeps me coming back for more.

2. LE CINQUE STATUE, *Largo S Angelo 1, Tel. 0774/20366. Closed Fridays. All credit cards accepted. Dinner for two L110,000.*

In front of the entrance to Villa Gregoriana this place has outside seating where you can enjoy the local cuisine. They make many of their pastas in house so they're sure to be fresh. They also specialize in meats, like *maialino* (baby pork) and *abbacchio* (lamb) *arrosto* as well as their *verdure fritte* (fried vegetables).

3. VILLA ESEDRA, *(near Hadrian's Villa), Via di Villa Adriana 51, Tel. 0774/534-716. Closed Wednesdays. All credit cards accepted. Dinner for two L70,000.*

You can get some interesting antipasti like the *insalatine di pesce* (small fish salad), then you can move on to their pastas, which are all made in house, and are all superb, especially the *spaghetti all'amatriciana* (with tomatoes, cream and spices) and the *penne all'arrabbiata* (with tomatoes, garlic oil and hot pepper). These and all their pastas are simply amazing. Perfectly Roman and bursting with flavor from the freshest ingredients. Not a fancy place but great food.

CASTEL GANDOLPHO

Located above **Lake Albano**, with a wonderful vista over the valley, **Castel Gandolpho** is the location of the summer residence of the Pope. From up at the Castel Gandolpho, you can enjoy a fabulous view of the wooded slopes that fall swiftly down into the murky waters of a volcanic crater. The one real sight is the **Palazzo Pontificio** (Papal Palace), built in 1624. During the summer months when the Pope is in residence, every Sunday at noon His Eminence gives an address in the courtyard of the palace. No permit is required to enter. First come, first served is the rule.

ARRIVALS & DEPARTURES

Castel Gandolpho is about 15 miles east of Rome. Take the Via Appia Nuova (SS7) for about 30 minutes. By train from Stazione Termini, it's about 35 minutes. From the station you will have to take a local taxi up to the Castel, unless you feel adventurous and want to walk the three kilometers uphill. Just follow the signs on the side of the road.

WHERE TO EAT

ANTICO RISTORANTE PAGNANELLI, *Piazza A Gramsci 4, Tel. 06/936-0004. Closed Tuesdays. All credit cards accepted. Dinner for two L90,000.*

This restaurant with a nice view of the lake has been in existence since 1882, and they still serve all the traditional dishes created with produce from the local countryside. They make a wonderful *strozzapreti all'amatriciana* (pasta with tomatoes, cream and spices), *risotto al'erbe* (rice dish with herbs), *maialino arrosto* (roast baby pork), *bracciole di cinghiale* (roast boar shanks) and other savory dishes. Rumor has it that the Pope even has stopped in once or twice.

FRASCATI

If wine is what you're looking for, **Frascati** is where you want to be. This town's wine is world famous, and this little town is simply dotted with wine bars where you can sample the vintages. The ambiance of this hill town is magnificent too.

Frascati is a great place to stay while visiting Rome if you can't stand the urban hustle and bustle. Since it's only 35 minutes and $5 away, Frascati's relaxing pace, scenic views, quaint little wine shops, excellent local restaurants, and winding old cobblestone streets should be seriously considered as an alternative to downtown Rome.

Since this is still primarily an excursion, I've listed more restaurants and wine bars than hotels – though I hope some of you will opt to stay here and enjoy Frascati's many charms.

ARRIVALS & DEPARTURES

Frascati is roughly 14 miles southeast of Rome. Take the Via Tuscolana (SS215) up to the hill town (25 minute drive). By train from Stazione Termini, board a local train that leaves every forty minutes or so from Track 27. The ride lasts a little over 35 minutes. Cost L6,500.

CONSIDER FRASCATI

Even though I spent 8 years living in Rome, and have grown to love it, the city can be a bit overwhelming both for a first time visitor and the Roman veteran. It's large, congested, noisy, polluted and challenging while also being one of the most beautiful, charming cities filled with some of the world's most well-known sights and prized artistic treasures. Another reason for staying in the countryside is that most prices at most hotels and restaurants seem to have gone through the roof.

So if you are someone who would rather not experience the hectic pace of a big city, but you still want to see all that Rome has to offer, stay in ***Frascati****. This quaint, charming, quiet, little hill town is the perfect place to get away from it all while still having access to everything. The town is only 35 minutes away by train (the fare is L6,500) and the trains run every 45 minutes or so until 10:00pm. Granted if you want to take a nap in the middle of the afternoon, your hotel would be way out here but that is what the* ***Borghese gardens*** *are for. Bring a picnic lunch and take a little siesta in the shade in one of the prettiest and peaceful gardens in any city in the world.*

In Frascati, you'll be able enjoy many good restaurants, sample the fine local wines from quaint little wine stores located all over the city. They serve you glasses or carafes from huge vats. You'll also be able to savor the ambiance of an ancient medieval town, with its cobblestone streets and twisting alleys. Here you'll be able to gaze out your windows and see lush valleys below, instead of looking out onto another building as you would probably do in Rome. And if you come in October, you'll be able to experience a wine festival of bacchanalian proportions.

So if you are used to the calm serenity of country life, but still want to experience the beauty that Rome has to offer, Frascati may be your answer.

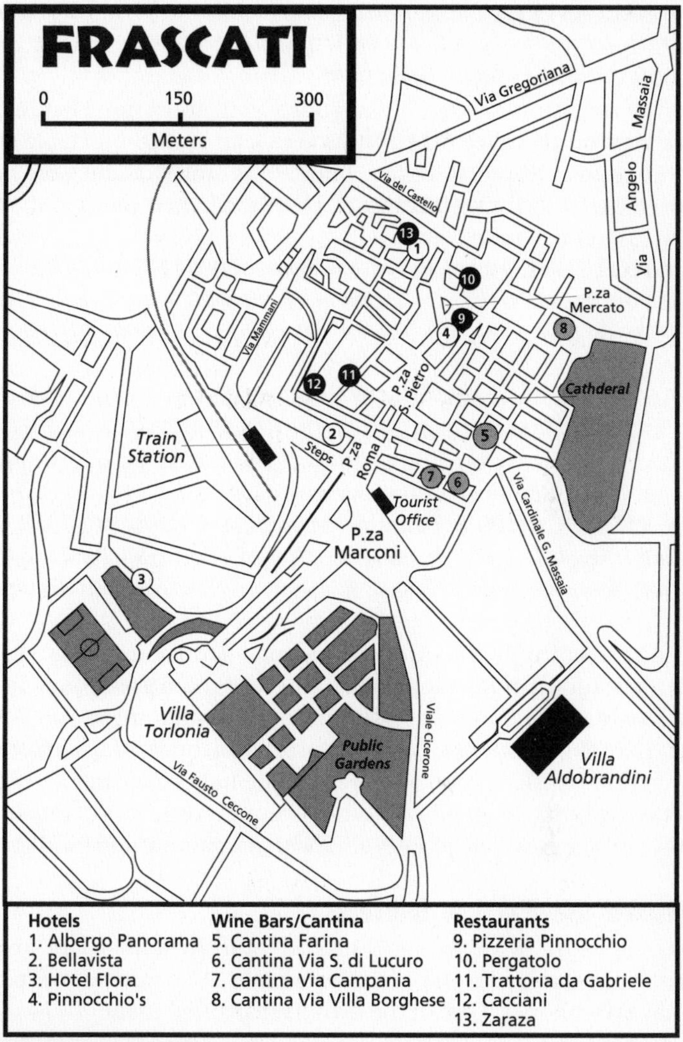

WHERE TO STAY

1. ALBERGHO PANORAMA, *Piazza Carlo Casini 3, Frascati 00044. Tel. 06/942-1800 or 941-7955. 9 rooms, two with bath. Single with bath L68,000-90,000; Single without bath L50,000-70,000; Double without bath L60,000-90,000. L15,000 for an extra bed. L30,000 for all meals. No credit cards accepted. ***

Situated in the *centro storico* with a beautiful panoramic view of Rome. This is a small but comfortable hotel for those on a budget. The rooms are kept spotlessly clean. A good inexpensive place to stay. Not much ambiance but clean and accommodating.

2. BELLAVISTA, *Piazza Roma 2, 00044 Frascati. Tel. 06/942-1068, Fax 06/942-1068. 13 rooms all with bath. Double L140,000-160,000. Breakfast L10,000. All credit cards accepted.* ***

You have room service, TV in your room, and a hotel bar, as well as a nice view of the valley. The rooms are clean and comfortable as befits a good country three star. The building is quite quaint and old, but restored perfectly for your comfort. I love the high ceilings in the rooms, making them feel much larger.

3. HOTEL FLORA, *Via Vittorio Veneto 8 00044 Frascati. Tel. 06/941-5110, Fax 06/942-0198. 33 rooms only 30 with bath. Single L120,000-170,000; Double L150,000-190,000. Breakfast L12,000. All credit cards accepted.* ****

An old hotel decorated with style, located in a central position in Frascati. Much better amenities than the Bellavista, but not as good a view. Located a little ways outside of town, this hotel is set in a wonderfully tranquil environment. A good place to stay.

4. PINNOCCHIO'S, *Piazza del Mercata 20, Tel. 06/941-7883, Fax 06/941-7884. Single L60,000-80,000 (Double used as a single); Double L100,000-130,000. Seven rooms all with bath, mini-bar, and TV. No credit cards accepted.* **

Large comfortable rooms with gigantic bathrooms, located upstairs from a restaurant of the same name, where you can grab yourself a snack until late in the evening. The office is in the restaurant so you'll need to enter there to get your key. Perfectly located on the central market square. The market is a sight you have to see while in Frascati and a great place to get some fruits, vegetables (you can even get fresh bags of mixed salad), meats, and cheeses. The place is alive with bargaining and local greetings.

WHERE TO EAT & DRINK

Some of the wine bars are so small and so nonchalant about the tourist trade that they don't even have names. Also many of the places do not have telephones. One of the owners explained to me, "*Why should we have telephones when we can walk over and talk in person?*" That makes sense, since Frascati is such a small intimate little town.

Don't be put off by this casual hill town attitude, since the ones without names or phones are some of the best places to visit. Enjoy.

Wine Bars

5. CANTINA FARINA, *Vini Propri, Via Cavour 20. No Telephone.*

A real wine bar, not a fern infested one. With a tile floor, collapsible wooden tables and chairs and great wine served from vats, here you can get a real taste for how the Italians enjoy life. Located near a school, so it can get periodically noisy during the day.

6. CANTINA VIA SEPULCRO DI LUCURO, *Via Sepulcro di Lucuro 6. No Telephone.*

Located just off the main road (Via Catone), this place has a small area for seating outside separated from the rest of the world by large planters. The inside is quite cool, like a wine cellar. Just inside the door is an antique wine press that they still use during the pressing season. Inside or out you'll get some of the best wines Frascati has to offer.

7. CANTINA VIA CAMPANIA, *Via Campania 17. No Telephone.*

Just down the road from the wine bar listed above, this place has one and a half of its four inside walls covered with wine vats, and the rest of the space taken up with strange looking tools used in the wine trade, as well as large empty bottles that you only wish you could take home with you ... full. The owner is quite friendly and if it's not too crowded will sit down and chat. Great wine. Wonderful atmosphere.

8. CANTINA VIA VILLA BORGHESE, *Via Villa Borghese 20. No Telephone.*

Small wine store filled with large 1,000,000 liter barrels called *botte*, and 500,000 liter barrels called *mezza botte*. Each cask is numbered and initialed with the vineyard it came from. Not very scenic atmosphere and no tables to sit at, but they will sell you a bottle of their finest for only L2,000. That's $1.50 for an excellent bottle of Frascati wine.

Restaurants

9. PIZZERIA/BIRRERIA PINNOCCHIO, *Piazza del Mercato 20, Tel. 06/941-6694 or 942-0330. Dinner for two L55,000.*

A large statue of Pinnocchio advertises this superb restaurant in Frascati's quaintest and most vibrant square (it's actually a triangle). There is outside seating with large planters separating you from the pace of this market-dominated piazza. Inside you'll find tiled floors and wood paneling giving the place a nice rustic flair. They serve great *canneloni ai quattro formaggi* (with four cheeses), as well as great Roman staples such as *amatriciana, carbonara, and vongole.*

For seconds try their *scampi alla griglia* (grilled shrimp) which is reasonably priced at only L16,000. If you find you've lingered too long over your Sambuca, Pinnocchio's has some wonderful rooms upstairs.

10. PERGATOLO, *Via del Castello 20, Tel. 06/942-04-64. L13,000-Cold plate with wine and bread; L20,000-First course of pasta, pizza, or meat, second course of the cold plate with wine and bread.*

Wild and fun atmosphere, a little on the touristy side with singers serenading the diners. You can either enjoy or ignore it in this large and spacious restaurant that has a deli counter displaying all the available meats, cheeses, breads, salamis, etc., that you'll be served. There are roaring fires behind the counter where your meats are all prepared.

If you've come to Frascati for the day or the week, this is one place you have to try, just for the fun of it. Say hi to the beautiful manager Tiziana for me.

11. TRATTORIA/PIZZERIA DA GABRIELE, *Via Solferino 5. No telephone. No credit cards. Dinner for two L35,000.*

You ladies will love the charming part owner Raphaele. He looks like something out of a movie with his piercing dark eyes and sultry glances. You can get pizza until 1:30am at wonderfully inexpensive prices. Just off the main piazza, this is a fun place to come in the late evening. Try their *pizza can salsiccia* (with sausage) or *con porcini* (mushrooms). I asked them to put both together, with extra cheese, and the pizza came out wonderfully, American-style.

12. CACCIANI, *Via Alberto Diaz 13, Tel. 06/942-0378. Closed Mondays. Holidays January 7-15 and 10 days after Ferragosto. Dinner for two L110,000. All credit cards accepted.*

One of the most famous restaurants in this region. It has a beautiful terrace that offers a tranquil and serene atmosphere. For starters, try the *crostini con verdure* (baked pastry appetizer filled with vegetables). Then try the home-made *fettuccine alla Romana* (made with tomatoes, chicken and spices) or *spaghetti con le vongole verace* (with clams in a hot oil and garlic sauce). For the entrée try the *fritto misto di carne* (mixed fried meats) the *saltimbocca*, or any of their grilled fish.

13. ZARAZA, *Viale Regina Margherita 21, Tel. 06/942-2053. Closed Mondays and the month of August. Dinner for two L70,000. Visa accepted.*

A simple rustic atmosphere with a few tables outside offering a limited view of the valley below. Inside tables are located in the basement of (but separate from) the Albergho Panorama hotel. It's warm and inviting in the winter, with the heat from the kitchen, the brick pillars, the whitewashed arched walls, and the friendly family service.

Traditional *cucina Romana* where you can get *bucatini all'amatriciana* (pasta with tomatoes, cream and spices), *gnocchi al ragu* (potato dumplings with tomato-based meat sauce), *capaletti in brodo* (pasta shaped like little hats in soup), *trippa alla Romana* (tripe with a tomato-based sauce) *abbacchio al forno* (grilled lamb), as well as some other Roman specialties such as *spaghetti all'amatriciana* and *penne all'arrabbiata* (with a hot spicy tomato-based sauce), as well as *lombata di vitello* (grilled veal chop) and *misto arrosto* (mixed roast meats).

SEEING THE SIGHTS

If you've driven to Frascati, you were able to savor the lovely scenic route along the old **Appia Antica** past the Catacombs and ruined tombs. The town is perched halfway up a hill, and on a clear day you will have splendid views of all of Rome and its scenic countryside.

Besides the great views, the wine, and the chance for some relaxation, Frascati has a wealth of villas and spacious parks that were formerly residences of princes and popes. One of these residences, **Villa Aldobrandini** which sits just above the town, and has a magnificent garden in which you can find solitude. To enter the villa's grounds you need to first get a free pass from the **Aziendo di Soggiorno e Turismo**, in Frascati's Piazza Marconi. *The hours are Monday-Friday 9:00am-1:00pm.*

Besides the beauty of its old villas, many of which were damaged in Allied bombings because the Germans had taken over the town for their headquarters, Frascati's draw is the fine **white wine** that bears its name. All wines seem to lose a special *qualcosa* when they travel, so if you are a wine lover, do not miss out on this chance to drink Frascati's wine directly at the source.

To enjoy this succulent nectar, there are old, dark wine stores, with heavy wooden tables and chairs located all over town. At one of these you can sit and enjoy this unspoiled and inexpensive wine, the way the natives have been doing for centuries. The **Cantina Vanelli**, just off Piazza Fabro Filzi, is a prime example of one such wine store, and a fine traditional location to sample Frascati's produce. Just ask for a *bicchiere di vino* (glass of wine). An alternative to the cramped quarters of these wine stores but with quite a bit less atmosphere would be to sit at one of the sidewalk cafés offering superb views along with great wine.

Frascati is the perfect place to wander through, getting lost in the alleys, side streets, steps leading nowhere, and winding roads (all cobblestoned). If you follow the sporadically placed yellow signs that say *Ferario Pedonale,* you'll be guided through all the major sights and sounds of this hill town. These signs are prominently displayed so that the revelers who come for the wine festival can find their way around even after having a glass or two of the local vintage. One distinguishing feature is that there seem to be more *alimentari* (little food stores) per person than in any other city I've ever seen.

If you are fortunate enough to be in Frascati during the month of October, the town celebrates a **wine festival** of pagan proportions that lasts several days and nights. Come out to witness and partake in the debauchery, but please do not drive back to Rome afterwards - take the train.

CERVETRI

Cervetri used to be the Etruscan capital of Caere, but today Cervetri is not known today for the town of the living, but the towns of the dead the Etruscans built. These **Necropoli** are large circular mounds of tombs laid out in a pattern of a street, like houses in a city.

Today these round roofs are densely covered with grasses and wild flowers. Inside they have been furnished with replicas of household furnishings carved from stone. Most of the original artifacts are in the **Villa Giulia Museum** or **Vatican Museums** in Rome, but the burial sites themselves are eerily significant. *The site is open Tuesday to Sunday 9:00am–4:00pm. Admission L7,000.*

After viewing the necropolis you can settle down among the mounds and have a picnic lunch, and imagine what life would be like during that time. After sightseeing you can return to the town by taxi, or by car if you have one, and take in the limited sights the little town has to offer. From the crowded main piazza you can climb steps to a **museum** with a lovely medieval courtyard. But the main sights out here are the Necropoli.

ARRIVALS & DEPARTURES

Cervetri is about 28 miles west northwest of Rome. A 45 minute drive up the Via Aurelia (SS1), which will give you a more scenic view, or the Autostrada A12, which connects to the 'beltway' around Rome by route 201. By train from Stazione Termini it takes 1 hour and 10 minutes; from Roma Tiburtina it takes 50 minute to get to Cervetri-Ladispoli. Once in the town, to reach the **Necropolis** you can grab a local taxi, or take the two kilometer walk along a little road. There are signs on the road to guide you where you're going.

WHERE TO EAT

DA FIORE, *near Procoio di Ceri, Tel. 06/9920-4250. Closed Wednesdays. Dinner for two L60,000. No credit cards accepted.*

A simple little local *trattoria* in the open country not far from the ruins and only four kilometers from the Via Aurelia. They make great pastas like *penne al funghi* (with mushrooms) *al ragu* (with tomato and meat sauce) or *con salsiccia* (with sausage). They also have grilled meats and their famous *bruschetta* (garlic bread as an appetizer) and pizza – all cooked in a wood burning oven.

OSTIA

OSTIA ANTICA

Founded in the fourth century BCE, **Ostia Antica** feels about as far away from Rome as you can get, but is actually only 15 miles southwest of the city, a mere 45 minutes by subway then a short train ride. As with excursions to Pompeii or Herculaneum, you get the sensation that the clock has been turned back nearly 2,000 years. And what most people do not know is that Ostia contains the largest sampling of mosaic floors anywhere in Italy. Some of which are as intricate as tapestries.

This city was once the bustling seaport of Ancient Rome, but today it is calm and serene respite from the hectic pace of modern Rome. The mosaic tile floors document the great variety of goods and services available in Ostia, documenting how busy the port was at one time. Commodities included furs, wood, grain, beans, melons, oil, fish, wine, mirrors, flowers, ivory, gold, and silk. Among the services offered were caulkers, grain measurers, maintenance men, warehousing, shipwrights, barge men, carpenters, masons, mule drivers, stevedores and divers for sunken cargoes.

As at Pompeii, the houses are the most interesting part of the city. There were large villas and average sized abodes but the majority of Ostian residences were apartment buildings. There were also many public amenities including a theater, baths, and a fire department. The theater is small but is still put to use today for modern renditions of Greek and Roman plays.

The city is well preserved despite having been subject to repeated attacks by pirates and hostile navies. The only invasions it undergoes now are from packs of marauding Italian school children on their cultural outings, rampaging through its archaeological excavations – the main reason to come here (see below).

Ostia was abandoned starting in the 5th century CE. By the late 4th century no new burials had been made in its cemetery and the road to Rome was overgrown with bushes and trees. What led to Ostia's decline was that its two harbors were silting up and were thus of no use to Rome anymore. And today the beach at Ostia (Ostia Lido) is three miles beyond the seawall of the ancient town. Without an identity or commercial base of its own – as Pisa had, Florence's old port city – archeological records indicate that citizens began leaving the decaying town of Ostia in droves. When Saint Augustine was passing through the city in the 4th century CE, it was already in full decline. By that time the Emperor Constantine had revoked its municipal status and assigned it to be governed by the village of Portus, which had grown up around a 'new,' harbor built by Trajan.

When in Rome, if you are interested in seeing an ancient Roman city being unearthed from its tomb and you do not have the time to get to Pompeii, Ostia Antica is an option which will not disappoint. Also, Ostia Antica is a wonderful respite from the hectic pace of Rome and is great place for kids to wander around.

ARRIVALS & DEPARTURES

Ostia Antica is about 15 miles southwest of Rome. Take the Via del Mare (SS8) for about 25 minutes. By metro and train, take Linea B to the

Piramide station, and catch the train to Ostia Antica or continue to Lido di Ostia (the beach). It takes about 45 minutes from Stazione Termini. Your Metro ticket is valid for both trips so it will only cost you L1,500. Once at Piramide follow the signs for "Lido."

On the way back you may catch a train that goes to the Magliana Metro station instead of Piramide. Don't panic, just follow the signs for "Linea B" and once there get on the train at the track that says "Direz. Termini-Rebibbia." Check the signboard at the Ostia station for the return train. There is a ticket booth in the station but it cannot hurt to have your return ticket already purchased.

WHERE TO EAT

On the way from the train station to the site there are a couple of cafes and a restaurant where you can grab a bite to eat. Inside the archeological site itself you will find a café to grab a bite to eat. None of them are worth writing home about, but they will satisfy your hunger.

SEEING THE SIGHTS

Ostia Antica gives an excellent notion of what life in the metropolis was like at the height of the Empire. This city presents to the modern world a picture of Roman life only a shade less vivid than that of Pompeii. The plan of the city is regular but not too regimented. It is scenic, monumental and functional. Its backbone is the major east-west street, the *Decumanus Maximus*, nearly a mile long, which was once colonnaded, and runs from the **Porta Romana** straight to the **Forum**.

You enter the excavations in Ostia at the aforementioned **Porta Romana**. The *Decumanus Maximus*, takes you past the well-preserved old **theater** and the **Piazzale dei Corporazione** (Corporation Square), a tree-lined boulevard once filled with over seventy commercial offices of wine importers, ship owners, oil merchants, or rope makers. All of these shops are worth a visit, but the well-preserved laundry and wine shop are best because these offices are tastefully decorated with more exquisite mosaic tiled floors representing their trades. A must see stop around this area is the site museum which has many of the excavated statues.

Farther down the *Decumanus Maximus* you arrive at the **Capitolium**, a temple dedicated to Jupiter and Minerva, located at the end of the **Forum**. The **insulae** (apartment blocks) are of particular interest since they are often four or five stories high. This is where the regular people and smaller merchants lived. Only the most wealthy of the merchants were able to build themselves separate villas. The *insulae* were well lighted, had running water, and a means for sanitation (i.e., garbage removal and toilets) on each floor.

Two private home of interest that should be visited are the **House of the Cupid and Psyche**, which is west of the Capitolium, and the **House of the Dioscuri**, which is at the southwest end of town.

My favorite way to tour this site as well as most other archeological sites is to go off of the beaten path. Leave the already excavated section and wander through the areas, which have not yet been dug up. This helps to give you an idea as to the amount of labor involved in actually excavating sections, and usually makes for great places to relax. And who knows maybe you'll turn up and ancient artifact or two.

The site is open daily 9:00am–6:00pm in summer, 9:00am–4:00pm in winter. Admission L10,000. The museum is open one hour less.

LIDO DI OSTIA

Lido di Ostia is the beach about four kilometers from the ruins of Ostia Antica. Take the same route that you took to the ruins but continue on a little farther either by car or by train (see *Arrivals & Departures* above for more details). This is a perfect place to visit after a day of wandering through Ostia Antica.

Treat yourself to a seaside celebration. There are rafts to rent, umbrellas to use, *cabanas* to change and cavort in, restaurants to go to, and hotels to stay at if you get to tired and don't want to get back to Rome. Lido di Ostia is a typical Italian beach and it's close to Rome. But don't go on the weekend unless you like mobs of people.

Try either of these restaurants if you're hungry:

LA CAPANNINA DA PASQUALE, *Lungomare Vespucci 156, Tel. 06/567-0143. Closed Mondays. Holidays in November. All credit cards accepted. Dinner for two L110,000.*

A little expensive but the location is supreme, especially the outside seating right on the sea. They have a superb antipasto table, which could serve as your whole meal if you're not too hungry. Their pastas and rice dishes are also good since many of them have been homemade at the restaurant. Try the *risotto ai frutti di mare* (rice with seafood ladled over the top). They are known for their seafood dishes so try anything *al forno* (cooked over the grill), with their wonderfully grilled potatoes. The service is stupendous, as it should be based on the price.

TRE PULCINI, *Viale della Pineta di Ostia 30, Tel. 06/562-1293. Closed Mondays. All credit cards accepted. Dinner for two L110,000*

A simple family-run place with mama Antoinetta in the kitchen and Renato in the restaurant. Here you'll experience some true down home Italian cooking. Try their *sauté di cozze e vongole* (sautéed muscles and clams), *zuppa di pesce* (fish soup), or their *fritto misto* (mixed fried seafood). You can also get some homemade *gelato* (ice cream) as dessert, which is made daily by the daughter Cristina. You can enjoy all of this either outside on the balcony or in the air-conditioned comfort of the interior.

POMPEII & HERCULANEUM

Thousands of people died and many more lost their homes when Vesuvius erupted in 79 CE, submerging Pompeii, Herculaneum, and Stabiae with lava and/or volcanic ash. The lava and ash created an almost perfect time capsule, sealing in an important cross-section of an ancient civilization. If you want to take a trip back in time come to one of these ancient towns. You will find nothing even remotely similar to this anywhere in the world, so if you have a free day, grab a tour bus, rent a car, hop on a train, but make your way to these cities buried in time.

ARRIVALS & DEPARTURES

By car from Rome, take the A2 south, past Naples, connect to the A3 and exit at Pompeii Scavi. Total time elapsed each way, 312 to 4 hours.

By train, first arrive at **Napoli Centrale**. Go one floor below the Central Station to the **Circumvesuviana** station for a local high-speed train to **Ercolano** (Herculaneum) or **Pompeii Scavi** (4 hours total journey).

The best way to get to either Pompeii or Herculaneum in a day (granted a rather long day) is by tour bus. This way you do not have to worry about driving or catching the right trains. You will leave early in the morning and arrive back in Rome late at night. See information on Tour Companies.

Pompeii

Before the city was buried in time, Pompeii was Rome's main seaport linking it to the rest of the Empire, and as such was an established city with a multicultural population of about 25,000. Because of successive waves of colonization Pompeii was home to Greeks, Egyptians, Gauls, Iberians and every other nationality in the Roman Empire. By 80 BCE, it was also a favorite resort of wealthy Romans.

Shaken by an earthquake in 62 CE, Pompeii recovered, but on August 24, 79 CE Pompeii's days were over. Mt. Vesuvius erupted, spewing ash and pumice pebbles which covered the city, preserving it and some of its unfortunate residents in time. For over 1,500 years Pompeii rested undisturbed, then was discovered in 1711 when a peasant was digging a well on his property. After which two centuries passed, during which time Pompeii and Herculaneum served almost entirely as a quarry for works of art, as a plaything for the various dynasties which misruled Naples, and as a romantic stop on the Grand Tour of Europe for elite European society.

Although rudimentary excavations began in 1763, systematic excavations did not get under way until 1911 and have been progressing slowly ever since. And now only about three-fifths of the site has been freed from the death grip of the volcanic ash. Herculaneum has suffered a less severe intrusion from amateurs interested in unearthing its treasures since on the afternoon of the eruption, rain turned the volcanic ash to mud, which solidified, burying the town thirty to forty feet deep. Electric drills and mechanical shovels are needed to dig here, so progress has been slow, but the town has been better preserved.

Despite this difference, Pompeii still offers the most fascinating introduction into ancient history. Strolling through this dead city is quite ominous. In places there are human forms and family pets forever preserved having died in the embrace of the volcanic ash. Along with these macabre scenes, you can easily imagine life going on here since many pieces of every day existence remain. You can see where people planted gardens, shops where they bought food, and walls are still covered with ancient graffiti. These range from erotic drawings advertising the world's oldest profession, to boasts by one of practitioners to having had over 1,300 men, to drawings of oral sex, to political slogans extolling the virtues of one candidate over another. It seems that a local election was taking place when the eruption occurred.

There are also abundant frescoes depicting mythological scenes in the wealthier homes, as well as frescoes indicating how the owners of the house made a living. The streets have characteristic deep ruts made by wheels of carts - the trucks of antiquity - and are bridged by massive stepping stones, which acted as both a conduit for pedestrians, and also as a traffic calmer.

Some of the best homes to see are the **House of the Faun** and the **House of the Vettii**, both in the residential area north of the **Forum**. Other homes of interest are the **House of the Melander** (located to the east of the Forum), the **Villa of the Mysteries** (located to the west of the main town), and the **House of Pansa** (located to the north of the Forum) that also included rented apartments. Also in evidence in the remains are symbols of the Greek cult of Dionysis, one of many that flourished in the city. **The Temple of Isis** (to the east of the Forum) testifies to the strong following that the Egyptian goddess had here. The public **Amphitheater**, in the east of the city, should not be missed because of its scale and level of preservation. There are locations on the stage area that if a whisper is spoken, even a person standing at the top-most part of the seating area can hear it clearly.

Pompeii is as a whole 160 acres, large enough for a population of between fifteen and twenty thousand souls. The city is surrounded by a wall, which was built in four phases. The earliest dates from the fifth century CE, the latest from just before the reign of Augustus and was allowed to fall in disrepair, evidence of the security of the peace of that era. Latin, Greek and another dead language Oscan were the tongues of choice in Pompeii. Latin because of the Roman influence, Greek because the area around Naples had originally been settled by Greeks and they kept their culture, and Oscan which was a hold over from ancient Italian tribes.

The city was well supplied with public amenities. Lead water pipes found everywhere show that all but the very humblest of houses were supplied with running water. There are all sorts of different housing in Pompeii including apartments and expansive villas. But it's not just the homes and their treasures that Pompeii reveals to us. Ancient tradesmen, their lives, works, and tastes about which literature tells us almost nothing, become more real for us here than anywhere else in the ancient world except for the abandoned port of Rome, Ostia Antica. Most houses either doubled as workshops, or had small workshops in them since the ancient world's slave economy did not foster the development of the factory system.

Pompeii has also enriched our knowledge of ancient Romans relations to their gods. Naturally the Imperial cult whereby Emperors were decreed to be gods, was adhered to, though generally only with lip service. Graffiti backs up this blasphemous stance. One such wall scribbling states "Augustus Caesar's mother was only a woman." The Egyptian sect of Isis was well represented, as was the Roman warrior sect of Mithras, and family cults flourished. This is evidenced by the fact that most houses and workshops had private shrines usually housing busts of ancestors. But the true god of Pompeii was, as with other cities ancient and modern, was the God of Gain. Money, the pursuit of wealth, and the accumulation of possessions were worshipped above all else.

Ironically, going back for their hoards of silver and gold spelled death for many of the residents of Pompeii. Under the hail of pumice stone and ashes many were asphyxiated or engulfed. A particularly disturbing cluster of victims, with their children and burdensome possessions is preserved near the **Nocera Gate**. But most of the remnants of the Pompeiian consumer society – the best-preserved artifacts – are not in Pompeii anymore, they are in the National Museum in Naples. So if you can, make a point of visiting there too. After many years of mismanagement, Pompeii is slowly re-emerging to be a true world wonder. An organization called World Monuments Watch has declared Pompeii one of the world's most imperiled cultural sites, but the good news is that they are helping to restore the ancient city to the wonder it once was. Pompeii is unique anywhere in the world, and is a must-see stop when in Italy.

Gates to the site open year round 9:00am to 1 hour before sunset. Admission L15,000. The best way to get here and back to Rome in a day, while also receiving the best that Pompeii can offer is via tour bus. See information on Tour companies.

Herculaneum

Seventeen miles northeast of Pompeii is the smaller town of Herculaneum. Most tour companies will combine a trip to one, with a visit to the other. At the time of the eruption Herculaneum had only 5,000 inhabitants, compared to the 25,000 in Pompeii, had virtually no commerce, and its industry was solely based on fishing. The volcanic mud that flowed through every building and street in Herculaneum was a different covering from that which buried Pompeii. This steaming hot lava-like substance settled eventually to a depth of 30-40 feet and set rock-hard, sealing and preserving everything it came in contact with. Dinner was left on tables, wine shops abandoned in mid-purchase, sacrifices left at the moment of offering, funerals never finished, prisoners left in stocks, and watchdogs perished on their chains.

Fortunately for the residents, but not for archeologists, the absence of the hail of hot ash that rained down on Pompeii, which smashed the buildings of that city and trapped many residents of that town, meant that many of the inhabitants of Herculaneum were able to get away in time. Despite the absence of preserved remains, Herculaneum offers complete houses, with their woodwork, household goods, and furniture well preserved.

Although Herculaneum was a relatively unimportant town compared with Pompeii, many of the houses that have been excavated were from the wealthy class. It is speculated that perhaps the town was like a retirement village, populated by prosperous Romans seeking to pass their retirement years in the calm of a small seaside town. This idea is bolstered by the fact that the few craft shops that have been discovered were solely for the manufacture of luxury goods. Archaeologists speculate that the most desirable residential area was in the southwest part of town, which overlooked the ocean in many different housing terraces. Here you will find the **House of the Stags**, famous for its beautiful frescoes, sculpted stags, and a drunken figure of Hercules. Farther north you can find the marvelously preserved **House of the Wooden Partition**. It is one of the most complete examples of a private residence in either Pompeii or Herculaneum. Near this house to the north are the **Baths**, an elaborate complex incorporating a gymnasium and assorted men's and women's baths.

Important to remember as you compare Herculaneum with Pompeii is that this town was only recently excavated since more modern tools were needed for the job, allowing for more advanced preservation efforts. But both sites are well worth visiting and are highly recommended by the author. Gates to the site open year round 9:00am to 1 hour before sunset. Admission L10,000.

ORVIETO

Umbria is Tuscany's understated cousin, quietly regal, unassuming, yet just as charming, and **Orvieto** is one of Umbria's best cities to visit. Umbria is a region of contrasts, where seemingly impenetrable, thick forests give way to sweeping, fertile valleys, where lush mountains and tranquil hills, dazzling waterfalls and still lakes mingle in a palette greener than any other corner of Italy. And just over the border with Lazio, the province that Rome is in, the stunning city of Orvieto rests picturesquely on the top of a hill bordered by protective cliffs, waiting for your day trip from Rome. It was a favorite refuge of the popes because of this defensible situation. One of the most beautiful towns in all of Italy, Orvieto has a rich array of winding medieval streets and stunning architecture. Its first inhabitants were Etruscan, after which the city became a protectorate of the Roman Empire.

With the empire's decline, Orvieto underwent the inevitable spate of barbarian invasion. It then became a free commune in the 12th century CE and enjoyed a period of artistic and political advancement, until the Papal States suppressed it into their fold in the 14th century. When Napoleon Buonaparte conquered it, he made it an essential center of his dominion until Orvieto was absorbed into the Kingdom of Italy in 1860.

Known not only for its architecture and natural beauty, the town is also famous for the wonderful Orvieto wine that flows from the local vines, as well as the tasty olive oil from the nearby olive groves. Besides its culinary pursuits, the town also is a ceramic center. Local artisans, especially the immensely talented Michelangeli, also create intricate wood carvings as well as delicate lace.

ARRIVALS & DEPARTURES

Orvieto is accessible from Rome by a train which runs every two hours, starting at 6:12am and ending at 8:30pm, and takes an hour and twenty minutes or less depending on the number of stops along the way. Returns start at 9:00am and end at 10:30am. Once at the train station you then take the funiculare (cable car) up the hill, through an avenue of trees before tunneling under the Fortrezza to the Piazzale Cahen. By the

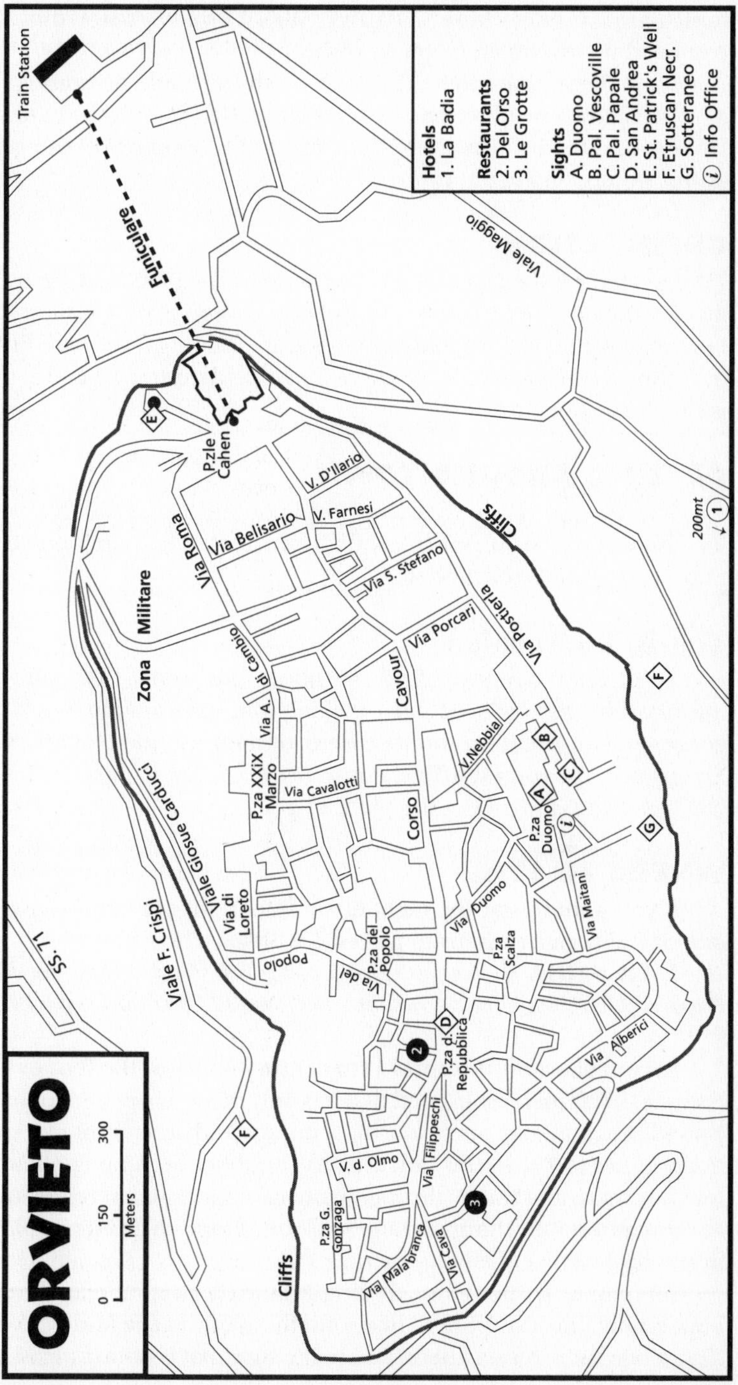
ORVIETO
0
150
300
Meters
Hotels
1. La Badia
Restaurants
2. Del Orso
3. Le Grotte
Sights
A. Duomo
B. Pal. Vescoville
C. Pal. Papale
D. San Andrea
E. St. Patrick's Well
F. Etruscan Necr.
G. Sotteraneo
Info Office
Train Station
Funiculare
P.zle Cahen
Zona Militare
Via Roma
Via Belisario
V. D'Ilario
V. Farnesi
Via S. Stefano
Via Porcari
Via Postierla
Cliffs
Viale Maggio
200mt
Via A. di Cambio
Cavour
P.za XXIX Marzo
Via Cavalotti
V. Nebbia
Corso
P.za Duomo
Via Maitani
Via Duomo
P.za Scalza
Via di Loreto
Viale Giosue Carducci
Viale F. Crispi
SS. 71
Via del Popolo
P.za del Popolo
P.za d. Repubblica
Via Filippeschi
Via Alberici
V. d. Olmo
P.za G. Gonzaga
Via Malabranca
Via Cava
Cliffs

funiculare station is where St. Patricks Well is located so stop there before you head up into town if you so wish.

From the station catch the bus 'A' – which should be waiting for you as you exit the funiculare since the bus is timed to its arrival – to the Piazza Duomo and the information office. From the Duomo you can get to all sights, hotels, and restaurants.

ORIENTATION

Located on the top of a hill surrounded by cliffs, the Corso Cavour divides the city east to west. On the east is the Piazzale Cahen and the Fortrezza – built in 1364 and now a pleasant public garden with fine views over the surrounding valley – where the funiculare arrives, and at the west is the Porta Maggiore.

GETTING AROUND TOWN

This town is easy to walk since being on the top of a bluff it is mainly flat. Once you take the funiculare up from the station there won't be many more serious hills to traverse.

Tourist Information

To arrange day trips, find out about bus tours, find train or bus information, get maps, detailed walking tour information, book a hotel, get general information about Orvieto, or book a guided tour for Orvieto Sotteraneo, the **tourist office**, *Piazza Duomo 4, Tel. 0763/301-507 or 301-508, Fax 0763/344-433,* is the place to go.

WHERE TO STAY

If you want to stay the night in Orvieto, right outside the city walls is one of Italy's most exquisite places, La Badia, The Abbey.

1. LA BADIA, *1a Cat., 05019 Orvieto. Tel. 0763/301-959 or 305-455, Fax 0763/305-396. All credit cards accepted. Single L250,000; Double L600,000.* ****

An unbelievably beautiful 12th century abbey at the foot of Orvieto is home to this incredible hotel that has only recently opened for business. You will be treated to one of the most unique and memorable experiences in the entire world. In the 15th century the abbey became a holiday resort for Cardinals, and today, through painstakingly detailed renovations, an ancient and noble Umbrian family, Count Fiumi di Sterpeto, plays host in this awe-inspiring environment.

The rooms are immense, the accommodations exemplary, the service impeccable, the atmosphere like something out of the Middle Ages. For a fairy tale vacation stay here, and make sure that you eat at least once at their soon to be world-renowned restaurant offering refined local dishes – many ingredients culled from Count Fiumi's farms and vineyards – in an incredibly historic and romantic atmosphere.

WHERE TO EAT

2. TRATTORIA DEL ORSO, *Via della Misericordia. Tel. 0763/341-642. Closed Monday nights, Tuesdays and February. Visa accepted. Dinner for two L80,000.*

Deep in the heart of Orvieto, nestled down a small side street off of the Piazza della Repubblica, is a small trattoria passionately operated by Gabrielle (doing the cooking) and Ciro (greeting and seating) where you can find genuine and simple Umbrian cuisine. You should start with the magnificent bruschetta (garlic bread) and proceed to the luscious fettucine alfredo. For seconds there are plenty of meat and vegetable dishes, as well as omelets to choose from. The desserts are home made, so you have to save room for at least one. A great place to sample the local flavor.

3. LE GROTTE DEL FUNARO, *Via Ripa Serancia 41. Tel. 0763/343-276. Closed Mondays. Dinner for two L80,000.*

Literally situated in a series of grotte (caves) carved into the tufo layer upon which Orvieto sits, this place offers you a unique dining experience to go along with their delicious food. The whole point of coming here is to eat downstairs in the caves, so avoid the terrace. The have a well rounded menu, but in truffle season that aromatic tuber is featured prominently and any dish seasoned with it should be sampled if you are here from October to December. Try Le Grotte when in Orvieto. You will not be disappointed.

SEEING THE SIGHTS

A. DUOMO

Stunning! Elegant! Mesmerizing! No words can really describe this amazing cathedral, located in the Piazza del Duomo, whose facade is covered with bas-reliefs, colorful mosaics, and radiating frescoes. The pointed portals on the facade literally jump out at you, and the rose window – flanked by figures of the Prophets and Apostles – is a treasure to behold. Bring binoculars to admire all the intricate detail, since the facade is an entire museum in and of itself.

Most of its ornamentation was created between the 14th and 16th centuries. The bronze doors are contemporary works by Emilio Greco (1964). A museum featuring more of his art is situated on the ground floor of the Palazzo Papale to the right of the Duomo. Above and beside the doors are the Bronze Symbols of the Evangelists. The exterior side walls are alternating horizontal layers of black basalt and pale limestone in the distinctive Pisan style.This same style is translated into the interior, covering both the walls, and the columns which divide the church into a nave and two aisles. The christening font is the work of several artists and is stunning in its intricacies. The apse is lit by 14th century stained glass windows by Bonino and contains frescoes by Ugolino di Prete Ilario.

In the right transept behind an artistic 16th century wrought iron railing is the beautiful Capella Nuova, which contains Luca Signorelli's superlative Last Judgment. It is purported to be the inspiration for Michelangelo's Last Judgment in the Sistine Chapel. A must see, since it is also considered one of the greatest frescoes in Italian art. The chapel also contains frescoed medallions depicting poets and philosophers ranging from Homer to Dante.

B. PALAZZO VESCOVILLE

Located to the right and at the rear of the Duomo, restored in the 1960s, it now houses the Archaeological Museum (open 9:00am - 7:00pm, Holidays 9:00am-1:00pm; admission L4,000), which has a collection of material excavated from the Etruscan Necropoli that are located nearby the city. A simple, basic introduction to the history of the region.

C. PALAZZO PAPALE

Situated to the right of the Duomo, this was once the residence of a long line of popes when they came to visit the city. This building dates back to the 8th century and is also known as the Palace of Bonifacio VIII. On the ground floor you can find the Museum of Emilio Greco (open 10:30am-1:00pm and 2:00-6:00pm in winter and 3:00-7:00pm in summer) exhibiting numerous works by this fine sculptor from Catania. On the first floor is the Cathedral Museum, which displays miscellaneous works of art, mostly from the Duomo or about the Duomo.

D. SAN ANDREA

On the edge of the Piazza della Repubblica, this plain church is best known for its dodecagonal campanile, a twelve-sided bell-tower. This masterful architectural complement to the church has three orders of windows and a turreted top section. Built between the 6th and 14th centuries on the site of a pre-existing early Christian church, the interior is a single nave with two aisles, a raised transept and cross vaults. The wooden altar by Scalza is worthy of note, as is the pulpit. Situated below the church and accessible by appointment are some ancient ruins dating from the Iron Age up to the medieval period.

E. ST. PATRICK'S WELL

Open daily from 9:00am to 6:00pm, this well, Orvieto Sotteraneo, and the Duomo are the most famous sights in Orvieto. Built by Antonio Sangallo the Younger for Pope Clement VII, the well served as a reservoir for the nearby fortress if the city was ever put under siege. Hence it is also known as the Fortress Well. Its ingenious cylindrical cavity design was completed in the beginning of the 16th century. Going to a depth of 62 meters, there are two parallel concentric staircases (each with 248 steps ... go on and count them if you want). The water carriers with their donkeys used one spiral staircase for going up and the other for going down. Each staircase has a separate entrance and is ringed by large arched windows. In the public gardens above the well are the overgrown remains of an Etruscan temple.

F. ETRUSCAN NECROPOLISES

Located on either side of the city the foot of the tufa cliffs, the Necropolis of the Tufa Crucifix is to the north and the Necropolis of Cannicella is to the south. Each date from around the sixth century BCE. Well preserved but ransacked and looted a long time ago, these tombs nonetheless are something to visit while in Orvieto. It's not often that you can come face to face with something that was created almost 2,500 years ago. Inquire at the information office about the ways and means to visit them.

G. ORVIETO SOTTERANEO

If you do nothing else while here, make sure that you sign up to go on one of the guided tours of the subterranean passages that snake underneath the entire city. Guided tours are held every day starting at 11am and go until 6pm, and cost L10,000. Inquire at the information about the times for the tours in English. At last inquiry they were at 12:15 and 5:15pm.Recently excavated and opened for tourists, the tours of these caves under the city take you on a journey through history, including Etruscan wells, a 17th century oil mill, a medieval quarry, ancient pigeon coops and much more, all thoroughly narrated by well-trained guides. These tours are an extraordinary trip back in time and shouldn't be missed.

SHOPPING

In general there is great shopping in Orvieto, but without the same run-of-the-mill, cookie cutter, international name brand stores you find in most tourist locations. There are many small artisans' shops, unique boutiques, ceramics re-sellers, all of which add to the rich local flavor that Orvieto cultivates. One store in particular you simply must visit is:

8. MICHELANGELI, *Via Gualverio Michelangeli 3B, 05018 Orvieto. Tel. 0763/342-660, Fax 0763/342-461. All credit cards accepted.*

An incredible store filled with intricately carved wooden sculptures, toys, figurines, and murals of the most amazing and appealing designs. A perfect store to find the perfect gift or keepsake. Michelangeli's work is slowly becoming recognized around the world. It is rustic but refined, and the very least you should stop in the store, check out the displays, take a look through his portfolios and treat the experience as you would a museum. A great store and a rewarding experience.

SIENA

Siena is generally described as the feminine counterpart to the masculine Florence, and even its nickname, **City of the Virgin**, belies this feminine quality. Located 42 miles south of Florence, this picturesque walled city is known for its many quality buildings, narrow streets, immense churches, and quaint little restaurants; but the two reasons why I love Siena are that cars are banned from the center of the city, making for a pleasant automobile-less environment (similar to Venice but without the water); and also for the biannual event called the **Palio**.

The well-preserved walls with towers and bulwarks of Siena are seven kilometers long and were built from the 13th to the 15th centuries. The ramparts on the outskirts are now used as public gardens. They are beautiful but not nearly as romantic or inviting as those from Lucca.

Siena was once a prosperous, stable, and artistic city in its own right even before she was absorbed into the Grand Duchy of Tuscany in 1559, which was ruled by Florence, after years of siege by Cosimo de Medici. Once it became a part of Florence, Siena was not allowed to continue to pursue its previously prosperous banking activities, nor were they allowed to continue their flourishing wool trade. Because of these actions, and the general despotic rule of Florence, Siena fell into a long period of decline. But today, as other Italian cities have also, Siena has learned how to succeed by marketing its ancient charm.

For tourist information in Siena, head to the tourist office, *Piazza San Domenico, Tel 0577/940-809; open 9:00am to 7:00pm.* You can get maps and hotel reservations if needed.

ARRIVALS & DEPARTURES

By Car

From Rome take the A1 to the Via di Chiana exit, then head west on route 326 into Siena. You'll have to leave your car at one of the many parking lots on the outskirts of the city center, since no automobiles are allowed into the city.

By Train

From Rome there are over a dozen trains a day. The trip takes 1 1/2 hours. The Siena train station is located one mile from the center of the city, but do not fear. Just exit the station, stand on the curb and catch either bus 15, 2, or 6 and they will all take you to a dropping off point near the information desk in the center of town, from which you can get a map (L500) and hotel reservations if needed. Everything else from that point on is walking distance.

If, or should I say when, the blue bus ticket machine in the lobby of the train station is out of order, simply go to the train ticket window and purchase a bus ticket for L1,200. It's good for an hour once you punch it in the machine on the bus. I recommend buying your return fare in advance if you're not going to stay the night, so you don't have to worry about that detail on your return to the station in the evening. If you don't want to catch the bus, the old town is a short walk up the hill.

Renting a Car

If you're staying in Siena for a while and want to view the magnificent countryside, you can always rent a car, van, or moped.

- **General Cars**, *Viale Toselli 20/26, Tel. 0577/40-518, Fax 0577/47-984.*
- **Avis**, *Via Simone Martini 36, Tel. 0577/27-03-05*
- **Hertz**, *Hotel Lea, Via XXIV Maggio, Tel. 0577/45085*

WHERE TO STAY

1. ANTICA TORRE, *Via di Fieravecchia 7, 53100 Siena. Tel. 0577/222-255, Fax the same. 8 rooms all with bath. Single L120,000; Double L160,000. Amex, Mastercard and Visa Accepted. Breakfast L15,000.* ***

This small hotel is located on a discrete and quiet street near Santa Maria de' Servi. The hotel itself is a tower built in the 1500s which makes the atmosphere here so unbelievably quaint. There are only two rooms per floor and to get to them you have to ascend tiny stairs so if you have a lot of bags or need an elevator don't bother staying here. And obviously the rooms are not that big since the tower itself is not gigantic, but what ambiance. From the top rooms you can look over the rooftops of the city and the green of the countryside. A very unique hotel. Stay here if you get the chance. Staying in a medieval tower is not your average run of the mill experience.

2. VILLA LIBERTY, *Viale Vittorio Veneto 11, 53100 Siena. Tel. 0577/449-666, Fax 0577/44770. 12 rooms all with bath. Single L100,000. Double L160,000. All credit cards accepted. Breakfast included.* ***

Just a little ways outside the walls of Siena near the *fortrezza* this hotel has been renovated in an eclectic Liberty style. Each room is elegantly furnished and comfortable. The best ones are in the upper area and come with more modern style furnishings. And each room has TV. Everything about this place is accommodating. More of a bed and breakfast than a Holiday Inn. Definitely not a 'cookie-cutter' hotel. A fine choice if you some to Siena.

3. LEA, *Viale XXIV Maggio 10, 53100 Siena. Tel. 0577/283-207, Fax the same. 12 rooms all with bath. Single L70,000; Double L115,000. All credit cards accepted. Breakfast included.* **

Situated in a small villa from the 1800s, in a tranquil residential area near the center, surrounded by a small garden which is set with tables and chairs. From the top floors you get a magnificently unique view into the heart of Siena. This hotel offers great prices, spacious rooms, direct dial telephones, simple but comfortable furnishings and well decorated bathrooms. In the morning breakfast is a basic continental fare served in the same room that accommodates the bar and reception area. A great two star in Siena. A budget travelers paradise.

4. PALAZZO RAVIZZA, *Pian dei Mantellini 34, Tel. 0577/280-462, Fax 0577/221-597. 30 rooms all with bath. Single L 120,000-245,000. Double L180,000-330,000. Breakfast L18,000. All credit cards accepted.* ***

A quaint little bed and breakfast type hotel in business since 1929. The building the hotel is located in has been owned by the same family for about two hundred years. Situated in a tranquil spot in the *centro storico* with good views over the city and the surrounding countryside, the furnishings are antique and the atmosphere wonderful. Buffet breakfast is served in their garden area and they are known to make a picnic lunch for you if asked. The evenings can be spent in the large tavern room. A quality place to stay in Siena, right in the middle of things. There is a public parking area just down the Via P. Mascagni and off of Via dei Laterino near a quaint little old cemetery if you come by car. Truly a great three star in Siena and the prices show it.

WHERE TO EAT

Since Siena is a university town, snack and fast food places abound, but there are also some excellent restaurants. Siena specialties include *cioccina* (a special variation on pizza) *pici* (thick Tuscan spaghetti with a sauce from ground pork), and *pancetta* (sausages and chicken breast added to tomatoes and cooked with red wine).

Siena is also known for its different varieties of salamis that you can buy at any *alimentari*. Some salamis you should try:

Soppressata, either sweet or hot, is an excellent boiled salami made from a mixture of rind and gristle with black peppercorns added. Don't let this description fool you. The sweet *soppressata* is the best.

Buristo is a cooked salami made from the blood and fatty leftovers of sausages. It is heavily spiced.

Finocchiona is a salami made of peppered sausage meat seasoned with fennel seeds. And *Salsiccioli secchi* are made from lean crusts of pork or boar, spiced with garlic and black or red pepper.

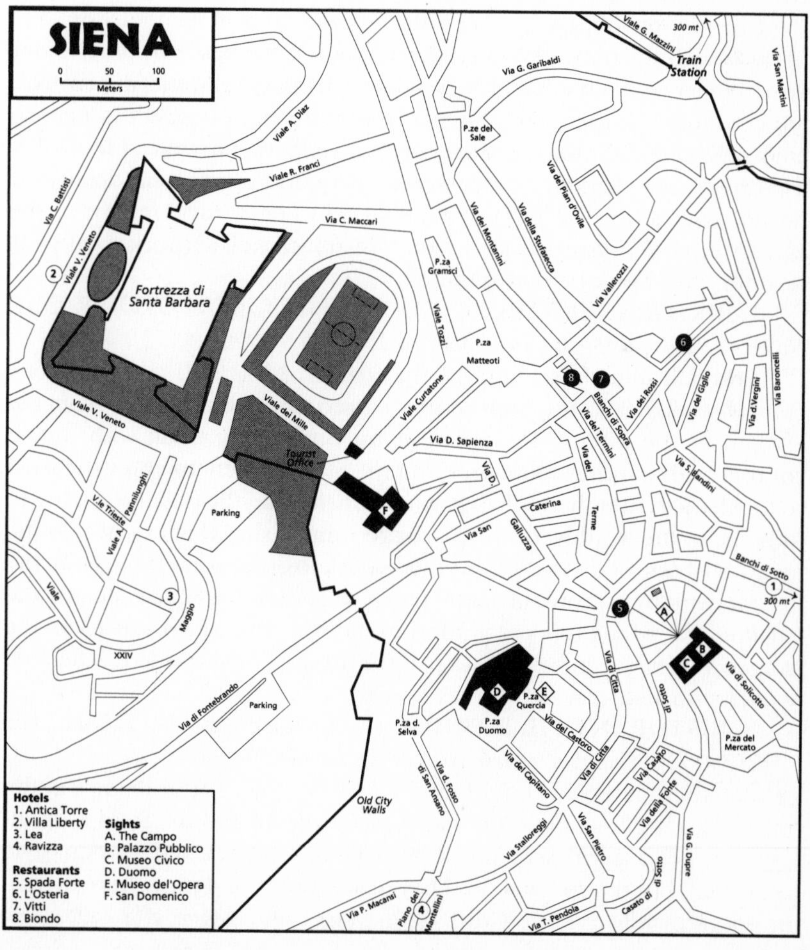

5. RISTORANTE/PIZZERIA SPADA FORTE, *Piazza del Campo 12. Credit cards accepted. Dinner for two L65,000.*

If you're at the top of the Campo looking down at the Palazzo Pubblico, this place is on your right at the end of the wall. They have scenic outside tables from which you can watch the goings-on in the Campo, as well as inside seating in a typically spartan Sienese restaurant environment. There is a huge antipasto menu which should satisfy you for lunch. If not, try one of their pizzas.

The *barrocciaia* (tomatoes, sausage and garlic), and the *salsiccia* (tomato, mozzarella and sausages) are both good. If you're into meats, try the *cinghiale alle senese* (wild boar cooked over the open flame) or the *agnello arrosto* (roasted lamb). A really good restaurant.

6. L'OSTERIA, *Via dei Rossi 79/81. Tel. 0577/287-592. No credit cards accepted. Dinner for two L50,000.*

Literally translated it's "The Restaurant" and it seems to be very popular with the locals. Located down a side street past two other more touristy places making it a little ways away from the thundering crowds. Squeeze through the worn hanging beads and cram yourself in here to enjoy a wonderfully local atmosphere with superbly prepared food. Try the *penne con melanzane e peperoni* (eggplant and pepperoni salami) for primo, and either the *pollo ai peperoni* (chicken with pepperoni), the *bistecca di vitello* (veal steak), or the *bistecca di maiale* (pork steak) for secondi. You won't be disappointed.

7. RISTORANTE VITTI, *Via Monatanini 14-16, Tel. 0577/28-92-91. No credit cards accepted. Dinner for two L55,000-60,000.*

Tranquil outside seating off the main road as well as in the *zona pedonale* (walking zone). Your food is passed through a window from the kitchen to the waiter. The inside is uncomfortably small with only a counter and standing room only, but the Sienese seem to enjoy the food so much they cram themselves in for lunch, leaving the outside seating to tourists. In the window of the place are some dishes that are not on the menu, so if one of them catches your eye ask to order something from the *finestra* (window). From the menu try some of their pasta, particularly the *tortellini alla panna* (cheese stuffed pasta in a rich cream sauce) or the *lasagna al forno* (oven baked lasagna) for primo. For secondo try the *petto di tacchino arrosto* (roasted turkey breast).

8. RISTORANTE IL BIONDO, *Via del Rustichetto 10, Tel. and Fax 0577/280-739. Closed Wednesdays. Dinner for two L80,000.*

Another place you should think of trying, since the ambiance at the outside seating is so peaceful and colorfully local and the food is great. You can get a good seat inside in a plain whitewashed Sienese-style restaurant, but try the outside. They make some good pasta here including *spaghetti alla vongole* (with clam sauce) and *penne alla puttanesca* (literally translated it means whore's pasta, made with tomatoes, garlic, black olives, olive oil and meat). For seconds, try the *saltimbocca alla Romana* (veal shank stewed in tomatoes and spices) or the *bistecca alla griglia* (beef steak cooked on the grill that would make a Texan proud).

SEEING THE SIGHTS

The Palio Race

The best time to visit because of the pageantry, and the worst time to visit because of the crowds, is during the biannual **Palio**, held on July 2 and August 16. The Palio is a festive time awash in colorful banners, historic pageantry, and a wild bareback horse race that runs three times around the **Piazza del Campo**. The race lasts all of 90 seconds but will leave you with memories to last a lifetime.

A *palio* literally is an embroidered banner, the prize offered for winning the race. The first official Palio was run in 1283, though many say the custom dates back farther than that. During the Middle Ages, besides the horse races, there were violent games of primeval rugby (which you can see in Florence twice a year during their *Calcio in Costume* festival) and even bullfights to settle neighborhood bragging rights.

The contestants in the horse race itself are jockeys from the seventeen neighborhood parishes or *contrade* in Siena. During a Palio ten horses ride in the first race and seven horses ride in the next since the square is not big enough to accommodate all the horses at once. The jockeys willingly risk life and limb for the pride of their small area of the city. At two places in the Piazza del Campo there are right angles at which the horses have to turn, and usually at these points you'll have at least one jockey lose his seat or a horse its footing.

But this is more than a horse race. It is really a sanctioned community-wide regression into the Middle Ages, with the coats-of-arms that represented each *contrade* at that time being displayed prominently by members of that neighborhood. The *contrade* used to be military companies, but these became outdated when the Spanish and Florentines laid siege to Siena and conquered it. At that time there were 59 *contrade*, but plagues and wars decimated the population until by the early 18th century there were only 23 left. Today only seventeen remain and the coats-of-arms for each *contrade* is as follows: *Aquila* (eagle), *Bruco* (caterpillar), *Chiocciola* (snail), *Civetta* (owl), *Drago* (dragon), *Giraffa* (giraffe), *Istrice* (porcupine), *Leocorno* (unicorn), *Lupa* (she-wolf), *Nicchio* (shell), *Oca* (goose), *Onda* (wave), *Pantera* (panther), *Selva* (wood), *Tartuca* (turtle), *Torre* (tower), and *Valdimontone* (ram).

Prior to the race there is a good two hour display of flag throwing by the *alferi* of each *contrada*, while the medieval *carroccio* (carriage), drawn by a white oxen, circles the Campo bearing the prized *palio* each neighborhood wants to claim as its own.

To witness this event, however, you have to plan way in advance since at both times of year the Palio is jam-packed. You can see the Palio in one of three ways: in the center of the Piazza where people are packed like sardines on a first come first serve basis; in the viewing stands which cost anywhere from L200,000 to L350,000; or in one of the offices or apartments that line the piazza. To get a seat in the viewing stand you'll need to plan at least 6-9 months in advance and get your tickets through your travel agent. To view the spectacle from an office or apartment you'll need to have connections. Maybe the company you work for has dealings with the banks and other companies whose offices line the square. However you witness this blast from Siena's medieval past, you will have memories for a lifetime.

A. THE CAMPO

Eleven streets lead into the square where, in the past, the people of Siena used to assemble at the sound of the **Sunto bell** to learn the latest news. Today it still is the gathering place for all the locals and tourists. You will see at most times of the day the young lounging on the stones and their elders congregating at cafés. The piazza is concave and irregular with a ring of rather austere buildings surrounding it, but even so it is a marvel of architectural harmony. On the curved side of the Campo sits the **Fonte Gaia** (Gay Fountain) made by Jacopo della Quercia. The water from this fountain comes here from 30 km away through a series of pipes and aqueducts from the 13th century. A feat of ancient engineering.

On the map the Campo looks flat, but it's actually a gradually sloping surface with bricks that seem to float down to the **Palazzo Pubblico**. A great place to grab a bite to eat at one of the many restaurants, sip a drink at one of the cafés, or to simply rest your tired tourist feet by relaxing on the cobblestone slope.

B. PALAZZO PUBBLICO

At the Campo. Tower open 10:00am–dusk. In the winter open only until 1:30pm. Admission L5,000.

One of the most attractive and imposing Gothic buildings in all of Tuscany. Most of it was built between 1297 and 1340, with the top story being raised in 1639. This building reflected the wealth and success of Siena, which was almost the same size as London and Paris during the fourteenth century. The little chapel underneath the tower was dedicated by the town to the Virgin Mary when the terrible plague known ever since as the *Morte Nera* (Black Death) came to an end. In Siena alone 65,000 people died of the plague in the summer of 1348. That was over half of their population. The intricate wrought-iron gate that covers the entrance was made in 1445.

The best part of this building is the **Torre del Mangia**. It offers the greatest sights in all of Siena. Unfortunately you have to climb up 400 small confined steps to top of the bell tower. It's 112 meters high, was built in 1334, and is still in amazing shape. The clock was made in 1360 and the huge bell was raised to its present position in 1666. Imagine having to haul a bell that weighs 6,764 kilos up a pulley system to the top of the tower? Remember to bring your camera because the views of the countryside and the city are stupendous. You can see past the old walls, look over the terra-cotta tiles of the city roofs, lush fields, and forests for as far as the eye can see. A definite must-see when in Siena.

C. MUSEO CIVICO

At the Campo. Open 9:30am–7:30pm Monday–Saturday. Open Sunday 9:30am–1:30pm.

Inside the Palazzo Pubblico is the **Museo Civico**, which is filled with many wonderful paintings, frescoes, mosaics, and tapestries. Upstairs is the famous **Sala del Mappamondo** (Hall of the Map of the World). From its large windows you can look out onto the market square. The other three walls are frescoed with scenes of the religious and civil life of the Siena Republic. In this museum you'll find many examples of the some of the finest Sienese art anywhere.

D. THE DUOMO

Piazza del Duomo. 7:30am–1:30pm and 3:00pm to dusk from December to March. From March to November open 9:00am–7:30pm. Admission L6,000.

The combination of Gothic and Romanesque architectural elements in the Cathedral of Siena is a result of the large amount of time spent completing it. Nonetheless it doesn't appear as if the two styles contrast too much with each other. Despite being incredibly elaborate the facade seems quite harmonious and attractive. The side walls and steeple are striped black and white like the *Balzana* that is the standard of the town. It was started in 1200 and finished in the 1400s.

Inside the cathedral there are even more elaborate and rich decorations. It has three naves and is 90 meters long and 51 meters high, and the walls are covered with the white and black *Balzana* stripes also. All around the nave you'll see a row of 172 busts of Popes, from Christ to Lucius III, all made in 1400. Beneath them are 36 busts of Roman Emperors. The graffito and inlaid floor is a succession of scenes from the Old Testament, which took from 1372 to 1551 to complete. The earlier ones are done in black and white, and the later scenes have a touch of gray and red in them.

You can't miss the intricate and elaborate pulpit which was made by **Nicola Pisano** from 1265 to 1268. It is of white marble and supported by nine columns resting on nine lions. There are 300 human figures and 70 animal figures decorating this delightful work. Besides the pulpit there are countless remarkable paintings, sculptures, reliefs, and stone coffins all attributed to famous Italian masters. The statues on the Piccolo altar have been attributed to **Michelangelo**. In the **Piccolomini Library** you'll find beautiful frescoes of the life of Pope Pius II made by the master Pinturicchio. As you leave the library you'll see the monument to Archbishop Bandini's nephews made in 1570 by Michelangelo.

There were plans to have made this cathedral a small part of a much larger place of worship; but those plans were stunted for a variety of reasons, including the plague and the eventual Florentine conquest of the city. Today only a few pillars and walls remain from the plans for that grandiose church.

E. MUSEO DELL'OPERA DEL DUOMO

Piazza del Duomo. 7:30am–1:30pm and 3:00pm to dusk from December to March. From March to November open 9:00am–7:30pm. Admission L6,000.

In the **museum of the cathedral** is a valuable collection of the treasure of paintings, statues, and fragments the cathedral once displayed. One of the best paintings is Duccio di Buoninsegna's *Maestra* (1308-1311) that was originally on the high altar. You'll find a group of three sculptures, the *Three Graces*, which are Greek works of the 2nd century BCE that were once in the Piccolomini Library. And you can't miss the exquisitely beautiful goldsmith's work, *Rosa d'Oro* (Golden Rose) that was given to the city of Siena by Alessandro VIII in 1658. Another work of interest is the plan of the unfinished facade of the Baptistery by Giacomo di Mino del Pelliciaio.

F. CHURCH OF SAN DOMENICO & THE SANCTUARY OF SANTA CATERINA

Costa San Antonio. Church is open from 9:00am–6:00pm. The Sanctuary is closed 12:30pm–3:30pm Monday–Saturday and all day Sundays.

The Basilica is indelibly linked with the cloistered life of the local saint. It rises monumental and solitary overlooking the surrounding landscape and city. Its simple brick architecture of the 13th century was modified in the 14th and 15th centuries but still remains more like the walls of a convent than a church. You can't miss the **chapel of St. Caterina** inside where the Saint's head is preserved today in the silver reliquary. In the other chapels of the church you'll find paintings by Sienese artists of the 14th through 16th centuries.

The house where St. Caterina used to live is now **Caterina Sanctuary**. The rooms she lived in as a youth have been frescoed by artists of all times with scenes from her life. It is a simple home but it is of cultural significance, since St. Caterina is one of the patron saints of Italy.

RURAL RETREATS AROUND ROME

I've provided a three day escape plan if you want to get outside of Rome. Peace and tranquillity are but a drive away in the hills surrounding the Eternal City. Some of these excursions are mentioned in greater detailed earlier in this chapter.

Day One

The perfect place to start is **Tivoli**, an ancient vacation spot famous for its large villas, lush gardens and picturesque waterfalls. The best way to get out to Tivoli from Rome is to make your way to the Raccordo Annulare, the beltway around the city. Follow this east until you get to the Via Tiburtina exit. This will take you all the way out. If it is easy for you to get directly on the Via Tiburtina downtown do so instead.

Drive first to **Villa d'Este**. Originally built as a Benedictine convent, it was transformed into a sumptuous villa by Cardinal Ippolito II of Este. Here you will be transfixed with the stunning beauty of the lush gardens and beautiful fountains.

After wandering the paths that cut through the vegetation, get back in the car for the short jaunt up to the **Villa Gregoriana**, in the town of Tivoli itself. Walking along the dirt path in the Villa's grounds you pass the Grotta delle Sibille and then are able to witness the panorama of the Grande Cascata with its wonderful waterfall.

After bathing in the beauty of these two villas it's time for some repast before you venture into the third, Hadrian's Villa.

For lunch stop in **Adriano** (*Via di Villa Adriano 194, Tel. 0774/529-174)* located just outside of Hadrian's Villa. Sample some of their *crostini di verdure* (fried dough with vegetables inside), or *raviolini primavera con ricotta e spinaci* (ravioli with spring vegetables, spinach and fresh ricotta).

After lunch venture onto the grounds of Hadrian's Villa. The building itself was begun in 125 CE and completed 10 years later, and was at the time the largest and most impressive villa in the Roman Empire. From his travels Hadrian, an accomplished architect, found ideas that he recreated in his palace.

Once you have satisfied all your architectural voyeurism, it's onto **Frascati** where we will spend the night.

To get to Frascati, take route 636 under the A24 highway, past the Via Prenestina and the Via Casalina. Once there we will check into our quaint old hotel, the **Bellavista** (*Piazza Roma 2, Tel. 06/942-1068*). Evening is the perfect time to spend at an outside café or wine bar in Frascati, savoring the quiet ambiance of this Roman hill town as well as the full bodied white of the region. If you want to be in the center of everything for dinner try **Pizzeria Pinnocchio** (*Piazza del Mercato 20, Tel. 06/941-6694*). If you want a quiet meal overlooking the fields of Frascati, try **Zaraza** (*Viale Regina Margherita 21, Tel. 06/942-2053*).

Day Two

The next day take a leisurely stroll through the thriving gardens of the **Villa Aldobrandini**. Afterwards simply wander the streets of this lovely medieval town, watching the tapestry of daily life unfold around you.

For lunch, let's go to **Pagnanelli** (*Piazza A Gramsci 4, Tel. 06/936-0004*) in **Castel Gandolpho**, only a few minutes drive away. Take route 216 through the town of Marino. There's not much to see here except for the wonderful **Palazzo Pontificio**, the summer residence of the Pope, located in the **Piazza del Plebiscito**. From the piazza and the restaurant you have wonderful views of the lake below. The scene is truly enchanting. After lunch take the car for a spin down to the lake and around the beautiful blue waters.

The afternoon and early evening will be spent getting to **Velletri** and **Anagni** then finally onto **Fiuggi** for the night and their curative baths the next morning. Don't hesitate to stop along the way and take some amazing photos of the picturesque Italian countryside.

To get to **Velletri** from Castel Gandolpho you can either take the less scenic Route 7, or the more pleasant route 217. You can get on Route 7 straight from Castel Gandolfo, but to catch the 217 you need to drive down to the lake and go south around it until the junction for 217. In Velletri we can admire the fourth century **Cattedrale di San Clemente** and walk slowly through the historical center of the town, taking in the small details of everyday life.

Next on our tour is **Anagni**, which we arrive at by taking Route 600 north out of town, which hooks up with Route 6 at Collefore and will take us to Anagni. This is a wonderful medieval town with steep, narrow streets winding around beautiful palazzi. The town's cathedral rises solitary on the highest point in town. Beside this eleventh century monument with its simple facade is the powerful twelfth century bell tower. If you're hungry stop for a small snack at one of the cafés in town, but don't eat too much; in Fiuggi we're going to have a great meal.

To get to **Fiuggi**, only a short drive away, we catch the Route 155r. Fiuggi is famous for its curative waters at the **Fonte di Bonifacio** or the

Fonte Anticolana. The waters and the tranquillity are always an excuse to linger here for a day. We will spend the night at the **Grand Hotel Palazzo Delle Fonte** (*Via dei Villini 7, Tel. 0775/5081*) a spectacular four star hotel, founded in 1913 with tennis courts, indoor and outdoor swimming pools, luscious gardens and more. If you don't want something so upscale, try **Hotel Fiuggi Terme** (*Via Prenestina 9, Tel. 0775/551-212*), another four star that runs about half the price since it has about half the amenities.

Fiuggi is a city split in two: Fiuggi Fonte where the curative waters are, and Fiuggi Citta with its quaint winding streets. We will be eating dinner in the old city at **La Torre dal 1961** (*Piazza Trento e Trieste 18, Tel. 0775/55382*) so you may want to drive to the restaurant. Eating here at Antonio and Maria Ciminelli's wonderful restaurant is a culinary delight. Everything they serve is exquisite. I especially like the filet of trout (*filetto di trota*) lightly cooked in extra virgin olive oil.

Day Three

Today will be leisurely, spent being 'cured' by the waters, savoring the peace and quiet of the hills, and sampling the fine food and atmosphere of Fiuggi. For lunch try **Villa Hernicus** *(Corso Nuova Italia 30, Tel. 0775/55254)* near the waters. Their *spaghetti con vongole e peperoncini verdi* (with clams and green peppers) is wonderful.

After you've had enough peace and quiet to last a life time ... it's back to Rome. We can get back by taking the Via Prenestina all the way.

20. FLORENCE

A visit to Italy is not complete without a trip to Firenze (Florence), one of the most awe-inspiring cities in all of Europe. The Renaissance reached its full heights of artistic expression here, and it was in Florence that countless master artists, writers, inventors, political theorists and artisans lived and learned their craft, then excelled at filling the world with the glow of their brilliance. Michelangelo and Leonardo da Vinci may be the best known outside of Italy, but I'll wager you've also heard of Dante, Petrarch, Machiavelli, Giotto, Raphael and many other learned and talented Florentines.

Strolling through the cobblestone streets of Florence is like being in an art history book come to life. The sights, smells, and sounds of this wonderful medieval city must be experienced first-hand to appreciate and understand the magical atmosphere. So read on, and I'll guide you through the amazing, lovely city of Florence!

Alive with History – Beautiful Firenze!

Florence started out simply as the market square for the ancient Etruscan town of Fiesole, located on a hill about three miles (five kilometers) to the northeast. Farmers displayed their fruits and vegetables on the clearing along the Arno, and the Fiesole people came down to buy. About 187 BCE, the Romans built a road through the marketplace, and later a military garrison was established here.

As the Roman roads extended through central and northern Italy, Florence grew and prospered, and it became a trade center for goods brought down from the north. Because of its significance invaders sought its spoils; and in 401 CE a horde of Ostrogoths besieged the city; then in 542 the Goths made an unsuccessful attack. Soon after, the Lombard conquest swept over Florence, and the city became the capital of a Lombard dukedom. In time, the Holy Roman Empire led by Charlemagne drove the Lombards out and in 799 ordered new fortifications built. Charlemagne's death in 814 ended the Holy Roman Empire's hold on Florence, at which time it became an independent city-state.

With its new-found freedom, Florence expanded rapidly. The Florentines became energetic merchants and bankers, expert workmen, brave soldiers, and shrewd statesmen. By the 1100s their guilds were among the most powerful in Europe, and Florentine textiles were sold throughout the continent. Florentine bankers financed enterprises in many countries, and in 1252 the city coined its first gold pieces, called **florins**, which became the accepted currency for all of Europe.

Although Florence was largely self-governing, for a long time the city was the property of German princes. The last to hold it was Countess Matilda of Tuscany. At her death in 1115, the countess bequeathed Florence to the papacy. In the early 1200s, the papal power was supported by a political group called the **Guelfa**, while the claims of the German emperor were backed by another group, the **Ghibellines**. This conflict lasted almost a hundred years and was formally initiated in 1215 when the rival factions each tried to seize control of the city.

Aided by several popes, the Guelfa held power in the city until 1260 when their army was almost wiped out at a battle near Siena. The Ghibellines held the reins for six years, until in 1266, Charles of Anjou, the champion of Pope Clement IV, marched down from France and smashed the forces of the German emperor at the battle of Benevento – at which point the Guelfa exiles were able to return to Florence.

In 1293, the **Ordinances of Justice** were passed, excluding from public office anyone who was a member of a Florentine guild. As a result many powerful people were barred from holding public positions, and the strength of the merchant-nobles was thus reduced for a time. Because of these laws, Florence remained a republic for about 150 years; but the control of the city, however, soon passed back into the hands of the wealthy.

The **Medici** family gradually took possession of Florence, installing their puppets throughout city government. Giovanni de' Medici was the first of this family to gain real wealth and influence. His son Cosimo was the real ruler of Florence for many years; it was he who brought exiled Greek scholars to the city. Under Cosimo's grandson **Lorenzo the Magnificent**, Florence ascended to its greatest heights as a cultural center.

After Lorenzo died in 1492, the city's excesses brought on a reform movement headed by **Girolamo Savonarola**, a Dominican friar. The Medici family was expelled in 1494 and Savonarola then ruled Florence himself until 1498, when a popular reaction to his rule erupted and he was put to death.

In 1512 *la familgia Medici* were restored to the city, and in 1537 it became part of the Grand Duchy of Tuscany. Upon the death of the last Medici in 1737, Tuscany passed to the Austrian Hapsburgs. In 1861 it was formally annexed to the newly formed Kingdom of Italy, of which Florence was the capital from 1865 to 1870.

REBIRTH OF ART & SCIENCE IN FLORENCE

Florence, rather than Rome, was the cradle of the Italian ***Renaissance.*** *This rebirth of classical knowledge soon gave way to new creativity in art and literature, and Florentines led the procession.* ***Dante's*** *magnificent poetry made the Tuscan dialect the official language of Italy.* ***Francesco Petrarch*** *composed his lovely sonnets here, and* ***Giovanni Boccaccio's*** *Decameron was penned here as well.* ***Niccolo Machiavelli,*** *another Florentine, set down his brilliant, cynical observations on politics based on the intrigue intrinsic to Florentine politics.*

Giotto *was the first of many immortal Florentine painters and sculptors.* ***Michelangelo*** *worked by day on the city's fortifications and by night on his paintings and statues.* ***Ghiberti*** *labored almost a lifetime on the doors for the Florentine Baptistery. Many other great artists studied or worked in Florence, among them* ***Leonardo da Vinci, Donatello,*** *and* ***Raphael.***

In World War II, Florence was a battleground, as was the entire country. Italy entered the war on the German side in 1940, and soon after German troops occupied Florence. When the Allies advanced in 1944, the Germans declared Florence an open city, yet in retreating they destroyed all the bridges except the Ponte Vecchio, and they demolished many medieval dwellings as well. Later the Allied Military Government restored the less seriously damaged structures helping to maintain the old charm the city retains today.

In 1966, Florence's many masterpieces were lost when the Arno River overflowed its banks, rising as high as 20 feet (6 meters) in some places. Many of the more important damaged works have since been restored, but thousands of irreplaceable treasures were lost to ruin brought by the mud and water.

TWO-DAY ITINERARY IN FLORENCE

DAY ONE

Morning

To ensure a fun, enjoyable stay without costing too much, make sure you get reservations at **Hotel La Scaletta**, *Via Guicciardini 13*. Centrally located, you can get to all major sights from here, and they have a wonderful roof terrace that looks out over the Ponte Vecchio and the Arno.

To begin, let's walk to the **Accademia** and see Michelangelo's *David*. Also take in all the other works by the master which are located here.

Lunch

Walk back to the **Piazza San Lorenzo** where there is a daily market. Go to **Nerbone's** in the **Mercato Centrale** for lunch. Try one of their amazing *Panini* (boiled beef or pork) served on a *Panino* bread roll. They'll ask whether you want some juice (*sugo*) placed on the roll. Tell them *si* (yes); it makes it much tastier. Order a beverage and sit at one of the tables directly in front of the quaint little place.

After your meal, wander through the market. Check out the different cuts of meat the Italians use in their recipes. Upstairs is the vegetable and fruit market. A good place to buy some healthy snacks for later.

Afternoon

Wander through the **San Lorenzo Market** until about 2:00pm. This is by far the best market in Italy. If you are going to buy something remember to bargain. After you're done shopping head to the nearby **Piazza Duomo**. Admire the bronze doors on the belfry, the simplicity of the baptistery, and the expanse of the church. Take the time to go all the way up top of the dome.

Late afternoon, if needed, take a little siesta. If it's not needed head to the **Piazza della Signoria** and admire the statues in the Loggia. Also go into the **Palazzo della Signoria** and admire the staircase that leads to their museum. This was the residence of the Medici until the Palazzo Pitti was made available. If you're interested go upstairs and pay the fee to see the inside.

Just outside of the Piazza dell Signoria is the **Uffizzi Gallery**, which you'll be going to tomorrow. Check to see if there is a long line since this will indicate how early you'll have to get here.

Now make your way to the **Ponte Vecchio** over the river **Arno**. Shop for jewelry in the many little stores if you want, but make sure you stop in the middle of the bridge and take each other's photo with the river as a background. Follow the bridge over to the other side of the Arno. From here we're going to the **Pitti Palace** and the **Boboli Gardens**. Each separate musem charges their own entrance fee. Each has beautiful artwork in the building, and the gardens offer peace and tranquillity are filled with many wonderful statues. If you bought some snacks at the **Mercato Centrale** you may want to take the time to have a brief picnic in the gardens. When you leave, check out the store **Firenze Papier Mache** in the piazza across from the palace.

Evening

Return to your room to freshen up and get ready for dinner. Tonight we're going to a wonderful local place called **La Bussola**, *Via Porta Rossa*

58, Tel. 055/293-376. You can either sit at the counter and have a simple meal of pizza or sit in the back and soak up all the ambiance and romance of Florence. Try their *spaghetti alla Bolognese* (with a meat and tomato sauce) or their *tortellini alla panna* (cheese or meat stuffed tortellini in a cream sauce).

After dinner wander over to the Piazza Santa Maria Novella and stop at the **Fiddler's Elbow** for a pint. This place has an authentic Irish Pub atmosphere, great Italian people and fun times. If dancing is your desire, try the **Space Electronic** nearby at *Via Palazzuolo 37, Tel. 055/292-082*.

DAY TWO

Morning

Get to the **Uffizzi Gallery** early so you can beat the lines. You'll probably spend all morning here.

Lunch

For lunch try a quaint basement restaurant between the **Duomo** and the train station and near Piazza Santa Maria Novella, **Buca Lapi,** *Via del Trebbio 1, Tel. 055/213-768*. There are old travel posters plastered all over the walls and ceiling, and the tables surround the cooking area so you can view quite a display while you wait for your food. Depending on the season, it may be closed for lunch. Try their *cinghiale con patate fritte* (roasted wild boar with fried potatoes) or their *pollo al cacciatore con spinacio* (chicken 'hunter style' which is made with tomatoes, spices and brandy and comes with spinach)

Early Afternoon

Remember the church in the piazza where the **Fiddler's Elbow** was last night? We're going there now (**Chiesa di Santa Maria Novella**) to check out the overall ambiance and to admire the frescoes painted by Michelangelo. While we're in this area of town, check out the store **Il Tricolore**, *Via della Scala 25*, just off the piazza. This is the official outlet for the police and military in Florence where you can buy a variety of items like pins, hats, shirts, badges, that you can take home as gifts. Some items they won't sell to you, like guns, knives, and uniforms.

Next we're walking slightly across town to get to the place where Michelangelo is buried, **Chiesa di Santa Croce**. Inside the church you will also find many other graves of prominent Florentines including Dante Aligheri. There is a leather shop attached to the church where you can find some of the best hand-made leather goods anywhere. It is also a treat to watch them work the leather. A great place to visit and/or shop.

Late Afternoon

From here, we're going up to the **Piazzale Michelangelo** to watch the sun set. Remember to take your camera and high speed film to catch all the light possible. You'll get some of the best shots of Florence from up here. On the way back into town stop at the **Il Rifrullo**, *Via San Niccolo 55, 055/213-631,* to get a pint of beer or glass of wine. At night this is an isolated and relaxing place to come and savor the Florentine evenings.

From here take the long walk across the river and to the train station to establish your itinerary for tomorrow's adventure. You may have to wait a little while in the information office, but it's worth it so you won't have to do it in the morning.

Evening

For dinner tonight we're going to the **Tredici Gobbi** (which means "13 hunchbacks") located on Via Porcellana. Situated down a small side street near the Arno, here you can enjoy a combination of Italian and Hungarian cuisine. For an after-diner drink wander over to the nearby **Excelsior Hotel** and go up to their roof deck. Enjoy a *sambuca con tre mosce,* literally translated it means "sambuca (a liquorice drink) with three flies," but in actuality the flies are coffee beans. When you bite into the beans as you sip the Sambuca the combination of tastes is phenomenal. Here you have a view over all of Florence as it lines the Arno.

IF YOU MISS THESE PLACES, YOU HAVEN'T BEEN TO FLORENCE

After spending all your time and money to come to this Renaissance paradise, there are a few sights that if you don't see you can't really say you've been to Florence. The first of which, the ***Duomo*** *with its campanile and baptistery, is hard to miss. The next, the* ***Ponte Vecchio,*** *is a gem of medieval and Renaissance architecture and is filled with gold and jewelry shops. And if you miss Michelangelo's* ***David*** *in the Accademia you shouldn't show your face back in your home town. That work of art is as close to sculpted perfection as any artist will ever achieve.*

Last but not least is the art collection in the ***Uffizzi Gallery****. To actually do this museum justice you may need to spend close to one day wandering through its many rooms. And don't forget to shop at the* ***San Lorenzo Market*** *or browse through the local* ***Mercato Centrale.***

There are countless other wonderful sights to see and places to go in Florence. Walking the streets is like walking through a fairy tale. But if you haven't seen the items above, you haven't been to Florence.

ARRIVALS & DEPARTURES

By Car

When arriving in Florence from Rome by care, for speed you will be on the **A1** (**E35**). If you were looking for a more scenic adventure, you would be on the **Via Cassia** which you can take all the way from Rome. Your trip should take between 3 1/2 to 4 hours.

By Train

From Rome the trip to Florence by high speed *rapido* train should take 2 1/2 hours each way. The station, **Stazione Santa Maria Novella**, is located near the center of town and is easily accessible on foot to and from most hotels. The **tourist information office** in the station, *Tel. 055/278-785,* is open daily from 7:00am to 10:00pm and is your first stop if you don't have a reservation at a hotel. The **railway office**, at the opposite end of the station from the tourist information office, is where you plan your train trip from Florence. To get served you need to take a number and wait your turn, a concept that is still foreign to many Italians.

The wait can be quite long, but it is entertaining watching Italians become completely confused about having to take a number, wait in a queue, and actually do something in an organized fashion. First your average Italian will attempt to assert his Latin ego to an information officer, whether they are serving someone else or not, get rebuffed, attempt to do it again with another information officer, get rebuffed again, finally look at the machine spitting out numbers and the directions associated with it, stare as would a deer trapped in an oncoming car's headlights, turn and glare at the long line formed since they first attempted their folly, then ultimately strut out of the office without getting the information they need. I've seen it happen so many times!

There are **taxis** located just outside the entrance near the tourist information office as well as **buses** that can take you all over the city.

GETTING AROUND TOWN

By Bus

There is no need to use public buses in Florence unless you're going up to Fiesole. But if you need to, first get information about routes from the booth at the **Piazza della Stazione** across the piazza from the station itself. A bus ticket costs L1,400 and is reusable within an hour.

At all bus stops, called **fermata**, there are signs that list all the buses that stop there. These signs also give the streets that the buses will follow along its route so you can check your map to see if this is the bus for you. Also, on the side of the bus are listed highlights of the route for your convenience. Nighttime routes (since many buses stop a midnight) are indicated by black spaces on newer signs, and are placed at the bottom of the older signs. In conjunction, the times listed on the signs indicate when the bus will pass the *fermata* during the night so you can plan accordingly.

Riding the bus during rush is very crowded, so try to avoid the rush hours of 8:00am to 9:00am, 12:30pm to 1:30pm, 3:30 to 4:30pm, and 7:30pm to 8:30pm. They have an added rush hour in the middle of the day because of their siesta time in the afternoon.

By Car

Florence is small and crowded and renting a car makes little sense unless you are staying on the outskirts. If you are staying in town, walking and taking cabs will suffice. Renting a car is relatively simple, as things go in Italy, but it is somewhat expensive. You can rent a car from a variety of agencies all over Florence. All prices will vary by agency so please call them for an up-to-date quote.

- **Avis**, *Borgo Ognissanti 128r, Tel 055/21-36-29 or 239-8826*
- **Avis**, *Lungarno Torrigiani 32/3, Tel 055/234-66-68 or 234-66-69*
- **Budget**, *Borgo Ognissanti 134r, Tel. 055/29-30-21 or 28-71-61*
- **Euro Dollar**, *Via il Prato 80r, Tel 055/238-24-80, Fax 055/238-24-79*
- **Hertz**, *Via Maso Finiguerra 33, Tel. 055/239-8205, Fax 055/230-2011*
- **Maggiore**, *Via Maso Finiguerra 11r, Tel. 055/21-02-38*

Most companies require a deposit that amounts to the cost of the rental, as well as a 19% VAT added to the final cost, which can be reimbursed once you're home (see Chapter 16, *Shopping*). A basic rental of a Fiat Panda costs L160,000 per day, but the biggest expense is gasoline. In Italy it costs more than twice as much per gallon as it does in the States. If you're adventurous enough to think of renting a car, remember that the rates become more advantageous if you rent for more than a week.

By Moped

Since Florence is so small, the areas in Tuscany I'm recommending are quite close together, and the drivers are not quite as crazy as Romans, a moped (50cc) or **vespa** (125cc) is one of the best ways to get around and see the countryside. But this isn't a simple ride in the park. Only if you feel extremely confident about your motorcycle driving abilities should you even contemplate renting a moped.

Rentals for a moped (50cc) are about L50,000 per day, and for a 125cc (which you'll need to transport two people) about L80,000 per day. From some companies you can rent even bigger bikes, but I would strongly advise against it. You can also rent the cycles for an hour or any multiples thereof.

- **Firenze Motor**, *Via Guelfa 85r. Tel 055/280-500, Fax 05/211-748. Located in the Centro section to the right of the station and north of the Duomo.*
- **Noleggio dell Fortezza** *(two locations), Corner of Via Strozzi and Via del Pratello, Open 9:00am to 8:00pm, the 15th of March to 31st of October; and Via Faenza 107-109r. Tel. 055/283-448.* **Scooter prices**: *1 hour L9,000/ half day L20,000/1 day L38,000.* **Bicycle prices**: *1 hour L3,000/half day L8,000/1 day L15,000.*
- **Motorent**, *Via San Zanobi 9, Tel. 055/490-113, in the Centro area.*
- **Sabra**, *Via Artisti 8, Tel. 055/576-256, in the Oltrarno area.*
- **Free Motor**, *Via Santa Monaca 6-8, Tel. 055/293-102, in the Oltrarno area.*

By Bicycle

Some of the moped rental places listed above also rent bicycles, but by far the best bicycle rental service and definitely the most professional is:

- **Florence By Bike**, *Via San Zanobi 120/122, Tel./Fax 055/488-992; Open from 9:00am-7:30pm every day; E-mail: ecologica@dada.it; Website: www.florencebybike.it. Credit cards accepted.* Not only do they offer bicycles for rent (1 hour, L4,000; 5 hours, L12,000; Day, L20,000; Weekend L35,000) at great prices, but they also offer guided city tours as well as countryside tours. Located near Piazza Santa Maria Novella, this is the place to come for good quality bike rentals and fun and informative bike tours.

By Taxi

Florence is a city made for walking, but if you get tired, taxis are good but expensive way to get around. They are everywhere, except on the streets designated for foot traffic so flagging one down is not a problem. But since they are so expensive I wouldn't rely on them as your main form of transportation. Also have a map handy when a cabby is taking you somewhere. Since they are on a meter, they sometimes decide to take you on a little longer journey than necessary.

The going rate as of publication was L4,500 for the first 2/3 of a kilometer or the first minute (which usually comes first during the rush hours), then its L500 every 1/3 of a kilometer or minute. At night you'll also pay a surcharge of L3,000, and Sundays you'll pay L1,000 extra. If you bring bags aboard, say for example after you've been shopping, you'll be charged L500 extra for each bag.

There are strategically placed cab stands all over the city.

WHERE TO STAY

Listed below are the best options to choose from for a short stay in Florence. If these are booked up and you need a place to stay, try the hotel locator services at the train station.

1. HOTEL CALZAIUOLI, *Via Calzaiuoli 6, Firenze. Tel 055/212-456, Fax 055/268-310. All credit cards accepted. 45 rooms all with private bath, TV, Telephone, mini-bar, and air conditioning. Breakfast included. Single 200,000; Double 290,000. Extra bed L70,000.* ***

Located in a recently renovated old palazzo and perfectly situated in the quiet pedestrian zone between the Duomo and Palazzo Vecchio. Some rooms have great views of the Duomo and with that view, its location, and all the amenities it offers this is a good place to stay. The rooms are spacious enough, as are the bathrooms, and have a nice floral and ribbon print motif. The rooms on the Via Calzaiuoli are perfect for people watching, but can be a little noisy on the weekend evenings. The hallways are small, so if you're there with a group of tourists getting in and out can be arduous. You can't beat the location or the service.

2. HOTEL CONTINENTAL, *Lungarno Acciaioli 2, 50123 Firenze. Tel. 055/282-392, Fax 055/283-139. E-mail: ricevimento@lungarnohotels.com. Website: www.lungarnohotels.it/ continental_e.shtm. All credit cards accepted. 48 rooms all with private bath. Single L360-390,000; Double L510,000-560,000; Penthouse Suite L565,000-860,000. Breakfast included.* ****

This place is *elegantissimo*. If only I could afford the penthouse suite I would be in heaven. One rung below that fantasy is the hotel's superb terrace with breathtaking views of the Arno and the Ponte Vecchio. It is breathtaking since they're basically right on top of the old bridge. You can't go wrong with the location, the ultra-modern rooms, the exquisite service. At the Continental you can truly live the experience of being in Renaissance Florence with all the modern amenities to keep you happy. A great place to stay.

3. ALBERGO FIRENZE, *Piazza dei Donati 4 (off of Via del Corso), 50122 Firenze. Tel. 055/268-301, Fax 055/212-370. No credit cards accepted. 60 rooms, 35 with private bath. Single without bath L55,000-65,000; Single L65,000-75,000; Double without bath L85,000-105,000; Double L95,000-105,000. Breakfast included.* *

This is two different hotels. One is new, the other's left in a time warp from the 1950s. My recommendation is based on the new section, so call in advance to get your reservations.

Even though this place doesn't have air conditioning, it should be higher than a one star. The lobby is all three star, as are the rooms in the new wing with their phones and TVs. Room 503 caught my fancy since it has a great view of the Duomo from the bed: when you wake up in the

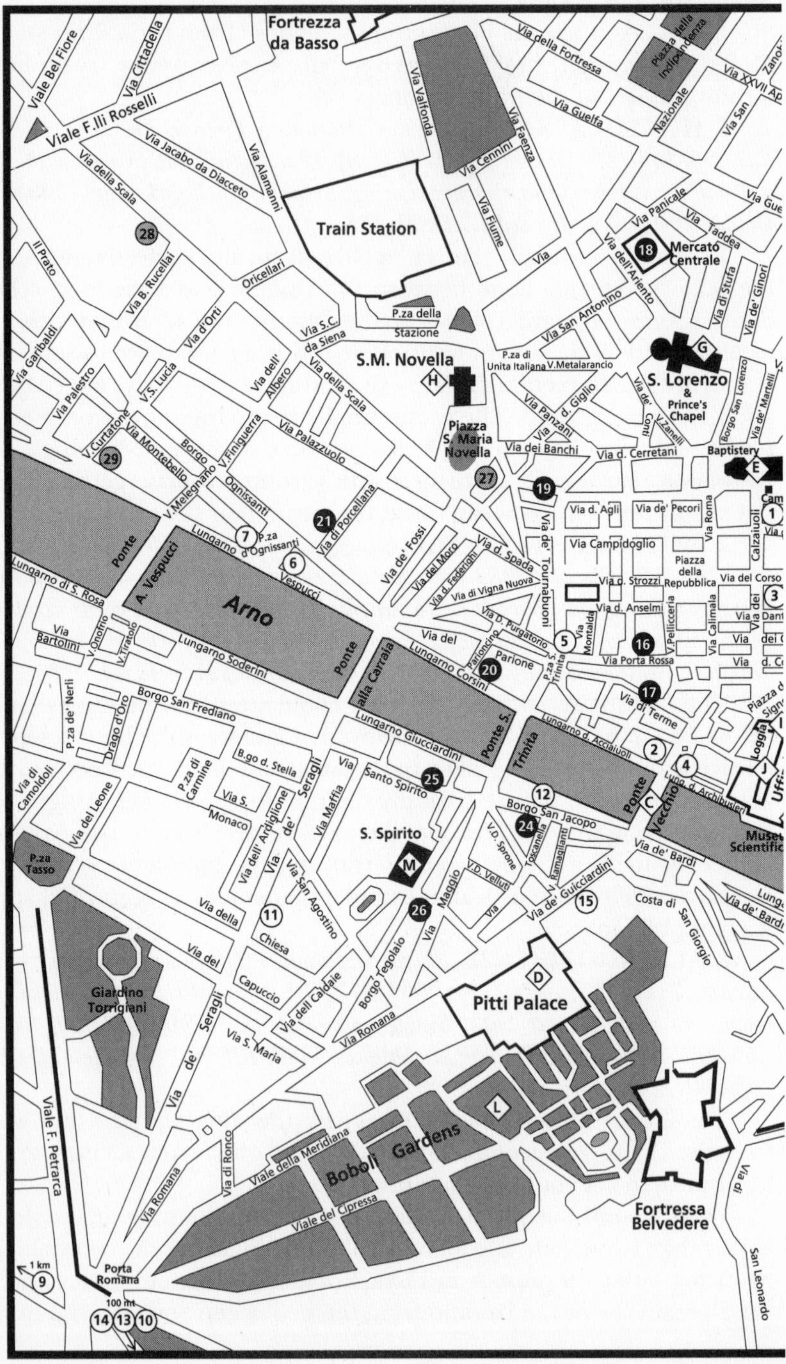
Fortrezza
da Basso
Via della Fortressa
Piazza della Indipendenza
Nazionale
Via XXVII Ap
Viale Bel Fiore
Via Cittadella
Viale F.lli Rosselli
Via Jacabo da Diacceto
Via della Scala
Via Alamanni
Via Valfonda
Via Cennini
Via Faenza
Via Guelfa
Via San
Train Station
Via Fiume
Via Panicale
Via Taddea
Via dell'Ariento
Mercato
Centrale
Via di Stufa
Via de' Ginori
Il Prato
Via B. Rucellai
Oricellari
Via d'Orti
Via S.C. da Siena
P.za della
Stazione
Via San Antonino
P.za di
Unita Italiana
V.Metalarancio
S.M. Novella
S. Lorenzo
&
Prince's
Chapel
Via Garibaldi
Via Palestro
V.S. Lucia
Via dell' Albero
Via della Scala
Via Panzani
d. Giglio
Via de' Conti
V.Zanetti
Borgo San Lorenzo
Via de' Martelli
V.Curtatone
Via Montebello
Borgo
V.Finiguerra
Via Palazzuolo
Piazza
S. Maria
Novella
Via dei Banchi
Via d. Cerretani
Baptistery
V.Melegnano
Ognissanti
Via di Porcellana
Via d. Agli
Via de' Pecori
Via Roma
Calzaiuoli
Ponte
A. Vespucci
Lungarno
P.za
d'Ognissanti
Vespucci
Via de' Fossi
Via del Moro
Via d. Federighi
Via d. Spada
Via de' Tornabuoni
Via Campidoglio
Piazza
della
Repubblica
Via del Corso
Lungarno di S. Rosa
Arno
Via di Vigna Nuova
Via d. Strozzi
Via d. Anselmi
Via D. Purgatorio
Via Bartolini
V. Onofrio
V. Tiratoio
Lungarno Soderini
Ponte
alla Carraia
Via del
Parioncino
Parione
P.za S. Trinita
Via Montalda
V. Pellicceria
Via Calimala
Via Porta Rossa
Lungarno Corsini
Via di Terme
Piazza d. Signoria
Loggia
P.za de' Nerli
Drago d'Oro
Borgo San Frediano
Lungarno Guicciardini
Ponte S. Trinita
Lungarno d. Acciaiuoli
Lung. d. Archibusieri
Via di Camoldoli
Via del Leone
P.za di Carmine
B.go d. Stella
Seragli
Via Maffia
Santo Spirito
Borgo San Jacopo
Ponte Vecchio
Via S.
Monaco
Via dell' Ardiglione
Via de'
S. Spirito
V.D. Sprone
Toscanella
Ramaglianti
Museo Scientifico
Via de' Bardi
P.za Tasso
Via San Agostino
V.D. Velluti
Via Maggio
Via de' Guicciardini
Costa di San Giorgio
Via de' Bardi
Via della Chiesa
Via del Capuccio
Via dell Caldaie
Borgo Tegolaio
Pitti Palace
Giardino Torrigiani
Via de' Seragli
Via S. Maria
Via Romana
Viale F. Petrarca
Via di Ronco
Viale della Meridiana
Boboli Gardens
Viale del Cipressa
Via Romana
Fortressa
Belvedere
Via di San Leonardo
1 km
Porta
Romana
100 mt

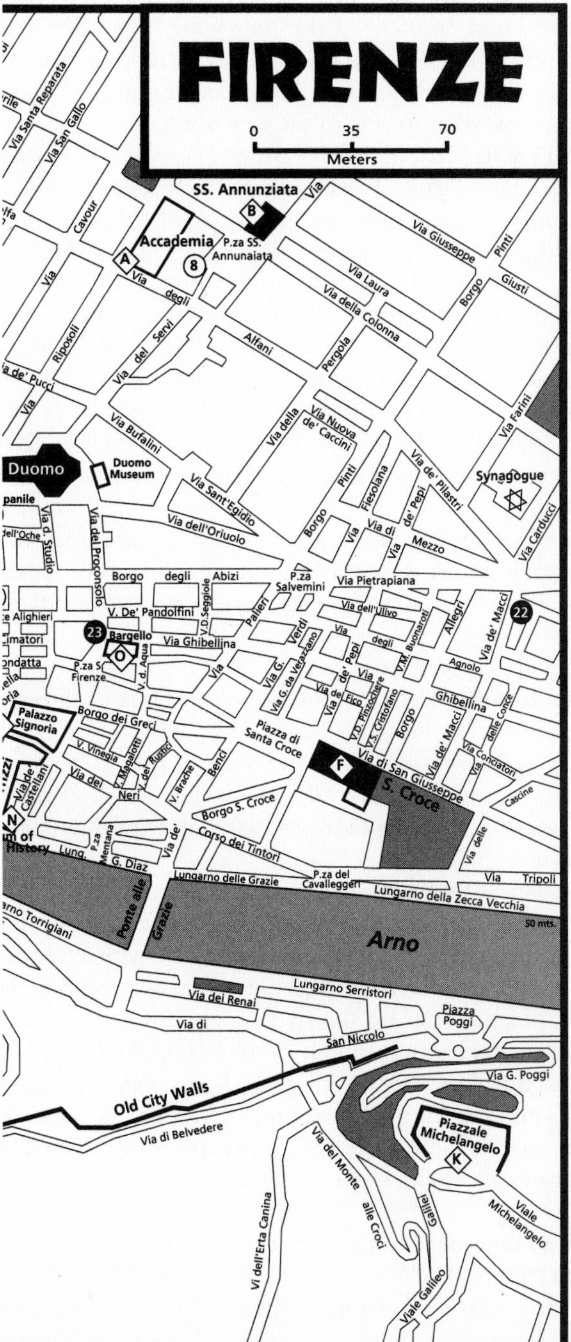

SIGHTS ◇

A. Academia
B. SS. Annunziata
C. Ponte Vecchio
D. Pitti Palace
E. Duomo, Baptistery, Campanile & Museum
F. Santa Croce
G. San Lorenzo
H. Santa Maria Novella
I. Piazza, Palazzo & Loggia della Signoria
J. Uffizzi Gallery
K. Piazzale Michelangelo
L. Boboli Gardens
M. Santo Spirito
N. Museum of Scientific History
O. Bargello

HOTELS ○

1. Calzaiuoli
2. Continental
3. Firenze
4. Hermitage
5. Beacci-Tornabuoni
6. Excelsior
7. Grand Hotel
8. Loggiato dei Serviti
9. Torre di Bellosguardo
10. Classic
11. Istituto Gould
12. Lungarno
13. Villa Carlotta
14. Villa Cora
15. La Scaletta

RESTAURANTS ●

16. La Bussola
17. Oliviero
18. Nerbone
19. Buca Lapi
20. Coco Lezzone
21. Tredici Gobbi
22. Il Cibreo
23. Mossacce
24. Mama Gina
25. Il Cantinone del Gallo Nero
26. La Casalinga

NIGHTLIFE ◉

27. Fiddler's Elbow
28. Space Electronic
29. Harry's Bar

morning there's the most romantically picturesque scene right in front of you. Besides the beauty and comfort of the new wing, the lobby and breakfast area is of a much higher standard than any other one star I've been in. It's beautiful and quite inexpensive. They speak English, so make sure you tell them that you want to stay in the new wing.

4. HOTEL HERMITAGE, *Vicolo Marzio 1 (Piazza del Pesce), 50122 Firenze. Tel. 055/287-216, Fax 055/212-208. E-mail: Florence@HermitageHotel.com. Website: www.venere.it/firenze/hermitage/hermitage.html. Mastercard and Visa accepted. 16 rooms all with private bath and jacuzzi. All rooms L350,000. Breakfast included.* ***

Only steps from the Ponte Vecchio but located above the tourist noise, this wonderful little hotel is on the top three floors of an office building and is reached by a private elevator. It has the most beautiful roof terrace, complete with greenery and flowers and a great view of the rooftops of Florence, as well as the Arno and the Ponte Vecchio. They serve breakfast up there in good weather and it is a great place to relax in the evenings.

The rooms are not that large but the ambiance and the location make up for it, as does the spacious terrace and common areas. The staff speaks a variety of languages. For a three star the place is great. Recently updated with jacuzzi style baths in every room so you can luxuriate here at the end of the day. A great hotel in a great location.

5. HOTEL BEACCI-TORNABUONI, *Via Tornabuoni 3, 50122 Firenze. Tel. 055/212-645, Fax 055/283-594. E-mail: Beacci.Tornabuoni@italyhotel.com. Website: www.venere.it/firenze/beacci_tornabuoni/beacci_tornabuoni.html. All credit cards accepted. 28 rooms all with private bath. Single L190,000; Double L300,000. Extra bed L60,000. Buffet breakfast included.* ***

Located on the top three floors of a 14th century palazzo on the world famous and elegant shopping street, Via Tornabuoni. There is a wonderful rooftop garden terrace that will make you fall in love with Florence every evening you spend up there. I preferred the rooms overlooking the garden for the quiet, but the ones on the street make for good people watching. A much better deal with infinitely better atmosphere than La Residenza which is just down the street. This place is coordinated like an old castle, with nooks and crannies everywhere, and plenty of common space besides the terrace to sit and write your postcards home. You'll be surrounded by antiques and will feel as if you've stepped into an Agatha Christie novel.

The breakfast is an abundant buffet which can be served to you in your room at no extra charge. The rooms are all furnished differently but with the finest taste and character. All have double beds. An excellent place to stay.

6. EXCELSIOR HOTEL, *Piazza Ognissanti 3, 50123 Firenze. Tel. 055/264-201, Fax 055/210-278. Toll free number in America 1-800-221-2340. All credit cards accepted. 200 rooms all with private bath. Single L790,000; Double L1,230,000. Continental breakfast L30,000. American breakfast L45,000.* *****

Directly across from its sister, The Grand Hotel, the prices here have really gone through the roof. Granted everything here is of the highest standard, especially the roof garden/restaurant where you can have your meal or sip an after-dinner drink, listen to the piano player, and gaze out at the splendor that is Florence, but wow, the prices have more than doubled in the past couple years. You don't have to stay here to enjoy the view; just come for dinner. Great rooms and perfect service. A superb five star luxury hotel. They have everything and more that you could want during your stay. If you can afford it, this is one of the best luxury hotels in Florence.

7. GRAND HOTEL, *Piazza Ognissanti 1, 50123 Firenze. Tel. 055/288-781, Fax 055/217-400. Toll free number in America 1-800-221-2340. All credit cards accepted. An ITT Sheraton hotel. 106 rooms all with private bath. Single L790,000; Double L1,230,000; Continental breakfast L30,000. American breakfast L45,000.* *****

Aptly named, this hotel is wonderfully grand. Located in a pale yellow and gray palazzo built in 1571, everything has been superbly restored to offer modern creature comforts while retaining the old world charm. Even though it is on a main thoroughfare, it is extremely quiet. The reception area is classically elegant. Each bedroom has beautiful neo-classic furniture and elegant decorations and frescoes; the bathrooms are a luscious oasis. Your breakfast is served on a small balcony overlooking an internal garden. More pleasant and comfortable than the Excelsior by maybe a whisker as a result of its recent renovation, but remember to go to the Excelsior for their roof-bar restaurant.

8. HOTEL LOGGIATO DEI SERVITI, *Piazza SS. Annunziata 3, 50122 Firenze. Tel. 055/289-593/4, Fax 055/289-595. E-mail: Loggiato.dei.Serviti@italyhotel.com. Website: www.venere.it/firenze/loggiato_serviti/loggiato_serviti.html. All credit cards accepted. 29 rooms all with private bath. Single L195,000; Double L295,000; Suite for L350,000-600,000. Breakfast included. L80,000 for an extra bed.* ***

Located in a 16th century *loggia* that faces the beautiful Piazza della SS Annunziata, this hotel is filled with charm and character. The interior common areas consist of polished terra-cotta floors, gray stone columns and high white ceilings. The rooms are pleasant and comfortable and are filled with elegant antique furnishings. All are designed to make you feel like you just walked into the 17th century, and it works. But they do have the modern amenities necessary to keep us weary travelers happy, especially the air conditioning in August. Some rooms face what many believe is one of the most beautiful piazzas in Italy (no cars allowed), while the rest face onto a lush interior garden. The bathrooms come with every modern comfort. The service, the accommodations, everything is at the top of the three star category. So, if you want to have a wonderful stay and also to feel as if you've stepped back in time, book a room here.

9. HOTEL TORRE DI BELLOSGUARDO, *Via Roti Michelozzi 2, 50125 Firenze. Tel. 055/229-8145, Fax 055/229-008. 16 room all with bath. Single L390,000; Double L530,000; Suites L550,000-650,000. All credit cards accepted.* ****

If you have the means, this is the only place to stay while in Florence. Once you walk in the gates you will love it. The ancient towered palazzo that is the hotel will make you feel like you have stepped back to the Renaissance. Besides this completely unique and accommodating building, this wonderful hotel has the best views over Florence. They are stunningly amazing. Also the grounds are filled with gardens and olive trees where horses graze; there is a huge open lawn in front flanked by fir trees; and they have a swimming pool with a bar – all of which overlook the magnificent city of Florence below.

The old palazzo used to be a small English language school, St. Michael's, that catered to 100 students (of which I was one). So you can imagine that currently, with only sixteen luxury rooms, the size of your accommodations are quite impressive. The interior common areas are like something out of a movie script, with vaulted stone ceilings and arches, as well as staircases leading off into hidden passages. You're a short distance outside of the old city walls but here you will find pure romance, complete peace, and soothing tranquillity. In fact the hotel is so magnificent that you have to reserve well in advance, since they are booked solid year round. I can't say enough about the view, it is simply something you have experience. Also, and most importantly, if you aren't already in love, you'll find it or rekindle it in this wonderfully majestic hideaway. This is *the* place to stay while in Florence.

10. CLASSIC HOTEL, *Viale Machiavelli 25, 50125 Firenze. Tel. 055/229-3512, Fax 055/229-353. All credit cards accepted. 20 rooms all with private bath. Single L160000; Double L230,000. Breakfast included.* ***

Located in a quaint little palazzo from the nineteenth century situated outside the old city walls, here you can get a taste of Florentine life without the constant clamoring of mopeds riding past your bedroom window. Piazzale Machiavelli is an exclusive address and this hotel shows it. The lush garden in the rear (there's a glassed-in section for winter guests) is your breakfast location as well as your mid-afternoon slumber spot, and there's a small bar just off the garden for evening drinks.

Your rooms are palatial, with immense ceilings and clean bathrooms. Each room is furnished quite differently. Some have antique furniture, others have newer but sill attractive pieces. The diversity lends a spot of charm. I would recommend this gem to anyone who likes to tour and then escape the hectic pace of the city. One minor note, they do not have air conditioning, but when I was there on a 90 degree day each room was very cool. These old palazzi were built to keep cool in the summer and remain warm in the winter. This place really is a classic and the choice for truly discerning vacationers.

11. ISTITUTO GOULD, *Via dei Serragli 49, 50125 Firenze. Tel. 055/212-576, Fax 055/280-274. No credit cards accepted. 25 rooms, 20 with private bath. Single L60,000; Double L50,000 per person.* (no star)

If you don't have your own bathroom here you're still okay, since you only have to share two toilets and two showers with four other rooms. The office is on the ground floor of a magnificent palazzo that you will enjoy exploring. There are limited office hours (9:00am–1:00pm and 3:00pm–7:00pm) but they do give you your own key so you can go in and out as your please. (A rarity in Florence for one-stars.) The rooms, on the second and third floors scattered all over the palazzo, are quite large. In your search throughout this wonderful building you'll find an immense common room with comfortable chairs and a quaint little terrace overlooking some rooftops in the rear, which is a great place to relax with a glass of Chianti and a makeshift meal of bread, cheese and salami.

The best part of your comfortable stay is that the proceeds generated by the Istituto Gould benefit a home for wayward children. Also, they separate the more mature budget travelers from the younger crowd, so the late night adventures of the rowdier set don't keep us older and wiser folks awake. This is a fantastic budget hotel in truly ambient surroundings.

12. HOTEL LUNGARNO, *Borgo S Jacopo 14, 50125 Firenze. Tel. 055/264-211, Fax 055/268-437. E-mail: ricevimento@lungarnohotels.com. Website: www.lungarnohotels.it/ungarno_e.shtm. All credit cards accepted. 66 rooms all with private bath. Single L360,000-390,000; Double L510-560,000; Suite L660,000-760,000.* ****

An excellent location right on the river, only a few meters from the Ponte Vecchio, and situated down a quaint, Florentine side street with some great restaurants and food shops. Even though most of the hotel is modern, it is a quaint, classic establishment. The lounge just off the lobby offers a relaxing view of the river and the Ponte Vecchio.

An ancient stone tower is part of the hotel, with a great penthouse suite. If you want the atmosphere of the tower, specify this upon making your reservation. Some of the rooms have terraces overlooking the river, which makes for a perfect place to relax after a tough day of sightseeing.

You need to specify this too.

A great feature of the hotel is the more than 400 modern paintings that line the walls. Some by Picasso, Cocteau, Sironi, Rosai and more. Another plus is the fact that hotel has bicycles available for guests to use free of charge. This is one of the great hotels in Florence.

13. VILLA CARLOTTA, *Via Michele di Lando 3, 50125 Firenze. Tel. 055/233-6134, Fax 055/233-6147. All credit cards accepted. 27 rooms all with private bath. Five more in a gatehouse building. Single L290,000; Double L410,000. Breakfast included. Can also get another meal at their fine restaurant for L55,000.* ****

The hotel is like something out of a dream, with its sunlit tea room used for breakfast, its small garden on the side with fish swimming in the fountain, and elegant dining in the magnificent restaurant below. To top it all off you have a real bar with stools from which you can get any type of concoction your heart desires.

The location is perfect for those who like to get away from it all. Off the beaten path in a quiet and calm section of town. The rooms are all pleasantly furnished with all necessary amenities. A truly great place to stay.

14. VILLA CORA, *Viale Machiavelli 18-20, 50125 Firenze. Tel. 055/229-8451, Fax 055/229-086. All credit cards accepted. 47 rooms all with private bath. Single L460,000; Double L850,000; Deluxe Double Room L950,000; Suites 2,000,000. A full buffet breakfast included.* *****

You'll find this extravagant and ornately decorated hotel (once a nineteenth century *palazzo*) on a residential street that curves up to the Florentine hills. It is truly magnificent with its chandeliers, statues, bas-relief covered walls, gilded mirrors and staff that will wait on you hand and foot. If you want to stay in the lap of luxury and are willing to pay for it, this is the place for you. There is a pool-side restaurant, Taverna Machiavelli, where you can eat and relax after a hard day's touring. Another important feature is the rooftop terrace garden, offering excellent views of Florence. And the rooms are superb, stupendous, *fantavolosso* – think of any adjective and the rooms will surpass it! A great place to stay if you have the money.

15. HOTEL LA SCALETTA, *Via Guicciardini 13, 50123 Firenze. Tel. 055/283-028, Fax 055/289-562. E-mail: lascaletta@italyhotel.com. Website: www.venere.it/firenze lascaletta. Mastercard and Visa accepted. 12 rooms, 11 with private bath. Single without bath L80,000; Single L140,000: Double without bath L140,000; Double L200,000. Breakfast included.* **

No ifs, ands, or buts about it, this is the best place to stay in the Oltrarno ... and maybe all of Florence, if you don't want to spend a lot of money. But you have to reserve your rooms well in advance. Let's say at least 4-5 months in advance, to guarantee you'll get a room overlooking the garden! Yes, there's no air conditioning, but it's not needed. This ancient building seems to soak up the cold air in the summer and retain the warm in the winter.

The rooms are large, clean and comfortable. The location is ideal and amazingly quiet and relaxing. And best of all there are two incomparable terraces overlooking all the best sights of Florence. Relaxing on these terraces after a day on the town makes a stay here sublime.

The furnishings are eclectic and simple, but comfortable; and the layout is scattered throughout the building, with everything connected by staircases. The prices are superb but they won't last forever. Management has already put air conditioning in three rooms, and when all are complete, the hotel should get its three star rating. That will send their prices through the roof, just like it did with La Scalinetta di Spagna in Rome. A great place to stay while in Florence.

WHERE TO EAT

TUSCAN CUISINE

During the Renaissance, Florence and Tuscany experienced a burst of elaborate cuisine, mainly the result of Catherine de Medici importing a brigade of French chefs, but today that type of cuisine has given way to more basic fare. Tuscan cooking has its roots in the frugal peasant cuisine that was the result of the region being agriculturally poor for so many centuries. The food is simple but healthy, with the emphasis on fresh ingredients which accentuates the individual tastes of each dish.

Grilled meats are a staple of the Florentine diet, with *bistecca alla Fiorentina* rivaling anything Texas could dream of producing. The Florentines tend to over-salt their vegetables and soups, but you can ask for them to be prepared *senza sale*, without salt, and no one will be insulted at all. You'll also find beans and olive oil prominently used in many dishes, as well as many types of game that populate the hills of Tuscany. And if you like cheese, my favorite is the full flavored *pecorino* made from sheep's milk.

Tuscany is not really known for its pasta dishes, but Tuscans do make an excellent *pasta alla carrettiera*, a pasta dish with a sauce of tomato, garlic, pepper, and parsley. If you want a simple, filling, healthy meal, you'll find one in Tuscany. Just don't expect some extravagant saucy dish. For that go to France.

Suggested Tuscan Cuisine

You don't have to eat all the traditional courses listed below. Our constitution just isn't prepared for such mass consumption, so don't feel bad if all you order is a pasta dish or an entrée with a salad or appetizer.

Antipasto – Appetizer

- **Crostini** – Chicken liver pate spread on hard, crusty bread
- **Pinzimonio** – Raw vegetables to be dipped in rich olive oil
- **Bruschetta** – Sliced crusty bread roasted over a fire covered with olive oil and rubbed with garlic; sometimes comes with crushed tomatoes, or another version has an egg on top (*Aqua Cotta*)

Primo Piatto – First Course

Zuppa – Soup

- **Ribollita** – means reboiled. A hearty mushy vegetable soup with beans, cabbage, carrots, and chunks of boiled bread.
- **Panzanella** – A Tuscan *gazpacho* (cold soup) made with tomatoes, cucumbers, onions, basil, olive oil, and bread.

Pasta

- **Pappardelle alla lepre** – Wide homemade pasta with a wild hare sauce
- **Pasta alla carrettierra** –Pasta with a sauce of tomato, garlic, pepper and parsley
- **Tortelli** – Spinach and ricotta ravioli with either cream sauce or a meat sauce

Secondo Piatto – Entrée

Carne – Meat

- **Bistecca alla Fiorentina** – T-bone steak at least two inches thick cooked over coals charred on the outside and pink in the middle. Welcome to Texas!
- **Fritto misto** –Usually lamb, rabbit or chicken, with peppers, zucchini, artichokes dipped in batter and deep fried
- **Arista di Maiale** – Pork loin chop cooked with rosemary and garlic
- **Spiedini di maiale** – Pork loin cubes and pork liver spiced with fennel and cooked on a skewer over open flames
- **Francesina** – Meat, onions, and tomatoes stewed in red wine
- **Trippa alla Fiorentina** – Tripe mixed with tomato sauce and served with a variety of cheeses

Pesce – Fish

- **Bacca alla Fiorentina** – Salted cod cooked with tomatoes and spices (usually garlic and fennel)
- **Seppie in Zimino** – Cuttlefish simmered with beans

Contorno – Vegetable

- **Fagioli all'ucceletto** – White beans with garlic and tomatoes and sometimes sage

- **Insalata Mista** – mixed salad. You have to prepare your own olive oil and vinegar dressing. American's lust for countless types of salad dressings hasn't hit Italy yet.

Formaggio – Cheese

- **Pecorino** – Cheese made from sheep's milk

Tuscan Wines

Tuscany is known for its full bodied red wines, especially the world famous **Chianti**. A bottle of Chianti has surely graced the table of every Italian home at least once. Robust, full-bodied and zesty, the many reds produced by the Chianti vines in Tuscany have attained worldwide acclaim. To be called Chianti a wine must be made according to certain specifications and the vines must be located in certain areas. Within this production zone seven different sub-regions are recognized: Chianti Classico, Chianti Colli Aretini, Chianti Colli Fiorentini, Chianti Colli Senesi, Chianti Colline Pisane, Chianti Montalbano and Chianti Rufina.

Produced between Florence and Siena, Chianti Classico is more full-bodied than the others in its family, and comes from the oldest part of the production zone. If the wine is a Chianti Classico you'll find a black rooster label on the neck of the bottle. An austere wine, ideal when aged and served with meat dishes, it is also well suited for tomato-based pasta dishes especially those with meat in them.

Chiantis can be called *vecchio* (old) if the wine has aged two years and is given the respected and coveted *Riserva* label when aged three years and *Superiore* if aged for five years. With Chianti wines you can expect the best, especially if it is a Classico.

From the Chianti region you should try the following red wines: **Castello di Ama**, **Castello di Volpaia**, and **Vecchie Terre di Montefili**. Outside the region try some **Rosso delle Colline Luchesi** from the hills around Lucca, **Morellino di Scansano** from the hills south of Grossetto, and **Elba Rosso**, made on the island of Elba.

The hills of Tuscany are filled with vineyards large and small supplying grapes to make some of the world's best vintages. When in Tuscany you must sample at least a little of this bounty. There are plenty of wine cellars and *enoteche* (wine bars) in every city in this region for you to sample the regional offerings. And you can't forget a glass of wine with your meal. Some Tuscans say that their food is bland so that they can enjoy the wine with their meals more. Whatever the reason, you'll love sampling the different varieties.

Most wines are classified by the type of grape used and the district from which the wines are produced. Some of the best wines come with a

DOC (*Denominazione di Origine Controllata*) label that indicates the wine comes from a specially defined area and was produced according to specific traditional methods. If the label reads **DOCG** (G stands for *Garantita*) the wine will be of the highest quality, guaranteed.

Some whites you might enjoy are a dry **Montecarlo** from the hills east of Lucca or a dry **Bolgheri** from the coast. The red wines mentioned above also have some excellent white wines to complement them.

Some of these wines may be a bit pricey in restaurants so you may want to buy them at a store and sample them back in your hotel room or on a picnic. At restaurants, in most cases the house wines will be locally produced and of excellent quality, so give them a try too. No need to spend a lot of money on a labeled bottle of wine, when the house wine is better than most that we get back home.

Listed below are the best places to sample Tuscan cuisine if you are on a day trip or an excursion from Rome.

16. LA BUSSOLA, *Via Porta Rossa 58, 50123 Firenze. Tel. 055/293-376. Visa and Mastercard accepted. Closed Mondays. Dinner for two L90,000.*

My favorite place in Florence. You can get superb pizza in this pizzeria/ristorante as well as pasta. The ambiance is like something out of a movie set, especially in the back. They have a marble counter where you sit and watch the pizza master prepare the evening's fare in the wood heated brick oven. Or, if you're into the formal dining scene, try the back with tablecloths, etc. Wherever you sit the food will be excellent.

For pasta, try the *quattro formaggi* (four cheeses) or the *tortellini alla panna* (cream sauce). You can get any type of pizza you want here and can even ask to mix and match ingredients. The pizza master is more than willing to accommodate.

17. OLIVIERO, *Via delle Terme 51r, 50123 Firenze. Tel. 055/287-643. All credit cards accepted. Closed Sundays and August. Dinner for two L120,000.*

The cuisine here is created with a little flair. The chef Francesco Altomare uses the finest fresh ingredients to prepare excellent meals that are unique every day and are based on what is available at the markets. The *insalata tiepida di polpo* (octopus salad) is exquisite as is the *tegamino di porcini gratinati al parmigiano e rosmarino* (lightly fried grated porcini mushrooms with parmesan and rosemary). I am not too enamored with their pasta dishes, but their fish and meat courses make up for it. A wildly creative *cotoletto di vitello farcite con cacio pecorino e pistacchi* (veal cutlet cooked with pecorino cheese and pistachio) may not sound delectable, but it is. At Oliviero's you will get a wonderful meal, creatively prepared. Dine here for a culinary adventure; skip it if you want something ordinary. This is where the 'in' crowd sups.

18. NERBONE, *Mercato Centrale. 50123 Firenze. No telephone. No credit cards accepted. Meal for two L10,000.*

In operation since 1872, this small food stand in the Mercato Centrale serves the absolutely best boiled meat sandwiches (pork, beef, or veal) for only L3,500. These traditional masterpieces are called *panini*. Your only choice of meats is what they have boiling in the big vats that day. The sandwich you get is just the meat, the bread, and some salt, but it is amazingly tasty. The 'chef' takes the boiled meat out of the steaming hot water, slices it right in front of you, ladles it onto the meat, pours a little juice over it for flavor (they usually ask if you want this ... say *si*), sprinkles it with a little salt, and *presto*, the best lunch you'll have in Florence. That is if you are a carnivore. You can stand at the counter and sip a glass of wine or beer, or take your meal to the small seating area just across the aisle. They also serve pasta, soups, salads, etc., but all the locals come here for their terrific *panini*.

19. BUCA LAPI, *Via del Trebbio 1, 50123 Firenze. Tel. 055/213-768. All credit cards accepted. Closed Sunday for dinner and Mondays. Dinner for two L70,000*

One of the very best restaurants Florence has to offer. On a small street, down in the basement of an old building, Buca Lapi treats you to the food of a lifetime (and the spectacle of one too). There is a small open kitchen surrounded on two sides by tables from which you can see all the food being prepared. The decor is bizarre in a fun way, with travel posters covering the walls and ceiling.

Try the *spaghetti al sugo di carne e pomodoro* (with meat and tomato sauce) for starters, then try either the *pollo al cacciatore con spinacio* (chicken cooked in tomato-based spicy sauce with spinach) or the *cinghiale con patate fritte* (wild boar with fried potatoes). A superbly intimate restaurant with wonderful culinary and visual experiences.

20. TRATTORIA COCO LEZZONE, *Via dei Parioncino 26, 50123 Firenze. Tel. 055/287-178. No credit cards accepted. Closed Saturdays and Sundays in the Summer and Tuesdays for dinner. In the winter closed Sundays and Tuesdays for dinner. Dinner for two L90,000.*

Located in what was once a dairy, Coco Lezzone's long communal tables contrast sharply with the white tiled floors. Despite the strange decor, Florentines and tourists alike pack themselves in to enjoy the authentic Tuscan cuisine and atmosphere. The portions are pleasantly large, the meats are amazingly good, especially the *arista al forno* (roasted pork). Also try the *piccione* (pigeon) cooked over the grill (don't worry, they're farm raised – they don't go out to the piazza and catch them for dinner.) Where else will you be able to eat pigeon? They also have *coniglio arista* (roasted rabbit), a must when in Florence since rabbit is a Tuscan specialty.

21. TREDICI GOBBI *(13 Hunchbacks), Via del Porcellana 9R. Tel. 055/ 284-015. Credit cards accepted. Dinner for two L70,000.*

Mainly Florentine cuisine, with a few Hungarian dishes added for flair. A moderately priced restaurant with some expensive meat dishes, such as the excellent *bistecca Fiorentina*. The pasta is average except for the exquisitely tasty rigatoni with hot sauce. They have menus in a variety of different languages so you'll always know what you ordered.

The atmosphere is simple and rustic and the back room with its brick walls is my favorite spot for dinner. Other fine dishes are the *fusilli* with rabbit sauce. 'Thumper' never tasted so good. For seconds they also serve wild boar and veal. After enjoying your meal, soaking up the delightful atmosphere, it's time for the dessert cart. These well-presented delicacies and a steaming cup of café will round out an excellent meal. Don't miss this place while in Florence.

22. IL CIBREO, *Via dei Macci 118r, 50122 Firenze. Tel. 055/234-1100. All credit cards accepted. Closed Sundays, Mondays and August. Dinner for two L130,000.*

They serve a combination of traditional and *nouvelle cuisine* and it is excellent. But, if you like pasta don't come here – there's none on the menu. Their mushroom soup is excellent as is the typically Roman buffalo-milk mozzarella. All the ingredients are basic and simple, but everything seems to be prepared in a whole new way. Their *antipasti* are abundant. Try the *crostini di fegatini* (baked dough stuffed with liver). Then for seconds sample the *salsicce e fagioli* (sausage and beans). If you want to try the *cibreo*, the restaurant's namesake, which is a tasty Tuscan chicken stew made from every conceivable part of the bird, you need to order it at least a day in advance while making reservations. If you want the same food for half the price, simply go to the *vineria* on the other side of the kitchen. That's where you'll find me.

23. TRATTORIA MOSSACCE, *Via del Pronconsolo 55, 50122 Firenze. Tel. 055/294-361. No credit cards accepted. Closed Sundays. Dinner for two L65,000.*

Great prices for great food. The meats are especially exquisite, especially the *ossobuco* (stewed veal knuckle in a tomato sauce). Try some *ribollita* (mixed boiled meats) too. I suggest you sit all the way in the back around the "L" of a dining area so you can enjoy your meal in front of the small open kitchen and watch the cooks prepare the food. That alone makes this restaurant a lot of fun. It's basically a place for locals but they accept the occasional tourist in their midst.

24. MAMMA GINA, *Borgo S Jacopo 37, 50125 Firenze. Tel. 055/239-6009, Fax 055/213-908. All credit cards accepted. Closed Sundays. Dinner for two L85,000.*

A large place with great food. I tried their *tortellini all crema* with apprehension since I do not believe that Florentines know how to make good pasta, and was more than pleasantly surprised. But first I had some great *bruschetta* (grilled bread covered with olive oil, garlic and tomatoes). For seconds I had the *petti di pollo alla griglia* (chicken breasts o the grill). You might also try the *penne stracciate alla Fiorentina* (a meat and tomato based pasta) and the *petti di pollo al cognac con funghi* (chicken breast cooked in cognac with mushrooms ... it gives it kind of a cacciatore taste). This is a really great place to get great food in a wonderful atmosphere. If you do not like smoke you have to ask them to seat you away from the people who do ... and most people do.

25. IL CANTINONE DEL GALLO NERO, *Via Santo Spirito 6r, 50125 Firenze. Tel. 055/218-898. Closed Mondays and August. AMEX and Visa accepted. Dinner for two L60,000.*

Go down the stairs and you'll find yourself in a large vault-like room, which is the *trattoria*. The menu is filled with Tuscan *antipasti* and soups, like the *minestra di pane* (a tasty bread soup); but my favorites are the series of *crostini* (stuffed pastry baked in the oven). You can get the crostini stuffed with mozzarella, *prosciutto* (ham), salami, and all manner of vegetable. They are delicious and filling, especially with a wonderful bottle of Chianti. Make sure you order one with the *gallo nero* (black rooster) label on the stem. It's the namesake of the restaurant and indicates that the Chianti is of the finest quality.

26. LA CASALINGA, *Via dei Michelozzi 9r, 50125 Firenze. Tel. 055/218-624. Closed Sundays and the first 20 days in August. No credit cards accepted. Dinner for two L50,000.*

Here in this authentic Oltrarno-style *trattoria* you'll find a few tourists intermingling with the local artisans and residents. The cooking is classic Tuscan that is simple, tasty and filling. The antipasto is a mixed salad with sliced meats and cheeses thrown in. For seconds you'll find some Tuscan favorites like *bolliti misti con salsa verde* (mixed boiled meats in a spicy green sauce), *lo spezzatino* (Tuscan stew), *le salsicce con le rape* (sausage with turnips), and *il baccala alla livornese* (cooked cod Livorno style – salty). Sample away and don't forget to wash it all down with some of the great house wine.

SEEING THE SIGHTS

The sights of Florence are fascinating, incredible – add your own superlatives after you've seen them! Florence is a living, breathing museum filled with inspiring open air sights, and some of the best museums in the world. The sights below are numbered and correspond to the Florence map on pages 294-295.

A. STATUE OF DAVID AT THE ACCADEMIA

Via Ricasoli 60. Open 8:30am–6:20pm Tuesday–Saturday. Sundays 8:30am–1:20pm. Closed Mondays Admission L12,000.

The **Accademia** is filled with a wide variety of paintings, sculptures, and plaster molds by artists from the Tuscan school of the 13th and 14th centuries; but the museum's main draw is a must-see for you in Florence. Here you will find a statue that is as close to perfection as can be achieved with a hammer and a chisel, Michelangelo's *David*. This masterpiece was started from a discarded block of marble another sculptor had initially scarred. Michelangelo bought it on his own – no one commissioned this work – since it was less expensive than a new piece of marble, and finished sculpting *David* from its confines at the age of 25 in the year 1504, after four years of labor. It was originally in front of the Palazzo della Signoria, but was replaced with a substitute in 1873 to protect the original from the elements.

Leading up to the *David* are a variety of other works by Michelangelo, most unfinished. These are called *The Prisoners,* since the figures appear to be trapped in stone. These statues were designed to hold the Tomb of Pope Giulio II on their sculpted shoulders, but Michelangelo died before he could bring the figures to life. And now they appear as if they are struggling to be freed from the marble's embrace.

Also included in this wonderful exhibit of Michelangelo's sculptures is the unfinished *Pieta*. Many art critics have spent their entire lives comparing this Pieta with the more famous one in St. Peter's in Rome. This statue looks older, sadder, more realistic, most probably since it was created by Michelangelo at the end of his life. The *Pieta* in Rome appears more vibrant, youthful, optimistic, and alive. Once again, this was probably because he sculpted the *Pieta* in Rome when he was a young man,

Also in the Accademia is the **Sala Dell'Ottocento** (The 19th Century Hall) that is a gallery of plaster model and other works by students and prospective students of the Academy. Despite the medium, plaster, these works are exquisite. The holes you see in the casts are iron markings used as guides so that when carved into marble the figure can be recreated perfectly.

B. PIAZZA & CHURCH OF SS ANNUNZIATA

Open 7:00am–7:00pm.

Just around the corner from the Accademia, this piazza is relatively isolated from the hustle and bustle of Florence's tourist center, and when you enter it you feel as if you walked back into Renaissance Florence. This is how all the piazzas must have looked and felt back then, no cars, only people milling around sharing the Florentine day.

In the center of the square you'll find the equestrian *Statue of the Grand Duke Ferdinando I* by **Giambologna** and **Pietro Tacca** (1608). The two bronze fountains with figures of sea monsters are also the work of Tacca

(1629).

The church was erected in 1250, reconstructed in the middle of the 15th century by **Michelozzo**, was again re-done in the 17th and 18th centuries, and remains today as it was then. The interior is a single nave with chapels on both sides and is richly decorated in the Baroque style. The ceiling is carved from wood and is wonderfully intricate. Throughout this small church you'll find simple but exquisite bas-reliefs, frescoes, sculptures and more.

C. PONTE VECCHIO

Literally meaning *Old Bridge*, the name came about because the bridge has been around since Etruscan times. The present bridge was rebuilt on the old one in the 14th century by **Neri di Fiorvanti**. Thankfully this beautiful bridge with its shops lining each side of it was spared the Allied and Axis bombardments during World War II. Today the shops on the bridge belong to silversmiths, goldsmiths, and some fine leather stores. In the middle of the bridge are two arched openings that offer wonderful views of the Arno. On the downstream side of the bridge is a bust of **Benvenuto Cellini**, a Renaissance Goldsmith and sculptor, done by Rafaele Romanelli in 1900. At night on the bridge you'll find all sorts of characters hanging out, sipping wine, and strumming guitars.

On the street from the Ponte Vecchio to the Pitti Palace there used to be a series of wonderful old palazzi. Unfortunately the bombers in World War II didn't avoid these buildings as they did the Ponte Vecchio itself. Even so, today the street is filled with lovely reconstructed buildings erected just after the war which makes them older still than most buildings in North America.

D. PITTI PALACE

Piazza dei Pitti. See hours for the different museums below.

Built for the rich merchant **Luca Pitti** in 1440, based on a design by Filippo Brunelleschi. Due to the financial ruin of the Pitti family, the construction was interrupted until the palace was bought by **Eleonora da Toledo**, the wife of Cosimo I. It was then enlarged to its present size. And from that time until the end of the 17th century, it was the family home for the Medicis.

Currently it is divided into six different museums; and since the upkeep and security for this building is so expensive, each museum charges an entrance fee:

The **Museo degli Argenti** contains precious objects collected over time by the Medici and Lorraine families. There are works in amber, ivory, silver, crystal, precious woods and enamel work. Located in the former

Summer Apartment of the grand dukes of Medici, the collection includes the *Salzburg Treasure* (gold and silver cups, vases and other articles) brought to Florence by the Archduke Ferdinand of Lorraine who was Grand Duke of Tuscany in 1790. (*8:30am-1:50pm. The 1st, 3rd, and 5th Mondays and 2nd, and 4th Sundays of the month closed. L12,000.*)

The **Museo delle Porcelane** is situated in the Boboli Gardens and housed in a quaint little building near the Belvedere Fortress at the top of the hill. This porcelain collection reflects the taste of the Medicis and the many families that resided in the Pitti Palace after the Medici's decline. There are pieces made in Capodimonte, Doccia, Sevres, Vienna, and Meissen and all are delicately exquisite. (*9:00am-1:50pm. The 1st, 3rd, and 5th Mondays and 2nd, and 4th Sundays of the month closed. L4,000 includes entrance to the Boboli Gardens.*)

The **Galleria Palatina e Apartamenti Reali**. Also known as the Pitti Gallery, this exhibit runs the length of the facade of the building and includes paintings, sculptures, frescoes and furnishings of the Medici and Lorraine families. This gallery has some fine works from the 16th and 17th centuries and the most extensive collection of works by Raphael anywhere in the world. Other artists included here are Andrea del Sarto, Fra' Bartolomeo, Titian and Tintoretto, Velasquez, Murillo, Rubens, Van Dyke and Ruisdal.

The royal apartments feature an elaborate display of furnishings, carpets, wonderful silks covering the walls, as well as some fine paintings collected and displayed by the house of Savoy – the most notable of which is a series of portraits of the family of Louis XV of France. (*Tuesday-Sunday 8:30am-6:50pm. Holidays 8:30am-1:50pm. Closed Mondays. L12,000 includes entrance to the Museo delle Carozze.*)

The **Museo delle Carrozze** houses carriages used by the court of the houses of Lorraine and Savoy when they ruled Florence. This was my favorite museum in Florence when I was a child. The carriages are extremely elaborate and detailed, especially the silver decorated carriage owned by King Ferdinand II of the Two Sicilies. (*Same hours as and admitted with Galleria Palatine e Apartamente Reale.*)

The **Galleria d'Arte Moderna**. The gallery occupies thirty rooms on the second floor of the palace and offers a thorough look at Italian painting from neo-classicism to modern works covering the years up to 1945. The emphasis is on the art from Tuscany and has some works similar to French impressionists. Organized chronologically and by theme. (*8:30am-1:50pm. The 1st, 3rd, and 5th Mondays and 2nd, and 4th Sundays of the month closed. L8,000 includes entrance to the Galleria del Costume.*)

The **Galleria del Costume** contains clothing from the 16th century to modern day. All are exhibited in 13 rooms of the Meridiana Wind. It is an excellent way to discern the changes in fashion from the 18th century to the 1920s. Today, because of television, major fashion changes occur almost every year; but back then it could take generations before any noticeable change occurred. Also included are historical theater costumes created by the workshop of Umberto Tirelli. (*Same hours as and admitted with Galleria d'Arte Moderna.*)

E. DUOMO & BAPTISTERY, CAMPANILE, & CATHEDRAL MUSEUM

All located at the Piazza del Duomo. Hours: ***Duomo*** *– Church open Mon.-Sat. 10:00am–5:00pm, Sun. 1:00pm-5:00pm. Entrance to the dome costs L6,000.* ***The Baptistery*** *– Open Monday – Sunday 1:30pm–6:30pm and Holidays 8:30am–1:30pm. Entrance L3,000.* ***The Campanile****– Open 9:00am–5:00pm, Summer 8:30am–7:00pm. Admission L6,000.* ***Cathedral Museum*** *(Museo dell'Opera del Duomo) – Open 9:00am–6:00pm Tuesday–Saturday. Until 7:30pm in the summer. Holidays open 9:00am–1:00pm.*

Duomo

When you're in Florence the one sight you have to visit is the **Duomo**, Florence's cathedral. It was consecrated in 1436 by Pope Eugenio IV as **Santa Maria del Fiore** (Saint Mary of the Flowers), and that is still its official name, but everybody calls it "The Duomo" because of its imposing dome. It was started in 1296 by Arnolfo di Cambio on the spot where the church of Santa Reparata existed. After di Cambio's death in 1301, the famous Giotto took over the direction of the work, but he dedicated most of his attention to the development of the Bell Tower (*Campanile*).

When Giotto died in 1337, Andrea Pisano took over until 1349 (death didn't cause his departure, he just moved on to other projects). By 1421 everything else was finished except for the dome, which **Brunelleschi** had won a competition to design and build. It took 14 years just to construct the gigantic dome. Over the years, slight modifications and changes have been made, and in 1887, the current facade of the Duomo was finished by architect **Emilio de Fabris**.

The interior of the Duomo is 150 meters long and 38 meters wide at the nave and 94 meters at the transept. There are enormous gothic arches, supported by gothic pillars, which gives the interior a majestic quality. The dome is 90 meters high and 45.5 meters in diameter and is decorated with frescoes representing the Last Judgment done by Giorgio Vasari and Federico Zuccari at the end of the 16th century. In the niches of the pillars supporting the dome are statues of the Apostles.

The central chapel is home to the **Sarcophagus of San Zanobius** that contains the saint's relics. The bronze reliefs are the work of Lorenzo Ghiberti (1442). When you've finished wandering through the cathedral and admiring the art and stained glass windows, you can go to the top of the Duomo and get some great views of Florence. The way up is a little tiring, but the magnificent photo opportunities – both inside and out – are fabulous. Don't miss these views!

The Baptistery

Definitely considered one of the most important works in the city, the **Baptistery** was built on the remains of an early Roman structure which was transformed into a paleo-Christian monument. The Baptistery, built in the 10th and 11th centuries was dedicated to Saint John the Baptist, the patron saint of Florence. Up until 1128, it was the cathedral of Florence. This small structure just didn't reflect the growing stature of the city of Florence, so they erected the Duomo.

Its octagonal shape is covered with colored marble. On the pavement by the Baptistery you'll find the signs of the Zodiac. Inside is the tomb of Giovanni XXIII by Donatello and Michelozzo in 1427. Next to the altar, you'll see the *Angel Holding The Candlestick* by Agostino di Jacopo in 1320. To the left between the Roman sarcophagi is the wooden statue *Magdalen* by Donatello in 1560.

But the true masterpieces of the Baptistery are the bronze paneled doors by **Ghoberti** and **Andrea Pisano da Pontedera**. The public entrance is the **Southern Door**, created by Andrea Pisano da Pontedera and is of least interest. The east and north doors are far more beautiful and intricate. Michelangelo described the east door as "the door to paradise." On it you'll find stories of the Old Testament, beginning as follows from the top left hand side:

- Creation of Adam; original sin; expulsion of Adam and Eve from Paradise
- Stories of Noah and the universal deluge (coincidentally some of these panels were almost lost in the flooding of 1966)
- Jacob and Esau; Rachel and Jacob; Isaac blesses Jacob
- Moses receives the Ten Commandments on Mount Sinai
- The battle against the Philistines; David and Goliath.

From the top right hand side:

- Adam works the soil; Cain and Abel at work; Cain kills Abel
- Three angels appear to Abraham; Abraham sacrifices Isaac
- Joseph meets his brothers in Egypt; Stories of Joseph
- Joshua crosses the Jordan River; The conquering of Jericho
- Solomon receives the Queen of Sheba in the Temple.

The Campanile

Giotto died while he was attempting to complete the **Campanile**, but after his death **Andrea Pisano** and **Francesco Talenti** both scrupulously followed his designs until its completion. The only part they left out was the spire that was to go on top, which would have made the Campanile 30 meters higher than its current 84. The tower is covered in colored marble and adorned with bas-reliefs by Andrea Pisano and Luca della Robbia and Andrea Orcagna. Sculptures by Donatello, Nanni di Bartolo, and others used to be in the sixteen niches but are now in the Cathedral Museum.

Cathedral Museum

The Cathedral Museum, or **Museo dell'Opera del Duomo**, is the place where many pieces of artwork that used to be in the Cathedral or the Campanile are now located. Their removal and placement here was mainly done to help preserve them from the environment as well as the onslaught of tourists hordes. Most of the items are statues and bas-relief work. The most famous ones to keep an eye out for are *St. John* by **Donatello**, *Habakkuh* by Donatello, *Virgin with Infant Jesus* by **Arnolfo**, and *Choir Gallery* with many scenes by Donatello.

F. SANTA CROCE

Piazza Santa Croce. Open weekdays 8:00am–12:30pm and 3:00pm–6:30pm. Easter through October open 8:00am-6:30pm. Sundays and Holidays open 8:00am-1:00pm.

The church of **Santa Croce** sits in the Piazza Santa Croce, surrounded by ancient palazzi renowned for the architecture. The one opposite the church is the **Palazzo Serristori** by Baccio D'Agnolo in the 16th century. Facing the church on the right hand side at #23 is the **Palazzo dell'Antella** built by Giulio Parigi in the 17th century. In this piazza, on any night, when all the shops are closed, you will feel as if you've stepped back into the Renaissance.

In the center of the square is a statue of **Dante Aligheri**, he of *Divine Comedy* fame, sculpted by Enrico Pazzi in 1865. This is a wonderfully ornate yet simple church belonging to the Franciscan Order. Construction was begun in 1295 but its modern facade was created in 1863 by Nicolo Matas. The frescoes on the facade were created in only 20 days by 12 painters working non-stop. It has a slim bell tower whose Gothic style doesn't seem to fit with this modern exterior. The interior, on the other hand, fits perfectly with the simple stonework of the bell tower.

Initially, the walls inside had been covered with exquisite frescoes created by Giotto but these were covered up by order of Cosimo I in the 16th century. What remains is a basic monastic church that conveys piety and beauty in its simplicity. Of the many Italian artistic, religious, and political geniuses that lie buried beneath Santa Croce, the most famous has to be that of **Michelangelo** himself. Other prominent Florentines buried here are **Niccolo Machiavelli**, **Galileo Galilei**, **Dante Aligheri** and **Lorenzo Ghiberti**.

Besides the beautiful bas-reliefs, exquisite sculptures, and other works of art in Santa Croce you can find an excellent and relatively inexpensive **leather school** *(Scuola del Cuoio)*. To get there go through the sacristy and you'll end up in the school that was started by the monks more than three decades ago. Here you'll find all kinds of fine leather products for sale but the best part is being able to see them being manufactured right in front of you in what were once cells for the monks. The prices and selection are good and seeing the artisans at work is something that shouldn't be missed when in Florence *(Tel. 244-533, Tuesday–Saturday, 9:00am–12:30pm and 3:00pm–6:00pm. All credit cards accepted.)*.

G. SAN LORENZO

Piazza San Lorenzo. Open every day 7:00am–noon and 3:30pm–6:00pm. Holidays 8:00am-9:30am and 11:00am-6:00pm.

One of the oldest basilicas in Florence. The architecture is the work of **Filippo Brunelleschi**, done from 1421-1446, but the church was finished by his pupil **Antonio Manetti** in 1460. The facade was never completed even though Michelangelo himself submitted a variety of designs for its completion.

The interior is made up of three naves with chapels lining the side walls. In the central nave at the far end are two pulpits that are the last two works of **Donatello** who died in 1466 after completing them. You'll find plenty of works by Donatello in this church, including:

- The stucco medallions in the Old Sacristy that represent the *Four Evangelists* that are *Stories of Saint John the Baptist*
- The terra-cotta *Bust of Saint Lawrence* in the Old Sacristy
- The bronze doors with panels representing the *Apostles and Fathers of the Church* in the Old Sacristy.

H. SANTA MARIA NOVELLA

Piazza Santa Maria Novella. Open 7:00am–noon and 3:30pm–5:00pm Monday–Saturday and Sundays 3:30pm–5:00pm.

Built in 1278 by two Dominican friars, **Fra Ristoreo** and **Fra Sisto**, the church was created in the Gothic style with green and white marble decorations that are typically Florentine in character. The church was completed in 1470. To the left and right of the facade are tombs of illustrious Florentines all created in the same Gothic style as the church.

The interior of the church is in a "T" shape with the nave and aisles divided by clustered columns that support wide arches. Down the aisles are a variety of altars created by **Vasari** from 1565 to 1571.

As a young artist, Michelangelo worked on many of the frescoes as commissioned by his teachers. This is where he got his initial training that helped him create the now famous frescoes in the Sistine Chapel in Rome.

You can spend hours in here admiring these magnificent frescoes created by many Florentine artists including **Domenico Ghirlandaio** (Chapel of High Altar), **Giuliano da San Gallo** (Gondi Chapel), **Giovanni Dosio** (Gaddi Chapel), **Nardo di Cione** (Strozzi Chapel) and more. And if you're tired of sightseeing and need a little break, Florence's best pub, The Fiddler's Elbow, is in the piazza outside the church.

I. PIAZZA, PALAZZO, & LOGGIA DELLA SIGNORIA

Piazza della Signoria

This piazza, with the Palazzo, the Loggia, the fountain, the replica of the statue of David, the cafes and *palazzi* is incomparable in its beauty. Over the centuries great historical and political occurrences, as well as the lives of average Florentines, have all flowed through this piazza.

Today the square is the site of the annual sporting event, **Calcio in Costume** (soccer played in period garb), where the different sections of the city vie for dominance in a game that is a cross between soccer, rugby, martial arts and an all-out war. This annual contest used to be played in the square of Santa Croce but was moved here during modern times. If you are in Florence during June, when the event covers three of the weekends in that month, you definitely have to try and get tickets. The entire piazza is covered with sand, and stadium seats are put up all around the makeshift field, and then the fun begins. The event is a truly memorable experience.

In the small square on the left is **Ammannati's Fountain** with the giant figure of *Neptune*. The statue is commonly called *Biancone* (Whitey) by the locals because of its bland appearance. Giambologna created the equestrian statue representing *Cosimo I dei Medici* on the left of the square.

Palazzo della Signoria – Palazzo Vecchio

Piazza della Signoria. Open Monday-Friday 9:00am–7:00pm, and Sundays 8:00am–1:00pm. Admission L10,000 for upstairs galleries.

The most imposing structure in the square is the **Palazzo Signoria**. It is 94 meters past the fortified battlements to the top of **Arnolfo's Tower**. The entire structure is rather severe, but at the same time elegant. Its construction began in the late 13th century and took hundreds of years to finish. It was once the home of **Cosimo de Medici** and other members of the Medici family before the Pitti Palace was completed.

In front of the building on the platform at the top of the steps, ancient orators used to harangue the crowds, and for this reason this section of the building is called *Arringhiera* (The Haranguing Area). Located here are several important sculptures including the *Marzocco* (a lion symbolizing the Florentine Republic; a stone copy of the original sits in the National Museum); *Judith and Holofernes* created by Donatello in 1460, which is a record of the victory over the Duke of Athens; the copy of Michelangelo's *David* (the original is in the Accademia), and *Hercules and Cacus* created by Baccio Bandinelli.

Above the main door is a frieze with two lions and a monogram of Christ with the inscription *Rex Regum et Dominus Dominantium* (King of Kings and Lord of Lords), which used to record the time that the Florentine republic elected Christ as their King in 1528. The inscription used to read *Jesus Christus Rex Florentinei Populi S P Decreto Electus* (Jesus Christ elected by the people King of Florence) but was changed in 1851.

The interior is mainly filled with artwork glorifying the Medici family who ruled the Florentine Republic for centuries. So if you need a break from religious art and all those paintings of the Madonna and Child, this is the respite you've been looking for. Everything is elaborate and ornate, as befitting the richest family in the world at that time.

You enter through the courtyard which was designed by Michelozzo in 1453. The elaborate stucco decorations on the columns and frescoes on the arches were added in 1565 on the occasion of the wedding between Francesco dei Medici and Joan of Austria. The fountain in the center, *Graceful Winged Cupid* was done by Verrochio in 1476. From here most of the art to see is upstairs, so either take the staircase up or use the elevator.

What follows is a description of the important works to see in each room of the palazzo:

Hall of the Five Hundred – Salone dei Cinquecento

This is the most splendid and artistic hall in Florence. It was designed for public meetings after the Medicis had been thrown from power. When Cosimo I regained the family's control over Florence, he had the hall enlarged and used it for his private audiences. On the wall opposite the entrance you'll find three large magnificent paintings by Baccio D'Agnolo, Baccio Bandinelli and Giorgio Vassari: *The Conquest of Siena; The Conquest of Porto Ercole; The Battle of Marciano*. On the wall across from this you'll find: *Maximilian Tries to Conquer Livorno; The Battle of Torre San Vincenzo; The Florentines Assault Pisa*. Underneath these painting you'll find sculptures by Vincenzo de Rossi representing *Hercules Labors*.

The ceiling is divided into 39 compartments with paintings by Giorgio Vasari that represent *Stories of Florence and the Medici*. The coup de grace is in the niche of the right wall at the entrance. Here you'll find

Michelangelo's unfinished work, *The Genius of Victory*, which was designed for the tomb of Pope Julius II. If you only have a little time, spend it here. This room is magnificent.

Study of Francesco I de Medici

Here you'll find the work of many of Florence's finest artists crammed into as small a space as imaginable. The walls and even the barrel shaped ceiling are covered with paintings, and niches are filled with a variety of bronze statues. Elaborate, ostentatious and overwhelming.

Hall of the Two Hundred – Salone dei Duecento

It is called thus since this is where the Council of two hundred citizens met during the time of the Republic for their important decisions. The walls are adorned with tapestry, the ceiling is ornately decorated, chandeliers hang low, and statues and busts adorn any free spot. The center of the room is occupied by the seating for the Council of 200.

Monumental Quarters – Quartieri Monumentali

These are a series of rooms that get their names from a member of the Medici family. Each are elaborate in their own right, filled with paintings, sculptures, frescoes, and more. From here you'll find many more interesting rooms and paintings as you explore, both on this floor and the one above, but this is the bulk of the beauty in the Palazzo Signoria.

The Loggia della Signoria

In the Piazza, on the right of the Palazzo as you face it, is the expansive and airy **Loggia della Signoria**, a combination of Gothic and Renaissance architecture. It was built by Benci di Cione, Simone Talenti and others during the years 1376–1382. At either end of the steps are two marble lions, one of which is very old, the other made in 1600.

Underneath the arch are some wonderful sculptures: *Persius* by Cellini in 1553 under the left hand arch; *The Rape of the Sabines* by Giambologna in 1583 under the right arch; *Hercules and the Centaur* by Giambologna in 1599 under the right arch also. There is also *Menelaus supporting Patroclus* and a few other less important works. All of them, since they are open to the elements and pollution, have been stained and discolored, but all are excellent studies in human anatomy.

J. UFFIZZI GALLERY

Piazza del Uffizzi. Open Tuesday to Saturday 8:30am–6:50pm and Sundays 8:30am–1:50pm. Admission L12,000.

The building housing the **Uffizi Gallery** was begun in 1560 by Giorgio Vasari on the orders of the Grand-Duke Cosimo I. It was originally designed to be government offices, but today holds the most important and impressive display of art in Italy, and some would say the world. The gallery mainly contains paintings of Florentine and Tuscan artists of the 13th and 14th centuries, but you'll also find works from Venice, Emilia, and other Italian art centers as well as Flemish, French, and German studies. In conjunction there is a collection of ancient sculptures.

These fabulous works of art were collected first by the Medici family, then later by the Lorraine family. The last of the Medici, the final inheritor of that amassed wealth, Anna Maria Luisa donated the entire Gallery to the Tuscan state in 1737 so that the rich collection gathered by her ancestors would never leave Florence. Not everything would go as planned, since in the 18th century some pieces were stolen by Napoleon's marauding forces, but most of these were later ransomed for their return. Some items were damaged in the great flood of 1966, and still others were damaged in 1993 when a terrorist car bomb ripped through parts of the Gallery. Even with all these occurrences, the Uffizzi is still one of the finest galleries in the world.

Its collection is so rich and so vast that it has caused some tourists to grow queasy, feel faint, and generally feel ill. A medical study has determined that some people become completely overwhelmed with the large amount of artistic beauty and cannot handle the input. Others postulate that it is the abundance of religious paintings, mainly of the Madonna and child, that make people disoriented by the constant repetition of the same theme. Whatever the reasons for the symptoms, if you start to feel queasy, or feel as if the paintings are moving, don't be shy to ask for a place to rest.

As you enter the Uffizzi, you will find the statues of Cosimo the Elder and Lorenzo the Magnificent, as well as several busts of the rest of the Medici rulers. It is ironic that they are so prominently displayed since when they ruled most Florentines despised their despotic ways. But now they are immortalized in time because of the philanthropic gesture of their last heir.

It would be virtually impossible to list all the paintings and sculptures exhibited, so let me make a list of those that you absolutely must see if you visit the gallery. If you want a more complete listing or an audio guided tour, you can get those as you enter.

- *Madonna of the Pomegranate* – Botticelli – Room X
- *Self Portraits of Titian, Michelangelo, Raphael, Rubens, Rembrandt and more* – Third Corridor
- *Madonna of the Goldfinch* – Raphael – Room XXV
- *Holy Family* – Michelangelo – Room XXV

- *Venus of Urbino* - Titian - Room XXVIII
- *Young Bacchus* - Caravaggio - Room XXXVI
- *Portrait of an Old Man* - Rembrandt - Room XXXVII
- *Portrait of Isabelle Brandt* - Peter Paul Rubens - Room XLI

K. PIAZZALE MICHELANGELO

From this piazza you have a wonderful view over the city of Florence being dissected by the river Arno. Remember to bring your camera since this is the best public view of the city. The best view, public or private is from the Hotel Torre di Bellosguardo, but if you desire that vista you have to spend the night since they don't allow sightseers on their grounds. At the center of the Piazzalle Michelangelo is a monument to **Michelangelo** dominated by a replica of the statue of *David.* Round the pedestal are four statues that adorn the tombs of famous Medicis which Michelangelo created. If you are up here around dinner time and want to grab something to eat, try the restaurant La Loggia on the opposite side of the piazza from the vista, across the road.

If you don't want to walk up the steep hill to the Piazza, take bus number 13 from the station.

L. THE BOBOLI GARDENS

Located behind the Pitti Palace. Open 9:00am until one hour before sunset. Closed the first and last Mondays of each month. L4,000 with Museo delle Porcelane.

Hidden behind the Pitti Palace is your respite from the Florentine summer heat and the hordes of tourists. Began in 1549 by Cosimo I and Eleanor of Tudor, the gardens went through many changes, additions, and alterations before they reached their present design. Among its many pathways and well-placed fields, the **Boboli Gardens** are the only true escape from the sun, humidity, and crowds that swarm through Florence in July and August. If you are inclined to walk in a calm, peaceful garden, far from the bustling crowds, or if you wish to enjoy a relaxing picnic, the Boboli is your place.

In the groves and walks of the Boboli you can find many spots to sit and enjoy a picnic lunch, or you can simply enjoy the platoons of statuary lining the walks. Some of the most famous works here include: *Pietro Barbino Riding a Tortoise,* commonly called 'Fat Baby Bacchus Riding a Turtle' (you'll find reproductions of this statue in almost every vendor's stall in Florence); a Roman amphitheater ascending in tiers from the Palazzo Pitti, designed as a miniature Roman circus to hold Medici court spectacles; and *Neptune's Fountain* at the top of the terrace, created in 1565 by Stoldo Lorenzi.

From this fountain a path leads to the adorable **Kaffeehaus**, a boat-like pavilion that offers a fine view of Florence and drinks to quench your thirst. Keep going up until you reach the **Ex Forte di Belvedere**, which offer magnificent views of all of Florence, and **Cypress Alley**, lined with statues of many different origins.

Also in the gardens is the **Museo delle Porcelane** with a delicate porcelain collection from the Medici and Lorraine families.

La Limonaia

Even if you are not looking for it, you can't miss the **Limonaia**, a room 340 feet long and 30 feet wide that became the 'hospital' for all the devastated works of art during the Flood of '66 (see story below). Originally used to house the Boboli Gardens' lemon trees during the winter months, this room, many experts felt, was the savior of the Florentine masterpieces, because of its insulation from the Florentine humidity. Most of the art treasures from the disastrous flood of '66 were brought here to be rehabilitated. I guess you could say that all art lovers can be thankful that the Medicis had a passion for lemons.

Porta Romana

This garden stretches seemingly forever, and it hides some of the best green spaces at its farthest corners, near Florence's **South Gate** (**Porta Romana**). If you exit here and take the big road to your left, Piazzale Michelangelo, you will walk through some incredibly bucolic Florentine neighborhoods.

M. SANTO SPIRITO

Piazza Santo Spirito. Open 8:30am-Noon and 4:00pm-6:00pm.

Begun in 1444 by Brunelleschi, and continued after his death in 1446 by Antonio Manetti, Giovanni da Gaiole and Salvi d'Andrea. The last of these built the cupola that was based on Brunelleschi's design. It has a simple, plain, seemingly unfinished facade, in contrast to the interior.

Divided into three naves flanked by splendid capped Corinthian columns, this church looks very similar to San Lorenzo. There is a central cupola with two small naves in the wings of the cross that have small chapels just off of them. Lining the walls are some small chapels capped by semi-circular arches are adorned with elaborate carvings. The main altar, created by Giovanni Caccini (1599-1607), is Baroque in style and intricately displayed. In the chapels off the wings of the cross to the right and left of the main altar are many fine works of art to be enjoyed (two of which are *Madonna con Bambino* by Fillipino Lippi and *San Giovanni and Madonna with Baby Jesus and Four Saints* by Masi di Banco).

Many of these works are difficult to see since light does not find its way into this church very well.

N. MUSEUM OF SCIENTIFIC HISTORY

Piazza dei Guidici. Open 9:00am-noon and 3:00pm-7:00pm.

Located along the Lungarno and near the Uffizzi is the **Museo di Storia della Scienza**. Situated in the severe Palazzo Castellani which was built in the 14th century, the building was first used as a civil courthouse from 1574 to 1841, and up to 1966 one part of the building was the *Accademia della Crusca*, but the massive flood of that year forced the relocation of that organization.

Since 1930 the Museo di Storia della Scienza has been housed here. The exhibit is mainly a collection of scientific instruments from the 16th and 17th centuries. There are astrolabs, solar clocks, architectural tools and more. Of great interest are the original instruments used by Galileo (rooms IV and V). Also of interest are the map-making materials and ancient geographical tools (room VII). There is also a splendid reconstruction of the map of the world made by Fra Mauro.

On the second floor you will find the precious astronomical clock from the 15th century (room XII) and many instruments created and used in the 17th century, including the amazing mechanical *mano che scrive* (hand that writes) and *l'orologia del moto perpetuo* (clock of perpetual motion). For those interested in scientific discovery, or for those who need a break from art, this is a wonderful museum to visit.

O. MUSEO NAZIONALE DEL BARGELLO

Via del Proconsolo. Open Mondays, Wednesdays, and Saturdays 8:30am-1:30pm and Tuesdays, Thursdays, and Fridays 8:30am-4:00pm. Holidays 8:30am-1:50pm. L8,000.

Located almost behind the Palazzo Signoria in the quaint Piazza S. Firenze, you will find one of the most important collections of art and artifacts in the world. Located in the building that was the first seat of government in Florence, and was in 1574 the seat of the justice department, police, and customs, this is a rather severe, austere palazzo that was restored from 1858 to 1865. After the great flood of 1966 most of the ground floor had to be redone.

You will find great sculptures from the Renaissance. Featured prominently are those created in Tuscany, which are some of the best ever made. After entering into the small area called *Torre Volognana* you are ushered into the *Cortile* (courtyard) area complete with a fountain and six allegorical marble statues by Bartolomeo Ammannati, *Oceano* by Giambologna, *Allegoria di Fiesole* by Tribolo and *Cannone di S. Paolo* by Cosimo Cenni.

Elsewhere in the museum you will find some beautiful works by Michelangelo including *Bacco* (1496-97) *David-Apollo* (1530-32) which is the first large classical sculpture by the artist, and *Bruto* (1530), which means ugly, and is the only bust created by Michelangelo of Lorenzino di Medici. On this floor are also some beautiful bronze statues by a variety of artists.

On the second floor (which you get to by stairs constructed by Neri di Fioravante from 1345-1367) are some interesting bronze animal sculptures including the famous *tacchino* (turkey) made by Giambologna. The other featured artist in the museum is Donatello whose works are displayed in the *Salone del Consiglio Generale,* constructed by the same architect who built the stairs. Here you'll find *S. Giorgio* (1416) accompanied by two statues of *David,* one younger in marble (1408-9) and the other more famous one in bronze (circa 1440). Other works by Donatello include the *Bust of Niccolo of Uzzano* made of multi-colored terra-cotta, *Marzocco* (1418-20), a lion that symbolizes the Florentine Republic, *Atys-Amor,* a wonderful bronze, and the dramatic *Crucifixion.*

There are many other works here, too many to mention, but suffice to say that this is a museum that shouldn't be missed while in Florence, especially if you like sculpture. The Accademia and the Uffizzi get all the press in Florence, but this is one of the best museums of sculpture anywhere in the world.

NIGHTLIFE & ENTERTAINMENT

Florence is definitely not known for its nightlife since Florentines usually only engage in some form of late night eating and drinking at a restaurant that stays open late. Heated dancing and wild debauchery don't seem to part of the Florentine make-up, except for a few places mentioned below. Here are some places to go if you get that itch to be wild; you'll find each listing on the Florence restaurants map, pages 308-309.

27. THE FIDDLER'S ELBOW, *Piazza Santa Maria Novella 7R, Tel. 055/215-056. Open 3:00pm–1:15pm everyday. Harp, Kilkenny, Guinness, and Inch's Stonehouse Cider on draught. Pint L7,000, half-pint L4,000.*

If you want to enjoy a true Irish pub outside of Ireland, you've found it. Step into the air conditioned comfort, sit among the hanging musical instruments, belly up to the dark wooden bar, eye yourself in the mirror, and have a pint. For snacks (you have to pay for them), they have peanuts, salami sticks for the Italians, and four types of Highlander Scottish potato chips (they call them crisps): Roast Beef Taste, Cheddar & Onion, Caledonian Tomato, and Sea Salt.

If you want to be a part of the ex-pat community here in Florence, this is one of the places to go. But it is also one of the main nightspots for young

Italians in Florence too. If you want to meet people, Italian or otherwise, this is the place to come. Whether it's sitting on the patio or inside at one of the many tables you're bound to have some fun.

There is also a TV in the back room that is usually commandeered for soccer or rugby games. You can also enjoy Fiddler's Elbows in Rome, Venice and Bologna.

28. SPACE ELECTRONIC, *Via Palazzuolo 37, 50123 Firenze. Tel. 055/ 292-082, Fax 055/293-457.*

The largest and loudest discotheque in the city. They've had music videos playing here before anybody knew what music videos were (I still remember seeing Mick Jagger crooning the words to Angie); and they continue to be the trendsetters when it comes to club antics. They play all sorts of music, so no one is left out. A fun place with many different levels and dance floors, where you can enjoy the company of your friends, or leave in the company of a newfound one.

29. HARRY'S BAR, *Lungarno a Vespucci 22, 50123 Firenze. Tel. 055/ 239-6700. All credit cards accepted. Closed Sundays.*

Based on the famous Harry's Bar in Venice (see the Venice chapter in this book), but with no business connections (Italians obviously have different trademark laws than we do). This is now the place to find the best burgers in Florence. They also mix some strong drinks in the evening, so if you have nothing to do and just want to get out of the hotel room, pop in here.

Opera

If you are in Florence from December to June, the traditional opera season, and have the proper attire (suits for men, dresses for women) and a taste for something out of the ordinary, try the spectacle of the opera.

- **Teatro Communale**, *Corso Italia 16, 50123 Firenze. Tel. 055/211-158 or 2729236, Fax 055/277-9410*

Movies in English

If you need a little video fix, try **Cinema Astro**, *Piazza San Simone (near Santa Croce), closed July 10–August 31 and Mondays. Tickets cost L8,000.* There's a student discount on Wednesdays for L6,000. Films are in English here every night at 7:30pm and 10:00pm. Either call for the schedule or stop by and pick one up.

SPORTS & RECREATION

Balloon Rides in Tuscany

Contact **The Bombard Society**, *6727 Curran Street, McLean VA 22101-3804. Outside Virginia, toll-free Tel. 800/862-8537, Fax 703/883-0985. In*

Virginia or outside, Tel. 703/448-9407; you can call collect. Call for current price and information about the most amazing way to view the most spectacular scenery in the world.

SHOPPING

Antiques

Many of the better known antique stores have been located in the **Via dei Fossi** and **Via Maggio** for years, but there are some interesting little shops in the **Borgo San Jacopo** and the **Via San Spirito**, all located in the **Oltrarno** section of Florence across the river.

When shopping for antiques in Florence, there is one important thing to remember: the Florentines are excellent crafts people and as such have taken to the art of antique fabrication and reproduction. But they do not consider what they are doing illegal or unethical because under Italian law, furniture made from old wood is considered an antique. And these products can be sold exported under the designation antique. If you find a 'real' antique by American standards, it is usually designated by a stamp indicating that it cannot be taken out of the country.

Artisans

If you want to see some of this excellent antique fabrication and reproduction work, as well as genuine restoration in progress, you need venture no further than across the river to the Oltrarno section. In these narrow streets you'll find small workshops alive with the sounds of hammers and saws, intermingled with the odors of wood, tanning leather, and glue. When I lived in Florence this was my favorite area to come to. Watching someone creating something out of nothing has always been a relaxing adventure, and besides, not many tourists even venture into these tiny alcoves of Florentine culture.

Some of the best known shops are located in the **Via Santo Spirito**, **Viale Europa**, **Via Vellutini**, **Via Maggio** and the **Via dello Studio**. Strangely enough, on these same streets are your real antique shops. How convenient to have the fabricators and reproducers next door to the 'legitimate' antique dealers. In other words, inspect your goods carefully.

Books & Newspapers in English

BM BOOKSHOP, *Borgo Ognissanti 4r, Tel 055/294-575. Open Winter: Mondays 3:30pm-7:30pm, Tuesday-Saturday 9:00am-1:00pm and 3:30pm-7:30pm. Open Summer: 9:30am-1:00pm and 3:30pm-7:30pm daily.*

An extensive collection of English language books in both hardcover and paperback. This is also one of the meeting places for the English-speaking community in Florence. Located in the Centro area.

ENGLISH BOOKSTORE PAPERBACK EXCHANGE, *Via Fiesolana 31r, Tel 247-8154. Open Monday-Saturday 9:00am-1:00pm and 3:30pm-7:30pm. Closed in August. Closed Mondays November–February.*

The unofficial English-speaking bibliophile meeting place, this store has the largest and best priced selection of new and used English-language paperbacks in Florence. If you want to exchange a book you have already read they are very generous with trade-ins. The only stipulation is that the book you select as your trade-in has to be used. Located in the Santa Croce section of Florence, just around the corner from an excellent pottery shop, **Sbigoli Terrecotte** (see next page for details).

LIBRERIA INTERNAZIONALE SEEBER, *Via Tornabuoni 68r, Tel. 055/215-697. Open regular business hours.*

This is an extensive and old fashioned bookstore that's been around since the 1860s to serve the expatriate community. An entire room is devoted to foreign books, not all of which are in English. Even if you can't find what you want, this is a fun place to browse.

FELTRINELLI INTERNATIONAL, *Via Cavour 12. Tel 055/292-196. Open regular business hours.*

One of Italy's largest and best bookstore chains, this location is dedicated to books in languages other than Italian, with a concentration on the English language.

THE PAPIERMACHE STORE

One store you simply cannot miss is the small studio/gallery of the artist Bijan, ***Firenze of Papier Mache****, Piazza Pitti 10, 50125 Firenze, Tel. 055/230-2978, Fax 055/365-768. He makes beautiful masks covered with intricate sketchings of famous paintings, as well as beautiful anatomical forms, all from papiermache. Even if you don't buy anything, simply browse and savor the beauty of his work. Since the shop is near the Palazzo Pitti, one of your 'must see' destinations while in Florence, there's no reason why you shouldn't stop here.*

Cartolerie - Stationary Stores

L'INDICE SCRIVE, *Via della Vigna Nuova 82r. Tel. 055/215-165. Mastercard and Visa accepted.*

A wide variety of stationary products and unique pens are featured in this store. Most of the items are hand-made, including the diaries, ledgers, guest books, desk sets. etc. A great place to get a gift for someone back home.

IL PAPIRO, *Piazza Duomo 24r, Tel. 055/215-262. Credit cards accepted.*

If you like marbleized paper products, this is the store for you. You can get boxes, notebooks, picture frames, pencil holders, basically anything you could imagine. The prices are a little high but that's because of the great location and high quality products. They also have three locations in Rome, all around the Pantheon.

Ceramics

If you are interested in the famous painted ceramics from Tuscany and Umbria, you don't have to go to the small towns where they are manufactured – there is a great store behind the stalls in the San Lorenzo market called **Florentina** (*Via dell'Ariento 81r, 50123 Firenze, Tel. 055/239-6523*). Owned by a stereotypical friendly Irish woman and her Italian husband, this store has everything you could want at prices similar to what you would get if you traveled to Deruta in Umbria or Cortona in Tuscany.

Another ceramics store is located near Santa Croce around the corner from the English Bookstore Paperback Exchange. The **Sbigoli Terrecotte** (*Via S. Egidio 4r, 50122 Firenze, Tel/Fax 055/247-9713*) has works from Deruta priced virtually the same as if you were in that town. This store also has a laboratory of its own where they make, bake and hand paint their own ceramics.

Markets

The markets in Florence are all hustle and bustle, especially in the high tourist season. But despite the crowds you can have a great time browsing and shopping. And of course, the prices are sometimes close to half what they are in stores. Remember to bargain because usually the starting price is rather high. The best bet when bargaining is to make a counter offer at half of the initial price. Then let the games begin. Bargaining is half the fun of buying something in an Italian market.

MERCATO CENTRALE, *immediately north of Piazza San Lorenzo, near the Duomo, open Monday–Friday, 7:00am–2:00pm and 4:00pm–8:00pm, Saturday 7:00am-12:15pm and 1:00pm-5:00pm. Sunday 3:00pm-5:00pm.*

This is Florence's main food market for wholesale and retail fish, fresh meat, vegetables, cheeses, oils, breads, and many other delicacies. The meat and fish section is on the ground floor, with a few vegetable stands thrown in, but if you're into healthy food, make your way upstairs to their fruit and vegetable market. The aroma is enough to make you want to come back every day you're in Florence. Try to find some *caciotta* (sheep's milk cheese) and *finocchiona* (salami flavored with fennel) because they are an exquisite local delicacy. This is the best place to shop for your picnic supplies as well as a must see while in Florence. The market itself is surrounded by the large clothing market of San Lorenzo.

When you visit the Mercato Centrale, don't think of leaving without getting a sandwich at **Nerbone's** (see review above in *Where to Eat*). In operation since 1872, this small food stand serves the absolutely best boiled pork, beef, or veal sandwiches, for only L3,500. They're simply called *panini* and your only choice of meat is what they have boiled for the day. The sandwich is just the meat, the bread, and some salt, but it is amazing. You can stand at the counter and sip a glass of wine or beer, or take your meal to the small seating area just across the aisle.

MERCATO DI SAN LORENZO, *located near the Duomo, everyday from 8:00am-dark. Closed Sundays in the winter.*

This is the largest and most frequented street market in Florence, and it completely dominates the church of San Lorenzo and its piazza, as well as spilling into most adjacent streets. You can find everything from shoes to pants, T-shirts, belts, and much more, most at prices close to half of what you would pay in a store. Both Florentines and tourists come here looking for bargains. Again, remember to bargain, because once a merchant marks you as a tourist the price quoted is usually higher than that quoted to Italians.

MERCATO NUOVO, *located in the Logge del Mercato Nuovo off the Via Por San Maria near the Piazza del Signoria, open daily 9:00am–5:00pm.*

This is the famous Straw Market. They sell traditional products made from straw but also exquisite leather products, ceramics, linens (like table clothes and napkins), statues, and other hand-made Florentine crafts.

MERCATO DELL PULCI, *located in the Piazza dei Compi about four blocks north of the church of Santa Croce, open Tuesday–Saturday, 8:00am–1:00pm, 3:30pm–7:00pm, and the first Sunday of each month from 9:00am-:007pm.*

This is Florence's famous flea market. If you want antiques and junk at obviously trumped up prices, come here. They think tourists will pay anything for a true Italian antique - so remember to bargain. The next market, Mercato di Sant'Ambrogio, is located just to the east of this market.

MERCATO DI SANTO SPIRITO, *Located in the piazza in front of Santo Spirito. Open the second Sunday of every month from 8:00am-7:00pm.*

A great market filled with antiques, junk, clothes, imported figures from Africa, military surplus, and much more. A great place to people watch, grab a great boiled meat sandwich, pick up some cashews to snack on or buy a gift to bring home. In my book, one of the best in Florence. Come here if you happen to be in the city the second Sunday of the month. In conjunction, the only *alimentari* in the city open on that Sunday is in the piazza.

Picnic & Food Supplies

If you can't make it to the **Mercato Centrale** or the **Mercato di Sant'Ambrogio** for your Boboli Garden or day trip picnic supplies, here's a small list of food stores from which you can get almost everything you want. The perfect amount of meat for a sandwich would be *mezzo etto* (about 1/8th of a pound) and the same goes for your cheese. Also, at most bars you can order a sandwich to go if you're too lazy to make your own, and you can also get some *vino* or *birra* to take with you.

VERA, *Piazza Frescobaldi 3r, Tel. 055/215-465. No credit cards accepted.*

Located in the Oltrarno section of Florence, this store is a food connoisseur's delight. It is indisputably Florence's best stocked food store, conveniently located close to the Boboli Gardens. It has the best fresh cheeses, salamis, hams, roasted meats, freshly baked breads, olive oil, soups and salads. If you want fresh fruit you're also in luck – but not here, you have to go to the store across the street.

ALIMENTARI, *Via Arione 19r, Tel. 055/214-067. No credit cards accepted. Closed Wednesday afternoons.*

Located in the Centro area of Florence near the Piazza San Trinita, this is your classic Italian grocery store. There's a sandwich counter from which you can have the sandwich of your choice made with a wide variety of meats (try the *prosciutto*), cheeses (get some of the fresh buffalo-milk *mozzarella*), salamis, and fresh bread. You can also get *vino* to go here. If you want to eat or enjoy a glass of Chianti at the bar; upside-down barrels serve as seats.

VINO E OLIO, *Via dei Serragli 29r, Tel. 055298-708. No credit cards accepted.*

You can find any type of wine or olive oil you could dream of in this store. Since it is slightly expensive you may not want to get your wine for the picnic here, but it is a great place to buy gifts for friends at home. If you don't want to carry them with you on the rest of your trip, the owner will arrange to have them shipped to wherever you choose.

ALESSI PARIDE, *Via delle Oche 27-29r, Tel. 055/214-966. Credit cards accepted.*

This store is a wine lovers paradise. They have wines from every region of Italy and there's one room entirely dedicated to Chianti. This store may also be a little expensive for picnic supplies, but you can get any manner of wine imaginable here, as well as selected liquors, chocolates, marmalades, and honeys.

INDEX

THINGS CHANGE!

Phone numbers, prices, addresses, quality of food, etc, all change. If you come across any new information, we'd appreciate hearing from you. No item is too small! Drop us an e-mail note at: Jopenroad@aol.com, or write us at:

Rome Guide

Open Road Publishing, P.O. Box 284

Cold Spring Harbor, NY 11724

TRAVEL NOTES